Beyond Borders

Writings of Virgilio Elizondo and Friends

Timothy Matovina

Editor

ORBIS BOOKS

Maryknoll, New York 10545

The Catholic Foreign Mission Society of America (Maryknoll) recruits and trains people for over-seas missionary service. Through Orbis Books, Maryknoll aims to foster the international dialogue that is essential to mission. The books published, however, reflect the opinions of their authors and are not meant to represent the official position of the society. To obtain more information about Maryknoll and Orbis Books, please visit our website at www.maryknoll.org.

Grateful acknowledgment is made to the original publishers of previously published essays by Virgilio Elizondo. These permissions are acknowledged in the Table of Original Publication on p. 292.

Queries regarding rights and permission should be addressed to: Orbis Books, P.O. Box 308, Maryknoll, New York 10545-0308.

Published by Orbis Books, Maryknoll, NY 10545-0308
Manufactured in the United States of America

Library of Congress Cataloging-in-Publication Data

Beyond borders : writings of Virgilio Elizondo and friends / Timothy Matovina, editor.
    p. cm.
  Includes bibliographical references and index.
  ISBN 1-57075-235-4 (pkb.)
  1. Elizondo, Virgilio P. I. Elizondo, Virgilio P. II. Matovina, Timothy M., 1955-

BX4705.E454 B49 2000
230'.2—dc21

                                      99-087499

Contents

PART ONE
RELIGIOUS EDUCATION AS PASTORAL THEOLOGY

Introductory Essays

Essays by Virgilio Elizondo

PART FIVE
BEYOND BORDERS

Introductory Essays

Essays by Virgilio Elizondo

Editor's Acknowledgments

The process of putting this volume together was the smoothest I've ever experienced in a collaborative effort of this sort. Once the contributors heard it was an *homenaje* for Virgilio Elizondo, they enthusiastically accepted the invitation to participate. Their superb essays illuminate Virgil's incredible theological contribution and honor him as an esteemed friend and colleague. My only regret as editor is that space limitations precluded essays by other collaborators among Virgil's many friends and associates from every continent of the globe.

I am deeply grateful to the volume's fourteen contributors, especially Orlando Espín, who had the vision to set this project in motion. Susan Perry, Geri DiLauro, and their colleagues at Orbis Books did outstanding work on the project. D. J. Mitchell, my student assistant at Loyola Marymount University, provided superb help with the bibliography, transcriptions of previously published essays, and other editorial tasks; this volume would not have been possible without his tireless efforts. Thanks also to Craig Dykstra, Jeanne Knoerle, Christopher Coble, and their colleagues at the Lilly Endowment for their generous support that afforded us expert copy editing, fees for reprinting Virgil's previously published articles, and (where necessary) translation services for the various essays that comprise this book.

Above all, *muchísimas gracias* to Virgil, whose visionary writings, constancy in friendship, and life of serving, mentoring, guiding, leading, challenging, and encouraging are the inspiration for this volume. Like so many others, the debt of gratitude I feel toward Virgil cannot be adequately expressed in the lines we dedicate to him here. Thank you, Virgilio, for the treasure of your friendship and for a life that has changed the contours of theology and pastoral ministry and, more importantly, the contours of our hearts.

Timothy Matovina

FOREWORD

Virgil Elizondo's Vision as a Hermeneutics of Hope

Gustavo Gutiérrez

In the early 1970s, I received a kind letter from a pastoral center located in San Antonio, Texas, inviting me to give some classes for a summer course. I did not know anything about the institution or about the person who signed the letter. The facts and the purposes expressed in the letter, however, aroused my interest. The letter dealt with a new project seeking to start from a solid anchoring in the Mexican American world. That is how in the distant (and without trying to play on words, always close) summer of 1974, I had my first contact with the Mexican American Cultural Center (MACC), with its director, Virgil Elizondo, and with the team working with him. I did not know that the days I would spend there (the first of many visits) would comprise one of the most significant experiences in my life. Thanks to Virgil and other friends whom I met in San Antonio, I discovered a people who were not only fighting to defend their severely threatened cultural identity, but who were also open to dialogue with other human worlds.

With many similar and, at the same time, different elements from the Latin American world with which I was familiar, Mexican Americans were becoming aware that they were at a place of encounter of various cultural heritages: indigenous, Hispanic, and North American. In the past and even now, these cultures had, at times, cruelly clashed and produced deep wounds. This is the reason why I was surprised by Virgil's desire not to leave aside any of those aspects and, at the same time, to prevent any one of them from invalidating the others. This is not an easy task and it is still unfinished. It is a costly journey because we have to accept the fact that we need to learn by "trial and error," as is the case whenever we travel along uncharted roads.

In that complex context and without renouncing any of its elements, Virgil and his friends asked themselves what role Christian faith and the proclamation of the Gospel had to play in the life of their people. These are the kind of questions that lead to theological reflection in which we see the ongoing creativity of reading the Gospel in a way that accepts without fear the challenges emerging from a constantly changing reality. From this perspective, Virgil and MACC have done pioneering work that goes far beyond the Mexican American world and is enriching all of us. I have experienced this firsthand and this is why I have taken the liberty of starting this account in the first person.

At this point, I would like to suggest some characteristics of Virgil Elizondo's works. This is just a sketch, since the articles of this book will deal more in depth with several aspects of his valuable contribution to contemporary theology.

Member of a People

Virgil's theological reflection bears the seal of his belonging to a people. All his writings express this and, in addition, we have clear personal testimonies to that effect. They are found, for example, in his book *The Future Is Mestizo*. In this book, with simplicity and sensitivity, he speaks to us of his childhood surrounded by his family's love and lived with a solid and spontaneous reference to the church that was, he says, "the center of life" (p. 11), the nucleus of crystallization for the world of all the people who were near him. He also tells us how, little by little, he initiated the arduous search for identity from within a people who did not seem to have their own place either in North American society or in relation with their original homeland, Mexico. Virgil calls this an experience of "non-being" (p. 20) or, if you wish, an experience of not being anyone. He does not feel like a spectator vis-à-vis this search. At a very personal level, it is his search, and his "I am" seems inseparable from the "we are." That was the starting point for an affirmation of identity that was necessary for giving meaning to existence and coherence to the options at hand. In that search, his greatest incentives were his family experiences, memories of the *barrio*, the efforts of so many Mexican Americans (many of them his close friends), and the encouragement of the bishops of San Antonio.

Between Mexican people who are proud of their past and people of the United States who seem turned to the future, how was he to live the present without feeling torn apart (as Virgil says several times, "disintegrated") in their misencounters and confrontations? At the time, many people were pondering the same dilemma and there was no easy answer since several factors were involved. Such a search is, however, essential for a people (and any person) who do not want to be wooden logs in the ocean, tossed back and forth by the waves. Besides, and Virgil sees it clearly, this search for meaning is also decisive to the experience of faith and the proclamation of the Gospel. For him, this is the "birth of a new race." He writes, "I am one of this race and the pains and joys of this new existence are the core of my daily life" (*The Future Is Mestizo*, p. xi). The message of the One who, according to Saint John, chose to pitch his tent in the midst of history is truly welcomed when we live human communion to the fullest. Human joys and sufferings, dreams and frustrations, selfish withdrawals and the generous openness that we all experience are the soil that welcomes the seed of Christian faith and leaves its imprint in the taste of the fruit it produces.

Hence, the enormous attention that Virgil pays to the interminable and misunderstood sufferings of a people who, as he often states, were "twice invaded, colonized and mestized," first by Europeans and later by North Americans. For my part, I clearly remember the stories of the friends whom I met at MACC during my first visits, regarding the thousand postponements and humiliations that they had endured trying to receive a fair remuneration for their work and to defend their legal rights, all on account of their skin color or because they were speaking a language considered inferior. Those injustices were ways of telling them that they could only alleviate their difficulties if they accepted assimilation by the dominant culture and if they gave up any claim to their own identity. Without a doubt, the present situation is not the same as it was several decades ago, but open and subtle forms of marginalization still continue.

Those painful experiences form part of daily life (they are also experienced by other people arriving in the United States from different Latin American countries), but they do not exhaust the experiences of Mexican Americans. Thus, Virgil's attention is equally focused on the many happy moments he experienced as a child with his people and that he reencounters as an adult. There is a sincere and profound joy in people who do not renounce their condition as human beings, something that is expressed, for example, in fiestas, a moment of creativity and imagination that Virgil analyzes with interest and perspicacity. Significantly, he analyzes fiestas from within since he not only takes part in them, but has also organized them. A fiesta can also mean an authentic and liberating experience, as Virgil shows with regard to the Fiesta Week of San Antonio (cf. *The Future Is Mestizo*, pp. 48-50). In one of his first works, he states: "The totality of life [is reflected through the fiesta] . . . it is not an escape from the world of problems but a bringing of the whole day into the celebration of the fact that life is a gift. Life is to be lived, appreciated, and celebrated" (*Christianity and Culture*, p. 173). That point of view permeates his theological reflection.

Toward Universal *Mestizaje*

Being firmly inserted in a people's life, history, and culture does not necessarily mean being withdrawn and closed to what does not pertain to that tradition. It is true that this can be the case, and the world today is living the tragedy of such attitudes, which some people have adopted because of the marginalization and the sufferings that they have endured for centuries. This could not be further away, however, from what Virgil postulates.

Here I would like to recall Manuel Castells's note (cf. *The Power of Identity*) on what he rightfully considers one of the great contemporary tendencies: constructing identity as the source of meaning. This author distinguishes between an identity of resistance and an identity of project. The first one is generated by people in positions or conditions that are devalued by the logic of domination. Under those circumstances, they tend to build trenches of resistance and survival, based on principles different from or contrary to those that permeate the institutions of society. Among many other things, some of this "identity of resistance" was present in the Chicano movement of the 1960s that Virgil knew from up close; that experience helped him to raise decisive questions.

But, continuing to follow Castells, there is also an identity project that takes place when, on the basis of the cultural materials at their disposal, society's actors build up a new identity that redefines their social location and, in the process, attempts to transform the entire social culture. Conscious of his people's values,

Virgil is also conscious of the universal dimension of those values. This is not to say that resisting the enslavement of a culture and of the people who live in that culture does not make sense. What happens is that it is necessary to go beyond. Castells himself states that "identities that start as resistance can lead to projects." This takes place when we perceive that cultural values are not only to be defended but also are offered as human dimensions that can enrich others. It seems to me that this is one of Virgil's greatest insights. Only in this way will it be possible, in a fruitful manner, to build the path of humankind toward "a universal *mestizaje*" (cf. *The Future Is Mestizo*, pp. 87-111). This entails a biological *mestizaje* but also a cultural one.

Far from suppressing the differences in sterile uniformity, *mestizaje* brings them out and values them. In this vast horizon, Virgil situates his reflections on the people to whom he belongs and on the role that they have to play in the proclamation of the gospel. The dominant theologies in Christian churches do not seem to take this challenge into account. What is needed is a reflection that pays close attention to the creativity and the religious practice of the Hispanic people in the United States, a theology that starts from the simple faith of a marginalized people who confront life and the different forms of death they are experiencing with their faith and their hope. For that to happen, we must know how to listen to this faith-filled people. Virgil writes, "The people *can* teach the church—if the church will only listen to them" (*San Fernando Cathedral: Soul of the City*, p. 15). The church has to be ready. In *Evangelii Nuntiandi*, Paul VI spoke of an "evangelizing and evangelized church." Similarly, the Puebla Episcopal Conference reaffirmed the "evangelizing potential of the poor."

As the first priest born in San Antonio to be in charge of the cathedral, Virgil's experience was precisely an experience of the universality to which I was referring a moment ago. While the great majority of the participants at the cathedral's Eucharists belong to the poor Hispanic people, they also attract people "from all ethnic groups and social backgrounds" (*San Fernando Cathedral*, p. 101). In addition to being beautiful and imaginative, this pastoral experience is profoundly challenging because it is done by a people who live, in their own flesh, poverty and social insignificance.

That experience calls for a theological reflection capable of following the journey of a people who are becoming aware of their own being and finding one axis of their identity in the Christian faith. This very fact invites us to take a further step and explore the perspective in which this discourse on faith is situated.

From Our Own Galilee

Virgil's objective, to reflect on the life of the Mexican American people in the light of faith, led him to look in depth at a fruitful biblical theme that had been neglected for a long time: Jesus, the Galilean, who proclaimed the reign of God from the marginalized and despised land of Galilee. Through Virgil, we have become aware of the deep theological implications of something that could have seemed purely geographical. People of that territory were looked down upon by their compatriots from Judea because Galileans mixed with people considered as pagans, who had also impacted their customs and religiousness. The gospels are clear in pointing out to us that it was in that province that Jesus, who lived in the Galilean town of Nazareth, conducted most of his itinerant preaching. The doctors of the law sent spies there to observe this disturbing person and, if need be, to raise questions that set him up against Roman occupants and presented him as a violator of the Mosaic law.

Galilee was also the starting point of the evangelizing mission of Jesus' followers. It was there that they received the mandate to make disciples of all nations (cf. Matt. 28:19). The gospel comes to us from a despised land and through people who have experienced marginalization. With insight, Virgil used this perspective as the theme of his doctoral thesis in Paris. He says that as he was working on it, "I kept struggling to find a connection between what appeared to be two theses that did not connect: the socio-historical process of the twofold *mestizaje* of Mexican Americans and the socio-historical identity and mission of Jesus" (*The Future Is Mestizo*, p. 72). The Galilean paradigm enabled him better to understand his people and the task that was ahead of him (cf. *Galilean Journey: The Mexican-American Promise*). And this paradigm is helping many others like myself to become aware of the permanent historical starting point for all evangelization.

Then Virgil linked this perspective with a theme to which he had devoted a great deal of effort and reflection ever since his first works: the foundational Guadalupe event. Recently, he dedicated a very important work to this theme (*Guadalupe: Mother of the New Creation*), a theme that is also open to the cosmic dimensions of the event. We are all aware of the central place that devotion to the Virgin of Guadalupe has in the faith of the Mexican people. Virgil helps us note that Guadalupe provides an excellent illustration of Galilean evangelization. In this case, the gospel comes to us through the Indian Juan Diego, a member of a race that was starting to be subjugated. The roles were reversed as Juan Diego was the one put in charge of bringing the message to the mistrustful bishop who asked for proof. He did receive it. Juan Diego spoke from his "nonbeing" but he did not do so in vain. Virgil leads us to observe that the figure and the inspiration of Guadalupe are found again in all those who, in the course of history, in the heart of the Mexican and Mexican American people, have sided with the poor and their struggle for justice.

Speaking from another context, the very intuitive Walter Benjamin used to say that if we want to understand history, we have to look at it from a perspective that goes against the grain. That is what Virgil is doing by assuming the evangelical perspective of Galilee. From a historical point of view, he often refers to what has been called "the view of the conquered." However paradoxical it may seem at first, that is the way to reach authentic universality. Entering history through the back door, through the poor, through those whom the powerful of the world despise, is the biblical way of expressing God's love for every person without exception. This is not easy to understand from our categories. Virgil is conscious of his belonging to a people and their historical ups and downs. He knows the universal outreach of their values and he is attentive to the path taken by Jesus to proclaim God's reign. His reflections help us to look deeply into our faith by sharing the joy of a people who do not lose hope in God or the conviction that it is possible to create a more just and a more human world. Therefore, Virgil's theology is presented as the hermeneutics of that joy and hope.

Virgil's work and his personal testimony play a foundational role. His reflections on the gospel and culture anticipated the growing number of works dealing with the inculturation of the gospel in today's church. It is a very rich theme, essential for the Hispanic people living in the United States; all of us have something to learn from it. Virgil opened roads that others have probed with inventiveness and creativity. The commitment and the solid intellectual formation of women and men, laity and religious, who have been inspired by Virgil and are engaged in the task of inculturating the gospel in the United States have given Virgil's theological reflection a great relevance. Indeed, they have helped make his reflection a living reality in today's world. At the same time, Virgil's vision offers a promise that has much to teach the theology that is being developed in Latin America and elsewhere.

(Trans. Colette Joly Dees)

Introduction

Timothy Matovina

I first met Virgilio Elizondo in 1982 as his student at the Mexican American Cultural Center (MACC) in San Antonio, Texas. I still have my notes from the class sessions he led on christology, Guadalupe and other faith expressions, and the dynamics of oppressor and oppressed. Since then he has been a constant friend, mentor, and inspiration. I am deeply grateful for this opportunity to join with others and honor him on the occasion of his sixty-fifth birthday.

Virgilio P. Elizondo was born in San Antonio on August 28, 1935. While his scholarship, teaching, and ministry have taken him to places all around the world, he has lived in his hometown and neighborhood almost all his life. In fact, when he went to the seminary he never left his home parish, as the seminary was within the parish boundaries. After his 1963 ordination as a priest for the archdiocese of San Antonio, he served in parish ministry, as Director of Religious Education for the archdiocese, and as the Academic Dean of Assumption Seminary. Additionally, he established the pastoral institute at San Antonio's Incarnate Word College (now the University of the Incarnate Word). In 1968 he attended the meeting of Latin American bishops at Medellín and began studies at the Ateneo University and the East Asian Pastoral Institute (EAPI) in Manila; the following year he received his Master's in Pastoral Studies from the Ateneo and a Diploma in Pastoral Catechetics from EAPI. He founded MACC in 1972 and subsequently served as its first president until 1987. During his years at MACC he began an international speaking ministry; over the past three decades he has offered numerous addresses and conferences to such groups as the National Catholic Educational Association (United States), the Association of Catholic Educators (Australia), the Native American School of Ministry (Canada), the Ecumenical Association of Third World Theologians, the Catholic Theological Society of America, the National Catholic Conference of Bishops (United States), and episcopal groups from Brazil and Mexico. While president of MACC he also pursued doctoral studies at the Institut Catholique in Paris, completing his acclaimed thesis *Métissage, violence culturelle, annonce de l'Evangile* in 1978. From 1983 to 1995 he was rector of San Antonio's San Fernando Cathedral, where he revived the predominately Mexican-American congregation's cherished faith traditions. He also established the internationally televised "Misa de las Americas" that the San Fernando congregation still celebrates weekly with millions of worshipers who participate via television. Today he continues his pastoral work as the director of programming for San Antonio's Catholic television station.[1] The essays in this collection illuminate his life of pastoral service and the fascinating theology and vision for a united humanity that he has articulated along the way.

Heart of a Pastor

Virgil is first and foremost a pastoral minister. His initial assignment as a priest was to Our Lady of Sorrows parish in San Antonio and he has served in some form of parochial ministry ever since; his teaching, writing, lecturing, video producing, and other work are all rooted in and enhance the pastoral core of his life and ministry. In my experience, Virgil's strongest charism is to bring out the best in others. He consistently puts into practice the advice he wrote some twenty-five years ago: "To be willing to learn from the poor is already *the first proclamation of the Gospel*, because learning from someone is a very existential way of telling them that they are important and have something to offer." During his years as rector of San Fernando Cathedral, parishioners like Lionel Sosa confirmed this element of Virgil's pastoral style: "The genius of Father Virgil is his acceptance of people as they are . . . So many churches make us feel bad about who we are and try to motivate us with fear. At San Fernando people leave services feeling good about themselves and wanting to be the best they can. The appeal of San Fernando is not to the head, but the heart. People sense the goodness of their God and their own goodness in the eyes of God and this enables them to become what they're meant to be."[2]

Virgil's ability to help others claim their own wisdom and talents was especially evident to me in the summer of 1993 when we facilitated a workshop on "Hispanic Christology" at MACC. His persistent admonition throughout the week-long sessions was that each participant had wisdom to offer the group and that the workshop would not be complete until each one of us began to interpret the gospel stories for ourselves. He invited, cajoled, pressed, and humored the group into offering our honest responses and insights. Toward the end of the week, one participant who at first seemed reluctant to speak gave her response to the text about Joseph's dream which told him not to divorce Mary (Matt. 1:18-25). She began her reflection rather quietly, but then grew more vocal as she spoke about the passage that states Joseph "had no relations with her." Assuming this meant Joseph kept Mary at a distance because he was still angry about the pregnancy, she bluntly remarked that if she were Mary she would have left Joseph immediately. After all, Mary was pregnant and needed the comfort of her husband's embrace and caress. Who would want to be in a marriage that was so devoid of the love expressed through physical touch? Her gut reaction to this biblical verse provided a profound moment of insight that challenged my unconscious presuppositions (and those of others in the group) about the absence of physical affection and everyday concerns in Mary and Joseph's marriage. A lively conversation ensued as participants considered Joseph and Mary's human emotions and their efforts to establish a marital life under such unusual circumstances. Virgil's capacity to help the group connect directly with the gospel stories provided an incredible ambiance in which participants' wisdom, reflections, and honest questions about the scriptural text could be known and further explored.

The instinct to "trust the faithful" has marked Virgil's preaching, teaching, and writing for decades, as the weaving of pastoral concerns and scholarly analysis in this volume clearly illustrates. In particular, through his preaching Virgil consistently and passionately invites his hearers to embrace the core message that God cherishes, esteems, values, respects, treasures, forgives, and loves them. As Virgil put it in one of his sermons: "The realization that one has self-worth, fundamental dignity, radical equality, and love is the innermost and deepest beginning of liberation. It certainly does not stop there. But, on the other hand, there is no other authentic beginning."[3]

I had the wonderful opportunity to experience Virgil's gifted pastoral style and preaching ability when I was a San Fernando parishioner from 1992 to 1995, the last three years of his term as rector. Many of his memorable sermons come to mind, but the one that sticks out for me the most is a homily he gave on the feast of the Epiphany. Virgil pointed out that the Magi found the Christ child because they sought God in the events of their everyday lives. Herod and his advisors, on the other hand, failed to discover God's presence in their midst despite their advantage of knowing the scriptures. Given this turn of events in Matthew's Gospel, Virgil urged us to remember that our religious tradition can be a handicap if it causes us to stop searching for God in the unexpected moments and events of our daily lives. We can become so certain that God is with us and in us that we fail to see the new ways in which God is trying to break through. If our religious tradition leads us to stop the search, it is no longer serving us, nor are we serving it. God is ever the great surprise who will appear to us in ways and at times that we least expect; like the Magi, we need only keep our hearts and minds open to the moment of sacred encounter.

Much of Virgil's most visionary work is not published on the printed page. His sermons and numerous talks, keynote addresses, conferences, and workshops provide potent memories for those of us who have seen him at his best: when he is interacting with people and building on the energy that the group dynamic creates. Unfortunately, we cannot fully present the experience of this living engagement between the two covers of this book. My suggestion is that readers hear Virgil speak or experience one of his many video productions, such as his series on Our Lady of Guadalupe, his introduction to the Bible entitled *A Walk Through the Scriptures*, and *Soul of the City/Alma del pueblo*, the video he narrated on the San Fernando Cathedral congregation.[4] Better yet, go to San Fernando Cathedral for Holy Week, the feast of Our Lady of Guadalupe, or one of the other major liturgical celebrations. There you will see, hear, touch, sense, and smell the rich ritual life that illuminates Virgil's (and his successor David García's) pastoral vision in action.

Liturgical Virtuoso

During Virgil's twelve years as rector of San Fernando, he enabled the cathedral congregation to revivify and further develop their centuries-old tradition of public ritual. James P. Wind, a Lutheran priest and scholar who worshiped at San Fernando for the first time during Virgil's tenure, deemed Virgilio a "liturgical virtuoso" whose boundless creative energy builds on existing traditions and or-chestrates an annual cycle of liturgical celebrations that interweave with the popular feasts of the people and resonate with parishioners as well as cathedral newcom-ers. Numerous cathedral congregants confirm Wind's observations. As parishio-ner Zulema Escamilla Galindo summed it up, "I've loved San Fernando since my mother-in-law took me there in 1938, but I've felt even more animated by the fervent celebrations led by Father Elizondo."[5]

Virgil's liturgical leadership and promotion of Mexican Catholic traditions is readily evident in the San Fernando congregation's annual public rituals. For the vigil of the feast of Our Lady of Guadalupe, the San Fernando congregation cel-ebrates a *serenata* of songs to their celestial mother which is transmitted through-out the Americas via television. *Las Posadas* (literally the "dwellings" or "shel-ters") reenact the pilgrimage of Mary and Joseph on the way to Bethlehem. These festive Advent processions are organized in various parishioners' homes and neigh-borhoods and one grand *posada* is enacted through the streets of downtown San Antonio, with the holy pilgrims denied entry at sites like the city hall and county courthouse before finally receiving shelter at the cathedral. The proclamation of Jesus' passion and death on Good Friday begins in the public market, winds through the city's downtown streets, and ends with the crucifixion on the steps of the cathedral. Later that evening the *servicio del santo entierro* (entombment or wake service) includes a candlelight procession with the body of Jesus through the plaza and streets around the cathedral. Each Sunday San Fernando's eight o'clock bilingual Mass is televised internationally. Frequently these celebrations incorpo-rate Mexican Catholic traditions such as an Epiphany entrance procession with parishioners dressed as the Magi, the blessing of children on a Sunday near the feast of the Presentation, and the remembrance of the community's deceased he-roes and leaders on a Sunday proximate to the feasts of All Saints and All Souls (popularly known as *el Día de los Muertos*, the Day of the Dead).[6]

At San Fernando Virgil did far more than accentuate his parishioners' Mexi-can Catholic ritual heritage, however; his openness to other peoples and religious traditions paved the way for numerous other devotees to join with the worshiping community at the cathedral. While congregants of Mexican descent are still the parish's mainstay, today San Fernando is a spiritual home for an incredibly di-verse assemblage of peoples. Under Virgil's guidance, the development of the internationally televised Sunday Mass and special celebrations like the Guadalupe *serenata* have attracted numerous people from various religious, cultural, and socioeconomic backgrounds who worship at the cathedral via television. Promi-nent public rituals like the grand *posada* and the passion proclamation on Good Friday also draw an increasingly diverse body of participants. New celebrations like the citywide Thanksgiving service and the annual Pilgrimage of Hope for those afflicted with HIV/AIDS gather Hindus, Buddhists, Muslims, Jews, and Christians from various denominations for interfaith services at the cathedral. As one San Antonio newspaper reporter wrote, contemporary San Fernando is the "celestial center of San Antonio," a place that renowned poet Sandra Cisneros deems "a sanctuary of the spirit" embraced by a vast array of city residents and visitors.[7]

For many San Antonians, Virgil's inclusive pastoral approach is his greatest gift to his hometown and numerous places beyond. City officials recognized his outstanding contribution to all San Antonio citizens by naming the plaza next to the cathedral "Elizondo Plaza" in his honor. J. Michael Parker, a religion writer for the *San Antonio Express-News*, admiringly observed that Virgil's vision as San Fernando rector enabled the cathedral to become a cultural, social, and religious center where "no one is a stranger." He then added rhetorically: "Where else would one see a Buddhist monk, a Muslim imam, a Jewish rabbi, a Protestant minister, and a Catholic priest offering prayers—each in his own way—for the needs of this rich, multicultural community?" Similarly, former San Antonio mayor Bill Thornton noted: "I can feel just as comfortable at San Fernando in silk tie and dark suit as the homeless person sitting next to me. We would both be asked to participate . . . Thanks to Father Elizondo, San Fernando is a place where we can all come together as San Antonians." Local Baptist pastor Buckner Fanning concurs with this assessment of Virgil's pastoral leadership at the cathedral: "There's an old saying that when the tide comes in, every boat in the harbor rises. San Antonio is a much finer spiritual community—in all denominations—because of Father Virgil Elizondo. His life and work at the cathedral have created a renaissance, not only in the cathedral, but in the whole community. He's helped the tide of spirituality to rise."[8]

Mestizo Theologian

Virgil's theology provided the pastoral vision that underlies the rejuvenation he led at San Fernando. As he himself recalled looking back on the invitation to become San Fernando's rector, he accepted the challenge of this assignment as an opportunity to put into practice the theology he had developed with others at MACC. During his years at San Fernando Virgil sought to fulfill Archbishop Patricio Flores's commission when he invited Virgil to serve as cathedral rector: "Now is the chance to prove that what you have been saying needs to be done. Let's show what our people have to offer."[9]

The theological vision that underlies Virgil's pastoral praxis is based on his insight that historically Mexican Americans have been externally conquered and oppressed, yet never crushed or dominated. In his preaching, teaching, and writing he outlines two conquests his people have endured: the Spanish conquest of the indigenous peoples in the territories that became New Spain (and later Mexico) and the U. S. conquest of what is now the Southwest. The effects of the second conquest continue in the pressure put on Mexican Americans to assimilate, to abandon the Mexican way for the American way. Despite this pressure, he perceives in his people a *mestizo* identity that is neither Mexican nor North American, neither Spanish nor indigenous, but a dynamic mixture of all these root cultures. He enjoins his fellow *mestizos* not to identify themselves in a negative way as "not Mexican" or "not American" but to claim the positive identity of *mestizos* who have the advantage of knowing two (or more) cultures. Celebrating their culturally conditioned expressions of faith is a powerful means of ritually embracing their *mestizo* heritage and identity. At the same time, however, Virgil insists that this *mestizo* identity entails a calling and mission; it is precisely those who know multiple cultures and have borne the pain of conquest and rejection who can lead the way to build a society in which the divisive barriers between peoples are broken.[10]

Virgil was ordained during Vatican II and his theology reveals his fascination with the conciliar documents and vision, especially the call for a return to the sources of faith. Following this directive of the Council, Virgil's theology and pastoral praxis are rooted in his creative reexamination of two foundational faith sources: the image and narrative of Our Lady of Guadalupe and the Jesus stories of the Gospels. In both of these sources Virgil finds rich treasures for theological reflection on the life and mission of a *mestizo* people. He encourages his fellow *mestizos* to embrace their identity and mission by his proclamation of Jesus' *mestizo* origins as a Galilean, a borderland reject caught between the Roman occupation force in Palestine and the Jewish temple elite who claimed Galileans were "impure." Yet it is the *mestizo* Galilean caught between two cultures who rejects rejection and opens the road to a new Pentecost in which the destructive barriers that separate peoples are removed. Similarly, he states that Guadalupe "is neither an Indian goddess nor a European Madonna; she is something new. She is neither Spanish nor Indian and yet she is both and more . . . She is the first truly American person and as such the mother of the new generations to come." Thus Guadalupe provides hope and inspiration for a *mestizo* people called to create a new future and a new humanity.[11]

Virgilio Elizondo is one of those rare theologians who has insights so imaginative that they influence grassroots devotees and pastoral ministers, scholars and activists, artists and poets, church officials and civic leaders, believers and even nonbelievers, in short, people of widely diverse perspectives, ages, and backgrounds. Commenting on Virgil's theological exploration of Our Lady of Guadalupe, journalist and writer Demetria Martínez opined that "Elizondo's brilliant work gives hope that Catholicism might yet live up to its potential in the new world." Author and editorialist Richard Rodriguez wrote that "Virgil Elizondo teaches me what it means to be related to Mexico. He writes of the soul of Mexico and teaches us all what it means to be Catholic." Poet Sandra Cisneros deems Virgil's writing "wise, compassionate and visionary," while former cabinet member and San Antonio mayor Henry Cisneros states: "Father Elizondo's analysis and wisdom help us to understand one of the major trends of our times: the convergence of cultures."[12]

The most direct and persistent influence of Virgil's theological reflection, pastoral action, and activism has been in Hispanic ministry and theology. Along with his collaborators at MACC, Virgil was the catalyst for many of the changes in Hispanic ministry over the past three decades, particularly the prophetic insistence that church leaders respect Hispanic faith expressions and cultures. In the process of promoting these vital changes in Hispanic ministry, he also led the way in establishing U. S. Hispanic/Latino theology. Fellow theologian and pastor Arturo Bañuelas states that "Virgilio Elizondo is the most prominent U. S. Hispanic theologian. What Gustavo Gutiérrez is to liberation theology, Elizondo is to U. S.

Hispanic theology." Similarly, African American theologian Shawn Copeland contends that Hispanic/Latino theology "would be unimaginable without his [Elizondo's] creative intellect." Allan Figueroa Deck claims that "the history of contemporary U. S. Hispanic theology must begin with the work of Virgil Elizondo." Virgil's colleagues in the Academy of Catholic Hispanic Theologians of the United States (ACHTUS) recognized his status as the premier Latino theologian by founding the Virgilio Elizondo Award, an annual prize given to an honoree for "outstanding contributions to a theology of and for U. S. Hispanics."[13]

While Virgil's theology is primarily focused on the experience of *mestizos* in the Southwest, the influence of this theology is not limited to Latinos nor to the borders of the United States. Leading European theologians like Jacques Audinet assert that "the writing of this Mexican American man of thought and action has had a deep resonance" with them and that, although "expressly treating a relatively small section of the earth's inhabited surface," Virgil "points to solutions of global problems." Similarly, Latin American theologians as distinguished as Gustavo Gutiérrez attest that "the work of Virgilio Elizondo plays a foundational role" in the development of U. S. Hispanic theology, which "is watering with its spring other areas of the world of Latin origin."[14] Virgil's prominent participation in the Ecumenical Association of Third World Theologians (EATWOT) and on the editorial board of the *Revista Latinoamericana de Teologia* further illuminate his international influence. From 1979 to 1999 he also served on the editorial board of *Concilium*, a widely acclaimed publication that arguably is as much an international forum for theological and church reform as it is a theological journal. These commitments and his extensive travel to teach and lecture in numerous places around the globe have facilitated the wide-ranging appeal and impact of Virgil's *mestizo* theology.

Our *Homenaje*

Virgilio has received the prestigious Laetare Medal from the University of Notre Dame, the Johannes Quasten Medal for excellence in scholarship and leadership in religious studies from the Catholic University of America, the Humanitarian Award of the National Conference of Christians and Jews, the President's Award of the National Federation of Priests Councils for distinguished priestly leadership in the United States, the Imagineer's Award of the National Mind-Science Foundation, the Mission Award of the U. S. Conference of Mission Associations, the Sadlier-Dinger Award for outstanding contribution to religious education in the United States, three honorary doctorates, and other awards and recognition too numerous to mention. The contributors to this volume desire to further honor him with our collective reflection on his theological contribution and his professional and personal influence on our lives.

This book does not follow the usual format for an *homenaje* or "festschrift" volume. Rather than write essays on a variety of topics to honor our friend, colleague, and mentor, the collaborators prepared introductory essays on various elements of Virgil's thought and contribution. The diversity of personal and disciplinary backgrounds among the various authors is part of our tribute to Virgil, whose life and work have consistently moved "beyond the borders" between pastoral ministers and professional scholars, laity and clergy, fields of specialization within the academy, religions, denominations, races, ethnic groups, genders, age groups, and nationalities. In addition to these introductory essays, the book contains fourteen of Virgil's previously published articles brought together in a single collection for the first time. A few passages from the original essays have been omitted, edited, or updated, but in large part the essays are reprinted in their original form. One-third of the articles are from *Concilium*, the others are from various select sources. They are arranged thematically in five major sections, although Virgil's integrative approach illuminates significant complementarity and overlap between the various themes. Indeed, as editor I wasn't always sure where some of Virgil's essays (as well as those of several contributors to this volume) best "fit" in the book as many of the articles cross and transcend the chosen thematic categories. This thematic presentation of Virgil's work does not follow a traditional theological schema. Rather, it reflects the emergence of key breakthroughs and concepts in Virgil's thought: his initial and ongoing focus on religious education as pastoral theology; popular religion, especially Our Lady of Guadalupe, as a locus for theology and pastoral praxis; *mestizaje* and the Galilean identity of Jesus; God's demand that Christians confront the personal and structural realities of sin and evil; the wider implications of the *mestizo* experience for theology, religious studies, the life of the church, and the future of humanity.

The reader should note that this volume does not include reprints of material from Virgil's books, since most of these works are well known and readily available. The volume's thematic schema, however, closely parallels the evolution of Virgil's thought as revealed in his major works, such as *The Human Quest: A Search for Meaning Through Life and Death* (1971), *Christianity and Culture: An Introduction to Pastoral Theology and Ministry for the Bicultural Community* (1975), *La Morenita: Evangelizer of the Americas* (1980), *Galilean Journey: The Mexican-American Promise* (1983), *The Future Is Mestizo: Life Where Cultures Meet* (1988), *Guadalupe: Mother of the New Creation* (1997), and *San Fernando Cathedral: Soul of the City* (1998). The introductory essays in this book provide helpful insights on these and Virgil's other publications; additionally, an extensive bibliography of his writings is included at the end of this volume.

While by no means a comprehensive treatment of Virgil's life and thought, this book contains various essays, insights, personal testimony, and anecdotes that illustrate Virgil's pastoral and theological contribution. Whether the reader is well acquainted with Virgil's work or encountering it for the first time, there is much between these two covers to fascinate, enlighten, animate, provoke, invigorate, and encourage you. I thank our readers in advance for joining with this volume's authors to honor Virgilio Elizondo by examining, appreciating, and learning from his scholarly, pastoral, and personal legacy. Above all, I am delighted to note that this vibrant legacy, now more than six decades in the making, continues to develop and flourish in Virgil and in the lives of countless others whom his vision has inspired and his kindness embraced.

Notes

[1]Further background material on Virgil's life can be found in his autobiographical work *The Future Is Mestizo: Life Where Cultures Meet* (Bloomington, IN: Meyer-Stone, 1988; reprint, New York: Crossroad, 1992; reprint, San Antonio: Mexican American Cultural Center Press, 1998).

[2]*Christianity and Culture: An Introduction to Pastoral Theology and Ministry for the Bicultural Community* (Huntington, IN: Our Sunday Visitor, 1975; reprint, San Antonio: Mexican American Cultural Center Press, 1978) 147 (first quotation); interview, Lionel Sosa, 30 March 1994 (second quotation). I conversed with all interviewees cited in this essay when I collaborated with Virgil on the San Fernando Cathedral Project, a congregational study conducted by the Mexican American Cultural Center and funded by the Lilly Endowment.

[3]Virgilio P. Elizondo, "A Child in a Manger: The Beginning of a New Order of Existence," in *Proclaiming the Acceptable Year*, ed. Justo L. González (Valley Forge: Judson, 1982) 69.

[4]The Guadalupe and scripture videos are available from Resources for Christian Living in Allen, Texas (800-822-6701); the San Fernando video can be obtained from JM Communications in Houston (713-524-1382). Various publishers have also distributed audio tapes of Virgil's talks, such as St. Anthony Messenger Press in Cincinnati (800-488-0488), which has his 1996 address to the Los Angeles Religious Education Congress, "Jesus of Nazareth: The Heart of Catechesis." The best single resource for Virgil's audio and video materials is the bookstore at the Mexican American Cultural Center in San Antonio (210-732-2156).

[5]James P. Wind, comment made at consultation on the San Fernando Cathedral Project, 29 August 1994; interview, Zulema Escamilla Galindo, 18 March 1994. The second quotation is my Spanish-to-English translation of Mrs. Galindo's comments.

[6]For a further treatment of public ritual at San Fernando, see Virgilio P. Elizondo and Timothy M. Matovina, *San Fernando Cathedral: Soul of the City* (Maryknoll, NY: Orbis, 1998); Roberto S. Goizueta, *Caminemos con Jesús: Toward a Hispanic/Latino Theology of Accompaniment* (Maryknoll, NY: Orbis, 1995).

[7]Jan Jarboe, "Celestial Center of San Antonio," *San Antonio Express-News*, 21 December 1986, 1C; Sandra Cisneros, "The Tejano Soul of San Antonio," *New York Times Magazine*, 17 May 1992, 25.

[8]*San Antonio Express-News*, 29 May 1995, 3B (first, second, and fourth quotations); interview, Bill Thornton, 18 February 1994 (third quotation).

[9]Elizondo and Matovina, *San Fernando Cathedral: Soul of the City* 9, 11 (quotation).

[10]For further elaboration of these foundational insights, see especially Virgil's *Galilean Journey: The Mexican-American Promise* (Maryknoll, NY: Orbis, 1983).

[11]Elizondo, *The Future Is Mestizo* 65 (quotation). See also Virgil's *La Morenita: Evangelizer of the Americas* (San Antonio: Mexican American Cultural Center Press, 1980); *Galilean Journey: The Mexican-American Promise*; *Guadalupe: Mother of the New Creation* (Maryknoll, NY: Orbis, 1997).

[12]The first quotation cited here is on the cover of *Guadalupe: Mother of the New Creation*; the others are from the cover of *The Future Is Mestizo* (1998 reprint).

[13]Arturo Bañuelas, "U. S. Hispanic Theology," *Missiology: An International Review* 20 (April 1992): 276 (first quotation); M. Shawn Copeland, "Black, Hispanic/Latino, and Native American Theologies," in *The Modern Theologian*, ed. David F. Ford (Oxford: Blackwell, 1996) 368 (second quotation); Allan Figueroa Deck, ed., *Frontiers of Hispanic Theology in the United States* (Maryknoll, NY: Orbis, 1992) xii-xiii (third and fourth quotations).

[14]Jacques Audinet, "Preface," in Elizondo, *Galilean Journey: The Mexican-American Promise* xi; Gustavo Gutiérrez, "Discovering a People," *Listening: Journal of Religion and Culture* 32 (Fall 1997): 177.

PART ONE

RELIGIOUS EDUCATION AS PASTORAL THEOLOGY

INTRODUCTORY ESSAYS

Religious Education

A Portrait Based on Virgilio Elizondo's Vision

Gloria Inés Loya

Introduction

As I began to enter into and to review the many works of Virgil Elizondo regarding his vision and leadership in religious education and Hispanic cultures, I also found myself reflecting on how much his commitment and thoughtful reflection have been an influence on the church as well as on me. My first recollection of participating in a conference given by Virgil was during the summer of 1978 at the Mexican American Cultural Center. To this day I still remember how I was inspired during the presentation by his scholarly investigation in theology; by his love of Jesus; by his commitment to the church; by his passion for the Hispano community; by his ability to be a friend to so many; by his constant hope; and by his sense of humor and the insights through which he challenges us to love the gospel. He would encourage his students to believe that with God's grace we can become architects creating a new future, the reign of God. Virgil was also a source of inspiration, because he was the first Mexican American theologian I had ever met, and as a Mexican American from California, I felt a sense of pride and joy for all Hispano people.

In this essay I will focus on Virgil's vision and imagination as expressed through his early work in religious education. Virgil responded to the challenge of the Second Vatican Council as he developed his pastoral theology which was deeply integrated with his views and commitment to religious education. He became a prolific writer, a challenging teacher, and a prophetic voice from within the Hispano community. His ideas and vision have been welcomed and listened to by all of the varied social, economic, and cultural dimensions of the church in the U.S., as well as in Latin America, Asia, and Europe. While he addresses the Hispano community, his writings and his theology go beyond national and cultural boundaries and frontiers to all who see and thirst for the gospel as the foundation for a commitment to a new creation which respects and welcomes the diversity of all peoples. From the locus of religious education, he has contributed to and enriched the

13

fields of catechetics and culture as well as the development and formation of religious educators who are ministers. In the following I will develop and describe a portrait of Virgil Elizondo and his vision of religious education. His earliest works express his principles and foundations regarding religious education and ministry. It would be impossible to present the essence of Virgil and his message in its totality; however, it is hoped that in this hermeneutical approach the reader will discover the contributions that this visionary theologian and religious educator has made to the church. By hermeneutics I mean the classic manner of interpreting the material of the author, Virgil, and "seeking to establish the original meaning of the material in its historical context and expressing that meaning for us today, while recognizing that a text can contain and convey meaning that goes beyond the original author's explicit intention."[1] A portrait from the roots or beginnings of his vision in religious education is also tied to a portrait of a dedicated priest who loves his Texan roots and who is grounded in his Mexican American heritage.

In this essay an analysis and word portrait will be presented that flows from his published work on religious education. Three hermeneutic gates or *puertas* will become the prisms through which the reader can recognize Virgil's contributions and our common challenges as we enter into the new millennium. The three hermeneutic *puertas* that will be described as windows into Virgil's view of religious education and his vision of evangelization are:

I.   The Hispanic Culture: Out of Chaos Comes Life
II. The Kerygma: The Proclamation of the Message
III. The Religious Educator: Becoming a Minister.

I. The Hispanic Culture: Out of Chaos Comes Life

In "Educación Religiosa para el México-Norteamericano"[2] (1972), written three years before Pope Paul VI's apostolic exhortation *On Evangelization in the Modern World*, Virgil proposes clear principles and values regarding the need for the religious educator to be a good communicator who respects and includes the Spanish language for effective Hispano catechetical programs. He establishes the principle that effective catechesis is based on solid and clear communication systems which welcome and include the Spanish language and Hispanic culture. He insists that this is more than simply transmitting or translating the concepts through words. Those who are religious educators and catechists not only need to understand the language of the other, they must also be sensitive to and aware of those receiving the communication. This means that the catechist must have a clear sense of the culture, the traditions, and the expressions of the people and be able to understand the meanings these have for those who are receiving the message from the catechist or religious educator. The catechist is also one who is open to and capable of receiving from the Hispano people through their culture.

In his early work on religious education, Virgil presents a picture of the reality of the Hispano in which he emphasizes the emerging Chicano of the 1970s.[3] Consistently, he reminds us that during the struggles of the Chicano Movement, a new awareness of a bilingual and bicultural people was rising up in the Southwest. The church of the United States was blessed with the presence of the Hispano-Chicano, born in the United States. He also addresses the presence of the new immigrants who crossed the border in search of a better life. For Virgil, the religious educator is one who recognizes and affirms the beauty and the faith of the Hispano culture and its rich contribution to the whole church. He sees the catechist-religious educator as one who has a pastoral vision which includes the struggle for social justice as well as the teaching of the faith tradition. Catechesis and religious education programs "imported" from Mexico, Latin America, or Spain could not respond to what was, and in many ways still is, a larger pastoral and ministerial challenge.[4] These concerns continue as critical issues in many dioceses and parishes. In the 1970s Virgil laid the cornerstone for teaching the faith and evangelization as he emphasized the need for attention to inculturation. Some may contend that this is not a new concept. Yet the church continues to face an urgent challenge for a pastoral vision that includes structures for catechetical programs developed from the faith symbols and values of the Hispano-Chicano culture. For Virgil a pastoral and holistic approach to catechetics becomes more dynamic when it includes those dimensions and issues pertaining to the family, social justice, the scriptures, and the church's living tradition. I believe that this is more than building a program or than discovering the "best" religious education book or resource material. Three decades ago Virgil wrote that the church was beginning to move in such a direction, and he vitally identified the Hispano-Chicano community with the Roman Catholic tradition.[5]

Virgil opened a *puerta* for the Hispano-Chicano in the church and he urged the consideration of bilingual and bicultural catechetics as well as the evangelization of cultures. The process of respecting the cultural context is a complex one, but one that started in ancient times with the gospel and with the incarnation of Jesus. It is a constant challenge for the church and for religious educators. Those who have committed themselves to be creative in planning pastoral-catechetical programs and processes based on the experience and culture of God's people have planted strong seeds for the faith to flourish.[6]

While excellent religious education programs continue to emerge, the critical pastoral questions raised by Virgil still remain. As we enter into the new millennium, where is the second-generation bilingual and bicultural Hispano whose parents are Roman Catholic? Does the Mexican American or Chicano vitally identify with the church today? Has there been a strong effort to prepare bilingual and bicultural Hispanos as religious educators and ministers to serve the growing Hispano Roman Catholic community? What is happening in our local churches regarding our youth? How are we passing on our faith and traditions to our youth? The questions raised by Virgil in the 1970s are still essential for committed catechists today. Our vision must be pastoral and it must be grounded in an evangelization of cultures. Inculturation is the incarnation of Christian life

and of the Christian message in a particular cultural context, in such a way that this experience not only finds expression through elements proper to the culture in question, but becomes a principle that animates, directs, and unifies the culture, transforming and remaking it so as to bring about "a new creation."[7]

The work of Virgil in catechetics and religious education from the perspective of Hispano Mexican American culture made a major contribution to the church's mission of evangelization. His manner of communicating in numerous conferences and classes at the Mexican American Cultural Center in San Antonio quickly inspired others to become religious educators or evangelizers who live by an authentic witness to the gospel of Jesus. The thousands of catechists and ministers that attended his conferences and classes throughout the country during the 1970s became more committed and better prepared to serve the Hispano community, even while chaos and social upheaval were taking place on college campuses and in the cities. His work echoed the powerful teachings of *Evangelii Nuntiandi* (On Evangelization in the Modern World) by Pope Paul VI (1975). "Truly the effort for evangelization will profit greatly at the level of catechetical instruction given at church, in the schools, where this is possible, and in every case in Christian homes. The methods must be adapted to the age, culture, and aptitude of the persons concerned; they must seek always to fix in the memory, intelligence, and heart the essential truths that must impregnate all of life."[8]

II. The Kerygma: The Proclamation of the Message

Virgil spoke of the pedagogy of evangelization and of religious education from a biblical perspective. He identified the teaching of the faith as part of the larger process of evangelization.

When the Pope called the Synod of Bishops for this coming fall (1974), all of us who are involved in evangelization and catechetics were overjoyed that he had taken what we are convinced is the core issue in the world today—how do we make God's redeeming love visible, and appreciated in the world today?[9]

The gospel message of Jesus is the heart of the evangelization process and the catechist who is an evangelizer must be imbued with the word and capable of becoming transformed by the word which is proclaimed. Virgil sees the word not only as something to be taught and clarified, but also as a creative act which brings new life out of death, meaning out of confusion, order out of chaos.[10]

Jesus is the catechist-evangelizer par excellence who by his incarnation teaches us the way. Virgil sees that through Jesus and through the church we can learn to listen to and become one with humanity. From this position of oneness the catechist-evangelizer can begin to speak and teach as Jesus did. This is much more than simply "educating" the other. "The misery of the other becomes the center of my heart, and thus the suffering of my brothers and sisters becomes the guidelines for my action. The life of Jesus is presented in scripture as a life of *miseri-*

cordia."[11] For those who are catechists-evangelizers, following the way of Jesus, whose words and deeds are the proclamation, is paramount.

> Let those who preach the Gospel be familiar with their national and religious traditions, gladly and readily laying bare the seeds of the Word which lie hidden in them . . . Christ Himself searched the hearts of men and led them to divine light through truly human conversation . . . [so] they themselves can learn by sincere and patient dialogue what treasures a bountiful God has distributed among the nations of the earth.[12]

Virgil believes that the catechist proclaims the Word through Christian living. He holds up the preaching of the apostles in the Acts of the Apostles as a vibrant model and example of this witness and proclamation. "In Acts 2:43, we begin to find a very important aspect for contemporary catechesis and evangelization: They devoted themselves to the apostles' instruction and the communal life, to the breaking of bread and the prayers."[13] Virgil insists that the basis for all preaching is found in the life of the community. The catechist-evangelizer must also take seriously the following:[14]
- continual preparation and study of the way of the Teacher/Lord
- mutual concern for one another by sharing the common goods
- the nucleus of their lives is in the breaking of the bread.

In proposing that there must be a strong link between the catechist and the dynamic proclamation of the word, Virgil also raises critical considerations that obstacles do present themselves when we stand committed to a living testimony of the faith. The Hispano community is a people of deep faith; nevertheless, this faith cannot flourish when we, the ministers, are not prepared to evangelize and teach effectively. In 1979, Virgil reminded catechists and religious educators that we must teach and educate responsibly with a love and understanding of the Christian tradition:

> The people have often found more sacramental meaning in their sacramentals than in the official sacraments of the church, when the sacraments have been reduced to a mere clerical ritual, rather than experienced as the dynamic moments of encounter with the Lord which celebrate the various moments of the ongoing process of evangelization.[15]

> There is the failure of some U.S. Catholics to welcome, appreciate, and minister in a truly catholic way to the Hispanic Catholics, and many are moving to active and dynamic ecclesial life in other Christian denominations.[16]

During the 1970s Virgil opined that the Hispano community has been sacramentalized but the community has not been evangelized. He called for catechetical leadership that will teach and support the Hispano community in becoming "ecclesialized" rather than merely "institutionalized."[17] These critical concerns raised some twenty years ago remain for contemporary religious educators to review and consider at the local church level.

Virgil is also strongly convinced that the Hispano family is truly the "domestic church"[18] or the organic life environment in which the seeds of the faith begin to grow. The faith is lived in the nuclear family and is also shared within the larger extended family. The first "catechists" are the parents and the grandparents, who take responsibility for the baptism of the children and for providing a home that values a strong spiritual life. As Virgil said, "the home truly becomes the first and most important school of human relationships. In the *familia* the art of human dynamics is taught through the many cultural dynamics of everyday life."[19] The parents, grandparents, and *padrinos* (godparents) continue to be those who proclaim the faith within the family through their Christian lives. Virgil reminds us of the importance of the grandparents, who carry within their hearts and minds the living memory of the family, its spiritual journey, and its faith history. Catechists who are evangelizers bring the family into the heart of parish religious education programs.

In reviewing some of Virgil's works and conferences over the years, it is quite clear that, as in the documents of the church such as the *Puebla Conclusions,*[20] he insists on a catechesis that flows from the teachings of the church and from solid theological criteria.

- That catechesis demands the building up of the community
- That catechesis motivates and inspires the believer to fidelity to the Father, Son, and Holy Spirit.
- That catechesis invites one to love the church and renew their commitment to the diversity of cultures within the church of the United States.
- That catechesis is a lifelong process leading the believer to an ongoing conversion and growth in the faith.
- That catechesis evolves from a biblical base, particularly from the New Testament and the words and deeds of Jesus and his disciples.
- That catechesis challenges us to an integrative faith through the knowledge and proclamation of the Word, the celebration of the sacraments, the profession and living of the faith in our day-to-day life.[21]
- That catechesis and the teaching of the faith flow from a respect and understanding of the Hispanic people's cultural roots; this is the "soil" from which the seed of faith in Jesus the Lord is cultivated and proclaimed.

The kerygma and proclamation of the gospel at the center of a religious education process must stand on firm theological underpinnings. This is very much in consonance with current documents of the church, particularly with the *Catechism of the Catholic Church* (1994).

III. The Religious Educator: Becoming a Minister

After founding the Mexican American Cultural Center in San Antonio, Virgil served as the first president and initiated a new and creative approach for preparing religious educators and other pastoral ministers to serve in the U.S. Hispano community.

> In 1971, I was asked by the bishops of Texas to become director of what was to become the Mexican American Cultural Center; it had no budget whatsoever, no location, no personnel, and not even a name. I was to be director of an idea that did not yet exist. But it was an exciting assignment and filled [me] with faith in God. I was crazy enough to accept and to begin the work of what is today the Mexican American Cultural Center . . . the risk was tremendous . . . thousands of people have come through our Center and have been totally transformed.[22]

The spirit of faith and the willingness to risk, traits always present in Virgil's leadership, were the building blocks for MACC. This spirit of commitment to the Hispanic community and the church was communicated to the students who prepared for ministry at MACC. I attended the Mexican American Cultural Center in the 1970s for the long pastoral course as part of my Master's studies. There is no doubt in my mind that the experience of MACC was and continues to be such a tremendous resource for our Hispanic leaders preparing to become religious educators and pastoral ministers, to come together and study theological and pastoral ministry in light of Hispano culture. Frequently at Hispanic meetings or at national theological gatherings, I continue to find priests, lay ministers, and women religious whom I first met years ago at MACC. This national gathering place for serious theological study and research, for ecclesial and cultural meetings, for celebrating the sacred moments of the liturgical year, for heated debate, and for wonderful *convivencias* has been a source for the formation of thousands of Hispanic ministers who serve the church as religious educators. Because of his clear theological insight, Virgil and the MACC faculty, especially the now Bishop Ricardo Ramírez, developed course content based on Hispano culture and on the documents of the Second Vatican Council. Other new pastoral and ministerial training centers in the United States seem to have followed the MACC model, while adapting to their particular geographical regions. The tremendous welcome offered at MACC gave Hispanic students a powerful sense of being "home." At MACC the students were introduced to the documents of the Second Vatican Council, especially *Lumen Gentium* and *Gaudium et Spes*, for study and analysis, as well as the later documents of Medellín, Puebla, and *Evangelii Nuntiandi*. Hispanic evangelization and religious education were viewed through the lenses of the rich living tradition in these ecclesial documents and from the perspective of the scriptures. These then became the sources for preparing new religious educators with a prophetic, evangelizing vision of church. Virgil's particular speciality regarding *mestizaje* was woven into a new ecclesiology for the Hispanic community within the Roman Catholic Church of the United States.

Such theological reflection and study took place in both the English and Spanish languages. This was a means of inviting Spanish-speaking Hispanics, English-speaking Hispanics, and non-Hispanics to join in the discussions and participate in an energizing theological-pastoral forum. Perhaps the group which felt most welcomed was the Mexican Americans, who sensed that truly there is a unique borderland culture growing profoundly within the Mexican and the Euro-American cultures of the United States.

At MACC those preparing to be religious educators and pastoral ministers entered into a total environment of study, living community, and experiencing the Hispanic culture and faith in the surrounding social, cultural, economic, historical, and religious reality of San Antonio. It was a holistic approach to pedagogy which emphasized insertion and immersion as far as was possible within the specific time of one's course of study. This meant stretching the student's skills, personal growth, faith, knowledge, and point of view far beyond merely the cerebral dimension. Virgil had a vision of how to elaborate the core program of studies and to prepare new ministers who were going to return to their own local churches as catechists, pastors, social workers, and educators. He seemed to focus clearly on a methodology by which all courses were developed.

> Ministry and education in the church will be determined by the interplay among Christology-ecclesiology-anthropology. During my own personal life as a priest (ordained in 1963), I have experienced a fascinating evolution which, in effect, has been a total transformation of the way in which the church has understood itself, its founder, its members, and its mission.[23]

The nucleus of this methodology was the opportunity for students to reflect deeply on the *predilectos de Dios*, the "favored ones of God" who are the core of the proclamation of the Good News.[24] Virgil tirelessly called upon students in classes, conferences, and liturgies to take seriously the preferential option for the poor in our lives and in our ministries. In this methodology the starting point in preparing for Christian mission is the materially poor. For those preparing to become ministers in the Hispanic community there must be a commitment to enter into solidarity with the materially poor.

> At the root of Christian ministry is witness, the new lifestyle based on conversion from the way of the world to the way of the Lord. For those involved in Christian education, degrees, ordination, titles, and publications cannot be the final qualification for teaching.[25]

These are challenging words that clearly called students to live the gospel responsibly and be authentic disciples centered on the Lord Jesus. While knowledge and study are necessary in preparing for ministry, the ministers must see themselves as servants also in need of conversion (*metanoia*) and they must recognize God's grace on the journey.

> The Christian minister, in the style of Jesus, does not seek to do things alone, but to call others to recognize their talents and abilities for the good of the

community. The energy released by the minister in calling people forth to service is endless; such calling of others is the minister's main task. Everyone without exception has something of value to offer.[26]

Jesus is the Teacher, the Religious Educator, and the *Puerta* who shows us how really to live in this manner (Phil. 2:6-8). Virgil presents us with this image of Jesus as the nobody that is a scandal to all. He is despised and rejected but he is also love that invites his disciples to a new way of life. The catechist continues the mission and ministry of Jesus.

During the tumultuous decade of the 1970s and into the 1980s Virgil encouraged and animated new religious educators who are ministers. He respected the local church community and its creativity and, therefore, did not address so much the specifics of a pedagogy of catechesis or religious education. Rather, like theologian Paul Bernier in his *Ministry in the Church: A Historical and Pastoral Approach*,[27] Virgil delineated those pathways which the religious educator as minister must follow in order faithfully to continue the mission-ministry of Jesus and to read the signs of the times within Hispanic culture and within the church of the United States. The teaching and proclamation of the Good News evolves from the preferential option for and commitment to the poor. From within such a theological and pastoral vision the religious educator is responsible for the teaching of the Christian faith.

There are strong and clear principles regarding religious education and catechesis found throughout Virgil's early works. This essay has presented a "portrait" of his view. In summary, the religious educator-minister has clear tasks and responsibilities that include:[28]

1. *Building community*. God's saving love comes through human relationships and in our communion with one another. The religious educator strives to support and encourage small communities within the parish community as focal points for religious education and faith sharing.

2. *Storytelling*. As we teach and learn about the story of salvation history, we also exchange those histories that are central to our families and our collective memory as a people of God. These stories are communicated in the signs, the symbols, the rituals, the language, and the culture of the community.

3. *Prophesying*. In living the gospel we are committed to work for social justice and an emancipatory praxis which challenges the forces of oppression and sin in our society.

4. *Nurturing*. We are nurtured on our journey by the Bread of Life which we share together as the Eucharist, our profound thanksgiving to the Lord.

5. *Missioning*. Our call to serve as catechists-ministers comes by virtue of our baptism in Jesus. We are missioned in the name of Jesus by our church (cf. Matt. 28:19-20).

6. *Partnership*. Virgil articulates and expresses this mutual respect between laity, clergy, and religious working together as pastors and teachers. James and Evelyn Whitehead remind us of this much needed gift to be coworkers in the Lord.

Partnership, both in the Gospel and in contemporary life, is an experience of
shared power. In this communal process, we explicitly reject domination of
one by the other. Being partners does not mean that we bring the same thing
to our relationship or that each of us contributes equally . . . More than on
strict equality, partnership depends on mutuality. The giving and the receiving go both ways . . . Partnership thrives when we recognize and respect this
mutual exchange of gifts.[29]

7. *Our Lady of Guadalupe.* In this image of the woman, we find the proclamation of the Word in the Americas. She is the sign of hope for all catechists and for
all who serve in the name of her Son, Jesus.

Notes

[1]Gerald O'Collins and Edward Farrugia, *A Concise Dictionary of Theology* (New York: Paulist
Press, 1991) 90.

[2]Virgil Elizondo, "Religious Education for Mexican Americans" 58-61 below.

[3]Ibid.

[4]Ibid.

[5]Ibid.

[6]See the new video now being produced by Liturgical Training Publications, Chicago, based
on the Religious Education Program on Sacramental Preparation in Sacred Heart Parish, San Jose,
California, 1999. The pastoral associate who created this excellent family-centered sacramental
preparation is María Guadalupe Vital.

[7]Peter Schineller, S.J., *A Handbook on Inculturation* (New York: Paulist Press, 1990) 6.

[8]Pope Paul VI, *Evangelii Nuntiandi* (Washington, DC: USCC, 1975) 30. The writings of Virgil
and of Pope Paul VI regarding evangelization/catechesis and culture are closely interwined in
spirit and theological insight.

[9]Virgilio Elizondo, "Biblical Pedagogy of Evangelization," *The American Ecclesiastical
Review* 168 (October 1974): 526.

[10]Ibid. 527.

[11]Ibid. 533.

[12]Ibid. 538; quote taken from *Ad Gentes*, The Decree on the Church's Missionary Activity,
Second Vatican Council, 1965, #11.

[13]Ibid. 539.

[14]Ibid.

[15]Virgil Elizondo, "The Catechumen in the Hispanic Community of the United States," in
Becoming a Catholic Christian: Symposium on Christian Initiation, ed. William Reedy (New
York: Sadlier, 1979) 54.

[16]Ibid. 55.

[17]Ibid. 53.

[18]See Paul VI, *Evangelii Nuntiandi*, 51. "At different moments in the church's history and also
in the Second Vatican Council, the family has well deserved the beautiful name of 'domestic
church.' This means that there should be found in every Christian family the various aspects of
the entire church. Furthermore, the family, like the church, ought to be a place where the Gospel
is transmitted and from which the Gospel radiates."

[19]Virgil Elizondo, "A Bicultural Approach to Religious Education" 68 below.

[20]See "Part One, Pastoral Overview of the Reality that is Latin America," in *Puebla and Beyond*,
ed. John Eagleson and Philip Scharper (Maryknoll, NY: Orbis, 1979) 248.

[21]Ibid. 248. These criteria are outlined in the Puebla Documents.

[22]Virgil Elizondo, "Ministry in Education from a Pastoral-Theological Perspective," in

Ministry and Education in Conversation, ed. Mary C. Boys (Winona, MN: St. Mary's Press, 1981) 46.

[23]Ibid. 48.

[24]Ibid. 60.

[25]Ibid. 64.

[26]Ibid. 60.

[27]Paul Bernier, *Ministry in the Church: A Historical and Pastoral Approach* (Mystic, CT: Twenty-Third Publications, 1992) 8.

[28]Ibid. 8-9.

[29]James D. Whitehead and Evelyn Eaton Whitehead, *The Promise of Partnership: A Model for Collaborative Ministry* (San Francisco: Harper, 1993) 8.

Elements in the Catechetical Pilgrimage

Virgilio, El Catequista

Anita de Luna

Introduction

Virgil Elizondo's catechetical leadership began in the mid 1960s when he directed the catechetical programs of the San Antonio archdiocese and later participated in the key historical moments of catechesis in the International Study Week of Catechetics at the East Asian Pastoral Institute and at the Medellín Catechetical Study Week.[1] Thus, his claim to be a catechist is well founded.[2] Among numerous honors, in 1993 Virgil received the Sadlier-Dinger Award for outstanding contribution to the ministry of religious education in the United States.[3]

Virgil's thinking was firmly molded by the Vatican II documents that relate to catechesis, in particular by the breadth and depth of "The Church in the Modern World" and "The Missionary Activity of the Church." One of his friends remembers visiting Virgil and watching him underline every significant statement in these documents.[4] The inspiration of the conciliar documents and his early exposure to catechesis drew him into projects directly related to religious education, an area in which he continues to be a leading voice.[5] Virgil's work has been highly influential in various arenas and his initial catechetical experience, I hold, has been formative of his global pedagogy. Centered on his personal experience as a Mexican American, he has documented his thinking in volumes of insightful articles, ground-breaking books, and a growing number of audiovisuals that will be his invaluable legacy to the next generation of catechists, theological anthropologists, pastoral theologians, and many others.

Virgil's influence and work is expansive, international, and embracive of themes which touch the whole universe of humanity. His publications, lectures, and various forums have reached many in the United States, Latin America, and Europe. In this essay I will review only one very small part of his work, that which relates directly to catechesis.

In the works I review Virgil reflects his experience in a pastoral, socioreligious context as he challenges society and the church to be more open and inclusive. His contributions to catechesis are expressive of a profound sense of justice oriented toward liberation. Writing specifically on Mexican Americans in his early writing, he articulated:

> The global objective of catechesis is to lead human beings to the fullness of life. However, we will never be able to lead them to fullness unless we free

them from their present state of socioeconomic and personal slavery. As long as people are convinced that they are not worth anything, they will not be able to experience the redemptive love of the Father.[6]

Significantly, this recognition of the significance of the individual's perception of his or her personal worth and dignity is an important thread that is integral to Virgil's catechetical message. He has accurately translated that personal insight into the collective Mexican American ethos.

According to Virgil, what tore at the self-image of the Mexican American was a lack of corporate knowledge that would bring about communal pride from within the community and affirmation from outside of it. Making the cultural information accessible and taking the culture and its implications as a *locus theologicus*, Virgil recreated a collective memory that I believe has augmented the possibility of Mexican Americans becoming players in church and in society. Virgil has inspired his audiences and his readers and spent time mentoring many of us into educational levels to which we otherwise never would have ventured. He has been available to us in our particular journeys and has taken pride and expressed consistent interest in our work. It is that mentoring which translates into the practice of companioning for a catechist.

Catechesis is about transforming society by teaching the type of faith that does justice as the gospel requires. The catechist must first, however, strengthen the catechumen to receive the faith in its fullness. Virgil discerned that to raise a people, in particular the Mexican Americans, to full stature in the faith would require bringing their identity to consciousness. That identity would be strengthened by the reclaiming of a sustaining patrimony.

As I sketch Virgilio, *el catequista*, I am privileging his catechetical works and placing them in dialogue with several of the major catechetical documents. I address three areas: (1) the role and task of the catechist, (2) the explicit and the implicit audience of his catechesis, and (3) the pedagogy that is the effective means for delivering his message.

The Role and the Task of the Catechist

The role of the catechist has been consistently defined in the catechetical documents. The *General Directory for Catechesis* defines it in the following way:

> The catechist is essentially a mediator. He [or she] facilitates communication between the people and the mystery of God, between subjects amongst themselves as well as with the community . . . [the catechist's] cultural vision, social condition and lifestyle, rather than being obstacles to the faith journey . . . help to create the most advantageous conditions for seeking out, welcoming, and deepening the Christian message . . . the personal relationship of the catechist with the subject is of crucial importance.[7]

Thus, the role of the catechist as mediator requires that he or she be knowledgeable in the doctrines of the faith, know those being catechized, and mediate among them and between them and the community. The aspect of community is stressed throughout the documents.[8] The description of the qualities of the catechist in the National Directory, *Sharing the Light of Faith*, includes the catechist's response to a call, treating the role as a vocation and situating the catechist as emerging from within the community.

The roles that Virgil, the catechist, has assumed are those of teacher, mediator, and prophet. His role as teacher is beyond question. I have been fortunate to have had many opportunities to hear Virgil as he delivers conferences and homilies, directs seminars, and teaches courses—he is always passionate about his task! His vita shows the numbers of universities and educational institutes in which he is visiting professor. His students have sat in the many classrooms in which he has lectured throughout the world, and many others have heard him in the innumerable podia from which he has delivered his presentations. Modern technology has taken him to countless other learners.

He is a catechist who is always teaching. He delivers the message with enthusiasm. His message comes from both theory and praxis. The catechumen in him has an insatiable thirst for learning, and he reflects on his broad base of experience which effectively grounds his learning. His relevance as teacher comes from his keeping pace with change and from monitoring the pulse of contemporary trends.

Virgil is a mediator. He delivers his message with boldness. Mediating between the gospel mandate and today's world, he probes the sinfulness of society. He often includes himself among those who need to be transformed. He says:

Our civil rights acts and emancipation laws have failed to stop discrimination and prejudice because our cultures and prejudices are too deeply engraved in all the fibers of our being . . . What we need most of all is not new laws, but new attitudes of the heart. This call is the radical acceptance of other as "other."[9]

Virgil frequently mediates between minority cultures and the general population.[10] Whenever he addresses issues of culture he does so with pride as a Mexican American. He intercedes for the people and the church as well. His works have raised the religious expressions of the Mexican American before the institutional church. He has equally praised the church when the institution has moved toward the people. Shortly after the publication of *The Catechism of the Catholic Church* he gave a number of presentations in which he borrowed the following two passages from it:

Article 1674:

Besides sacramental liturgy and sacramentals, catechesis must take into account the forms of piety and popular devotions among the faithful. The religious sense of the Christian people has always found expression in various forms of piety surrounding the Church's sacramental life, such as the veneration of relics, visits to sanctuaries, pilgrimages, processions, the stations of the cross, religious dances, the rosary, medals, etc.[11]

Article 1679:

In addition to the liturgy, Christian life is nourished by various forms of popular piety, rooted in the different cultures. While carefully clarifying them in the light of faith, the Church fosters the forms of popular piety that express an evangelical instinct and a human wisdom that enrich Christian life.[12]

Virgil felt that however small this step was, it was significant and needed to be noted that the church's magisterium was validating the people's expressions of faith. Popular religion has become of great significance in theologizing for U.S. Hispanics in these recent decades, and Virgil has been at the forefront of this theological trend that promotes the people's faith. On behalf of the church, he took the time to boost the moment before the people. Common themes for him have been the arbitration between faith and culture as in his *Christianity and Culture*, between majority and minority cultures in works such as *The Future Is Mestizo*, and between the sensus fidelium and the official church in his many works on popular religion such as *Guadalupe: Mother of the New Creation* and *Galilean Journey: The Mexican-American Promise*. He has indeed been a mediator.

Finally, Virgil has accepted his role as prophet. Early in his ministry he took it upon himself to raise awareness about the causes of injustice. In the 1970s and 1980s he called the church, the bishops, the clergy, and the laity to address the increasing number of Americans of Mexican descent requiring ministry unique to their socioreligious situation.[13]

Today, while still challenging society to transform itself from its ethnocentric attitudes, he remains hopeful and preaches his theme of unity and complementarity. He urges us to see diversity as a gift and to grow in appreciation of difference. He has an affinity to the scripture images of the Tower of Babel in Genesis 11 and the Pentecost event in Acts 2.[14] While Virgil is prophetically bold about bringing to light the sinfulness and evil of oppressors, he also issues his summons to the oppressed. He writes:

Those who have been marginated, brutalized, abused, segregated, put down, ridiculed, or merely tolerated need also to recognize their sin: the sense of inferiority that some come to believe and accept. The victimizer's ultimate triumph is to get the victims to accept the blame for their situation of misery. The sin of the victimized is to accept this as true, resulting in a loss of dignity and self-worth. Attitudes of docility, embarrassment of color or heritage, and the many negative and self-destructive feelings grow out of the inner sense of shame at being who one is.[15]

In many of his works, Virgil clamors for a conversion from our ethnocentrism to an appreciation of a multicultural, multilingual, and multiracial reality. He proposes that we begin with an initial confession of our monocentric sinfulness, move toward a conversion of embracing the "other," and gradually progress toward what he calls a construction of the new world order.[16]

One project that Virgil initiated consolidated more than any other his roles as teacher, mediator, and prophet. The project was the realization of a dream to address the pastoral concerns of the very large majority of Mexican Americans. In 1972 Virgilio, along with a group of other gifted persons, founded the Mexican American Cultural Center in San Antonio, Texas, to empower leaders through faith and culture. From the specific perspective of the Mexican American Virgil envisioned bringing together experts from around the world to address the universal questions of faith and culture. Past its twenty-fifth anniversary, MACC today continues to build on that initial dream.

The role of the catechist, whether as teacher, mediator, or prophet, includes some essential tasks. The documents divide the tasks of catechesis into two parts: initiatory and ongoing. These are described by the 1997 *General Directory for Catechesis* (GDC) as follows: (1) to promote knowledge of the faith; (2) to enable the faithful to participate fully, consciously, and actively in liturgical and sacramental life; (3) to enter into a process of conversion evidenced by response to the social consequences of gospel imperatives; (4) to have all activity be permeated by the spirit of prayer; (5) to form genuine Christian communities; (6) to educate to a missionary dimension.[17]

Commenting on the GDC, Sister Catherine Dooley notes that the task of catechesis is conditioned by the particular concerns of society. During this century the emphasis of catechesis has moved from method to message to milieu.[18] Early in the century the conversation was dominated by the question-and-answer methodology used by the Baltimore Catechism of 1885. Midway through the century the conversation shifted to the question of the *kerygma*, which was in crisis at the time when catechetical giants like Johannes Hofinger, Josef Jungmann, Alfonso Nebrada, and others in Manila and at Medellín articulated the key moments in the historical development of evangelization. At the study weeks convened at the time, the emphasis turned to the adaptation of the message to the culture and milieu of the groups who would receive it. These were Virgil's catechetically formative years. *Sharing the Light of Faith*, published in 1979, also carried a strong emphasis on cultural consciousness.[19]

Moving somewhat away from cultural influence and closer to ecclesial dimensions, the 1971 *General Catechetical Directory* describes catechesis as a ministry of the word. The 1997 *General Directory for Catechesis* also envisions the catechetical tasks as ecclesial. Both of these documents define catechesis as a moment in the process of evangelization.

In summary, the task of catechesis is a lifelong process which pertains to the development and the growth of faith in an individual or group. Because the tasks are informed by society's questions, the catechetical accents tend to change. Catechesis addresses the primary mission of the church which is to evangelize, build community, and invite the faithful to conversion according to the Gospels.

Virgil's writing related to catechesis firmly grounds his approach within evangelization. He sees the task of the discipline as transformation with an emphasis on culture and conversion. He sees these emphases as significant for the shared pilgrimage toward a more just and peaceable world order. In his own words, he writes: "It is the task of the religious educator to reflect, teach, clarify, and celebrate this process of struggle and transformation as it takes place within our own historical and cultural journey."[20]

For Virgil, catechetical praxis is followed by hope-filled vision. Reminiscent of Chardinian thought, Elizondo is poetic and hopeful for the world and its inhabitants. He holds on to a hope for humanity and an acute optimism that humanity will grow toward greater wholeness—by their fruits they will know them. As he writes:

> In the end life will be the perfect and unending relationship with one another, with all of nature, and with God. In the interim we must work diligently for justice. In the end struggles for justice will no longer be necessary, for the justice of God will reign. The proper relationships will have been reestablished. Humanity will have truly been rehabilitated. There will finally be peace on earth because the orderliness of all of creation will be a reality. Beginning in Christ, God has placed us in the proper relationship. When what has started in Christ comes to perfection in all, life will indeed exist in its fullness—SHALOM.[21]

Virgil understands that the task of the catechist is taking everyday life and rereading it through the eyes of the gospel. He weaves steadfastly into his writing the aspects of culture and conversion, which are integral parts of evangelization. His works consistently explore and examine the status quo and in so doing he aims at unveiling sin and announcing the alternative of the gospel.[22]

Explicit and Implicit Audience

The second part of this essay reviews Elizondo's works related to catechesis and his intended audience. I find that Virgil's works invite a specific and a general audience. Explicitly, Virgilio writes for a general audience that is non-Hispanic, expounding on culturally related themes. His writing often adopts a reflective style.

Four of Virgil's articles are reprinted in this section; all are aimed at a general audience. Some are addressed to society at large, others to the church, and still others to non-Hispanics. In "Religious Education for Mexican Americans," Virgil exposes the urgency of attending to the needs of the growing number of Mexican Americans and writes in particular to pastoral agents. He writes: "If Chicanos do not see and experience the love of the church, the best catechetical programs will fall on an increasing number of deaf ears."[23] And again he urges:

> The church has many good things to teach but Chicanos are saying to the church: "Show us that we are really important to you . . . we are your children who have been trampled upon, put down, ridiculed, abused, robbed of our

rights. Help us in our search for liberation so that we may be able to fulfill our legitimate role in society on the same level as our brothers and sisters."[24]

In "A Bicultural Approach to Religious Education," Virgil uses a similar approach. He uses scripture to elucidate the praxis of the religious educator and the power of idol-making. Consequently, he particularizes his subject and edges toward a Hispanic perspective on blessing and enumerates the characteristics of the culture that relate to faith. Finally, he concludes with some universals and notes:

Religious education leads the people into a new way of seeing—with the eyes of the Gospel—thus being in a new way. It creates new attitudes and releases a new spirit. It leads people to see the other, the cultural other, with the heart and thus understand with the mind. When this takes place we cease to see cultural differences as threats and begin to see them as gifts. We begin to see the threat of the other as an invitation to die to ghettoism so that we may resurrect to a greater life.[25]

In "Cultural Pluralism and the Catechism," Virgil is commenting on the *Catechism of the Catholic Church* and he voices his stance on the text's recommendation for particular groups to write local catechisms. Here, as in the above articles, Virgil includes himself in what he is suggesting: "What we want is to be significantly included throughout any of the texts that are developed for the United States—not to appear as an appendix, but as an integral part of the text."[26]

Concluding his thoughts, Virgil ends the article by amplifying to the universal and away from the particular:

I hope and pray that our church may help to bring about a new paradigm of human existence: the reign of the God who watches over all the peoples of the world and who wants us to live in harmony and not in destructive fights and wars. To the degree that we can celebrate our unity in our diversity, we will have something truly new to offer today's divided world.[27]

Most typical of Virgilio's work is the cultural signature he gives his work. His point of departure is always his particular frame of reference—Mexican American. This identification which he makes public gives his work credibility because it emerges from his specific experience; he speaks from his particularity and then opens his themes to their universality. Theological anthropologists like Aylward Shorter and others have written extensively to establish that faith can only be expressed within specific cultures and can only be transmitted effectively when the receiving cultures can inculturate it. The inductive method in evangelization and catechesis has for a long time been recognized as the only credible way to understand faith. Berard Marthaler, commenting on the *General Catechetical Directory*, writes: "Catechesis [which leads the person to a mature faith] takes as its starting point the actual experience and knowledge, however limited, of the learner."[28]

The implicit audience that Virgilio addresses is the Mexican American. He is the voice for us and when one of us Mexican Americans reads his writing we feel we are on secure ground and we are able to stand with Virgil and say the things that he says—he is truly our voice. We are dignified when our particular cultural experience and expressions of faith can serve to elucidate issues of universal import. Virgilio as an international figure has access to many angles and perspectives to express his thought; the fact that he opts to use the Mexican American experience is a source of particular pride and profound validation for the culture.

Among the many contributions that Virgilio has made, in my estimation his greatest has been that in identifying himself as Mexican American he has become an identifiable hero/prophet for us. He has named and claimed a cultural and spiritual heritage for himself and in so doing has reclaimed it for all Mexican Americans. He has given all Mexican Americans a memory.

> People who have lost their memories no longer remember who they are. That means that they can no longer function effectively in the present and that they have no secure plans for the future. They have lost their past and that has emptied their present of meaning and clouded their future. We must have contact with the past if only for the sake of the present and the future.[29]

These are the words of John Westerhoff addressing the issue of catechesis and history. Civic and church history fail to lift the contributions of indigenous cultures and to raise the overwhelming sacred aura that surrounded the indigenous peoples who were the ancestors of today's Mexican Americans. Virgil saw the remnants of the ancient sacredness still discernible in contemporary faith expressions; placing this gift of Mexican American religious expressions before the church became his task.

By bringing to the foreground the best of Mexican American religion Virgilio has made this rejected ancestry acceptable and honorable. The meta-metaphor for many U.S. Hispanics and Mexicans, Our Lady of Guadalupe, is the pearl in Virgilio Elizondo's work. Guadalupe is God's alternative to the evangelization of the sixteenth century and she is the manifestation of God's favor to the poor. She is the vehicle for understanding and for teaching faith.

While there have been writers in other disciplines who also attempted to recreate the Mesoamerican history of the people,[30] Virgilio was the first to emerge from among the Mexican American people to tell the story of the past in its socioreligious context and make connections with their contemporary reality.[31]

The importance of honoring the past of a people in order to build a present and secure a future is a subject for a number of educators. In his famous work on religious education, Thomas Groome lists some assumptions for educators regarding time:

> We are motivated to educate so that out of the past heritage of our people we may build a present and future for ourselves and our students . . . part of the task of education is to ensure that our "funded capital" [past] is conserved and made available to people in the present. Without it our present is impoverished and our future is diminished.[32]

Virgil has led us to become familiar with our own indigenous beauty by placing a mirror before us; hence, he has placed the reflection of the image before non-Hispanics to facilitate a cultural consciousness. His books *La Morenita* (1980) and *Galilean Journey* (1983), in my view, mark major moments of catechesis. Thus, when we struggle with identity questions within a deeply religious bicultural existence we find consolation in reading Elizondo whose images are extremely compelling and identifiable. The printed word gives the reader time to meditate and reflect at her own pace and at his own point of readiness.

Virgil has placed many in a position of strength from which to encounter the "other" and promote life's chances in the church and in society. The security of knowing ourselves as good is essential to the catechetical message. This is the best gift any catechist can give his or her companions on the journey.

Pedagogy

The *General Directory for Catechesis* reads: "Catechetical pedagogy will be effective to the extent that the Christian community becomes a point of concrete reference for the faith journey of individuals. This happens when the community is proposed as a source, *locus*, and means of catechesis."[33]

Virgil is well integrated into the San Antonio parish community in which he serves, a community that has grown into the global perimeters in which he moves. He does not discriminate in his choice of subjects from whom he learns. He easily engages the conversations of his European and Latin American theologian colleagues. He is equally at ease with the uneducated but very wise people from San Fernando Cathedral in San Antonio from whom he learns just as much and from whose experience he draws such gems as his current work-in-progress on the spirituality of the *Mestizo*.

John Westerhoff, a contemporary expert in religious education, tells us that "to catechize is to participate with others in the life-long pilgrimage of catechesis."[34] The genius of Virgil's pastoral pedagogy has been that he has remained close to the people he catechizes. His way of keeping an audience, a congregation, or any hearer captive with his message is by continuing to identify and speak from the perspective of personal experience and by having his message remain fresh and relevant. His personal story, seen through the eyes of the Gospels, the prophets of old, or the crucified Jesus is a subject that draws and keeps an audience listening attentively. Virgil has earned his credibility and has refined his pedagogy so that he can create an instant forum for his message. That, in essence, is the kind of creativity required of a good catechist.

Virgil produces books which have gained popularity across the globe, yet he can stand before a parish scripture class with some newsprint and markers and be perfectly happy. He successfully initiated the only weekly, live, televised Mass in the Americas. The Mass is transmitted from San Fernando Cathedral in San Antonio, Texas. He established a tradition that involves the city of San Antonio in a celebration of the drama of Passion Week which has grown to international repute. Yet he is equally pleased broadcasting a program for catechetical formation in the archdiocese of San Antonio through the Catholic channel. He recognizes the potential and uses many media for evangelizing. An excellent catechist, his pedagogy is consistently creative, varied, and effective.

"To be a catechumen is to be a pilgrim; to be a catechist is to be a compassionate companion and guide to pilgrims."[35] Virgil is an effective catechist and reaches his audience because he is such a willing learner and only then is he an effective teacher. He has certainly been a good companion on the shared journey toward mature faith and has led many to a recognition and a reclaiming of their personal goodness, beauty, and potential as prerequisites to continuing on a journey toward maturity of faith.

Virgil is a prolific writer. His works have a disarming simplicity which appeals to the ordinary person, the researcher, and the scholar. While being comprehensible to a general audience, his works are also profoundly substantial. The beauty of Virgilio's work is that his message is accessible to so many because he is so readable.

Conclusion

Catechetics requires a past to understand the present and to build a future. Virgil has given Mexican Americans a memory for the personal and corporate survival of the individual and the collective soul and has invited society-at-large to be transformed. Within his *mestizaje*, set within a Mexican American reality, he has provided a locus for theology, inspiration, and reflection that ignites imaginations and opens the mind to broad and universal insights.

The test of good evangelization is its potential to unsettle the comfortable, to touch hearts and stir imaginations; all these elements coalesce in the invitation to convert. Elizondo has the gift of doing that for us. It is impossible not to get caught in his spellbinding and optimistic desire to enhance the development of a consciousness that envelops all of humanity, calling forth the best in us and drawing us together in respect and dignity.

Elizondo has been a genuine cultural interpreter, beginning each of his works by claiming his specific reality. His strength as catechist, scholar, and evangelizer comes from his committed faith in God and people, an interdisciplinary knowledge, and a solid grounding in his authentic personal identity. He is well anchored in the culture, the faith, and the posture from which he speaks and writes. Virgil's creativity has no limits and his gift to the church, the Mexican American community, and all other cultures is a boundless treasure. It is grace. In one of his commentaries, Marthaler says of catechists: "There is more to catechetical formation than training in skills, learning an art, getting an academic degree. It presumes a deep Christian commitment and involves the whole person, his [or her] cultural, social, psychological, intellectual, moral, and spiritual growth."[36] Virgilio, *el catequista,* has gifted the church with his whole person. He has placed himself in the path of the Spirit's blowing and has allowed the spontaneity of his God-given gifts to come alive; hence, he has been used for the good of all. I conclude with a quote from the GDC that is applicable to Virgil, who has responded so totally to the call to catechize: "No methodology, no matter how well tested, can dispense with the person of the catechist in every phase of the catechetical process. The charism given to him [or her] by the Spirit, a solid spirituality and transparent witness of life, constitutes the soul of every method."[37]

Notes

[1]Virgil's extensive curriculum vitae includes a Diploma in Pastoral Catechetics from the East Asian Pastoral Institute (1969).

[2]Virgil Elizondo, "Cultural Pluralism and the Catechism" 72 below.

[3]This piece of information and other specifics on Virgil's accomplishments are documented in his curriculum vitae which was graciously supplied by Ms. Janie Dillard, Virgil's administrative assistant at his MACC office in San Antonio, Texas.

[4]Sister Celia Ann Cavazos, MCDP, was instrumental in bringing to print some of the major catechetical documents and is one of Virgil's acompañantes in his catechetical pilgrimage. I am indebted to her for contributing to the sketch of Virgil's catechetical portrait.

[5]Virgil has collaborated with W. H. Sadlier, a catechetical text publisher, in the production of several texts from the mid 1980s to the present. He continues to be a popular lecturer on a variety of evangelization and catechetical themes at many national conferences. In 1995, for example, he presented a keynote address entitled "Excellence in Catechesis: Bridging the Centuries" to the National Catholic Education Association meeting in Cincinnati.

[6]Virgilio Elizondo, "Religious Education for Mexican Americans" 60 below.

[7]Congregation for the Clergy, "Elements of Methodology," General Directory for Catechesis (hereafter GDC) (Washington, D.C.: USCC, 1998) 150-151.

[8]For a description of the qualities of the catechist that details the importance of being part of and serving the community, see Sharing the Light of Faith (Washington, D.C.: USCC, 1979) 126-127.

[9]Virgil Elizondo, "A Bicultural Approach to Religious Education" 65 below.

[10]Ibid. 65-70.

[11]Catechism of the Catholic Church (New York: Doubleday, 1995) no. 1674.

[12]Ibid. no. 1679.

[13]"Religious Education for Mexican Americans" 58-61 below.

[14]"Cultural Pluralism and the Catechism" 72-86 below. This article is an example of Virgil's prophetic posture that arises from the scriptures and relates to the sinfulness of stereotyping cultures and perpetuating myths of superiority and inferiority.

[15]Virgilio Elizondo, "Benevolent Tolerance or Humble Reverence? A Vision for Multicultural Religious Education" 92 below.

[16]Ibid. 90-96 below.

[17]GDC, nos. 85, 86.

[18]For a very insightful review of catechesis in two major documents see Catherine Dooley, "The General Directory for Catechesis and the Catechism: Focus on Evangelizing," Origins 28 (4 June 1998).

[19]Sharing the Light of Faith, nos. 194, 242, 236, 137, and 139.

[20]"A Bicultural Approach to Religious Education" 63 below.

[21]Virgil Elizondo, "By Their Fruits You Will Know Them: The Biblical Roots of Peace and Justice," in Education for Peace and Justice, ed. Padraic O'Hare (San Francisco: Harper & Row, 1983) 63.

[22]"A Bicultural Approach to Religious Education" 63, 70 below.

[23]"Religious Education for Mexican Americans" 61 below.

[24]Ibid.

[25]"A Bicultural Approach to Religious Education" 70 below.

[26]"Cultural Pluralism and the Catechism" 84 below.

[27]Ibid. 85 below.

[28]Berard L. Marthaler, *Catechetics in Context: Notes and Commentary on the General Catechetical Directory Issued by the Congregation for the Clergy* (Huntington, IN: Our Sunday Visitor, 1973) 143.

[29]John Westerhoff III, "The Challenge: Understanding the Problem of Faithfulness," in *A Faithful Church: Issues in the History of Catechesis*, ed. John Westerhoff III and O. C. Edward, Jr. (Wilton, CT: Morehouse-Barlow, 1981) 8-9.

[30]For some excellent development from the perspective of cultural anthropology on the inculturation of Christianity in the sixteenth century, see the works of Miguel León-Portilla and Jorge J. Klor de Alva. There is also another fine resource by Robert M. Carmack, Janine Gasco, and Gary H. Gossen, *The Legacy of Mesoamerica: History and Culture of a Native American Civilization* (Upper Saddle River, NJ: Prentice Hall, 1996).

[31]The long-time classic from the perspective of the sixteenth-century evangelization of present-day Mexico was Robert Ricard's *La conquista espiritual de Mexico*, first issued in 1947. This work, however, made no connection to the U.S. Hispanic.

[32]Thomas H. Groome, *Christian Religious Education: Sharing Our Story and Vision* (San Francisco: Harper and Row, 1980) 7.

[33]GDC 151.

[34]Westerhoff, "The Challenge: Understanding the Problem of Faithfulness" 3.

[35]Ibid.

[36]Marthaler, *Catechetics in Context* 215.

[37]GDC 150.

Virgilio Elizondo as Religious Educator

Ever Removing Barriers

Thomas H. Groome

In college, I had a front tooth peremptorily removed in a football "accident." I was rushed to the local dentist, who referred me to an orthodontist, who referred me to a periodontist, who referred me to a prosthodontist, who referred me to an oral surgeon, who sent me back to my local dentist—who could have taken care of my problem in the first place. In my odyssey, I also encountered a dental nurse, a dental hygienist, a dental assistant, and a dental mechanic. And this was thirty years ago; other specialties have emerged since then. What a far cry from 1544 when King Henry VIII gave an official charter to the barbers of England to do what they had been doing for centuries, namely, perform all necessary dental procedures as well as clip beards and cut hair.

Specialization with attendant barriers of division among and within the sciences is a distinguishing feature of the modern era. Conventional distinctions based on the function or focus of a science have grown into walls of separation; and even within the sciences, subspecialties have emerged marked by hardened boundaries, turf protecting, and often antipathy.

Now, there have been blessings and benefits from modern scientific specialization. In-depth knowledge and advanced know-how regarding things that matter to our condition and world are always assets; they help to make and keep life human. Further, advances in all the sciences have been so vast and rapid as to require any one scholar to focus within a specialty; the solo encyclopedist, if ever possible, is now far beyond the realm. And though my local barber gives a fine haircut, I would hate to have to face him for a tooth extraction.

Echoing a favorite criticism among postmodernist authors, however, specialization that establishes barriers between or within the sciences—including the arts and humanities—has a debilitating underside. The resulting fragmentation can cause a whole science to "miss the wood for the trees," and discourages the cooperation and integration needed to serve the common good. If the specializations within dentistry do not retain a shared sense of purpose—dental healthcare—they become problematic to the welfare of society and even of their individual clients. To begin with, they are accessible only to the wealthy or well-insured in affluent societies and so generally neglect the poor of humankind. Would fewer specialists and more well-trained generalists—with the confidence and training to carry out all routine procedures—render more adequate and accessible dental healthcare to more people?[1]

In theology, too, the modern era has brought intense and often barrier-building specialization, with subspecialties within the specialties. One can find systematicians who concentrate solely on ecclesiology; and I have a scripture-scholar friend who says, only half-jokingly, that his "field" is Psalm 41—the theme of his dissertation. As within all the sciences, theological specialization can heighten scholarship but hardened separations can be debilitating to the overall enterprise—to the point of defeating the humanizing purposes of theology.

Insofar as theology could be called a *science* in the early church, it was unified in its focus on understanding, articulating, and encouraging the *life of Christian faith*. This unity held throughout the monastic era of theology (circa 500-1150), with its method of *lectio divina* and the purpose of spiritual wisdom to enhance Christian living. With the founding of the universities (beginning circa 1150), theology felt challenged to hold its own in this more academic setting. Now dogmatics emerged as a *scientific* endeavor—more intent on rational knowledge than on spiritual wisdom. Still, however, Aquinas saw dogmatics as requiring partnership with the study of philosophy and scripture, and all three providing the necessary foundations for the moral and pastoral training of priests. For the Scholastics, theology was dignified as "faith seeking understanding."

In the second half of the eighteenth century a fourfold division emerged, first in Protestant seminaries, and typically called dogmatics, Bible, church history, and practical theology. A little later a similar pattern began to divide the curriculum of Catholic seminaries, though practical was called pastoral—if named at all—and focused on moral theology as training for confessors. Thereafter, and as modern universities took up the academic study of theology, the subspecializations emerged with a vengeance. Now it is difficult to count them because disputes rage about their names and what precisely belongs where, especially when "subject matter" is made the basis of formal distinctions.

One attempt at a list might run as follows: *fundamental* or foundational theology, with subdivisions like theologies of God, of revelation, of the human condition; *systematics* or dogmatic theology, with a horde of subspecialties like christology, ecclesiology, sacramental or liturgical theology; *Bible* and exegetical theology, subdivided into Hebrew scriptures or Old Testament (with further subspecialties like the prophets and wisdom literature), New Testament (with subspecialties in the Synoptics, Johannine, Pauline, and pastoral literatures), and intertestamental studies or second-temple Judaism; *historical* theology, or church history, or history of theology, with various subspecialties like patristics (which sometimes combines with New Testament as "early Christian origins") and medieval; *moral* theology or Christian ethics—now preferring to separate from pastoral—and with subspecialties like theological and social ethics; and *pastoral* or practical theology with various subdisciplines such as religious education or catechetics, pastoral care and counseling, spirituality (which can also locate under systematics), liturgy (ditto), and more; an emerging discipline called *comparative* theology that promotes dialogue between Christianity and other religious traditions; and I'm sure I've left some out.

Of course, theologians in all of these subspecialties span the ideological spectrum from conservative to liberal to radical. Likewise, many self-consciously choose to "do" their theology from a particular perspective, interest, or social context; so there is Latin American liberation theology, African American theology, feminist theology, creation theology, postmodernist theology, and many more.

Though tempting, it would be cynical to dismiss this intense specialization as a new Tower of Babel, once more aspiring to reach to the very heavens—this time through erudition. Better to appreciate that contemporary theology has achieved an amazing breadth and depth of scholarship, enabling it to engage the scientific consciousness of our time. Bultmann's fear that the gospel miracles would pale by comparison with the modern light bulb has not come to pass, because theology has found ways to articulate and communicate old truths according to the mode of present receivers. Its scholarship can help people to find meaning through Christian faith in what Bonhoeffer called "a world come of age." Likewise, no sacred texts or traditions have been submitted to such historical analysis and contextualizing as in Christian theology, helping to offset fundamentalism and fanaticism, which are still serious threats to world peace from many religious traditions.

On the other hand, there are turf-claiming and barricade-building tendencies among theology's subspecialties that have serious liabilities. First, unless all the specializations are unified by a shared sense of purpose and procedure, their self-contained scholarship could defeat the defining purpose of theology—to enable people to engage and make meaning out of life from a faith perspective (traditionally stated as "faith seeking understanding"). The subspecialties of dentistry serve the common good to the extent that they render comprehensive dental healthcare made available to all. Why not likewise for theology? Instead of becoming rarefied discourses among separated cadres of scholars, theological specialties should coalesce as readily available resources to their faith communities for living and life-giving faith.

Second, theology's subspecialties have generally embraced the Enlightenment assumption that scientific scholarship should be value-free and objective—devoid of historical interest and influence—and should seek transcendental truths through critical rationality. But a conviction of these postmodern times is that such "pure reason" is a myth and a destructive one; better by far that all scholars become critically conscious of the influence of their social context. And instead of feigning "disinterest," they should become intentional about the historical responsibilities of their scholarship. Without such critical awareness and social commitment within academic theology, it becomes less likely to be a humanizing resource for the world—deserving, once again, of its old caricature of "how many angels can fit on the head of a pin?"

A third and perhaps most damaging liability of specialization within modern theology is its acceptance of the Enlightenment dichotomy and hierarchical ordering between "theoretical" and "practical" fields. In sum, systematics, Bible, and historical assumed the mantle of "theoretical" specializations, often posing as serious scholarship precisely by rising above pastoral issues. Then, presumed to be without scholarship in its own right, pastoral theology was reduced to a "delivery" system, a training in the skills needed to apply the theory—should it have any application—developed by the theoretical specialties.

This dichotomy and hierarchical ordering between the theoretical and practical has been particularly debilitating for the relationship between theology and religious education—my own alleged expertise. It has encouraged theologians to be indifferent to their profound responsibilities as religious educators (so much theology is taught poorly) and, likewise, has discouraged religious educators from developing the foundational scholarship—theological and social scientific—that their endeavor requires.

I recognize that my historical claims here are sweeping and need nuancing. Yet, until quite recently—when the priority of praxis began to be reestablished in Christian thought—many subspecialties within academic theology have been naïvely intent on proceeding by pure reason, and often appeared to have a supercilious attitude toward historical or pastoral concerns. The hope of our time, however, is that the foundations of the "theory to practice" paradigm are crumbling. Its feigned historical innocence is seen for what it is—at best naive and potentially dangerous. In its place, a paradigm is emerging that unites theory and practice as praxis, and prioritizes the historical responsibilities of all Christian theology. It invites theologians, regardless of their specialty, to be intentional about what their scholarship means for life and world, and likewise to become conscious of the influence of historical context on their theologizing.

The purpose of my brief foray into the history and state of theology is to situate and heighten appreciation for the work of Virgilio Elizondo. He has helped to forge the emerging praxis-based paradigm in theology, and has embodied the hope that the pitfalls of specialization can be avoided. Though he rightly enjoys a national and international reputation as a systematician and as a pastoral theologian—and I am about to review him as a bona fide religious educator—his specializations have enhanced each other, contributing to theological work of intellectual coherence and historical integrity. He has helped to erase the barriers between theological specializations precisely because his work and ministry have had one unifying and defining purpose since the beginning of his public career— "to make God's redeeming love visible in the world today" (1974).[2]

My particular assignment here is to write about Virgil's work as a religious educator and the contribution he has made to this aspect of theology and ministry. This is a ready task in that Virgil began his theological career as a religious educator and has remained one all his life. In fact, his initial assignment as religious educator is a clue to understanding his life work. But my broader intent is to highlight how he has avoided the barriers that can separate theology's subspecialties and, in particular, how he has transcended the divide between theology and religious education. By working throughout his life as religious educator and theologian, Virgil helps to redefine both in complementarity to each other.

The remainder of my essay has three sections: a brief review of Virgil's work and self-understanding as religious educator; the core themes of his specific writings on religious education—both reflecting and contributing to his theology; finally, I return to the issues raised in this introduction and reflect briefly on how Virgil's life work can help us to eradicate barriers of specialization and to forge a more adequate partnership between theology and religious education.

Ever the Religious Educator

A few years after his ordination to the priesthood in 1963, Virgil was appointed Director of Religious Education for the archdiocese of San Antonio. Recognizing his lack of professional training in the field, he sought and was granted permission to study at the East Asian Pastoral Institute in Manila. There he encountered such catechetical "greats" as Alfonso Nebreda and Johannes Hofinger and wrote his first book, *The Human Quest: A Search for Meaning through Life and Death.*

Upon returning to San Antonio, and in addition to his responsibilities as archdiocesan Director of Religious Education, Virgil was appointed Dean of Studies at Assumption Seminary. He was given the mandate to revise its curriculum to reflect the spirit of the Second Vatican Council. From this first experience of wearing the two hats, he likely began to recognize the correlation between theological and religious education and the challenges common to both. Thereafter, in 1972, he founded and became the first president of the Mexican American Cultural Center in San Antonio—again calling for partnership between theology and religious education.

Throughout his career, Virgil has published many writings specifically on religious education, the most recent being a major essay of 1997.[3] In addition, he has served as a consultant to three widely used catechetical curricula[4] and has long been a popular speaker at diocesan and national gatherings of religious educators. Across all cultural groupings, but especially within the Hispanic American community, Virgilio Elizondo is one of the most respected religious educators in North America. We have much to learn from his self-understanding as religious educator.

Religious Educator as Prophet. For Virgil, the religious educator is synonymous with the biblical prophet—situating oneself "in the midst of chaos, slavery, death, and division," in order "to point the way and clarify the vision for a new social order."[5] In this function, the model, as always for Christians, is the prophet Jesus.[6]

Virgil constantly turns his prophetic voice to challenge the "Americanism" of this society, "a totalitarian image which overshadows any cultural diversity or ethnic make-up and seeks to shut out anything 'other' than itself."[7] But he is likewise critical of the sins of the church. In an essay of 1979 he wrote that "the typical U.S. Catholic parish . . . has been more an obstacle to faith than an invitation to Christ" and that "the institutional Church has not radiated the image of Christ who welcomes all, especially the most rejected of society."[8] Some twenty years later he critiqued the continuing sinfulness of the mainline American Church as "the sin of dogmatic ethnocentrism"—the belief that white European Americans are "the superior race" and "the sin of arrogant pride"—that blinds us to the gifts of those who are "other."[9] And yet, like every true prophet in the biblical tradition, he both calls in question and holds out hope—hope for a new society of justice and freedom, and for a new church in which all are included, respected, and can find a home.[10]

Catechist as Evangelist. The recently published *General Directory of Catechesis* (1998) makes evangelization the defining focus of the church's catechetical ministry. Virgil, however, was "ahead of his time" on this theme. In 1974 he proposed that all catechesis be understood as having the purpose of evangelization. Further, instead of the traditional image of bringing converts into the church, he described evangelization as "the opening of one's eyes to the ultimate meaning of reality," and as "the process of conversion from self-centeredness to other-centeredness in the person of Jesus who is resurrecting in us."[11] Following on, he often pointed out that conversion must constantly engage the individual Christian, the whole church, and catechists themselves; all of us are forever in need of evangelization.

Catechesis for Lived Faith. Note Virgil's holistic sense of Christian faith, that it should permeate "every aspect of life . . . the economic, the social, the political, the cultural" and must care for the needs of "the total person."[12] We must catechize for Christian faith to be lived and life-giving, to be realized in every nook and cranny of life. He emphasizes "taking a stand" on behalf of the poor and those who suffer injustice of any kind; in response to the cries of those in need, "we cannot stand by and look the other way, for ignorance and neutrality in themselves already mean condemnation."[13] Precisely because Christian faith should be embodied as standing up for life in the midst of the world, "the questions in Christian education are: Who ultimately am I with? Who am I for? What am I against?"[14]

Catechesis in "the Dynamics of Life." We return to this theme below under Virgil's commitment to inculturation, but here I highlight it as his pedagogy of catechesis. In sum, he was convinced that "the Christian message" must always be presented "in the dynamics of life."[15] Stated another way, the catechetical process is interchange and correlation between "the stuff of everyday life" and "the Gospel."[16]

Core Commitments as Religious Educator

Virgilio Elizondo's life work and writings are marked by core commitments that define his contribution and lasting legacy. I'm sure other colleagues in this collection will highlight similar commitments from his specifically theological writings but I will draw solely from his publications on religious education. The significance of the correlation he maintained as theologian and educator—and what we might learn from this—will occupy us in the closing section. For now, let us review five of his core commitments as religious educator.

A Praxis Approach. Virgil's approach as religious educator takes "as its point of departure the living faith of the particular faith community."[17] He begins with what is "going on" in the world, then brings the scriptures and traditions of Christian faith as a "living word" into each life and social context, always with the intent of renewed Christian living.

Why does he make contemporary praxis the starting point instead of theoretical reflection—the more traditional approach? Because he is convinced that God's revelation begins in the events of our everyday lives as well as being reflected in God's great saving events in history. Thus, the religious educator must encourage people to "look at" and reflect upon both sources of God's self-disclosure—their contemporary reality and "the tradition that comes to us from the Lord himself."[18]

Further, the privileged locus of God's present revelation is in the struggle for freedom and justice: "today the starting point, the locus, of God's revelation is the present day tensions, crises, and emotions which arise out of [the human] struggle for a more human existence in our world."[19] And the people most privileged with God's present self-disclosure are "the poor" or "the nobodies of society."[20] These are the "predilectos de Dios, the favored ones of God"; "at the very core of the Gospel is the fact that those who seemingly have nothing to offer have in fact the greatest gift to offer the world."[21]

In Solidarity with the Poor. Following from my previous point, Virgil's chosen and ever-conscious social location—where and with whom he stands and from which he does religious education—is in solidarity with the poor and those who suffer. In fact, this should be the starting point for all Christian mission and ministry. "The starting point of Christian mission is the materially poor. The Gospel begins among the victims of injustice, the hungry, the ugly, the sick, the dying, the handicapped, the marginated, the rejected, the excluded of society . . . Only in solidarity with their struggle will the prosperous, the accepted, the dignified, the beautiful, the educated, the professional, the religious find salvation." Beyond all other qualifications, "Christians in ministry must be in solidarity with the poor of the world."[22]

Applying this commitment specifically to religious education, he writes, "The first and indispensable qualification for a Christian teacher is a personal lifestyle of freely chosen material poverty in solidarity with the poor, who alone can teach the world the full measure of the continual suffering brought about by sin."[23] Nothing less will reflect the *kenosis*—the self-emptying—modeled by Jesus. "It is important to see in the *kenosis* of Jesus the model for all Christian ministers. He who had all the power and the glory did not hesitate to empty himself of it in order to come into the world in full solidarity with the poor, the marginated, the unprestigious, the unlettered, the lay people."[24]

From the Perspective of the Hispanic Mestizo *Community.* A most compelling point made by postmodernist literature is that "the view from nowhere"—a disinterested and objective perspective as claimed by Enlightenment rationality—is a myth. Better, by far, to recognize and draw upon one's own socially constructed perspective, not as another blinding ideology but allowing it to illumine what one sees. In fact, the best hope of "objectivity" is to be radically aware of one's "subjectivity" and how perspectival we are in our view of the world. Virgil has an abiding commitment to self-consciously doing religious education from the perspective of the Mexican American *mestizo* community.

Over against the "classist-racist vision of a WASP America" that proposes a "melting pot" in which diversity is obliterated and all strive to become like the dominant group, Virgil favors a "stew-pot" in which all contributions are welcomed and each culture affects and enriches the others.[25] He offers a moving outline of the gifts that a Hispanic or Mexican American culture should bring to religious education and to the whole life of church and society. In general, this perspective is that "life . . . is to be lived to the fullest" because it comes from God who intends us to live it "as a beautiful gift."[26]

He lists the following specific gifts of a Hispanic perspective: (a) cherishing *the family*, extended to all related by blood or marriage ("even cousins-in-law"), to the *compadres*, and into the whole *barrio*, with great respect for the elders and offering hospitality to all; (b) accepting *suffering and death* as integral to the totality of life and with a deep sense of *la memoria*, forming community with those gone ahead; (c) valuing the present *time*, with determination "to live to the fullest today" and *mañana* as a "realistic acceptance of limitations" to what we can achieve by our own efforts; and (d) lastly, what he calls a *"prophetic-festive"* perspective that celebrates in spite of the tragic, that hopes against all hope, and enacts *fiesta* as a prophetic response to all that would deny life.[27]

For the Liberation of God's Reign. All of Virgil's work in religious education—both doing it and writing about it—is grounded in the conviction that Christian faith and the Jesus event in history must bear the fruits of liberation at every level of existence—personal, interpersonal, and social/political. Such liberation entails the realization of full justice for all, understood as "the proper relationship with each other, with nature, and with God."[28]

For Virgil, justice is symbiotic with true liberation and entails growth in personal holiness of life as well as commitment to social well-being. In fact, realizing justice demands personal holiness as well as social reconstruction because even the most equitable of social structures can function justly only as the hearts of their participants are converted to holiness. And such liberation, justice, and holiness of life amount to what Jesus intended by the reign of God.

For Christians, Jesus is the model and empowerment of God's reign. According as his disciples "accept the absolute sovereignty of God and God's way for humanity" as modeled in Jesus, we become agents of God's reign in history. "It is under God—the God of Jesus—that people will be able to gradually obtain their true greatness, their desired freedom, and their true fulfillment."[29] For Christian faith, "in Jesus and his followers, the kingdom of life—the reign of God—has indeed begun" but its completion is far from realized. Every Christian is called to the personal conversion and social reconstruction that will bring about God's ultimate promise of *shalom*.[30]

For Inculturated Faith. Virgil rightly places the incarnation of Jesus at the core of Christian faith. "The first ministry of Jesus was his ministry of becoming man—the mystery of the Incarnation." Further, "Jesus did not become an abstract sort of trans-cultural man. He became a very specific man, in a very specific setting, with the culture, traditions, problems, and religion of his people."[31] Now, religious education must help Christians to do likewise with their faith, "making it flesh" in the world, incarnating the gospel in every time and place. And such incarnation of the gospel demands its inculturation—making it indigenous to every culture.

On the theme of inculturation, Virgil was again "ahead of his time." It has now become part of the church's consciousness that there must be a "living exchange" (Pope John Paul II's term) between Christianity and culture. This means that the gospel should enrich each culture in which it is realized and likewise should be expressed and celebrated through the media of each local culture. Instead of any one cultural version of Christian faith being imposed on another cultural context, each context must come to its own expression of the living gospel, enriching both the local culture and the whole church. As far back as 1974, Virgil proposed such inculturation, and particularly as a task of religious education.

He was convinced that God is always already present in every culture—long before the arrival of any "catechist or preacher"—disclosing Godself "through the customs, traditions, art, and wisdom of each people."[32] Even as early as "the time the Gospels are written, the authors do not hesitate to bring out the meaning of the words and teachings of Jesus in the light of the problems, needs, customs, and vocabulary of their particular people."[33]

Likewise, today, "Christianity does not come to destroy native customs and traditions, but following in the steps of the Master, it takes them and ennobles and perfects them."[34] And Christian educators must always do likewise. Truth is that "every culture has its share of grace and of sinfulness, and it is the task of the Gospel to come through the culture and gradually to challenge the culture to go beyond itself—not to destroy but coming through it to begin to challenge it from within."[35]

Specializations in Partnership

Readers who are familiar with Virgilio Elizondo as a theologian—the other essays in this volume are a fine introduction thereto—and from the above review will readily recognize that there is profound cohesion throughout his work as theologian and religious educator. There is certainly no division between these functions; at most there is a distinction of emphasis. In this, his work symbolizes the hope of partnership rather than barriers between theological specialties, and particularly between theology and religious education.

Let me raise up his contribution to this emerging paradigm by returning to the three liabilities of divisive specialization and hierarchalization within modern theology that I raised in the introduction. We will note how he avoids such pitfalls and offers more life-giving possibilities.

First, instead of division and fragmentation, Virgil Elizondo's work is marked by a profound unity and cohesion, precisely because he has a consistent sense of the purpose and procedure of his work.

He understands the purpose of theology as the liberating realization of the reign of God. God's reign symbolizes the justice and peace, the freedom and fullness of life that God intends for all people, for society, and for creation; it is to be realized on every level of existence—personal, interpersonal, social/political, and ecological. It calls every Christian to lifelong conversion into holiness of life after "the way" of Jesus and to participate in the transformation of both church and society toward all the values that constitute God's *shalom*.

Virgil's procedure or method, regardless of the theological function, is to begin with historical praxis, especially in solidarity with those who struggle for justice. Then the task is to appropriate (or inculturate) Christian faith in that context of life, always with the intent of emancipatory Christian praxis by persons and communities in the midst of the world.

This praxis sense of purpose and procedure—nurturing living and life-giving

Christian faith—permeates and so unites everything he does, regardless of what "hat" he may be wearing. Now, when such intent and approach is truly one's own, in other words, when a person embraces such a *habitus* for doing theology, then barriers among specialties are erased and replaced by partnership between varied points of emphasis and function.

A second liability of modern theology—ignoring historical interest and social context—is certainly avoided by Virgil, in fact with a vengeance. By contrast and like all who embrace a praxis approach to doing theology or religious education, he explicitly places an emancipatory interest at the center of his work. Likewise, he self-consciously approaches his task from his cultural and social perspective— Mexican American *mestizo*; he draws upon it as an illuminating lens and questions its shortcomings when this seems warranted.[36]

Third, regarding the hierarchical ordering between the theoretical and practical, particularly between theology and religious education, Virgil clearly transcends such false consciousness. In fact, he helps us to reconceptualize both theology and religious education and embodies the partnership that should exist between them.

As already intimated, he sees all theology as having historical interest as life-giving faith. Note that he describes pastoral theology as "a science [that] studies and reflects upon every action of the church in relation to its mission and in view of the circumstances which confront the church today." And then he adds, "If there is a Christian theology, it is by nature Pastoral Theology, for it rises from Christian praxis and leads to Christian living."[37] In a sense, all Christian theology, eventually, has the interest of religious education.

On the other hand, religious education or catechesis—he uses the terms interchangeably—entails bringing people to their own theological reflection on their lives; in a sense, the catechist should enable people to "do" their own theology. He writes: "True catechesis will be the continuing task of the theological reflection of the Christian community—faith seeking understanding. Without this ongoing theological reflection which is, in effect, catechesis, religious education or catechetical programs may give much knowledge but they will not effect the growth in faith which catechesis intends to accomplish."[38] In other words, for Virgil religious education is guided by theological interest.

In conclusion. As both theologian and religious educator, Virgilio Elizondo is a powerful and prophetic voice to the church and the world from the Mexican American faith community. He has spent his life "doing" theology and religious education that promote liberation and justice, erasing barriers erected by race, ethnicity, and economics. But the very mode of his life and work also helps to erase false barriers that loom between theological specializations, replacing them with cohesive partnerships and unified efforts. This too will be his legacy.

Notes

[1] A significant experiment in this regard was the program of "village doctors" initiated by Mao Tse-tung in China. Essentially, these people were given about six months of basic medical training, prepared to care for most ordinary ailments and to recognize and refer the ones needing

a specialist. By all accounts, this was one of Mao's more successful social programs, bringing significant improvement in healthcare to the vast population of rural China.

[2]"Biblical Pedagogy of Evangelization," *American Ecclesiastical Review* 168 (October 1974): 526.

[3]See "Benevolent Tolerance or Humble Reverence? A Vision of Multicultural Religious Education" 87-97 below.

[4]Namely the *God with Us* series (1985), the *Coming to Faith* series (1991), and the *Keystone Coming to Faith* series (1997), all from W. H. Sadlier.

[5]"A Bicultural Approach to Religious Education" 63, 64 below.

[6]Ibid. 65 below.

[7]Ibid. 63 below.

[8]"The Catechumen in the Hispanic Community of the United States," in *Becoming a Catholic Christian*, ed. William J. Reedy (New York: Sadlier, 1979) 51, 53.

[9]"Benevolent Tolerance or Humble Reverence?" 90-92 below.

[10]See ibid. 92-96 below.

[11]"Biblical Pedagogy" 526-527.

[12]Ibid. 528, 542.

[13]Ibid. 531.

[14]"Ministry in Education from a Pastoral-Theological Perspective," in *Ministry and Education in Conversation*, ed. Mary C. Boys (Winona, MN: St. Mary's Press, 1981) 65.

[15]"Politics, Catechetics and Liturgy," *Religion Teacher's Journal* 10 (November-December 1976): 32.

[16]"A Bicultural Approach to Religious Education" 70 below.

[17]"Ministry in Education" 47.

[18]"Biblical Pedagogy" 540.

[19]Ibid. 530.

[20]"Politics, Catechetics and Liturgy" 30.

[21]"Ministry in Education" 60.

[22]Ibid. 62-64.

[23]Ibid. 64.

[24]Ibid. 68.

[25]Ibid. 57 ff.

[26]"A Bicultural Approach to Religious Education" 66 below.

[27]Ibid. 66-70 below.

[28]"By Their Fruits You Will Know Them: The Biblical Roots of Peace and Justice," in *Education for Peace and Justice*, ed. Padraic O'Hare (San Francisco: Harper & Row, 1983) 41. Read this whole section for a powerful instance of how a liberation/justice perspective can make even an old story—such as Genesis 1 to 11—come alive in a new way.

[29]Ibid. 60-61.

[30]Ibid. 62-63.

[31]"Biblical Pedagogy" 532.

[32]Ibid.

[33]Ibid. 537.

[34]Ibid. 532.

[35]Ibid. 538.

[36]See, for example, "Benevolent Tolerance or Humble Reverence?" 92 below, where he talks about "the sin of the marginalized" as "humiliating shame."

[37]Virgilio Elizondo, *Christianity and Culture: An Introduction to Pastoral Theology and Ministry for the Bicultural Community* (Huntington, IN: Our Sunday Visitor, 1975) 39-40.

[38]"The Catechumen in the Hispanic Community of the United States" 54.

Elizondo's Pastoral Theology in Action

An Inductive Appreciation

R. Stephen Warner[1]

Much of Virgil's most visionary work is not published on the printed page . . . [Elizondo is seen] at his best . . . when he is interacting with people and building on the energy that the group dynamic creates. Unfortunately, we cannot fully present the experience of this living engagement between the two covers of this book. My suggestion is that readers . . . go to San Fernando Cathedral for Holy Week . . . There you will see, hear, touch, sense, and smell the rich ritual life that illuminates Virgil's . . . pastoral vision in action. (Timothy Matovina, Introduction to this volume, p. 3).

Introduction

Five years before this book went to press, I did just what Timothy Matovina recommends, going to San Fernando Cathedral for Holy Week. As an ethnographer, I had been asked to join a team of scholars at the Mexican American Cultural Center who were working on an interpretation of the ritual language employed at the cathedral under the tutelage of its then-pastor, Virgil Elizondo. My host, the project's associate director, was none other than Tim Matovina, a perfectly bilingual active Catholic. Knowing that I was neither Catholic nor bilingual and that I was unfamiliar with Elizondo's work, Tim agreed to serve as an interpreter and informant, and he shared a great deal of his wisdom with me during my three days in San Antonio. But for the rituals themselves we consultants were invited to "lose ourselves among the people"; thus I was often on my own to observe ceremonies whose literal sense I could not understand. So I had to pay heed to a lot of nonverbal messages, and my perspective was that of an outsider.

The text immediately following, including the numbered endnotes, is the bulk of the report I wrote for Tim and Virgil and their project upon my return to Chicago but before I had read any of their writings. In the intervening years, inspired by my experience at San Fernando, I have read many of Elizondo's writings, including those reprinted in this volume, and have testified to his influence on my own work.[2] My report will thus serve as relatively uncoached testimony to the effect that as a pastoral theologian Elizondo practices what he preaches. The field report to follow describes Elizondo's practice as I saw it; the added lettered footnotes reference his preaching from the essays reprinted in this book. The essay concludes with reflections on Elizondo's pastoral theology in action.

An Outsider's Experience of Holy Week Observances at San Fernando Cathedral[3]

I was invited to San Antonio to share my reactions to the Holy Week observances. My hosts particularly wanted me to interpret the ritual language employed in the massive Passion play held on Good Friday—the *Via Crucis* pageant, in which a young man of the parish appointed for the day to be Jesus drags a heavy wooden cross from "Pilate's palace" in the tourist-oriented Mercado (Mexican market) to "Calvary" in the town plaza half a mile away. I did what I was asked and joined the crowd in the procession down the street—actually named Dolorosa in San Antonio—and witnessed with them the graphically sanguinary reenactment of the crucifixion. It was a big event, worthy of a front-page photo in the next day's *San Antonio Express-News*, where "Jesus," seen "crucified" on the steps of the cathedral with women mourning at his feet, was identified as Javier Gómez and the crowd was estimated at 8,000.[4] For me, it was an unforgettable experience.[a]

Yet it is not Holy Week, San Fernando Cathedral, or Mexican religious practices that come to the attention of the tourist visiting San Antonio. To those arriving in town, San Antonio proclaims itself to be the site of the Alamo, dedicated to the memory of William Travis, James Bowie, Davy Crockett, and the other "martyrs" of the 1836 war of Texas independence. Photos, paintings, and drawings of the Alamo—one of the top tourist attractions in the United States—are everywhere. The word appears in the names of streets, buildings, and businesses, and the scalloped outline of the building's distinctive façade is an ever-present visual trope. I found no postcards of the cathedral in the airport shops, and even when I did find one later (in the Mercado), the Alamo's façade appeared in outline on the address side of the card, as it does on every postcard in the "San Antonio collection."[5] From the same tourist perspective, San Antonio's Mexican American culture is represented primarily in terms of margaritas and salsa, written in neon lights on cream-colored stucco.

I do not doubt that the Hispanic residents of the city—some descended from Spanish families tracing their roots in San Antonio more than two and a half centuries back, long before Mexican independence, and others who have arrived from Mexico in the past decade—are fully conscious of this contradiction. The city is publicly identified by a symbol precisely of its alienation from the coun-

---

[a] "Pilgrimages . . . can definitely be privileged moments in everyone's personal journey of faith, as well as fascinating adventures full of unsuspected experiences . . . In discovering ourselves to be in community with others, even total strangers, we experience the ultimate reality of the church as the people of a God who has no boundaries and is open to everyone without exception . . . No one should leave for home as they departed from home" ("Pastoral Opportunities of Pilgrimages" 133, 138-139 below).

try—New Spain or Mexico—of their or their ancestors' origins, despite the fact that San Antonio is near to the border, historically a frontier town, sometimes called "the northernmost city in Mexico." Yet as Americans, residents, and citizens of the United States, many Hispanics wish also to embrace the values of liberty and courage and the national loyalties that the Alamo is said to enshrine.[6]

San Antonio's Hispanics, who constitute 56 percent of the population of the city,[7] thus live in a public culture that holds them at arm's length. The *San Antonio Express-News*, the city's only daily, is published solely in English, unlike the *Miami Herald*, whose every issue is published doubly, one whole paper in English, the other, editorially identical, in Spanish.[8] Were it not for the fact that 80 percent of San Antonio's Hispanic residents speak English,[9] the *Express-News* would go unread by most residents of the city.

It is in this context that Virgilio Elizondo, as pastor of the cathedral parish of San Fernando, determined to revitalize Mexican religious traditions at the cathedral, to valorize and inculcate Mexican religious culture in the heart of the ninth largest city in the United States. The Holy Week rituals I was invited to observe there are the climax not only of the liturgical year but—along with the December 12 feast of Our Lady of Guadalupe—of his program of cultural *mestizaje*. Over the three days of my visit, there were The Last Supper (*Ultima Cena*) and the candlelit procession to Gethsemane, *Oración en el Huerto*, on Holy Thursday; the *Pasión*, *Via Crucis*, Crucifixion, *Las Siete Palabras*, and Veneration of the Cross during the day on Good Friday; *Pésame*, the poignant wake in the company of the grieving Mary, and *Servicio del Santo Entierro*, burial service, on Friday night; and finally the *Resurreción Gloriosa* on Holy Saturday night.

The rituals were vivid and involved all one's senses and faculties.[b] On Thursday night, a procession followed the Blessed Sacrament as it was carried through the cathedral and out the door to the plaza across the street, all of us carrying candles and chanting, *caminemos con Jesús*, let us walk with Jesus. Burning candles created islands of heat and wafts of scent all over the church. In the sanctuary leaving the service, everyone was given a small loaf of bread to share with family members. Next day, on the *Via Crucis*, parishioners dressed as Roman legionnaires flailed Gómez's back, leaving garish marks of red, while pious women in black lace led the people in another chant of contrition, *Perdona tu Pueblo, Señor*. A few individuals came forward to bear the cross for Gómez for a block or so. (They were, in fact, Elizondo and fellow clergymen honored with the burden.) Loudspeakers carried the sound of hammer on metal as "spikes" were driven

---

[b]"The pilgrimage is not a time for doctrinal or moralistic catechesis, but rather a time for the catechesis of the heart which will come through new profoundly human experiences of friendships, relationships, wonder, gratitude, peace, and joy" ("Pastoral Opportunities of Pilgrimages"136-137 below). "The authentic inculturation of liturgical celebration . . . implies much more than just singing in the local language and using local materials for the vestments. It implies a deep respect and willingness to accompany the people's faith pilgrimage with the full liturgical celebration of the special events that have marked their life and that form part of their collective memory" ("Cultural Pluralism and the Catechism" 81 below).

through "Jesus' " hands into the truly heavy wood of the cross, and Gómez's screams echoed all over the plaza. To begin the service of the Seven Last Words, the cross—Gómez still attached, smeared with red, naked to the waist, wearing his crown of thorns—was carried up to the altar of the church. Later in the evening, with a full-size wooden figure of Christ now supplanting the actor, a bier with the body of Jesus was again carried through the church, there to be covered with hundreds of flowers brought forward by congregants.[c] A woman representing Mary followed the bier up to the altar, crying out in a heart-wrenching (and superbly performed) Moorish wail, as funeral torches filled the nave with pungent smoke.

Many of these rituals were foreign to me, but I doubt that their strangeness was due only to my Presbyterian background. Surely many of my Irish and German Catholic friends would similarly have been astounded by the vividness and the colorfulness of these *Mexicano* rites, which seemed to fill the imagination to over-flowing, to preclude escape into the merely symbolic. Right in front of us we saw realistically reenacted the suffering and death of Jesus, the cruelty of his tormen-tors, and the grief of his mother. There was nothing metaphorical, nothing merely figurative, nothing generic about these rites.

Yet, as an Anglo, I did not feel excluded.[d]

First of all, the rites were Catholic, and some of them were, to my ear, merely Spanish translations of the universal rites of the church. Thus, the scripture read-ings on Holy Thursday were, as elsewhere that night in Catholic churches, taken from Exodus, First Corinthians, and the Gospel according to St. John. The Seven Last Words were the same as those spoken the same day at the ecumenical Protes-tant service in my home town, Evanston, Illinois, only in a different language. The melody accompanying the words *caminemos con Jesús* is used with different words at Holy Name Cathedral in Chicago.[10] Some aspects of the ritual that I did experience as different, especially when everyone held hands for the Our Father, those on the aisles stretching out to reach those on the other side, felt warmly welcoming.[11]

Second, Elizondo, who introduced himself to me as Virgil, lives on cultural margins and conducts as much of the liturgy as he can in both English and Span-ish. Because they were broadcast internationally on UNIVISION, *Las Siete Palabras*, it is true, were said in Spanish (except for the closing solo, by parishio-

---

[c]"For the Indians [of 1531] . . . flowers and music . . . were the supreme way of communication through which the presence of the invisible, all-powerful God could be expressed. As the apparition [of Our Lady of Guadalupe] had begun with music, giving it an atmosphere of the divine, it reached its peak with flowers, the sign of life beyond life, the sign that beyond human suffering and death there was something greater-than-life in the dwelling place of the wonderful giver of life" ("Our Lady of Guadalupe as a Cultural Symbol" 122 below).

[d]"I . . . come to you as a pastor of a very active parish who is learning that the more local we are, the more universal we become. We televise a Sunday liturgy to the entire nation. It is a very Mexican celebration. Yet the appeal of this mass is far beyond the Hispanics of the United States" ("Cultural Pluralism and the Catechism" 72 below). "Even though our basic identity is very Mexican, we work hard at welcoming others" ("Benevolent Tolerance or Humble Reverence? A Vision for Multicultural Religious Education" 90 below).

ner Joe Castillo, of "Were You There When They Crucified My Lord?"). And, yes, the Passion play itself was proclaimed in Spanish. But Elizondo's narration and commentary at the Mercado and during the *Via Crucis* were bilingual, and the pageant was preceded by invocations in English from Archbishop Patricio Flores and guest pastor Buckner Fanning, a local Baptist. Whenever Elizondo spoke, he said first a paragraph or two in one language and then, in the other, a rough equivalent plus the next part of the discourse. He would then proceed stepwise through his prayer, his announcement, or his homily, never quite repeating himself, never quite leaving anyone in the dark as to his meaning.

Third, it became clear that Elizondo's inclusiveness was not only hospitality extended to Anglo visitors like me, but a feature of his teaching for Mexican Americans. There are others in the parish who don't know Spanish, and they include young Mexican Americans. I was told that 20 percent of San Antonio's Hispanics are, like me, monolingual English-speakers,[12] and in the cathedral I saw Mexican American parents leading their teenage children through the Spanish words on the song sheet that was handed out at the door. The officially Spanish policy of the cathedral is intended not only to accommodate Spanish-speakers but to foster them.

Thus it became clear to me over the several observances that Elizondo's cultural *mestizaje* is not simply a matter of admitting "folk" or "native" religious practices into his church but an intentional engendering of religious and cultural traditions[e] that he feels his parishioners have a right to embrace and to pass on to their children. Elizondo's *mestizaje*, rather than being a defensive concession to popular ways, is an assertive educational mission. Thus, on Thursday night, as Archbishop Flores prepared to wash the feet of the "disciples" (twelve young parishioners in apostles' costumes), Elizondo in his homily invited the children of the parish—a huge throng—to come forward to watch at the steps of the sanctuary, where they stayed until the communion rite. Thus also Mary Esther Bernal, as director of the cathedral's choirs, led the parishioners through the choruses of the Gloria, set to a catchy, folk-sounding but actually newly composed tune, indicating with her hands not only tempo but also relative pitch. Much of the color of the pageantry is evidently intended to fill the memories of onlookers with indelible religious images. In a society as drenched as ours in symbolic representations,[13] Elizondo wants his own message to have a competitive edge.

San Fernando's parishioners live in a busy city full of distractions. Despite the homespun dress of the "disciples" who showed up in church on Thursday night to have their feet washed by the archbishop, Elizondo knows that his church is not filled with peasants fresh from the fields, but with people who use their showers to make sure their feet are clean before exposing them to the archbishop, people who drive cars to church and who (he hopes) will watch services on television if by chance they can't make it in. So the pastor spoke less as the narrator and more as the prophet when, as he welcomed the crowd on Friday to the Passion play in

---

[e] "Catechetics needs to help in the creation of the local tradition of living faith" ("Cultural Pluralism and the Catechism" 81 below).

the Mercado, he said that they had come not to be entertained but to engage in an act of prayer. He wanted to use the color and drama of the pageant to teach religious and cultural lessons.[f]

Elizondo, Flores, Bernal, and the other shapers of the events I witnessed know that culture is not bred in the blood and bones. Culture is not tribal, automatically passed on from parent to child. "Hispanics" are made, not born. If it is to survive, a culture must be nurtured and learned.

There are two mixed cultures they are trying to teach at San Fernando, each of which they think is enhanced by the other: Christian, specifically Roman Catholic, and Hispanic, specifically Mexican American. The parish today contains some whose journey across the border is within living memory and whose English is rudimentary. Elizondo's Spanish-language policy serves them. But the parish also contains those well-situated Spanish speakers whose English is fluent, idiomatic, and Texan-accented but whose devotion to Catholicism has been sorely tried by the church's neglect of their heritage. At San Fernando, I met people whose ancestors came to the United States early in this century or late in the last—third-, fourth-, fifth-, and later-generation Mexican Americans whose culture Elizondo ennobles, giving them opportunities to pass it on as a valued legacy to their children.

Such parishioners use their English literacy in San Antonio's public life. They do not need the Mass to be said in Spanish for sheer linguistic comprehension. If they did, and if they wanted the Mexican traditions that often accompany the Mass said in Spanish, they could go to Our Lady of Guadalupe on San Antonio's west side, where the parishioners have been putting on their own *Via Crucis* for generations,[g] with one Andrés Camero playing the part of their Jesus during the year I visited San Antonio.[14] The Mexican American pillars of San Fernando that I met prefer to worship at the cathedral, just on the west edge of downtown, catacorner from the century-old Bexar County Court House, and they were honored to have Baptist Bill Thornton, who later became San Antonio's mayor, address the crowd gathered in the Mercado for the Passion play, and Robert Green, Bexar County Clerk, serve as one of Jesus' pallbearers on Friday night. To watch a dignified usher signal discreetly to a colleague in the back of the crowded nave that he has two seats available halfway to the front—all while the TV cameras are rolling[h]—is to sense the pride that is conferred by the centrality of the cathedral in

---

[f]"Fiestas without prophetic action easily degenerate into empty parties, drunken brawls, or the opium to keep the people in their misery. But prophetic action without festive celebration is equally reduced to dehumanizing hardness. Prophecy is the basis of fiesta, but the fiesta is the spirit of prophecy" ("*Mestizaje* as a Locus of Theological Reflection" 175 below).

[g]During Elizondo's youth in San Antonio, the neighborhood parish "was the only institution in the city where we felt fully at home, fully free to express ourselves in our own language, our singing, our festivities, our worship" ("Hispanic Theology and Popular Piety: From Interreligious Encounter to a New Ecumenism" 278 below).

[h]"Those who had nothing to offer now have the best thing to offer to everyone: new life. It is the rejected and marginated Galileans who receive the Spirit and, without ceasing to be Galileans, now see themselves in a new way as they begin to initiate the new humanity. Everyone is invited, but it is the very ones who had been excluded who now do the inviting" ("*Mestizaje*" 172 below).

the public life of San Antonio. It seemed to me that Elizondo intends San Fernando to play for the Mexican American west side the civic religious role that the Alamo plays for its Anglo north side.

It would be a mistake to dwell overlong on this theme of ethnic pride. What is celebrated at the cathedral—particularly on these days of Holy Week—is a message of humility. The archbishop washing the feet of twelve young men. (He told me later that he had recently undergone knee surgery.) Pastor Elizondo taking up the cross on the Via Dolorosa, while hundreds chanted in unison, *Perdona Tu Pueblo*, forgive thy people. More hundreds of mourners coming forward to kiss the cross. Hooded, anonymous *penitentes* bringing their petitions to the grieving *Madre de Dios*. The whole congregation on its knees for three long prayers during the afternoon service.

I sensed not only a message of humility this particular weekend but also a culture of humility at San Fernando. The photos, momentos, hospital bracelets, and miniature arms and legs that people array around the effigies of trusted saints (the black Christ of Esquipulas from Guatemala is a new favorite at San Fernando) to dramatize their petitions and expressions of thanksgiving—these humble artifacts are called *milagritos*, the diminutive of miracles, as if to underscore the diffident yet intimate spirit in which they are offered. Nowhere else have I felt so much sincerity behind the Catholic litany before communion, "Lord, I am not worthy to receive You, but only say the word and I shall be healed."

The contrast could not have been greater when Rev. Fanning spoke to the crowd in the Mercado before the Passion play began. He acknowledged the solemnity of the observance, but he refused to be saddened. He urged his listeners to see the cross not as an instrument of torture but as a gigantic "plus sign," representing God's triumph over death. Notwithstanding the fact that the parish was about to observe a long day of vivid, death-oriented rituals and would await the end of the Saturday night vigil before returning to an officially festive mood, Fanning, smartly dressed in a business suit, spoke to the crowd in the unamplified, hearty voice of the Baptist preacher. Elizondo, clad in red and white vestments, spoke softly into a microphone. Although at the moment I liked Fanning's message, it seemed by the end of the day radically inappropriate to the drama about to unfold.[i]

Later, during the *Pésame* service, when Elizondo invited people from the congregation to come forward to express their thoughts to the grieving Mary, one of those he recognized was County Clerk Green, who on behalf of the people of Bexar County thanked the parish for the honor of addressing them and thanked Mary for the gracious gift of her Son. His demeanor could not have been more unlike that of the weeping, grief-stricken Mexican American parishioners, whose condolences to Mary were spoken so softly, despite the microphone, as to be

---

[i]"For a people who have consistently been subjected to injustice, cruelty, and early death, the image of the crucified is the supreme symbol of life despite the multiple daily threats of death. If there was something good and redemptive in the unjust condemnation and crucifixion of the God-man, then, as senseless and useless as our suffering appears to be, there must be something of ultimate goodness and transcendent value in it . . . *Even if we are killed, we cannot be destroyed*" ("Popular Religion as Support of Identity" 131 below).

nearly inaudible. The flower-bedecked wooden corpse and black lace-draped effigy standing next to it in the sanctuary elicited literally inarticulate but physically palpable emotions from the Mexican American people of San Fernando.[j]

Lest these points about humility obscure what I said earlier about the intentionality of the observances, I must emphasize this: In speaking of the religiosity of the people of San Fernando, I do not mean to suggest the familiar image of pious huddled masses that is evoked when the news media report that "hundreds of the faithful gathered today to pay homage to their crucified Lord," as if the TV cameras had miraculously come upon Good Friday observances in a nineteenth-century Sicilian village. The religiosity at San Fernando is not naive and unreflective, but neither is it triumphalist. As I sat in a pew next to Esther Rodriguez, dressed in the widow's black that many women of the parish wear as an expression of their Good Friday devotion, it occurred to me that her clothes of mourning were a badge of honor, making a statement simultaneously of genuine humility and pride: humility before the greatness of God and the richness of *mestizo* tradition; pride that at San Fernando Cathedral she could call these things her birthright.[k]

Conclusion

Having experienced Elizondo's pastoring at first hand five years ago and now having read his work as represented in this book and elsewhere (particularly his 1983 book *Galilean Journey*), I conclude that (1) the situation of Mexican American culture of which he writes can be perceived by an outside observer; (2) he does as a pastor what he says should be done; (3) at least one element of his pastoral theology is clearer in his practice than from his writing; and (4) full appreciation of his pastoral theology requires access, as Matovina says, to his practice on the ground, as well as to his writing in books and journals.

1. While I was in San Antonio, I experienced at first hand many things about Mexican America of which Elizondo has written (no doubt partly under his influence and that of his disciple, Matovina). Comparing the culture San Antonio makes known to tourists with the San Antonio I saw in the cathedral and the west side barrio, Elizondo does not exaggerate when he writes, "Only the white Western way appears as the truly human way of life; all others continue to be relegated to an inferior status."[l] The fact that Mexican Americans "were made foreigners in their own lands,"[m] however, does not mean that they belong in Mexico, for, as Elizondo writes, "The love for the United States and the patriotic spirit of the

---

[j]"In the ridiculed, insulted and crucified Jesus, we knew that God had not abandoned us for the nice and fancy churches of our society, but that God in the person of the suffering Jesus carrying his cross was right there with us in our struggles . . . The silent suffering of Jesus had been our way of life" ("Hispanic Theology and Popular Piety" 288-289 below).

[k]"Popular piety . . . becomes liberating when used as a source of unity and strength in the struggle for dignity and subsequent change against the powerful of society" ("Our Lady of Guadalupe as a Cultural Symbol" 122 below).

[l]"*Mestizaje*" 162 below.

[m]"Benevolent Tolerance or Humble Reverence?" 95 below.

Hispanics for this country is certainly beyond question."[n] The truth is that Mexican Americans are made to feel marginated, in the Roman Catholic church as well as in secular American society, as Elizondo confesses in his autobiographical reflections: "As *mestizos*, our flesh and blood identity has consistently marginated us from both parent groups. We have been too Spanish for the Indians and too Indian for the Spaniards, too Mexican for the United States, and too 'Gringo' for our Mexican brothers and sisters."[o] Such margination is a critical context within which Elizondo pastors.

2. In the rites of the San Fernando Cathedral parish, I saw Elizondo practicing things I later read him saying. In the face of Alamo symbolism and *mestizo* margination he firmly decentered WASP hegemony:

> In the United States we cannot ignore the strong weight of the dominant and righteous WASP culture with its racism and ethnocentrism. Special emphasis must be made throughout the catechetical texts to attack every notion that consciously or unconsciously promotes white western culture as superior and normative for all others . . . We must become clearly aware of this and counter it in every way possible.[p]

Yet Elizondo carried out this attack in ways that were inclusive rather than exclusive, inviting rather than alienating. Five years ago, I recognized a number of ways in which Elizondo's verbal messages were directed to speakers of English as well as Spanish, but only later did I recognize the importance for his practice of inclusiveness of nonverbal modes of communication, especially music and motion.[15] Elizondo's "catechesis of the heart" transcends linguistic boundaries, but for this to be possible it must be rooted in real human experience, not only texts.

> The ultimate success or failure of a truly multicultural religious education program depends on the personality of the local congregation, the person of the religious educator, and the total environment of the church—its people, ministers, decorations, music, church order, and celebrations.[q]

As did early Christianity, the ritual practice at the Cathedral of San Fernando drew on the experience of marginated people to "affirm rootedness while destroying ghettoishness."[r]

3. I have encountered in Elizondo's writings only oblique references to what I witnessed as a key component of his pastoral practice, namely, a cultural catechesis that inculcates Mexican American culture as well as affirming its value. His writings often acknowledge the contingent quality of racial/ethnic identity, the fact that, in the Mexican American case, people experience themselves in between

---

[n]"A Bicultural Approach to Religious Education" 65-66 below.
[o]"Hispanic Theology and Popular Piety" 282 below.
[p]"Cultural Pluralism and the Catechism" 84 below.
[q]"Benevolent Tolerance or Humble Reverence?" 90 below.
[r]"Popular Religion as Support of Identity" 127 below.

opposed cultural forces and many are drawn to one side or the other, some wishing to assimilate to the dominant WASP model, ignoring the lesson that "simply to assimilate would be a sell out, an insult to our ancestors and a betrayal of our faith."[s] Elizondo's lesson that "for a colonized/oppressed/dominated group, [popular expressions of the faith] are the ultimate resistance to the attempts of the dominant culture to destroy them as a distinct group either through annihilation or through absorption and total assimilation"[t] must be understood as prescriptive as well as descriptive. "Through the pains and frustrations of trying to be what we are not, the uniqueness of our own proper identity begins to emerge."[u] As a priest, Elizondo does not merely accept the people's culture into the church, he teaches an inculturated faith.

4. Yet, it was necessary for me to read Elizondo to understand how the religion he preaches and practices combines the themes of what five years ago I awkwardly called humility and pride, how he encourages a faith that is reflective but not triumphalist. With respect to people of my background he says, "White Western Christians need to convert from their sins of arrogance and pride. Their righteous sense of superiority has blinded them to their own inadequacies and sinfulness and has kept them from appreciating the treasures God has bestowed on the peoples of the other races and cultures of the world." His own liturgical practice helped me recognize some of those treasures. To fellow *mestizos* he says, "On the other hand, those who have been marginated, brutalized, abused, segregated, put down, ridiculed, or merely tolerated need also to recognize their sin: the sense of inferiority that some come to believe and accept . . . Attitudes of docility, embarrassment of color or heritage, and the many negative and self-destructive feelings grow out of the inner sense of shame at being who one is."[v] Five years ago, I sensed that such a sin had been put behind by San Fernando's parishioners, who had come to a deep understanding of what Elizondo calls "biblical humility," which:

> does not mean putting ourselves down as if we were worthless. We are simply one of the fellowship. This biblical humility means that we accept ourselves as we are—historically and culturally conditioned. This is both our originality and our limitation. As original, we have much to offer; as limited, we have much to learn. It is in this same spirit that we accept all others—neither as superior or inferior, masters or students. It is this humility which gives us the

---

[s]"A Bicultural Approach to Religious Education" 66 below. In the wake of the conquest by the United States of northern Mexico, "the churches demanded that we break radically from the religious ways of our ancestors. Some of our people have tried and have found it very painful, others have managed to survive while still others have just given up altogether" ("Hispanic Theology and Popular Piety" 285 below). "In the first stages of the struggle to belong, the *mestizo* will try desperately to become like the dominant group, for only its members appear to be fully civilized and human" ("*Mestizaje*" 163 below).

[t]"Popular Religion as Support of Identity" 126 below.

[u]"*Mestizaje*" 164 below.

[v]Quotations from "Benevolent Tolerance or Humble Reverence?" 92 below.

spontaneous willingness to offer what we have without apologies and to receive from others without a sense of shame.[16]

It was biblical humility that I witnessed at San Fernando. I pray that I can learn to practice it.

Notes

[1]For their comments on the field report contained in this essay, I am indebted to Nancy Ammerman, Joy Charlton, Shoshanah Feher, Luin Goldring, Anne Heider, Luis León, Timothy Matovina, and Olga Villa Parra. For the project as a whole, I am deeply indebted to Timothy Matovina for advice and encouragement and to Virgil Elizondo for inspiration.

[2]R. Stephen Warner, "Religion, Boundaries, and Bridges," *Sociology of Religion* 58 (Fall 1997): 217-238.

[3]The first draft of this report was written on Easter Sunday (April 3) 1994, within forty-eight hours of the events described, and before I had read any of the writings of Elizondo or Matovina. This revision contains corrections, including numbered endnotes, made before August 1994, primarily on matters of fact and writing style. It also eliminates some extraneous material and adds new lettered footnotes referencing those of Elizondo's writings that are reprinted in this volume.

[4]J. Michael Parker, "Jesus's Cross Called 'Plus Sign for Life' by Baptist Pastor," *San Antonio Express-News*, 2 April 1994, 1A, 8A.

[5]Never mind that that very façade was added to the building years after the fabled events of 1836.

[6]Early on Good Friday morning, near the Alamo, I saw a recent sculpture of Toribio Losoya, one of nine officially recognized *Tejano* heroes of the Alamo who died alongside Travis, Bowie, and Crockett at the hands of Mexican general Antonio López de Santa Anna. True, the *Tejanos* fought more in protest of Santa Anna's abrogation of the Mexican constitution of 1824 than for Texan independence; nonetheless, the statue proclaims, despite the Daughters of the Texas Republic, that the Alamo is not the Anglos' alone.

[7]From the 1990 U.S. Census.

[8]From author's observations, confirmed by Professor Thomas A. Tweed. In this sense, whereas Miami is a bilingual city, San Antonio is a city of bilinguals.

[9]A figure reported to Timothy Matovina by San Antonio market researcher Lionel Sosa.

[10]According to J. Michael Thompson, director of music at St. Peter's Church in Chicago, the melody, as I sang it to him, is a variation on Gregorian Psalm Tone 1 in the Dorian Mode. See Warner, "Religion, Boundaries, and Bridges" 226-227, for details on the chant.

[11]I have since experienced this ritual—holding hands across the aisle for the Our Father—in Mexican American Catholic churches in Los Angeles, San Francisco, and Chicago.

[12]From Lionel Sosa and Associates, Market Researchers, as reported by Timothy Matovina.

[13]Friday morning in the *Express-News*, columnist David Anthony Richelieu anticipated the irony of the day to come when, recalling previous years' *Via Crucis* pageants, he wrote, "Nowhere else can Christ's anguished cry, 'Father forgive them, for they know not what they do,' echo across a crowded plaza as nearby, a meter maid slips a parking ticket under the wiper of a TV minicam van blocking traffic." David Anthony Richelieu, "How Tradition Makes Symbols Come Alive," *San Antonio Express-News*, 1 April 1994, B1.

[14]Parker (1994) 1A.

[15]Warner, "Religion, Boundaries, and Bridges" 226-233.

[16]Virgil Elizondo, "Conditions and Criteria for Authentic Inter-Cultural Theological Dialogue," *Different Theologies, Common Responsibility: Babel or Pentecost?* ed. Virgil Elizondo, Claude Geffré, and Gustavo Gutiérrez (Edinburgh: T & T Clark, 1984) 22-23.

ESSAYS BY VIRGILIO ELIZONDO

1. Religious Education for Mexican Americans

(1972)

Virgilio Elizondo

The technical ability of human beings to communicate among themselves has been one of the most remarkable developments of modern science and technology. Our world has really become a small village where news reaches the most remote areas at the very moment the news is taking place. Technically speaking, we have the tools to unite ourselves with the entire world by forming a closely united family through efficient and sophisticated systems of communication. However, in the same way as every discovery leads human beings toward new areas of investigation, the discovery and the production of world systems of communication have led to the discovery of a deeper problem: the very nature of communication. How do people communicate?

For a long time, communications have been taken for granted. People actually believe that once there is a common language, we will be able to understand one another. This idea may have been the greatest obstacle that effective programs of catechesis have confronted for Spanish-speaking Catholics.

Effective communication does not merely consist in the transmission of concepts through words. Words, by themselves, are very ambiguous. They have multiple uses and multiple meanings for different peoples. In order to communicate effectively, it is not sufficient for an orator to express himself or herself with great precision and clarity in the language of their audience. It is equally important for the orator to know what the audience is really receiving.

At the present historical time, the United States and Mexico are waking up to the phenomenon of the existence of a totally new socio-cultural group: Mexican Americans, often known as Chicanos. These people are neither North Americans nor Mexicans. They are residents of the United States and they have *mestizo* ancestors. They are not necessarily immigrants from Mexico, since many Chicanos had been living in the United States long before the latter took over vast areas of Mexican territory; indeed, many of them had been living in the Southwest long before this region was separate from Mexico and incorporated into the United States.

Other Mexican Americans are immigrants who came to the United States for the purpose of finding a new life, just as millions of European and Asian immigrants did. Most of the Chicano residents are happy in the United States. Otherwise, they would not be here. However, they are not happy about the way they have been treated by their Anglo-American compatriots. Chicanos make up a high percentage of the war dead and, yet, the country for which they have fought and died is treating them as second- or third-class citizens.

This discrimination with its subsequent second-class citizenship has been accepted up to the present time by many Chicanos as a normal way of life. The discrimination is not limited to individual citizens and to civil society. Today the church is also acknowledging that, in fact, it has only provided an inferior form of ministry to Chicano communities. With the objective of integrating them into parish activities, the church has frequently forced Chicanos to stop being Chicanos. In many areas, not only has the church failed to help solve the problems, it has even helped to perpetuate them.

The honest recognition of the problem is the first step toward an eventual solution. At the present time, several areas of the United States are showing serious interest in providing an effective ministry among Chicanos and among Chicano communities. The first point that has to be acknowledged is that Chicanos constitute an essential group that has a very legitimate place in our society.

The church cannot fall into the heresy of saying: "If you are going to live in the United States, you have to become North Americans." As Chicanos, we are North Americans! The church in the United States cannot make its ministry effectively reach Chicanos simply by bringing them liturgical and catechetical material from Mexico, Spain, or from South America. On the other hand, neither can the church conduct its ministry in an effective way by trying to use Anglo-Saxon material. This material may be excellent in the groups for which it was prepared and, perhaps, it can help Chicanos. However, it certainly cannot be the answer to the real pastoral problem. Nor will this problem be solved by bringing Spanish-speaking priests from other countries to the United States. Nor will it be solved by sending North American priests to study in the great Latin American centers of pastoral formation, such as the ones existing in Cuernavaca, Mexico City, or in Manizales.

These centers are excellent for their own objectives. But the Chicano problem is a special problem that has to be investigated and solved within the United States. We cannot pass on our own responsibilities to others. The church of the United States has to consider it as its own problem and pastoral opportunity. It is the responsibility of the whole church of the United States, bishops, the clergy and lay people, to face this problem seriously and to start to correct it at its roots.

Although lacking in coordination, priests and religious are now making many widespread efforts in the United States (Miami, Fresno, San Antonio, Toledo). All the efforts point to the need of having a serious socio-ecclesiastical center of investigation, research, formation of personnel, and production of pastoral material. Only a center of this type will start to provide an answer for an effective ministry with Mexican Americans.

However, since the people who are working in ministry cannot wait until such a center starts to function, it is important to at least involve Chicanos and try to know them as they are. Because of the type of existence in which they have been condemned to live, Chicanos have many inferiority complexes. They hate the way they are treated, humiliated, and seen as foul-smelling, lazy, irresponsible people who have a strange way of speaking.

The first step toward an effective program must be twofold:

1. It has to make the Anglo-Saxon communities start to reflect seriously on the way they have mistreated their Chicano brothers and Chicana sisters, to begin to look for ways to mend the infamous activity of the past and to reflect on positive aspects of Chicanas and Chicanos.

2. It is extremely important for people who work with Chicanos to develop programs that contribute to build up in them an image that is different from the one that they now have of themselves. It is important for them to be conscious of their rich cultural origins and of the greatness of their European and Indian ancestors.

It took four hundred years for Mexicans to recognize that their greatness was in their *mestizaje*. It is not surprising that it is taking time for Chicanos to discover that their greatness lies precisely within themselves in the mixture of two great cultural currents. The North American current brings its ability for practical things, efficiency, and productivity and the *mestizo* current its love for beauty, reflection, and art and its ability to develop in-depth feelings and emotional expression.

The new Chicano culture, which is in the process of being born at this historical moment, is, in fact, something to be proud of. It is truly a Christian culture since it crosses all the color barriers and Chicanos can easily have all shades of color, from the blackest to the whitest shade, with all the possible variations. This awareness must be awakened and it has to nourish all our programs of catechesis. Our main objective has to be the rebuilding of the image that people have of themselves.

What does all this have to do with the catechetical institution? The global objective of catechesis is to lead human beings to the fullness of life. However, we will never be able to lead them to fullness unless we free them from their present state of socioeconomic and personal slavery. As long as people are convinced that they are not worth anything, they will not be able to experience the redemptive love of the Father.

Because Chicanos know that they are separated from the main current of the church and from society, they are profoundly alienated people. This is why the church has to make special efforts to approach Chicanos in order to help them in the painful process of their own discovery, their liberation, and their complete entrance into the mainstream of life. In their efforts, Chicanos will make mistakes. As "Mater et Magistra," the church will not only have to help them in their efforts to become complete human beings, it will also have to use all its resources to show them the way to total liberation.

The church should neither fear nor prevent this movement. Its mission is to become part of the movement, to help Chicanos to follow the church's lead, and to serve Chicanos in the light of the Gospel. It is only to the extent that Chicanos see the church as the living sacrament of salvation that they will listen to its voice.

The church has many good things to teach but Chicanos are saying to the church: "Show us that we are really important to you . . . we are your children who have been trampled upon, put down, ridiculed, abused, robbed of our rights. Help us in our search for liberation so that we may be able to fulfill our legitimate role in society on the same level as our brothers and sisters." If Chicanos do not see and experience the love of the church, the best catechetical programs will fall on an increasing number of deaf ears.

The church in the United States is starting to make genuine efforts but this is merely the beginning. It is our hope that these beginnings will grow and develop so that, in the church, Chicanos and Chicanas may see and experience the visible sign of God's redemption and the presence of liberation in today's world.

(Trans. Colette Joly Dees)

2. A Bicultural Approach to Religious Education

(1981)

Virgilio Elizondo

The Human Struggle: The Praxis of the Religious Educator

In these times of growing international crisis and new rise of nationalism we are faced with a challenge that will not and cannot be dismissed: the world has become a crowded small village. Upheaval in a country that was once considered foreign and distant is now taken as a crisis in the international scene. The social struggle in countries like Nicaragua and El Salvador are no longer considered scuffles between unhappy peasants in an unhappy country. They have risen in stature because the ploys of those once distant lands are now the plights of neighbors with implications that go beyond the conventional models of nationalism and culturalism (racialism).

New models of living and perceiving the world are necessary for humanity to survive. We must pass from the competitive ghetto models to cooperative family models of human living. We must make the model of Jesus, whereby brothers and sisters freely give their lives that others may live, our model of living.

In our Judeo-Christian tradition we affirm that God enters our historical process. This entrance is not one of miraculous and apocalyptic comings. God enters the world by default: he has never left it. It is in the day-to-day grind, the mundane work-a-day world where God is most active. It is through him that the transformation from chaos to order takes place (Genesis), enslavement becomes freedom (Exodus), death becomes life (Death-Resurrection of Jesus), and division becomes harmony (Pentecost). Such is the work of God.

The work of humanity, however, often works contrary to that of God. In our sinfulness we seek to isolate ourselves and build cities surrounded by walls, to divide and conquer for personal self-gain even at the destruction of others. Our walls are made to separate us: keep what we like and is useful, and exclude what is foreign and different. Our walls are made of bricks: those of physical, social, and cultural differences that separate us and uphold our own narrow-minded vision of the world as God's way for all! The way of sinful humanity is one of self-fulfillment through material goods: prestige and power through the deprivation and destruction of others. Our way of life, our gain, our power, our possessions become our *idols*—our ultimate gods. This is the ongoing sin of the world.

In the present moment of history, we know that the transformation of humanity's

sinful ways has indeed begun, but we are a long way off before the final completion. The struggle between God's way and the ways of sinful humanity are at the
very core of the world's problems and potential self-annihilation.

It is the task of the religious educator to reflect, teach, clarify, and celebrate
this process of struggle and transformation as it takes place within our own historical and cultural journey. Religious educators must situate themselves (1) within
the tradition of their own people and (2) in the midst of chaos, slavery, death, and
division. This was the position of the first religious educators: the Prophets. They
stood within the dialectic of God's way and humanity's sinful ways and spoke the
truth—the concrete and specific truth about authentic good and destructive evil.

The Prophets did not hesitate to speak out against the idols of their time; they
did not hesitate to reflect and clarify the sin of humanity; they did not hesitate to
live the way of truth. They illumined the blindness of social sin, for once sin has
disintegrated to the level of becoming an idol, once it has been established as part
of the normative worldview, it is blind to the status quo. Out of these men and
women of prophecy, misfits as they were taken to be, we discover our tradition of
witnessing and teaching, clarifying and celebrating God's way into the praxis of
our human journey.

This is the tradition of the religious educator, this is his/her challenge: not to
uphold the cultural idols that we have grown comfortable with, but to shatter
them with the teaching of the Father.

The "American-U.S." Reality—The Makings of an Idol

If our religious tradition and the Prophets have spoken to us very directly, there
is another tradition that has asserted an even stronger influence in our society:
Americanism.

The core of what it means to be American was formulated in the foundational
moments of this country, solidified during the formative years of our history and
transmitted through the literature, folklore, and media of our society. The American image our tradition has built is the WASP image with the English language as
its base and the Protestant work ethic as its cultural philosophy.[1]

This normative image of "Americanism" is one that has permeated all streams
of life in the United States. It functions as a totalitarian image which overshadows
any cultural diversity or ethnic make-up and seeks to shut out anything "other"
than itself.

A person is considered foreign if he or she is not part of this "in" group and
becomes identified by the otherness he/she displays, i. e. "spic," "dago," "nigger."
One only has to look at the history of the Catholic Church in America as well as
the struggle of Eastern European immigrants to see this problem in the formative
years of the U.S. Catholic Church.[2]

The threat of the "other" has long been a problem in the United States. The
original inhabitants of this land were eliminated because they were labeled "diabolical savages."[3] Soon after the bombing of Pearl Harbor history tells of the mass
prejudices against Japanese Americans. They were not one of *us*. The random

discrimination against Mexican Americans because they appear to be foreigners still exists today. And the pain of one of this country's greatest sins still stares us in the eyes: slavery.

We do not deny that there have been and continue to be destructive segregation and malicious prejudices; too many of them are still too evident today. From flagrant violation of human rights to subtle systematic forms of economic disadvantage, our people, Americans as we all are, still suffer from cultural and racial discrimination. Believing that the "American," i.e., WASP, way is *the way* remains our biggest obstacle, our biggest idol, our biggest sin.

In spite of this a new image is beginning to rise. It is an image recognizing one's cultural tradition and searching for one's cultural roots. People are beginning to realize that they do not have to ignore their cultural heritage. They can be who they are, but "be" in a new way. The idolized idea that Americanism is equated with White Anglo-Saxon middle-class values is being threatened by the liberating discovery that the uniqueness and originality of the United States is precisely that it is a nation of nations.

The challenges we are faced with are many and the potential for a new creation is fascinating! We have to begin to discover models of living and relating that are new and unoppressive; that are not fearful of God-given otherness (difference) but welcoming. Our new model of biblical America must be inclusive rather than exclusive. Out of the chaos of many nationalities existing within one nation we have to create a truly new order—a *novus ordo seclorum*! Like the biblical prophets, today religious educators are called to point the way and clarify the vision for a new social order.

We have to turn the enslavement of stereotyping into the liberation of the children of God who can truly celebrate and appreciate their own uniqueness and originality. This means a celebration not of superiority/inferiority but of life-giving complementariness.

A Gospel Perspective

The quest for survival as the absoluteness of my way above all others must be transformed into dying to my own egocentric and ethnocentric ways so as to be enriched by the others. Recognizing the beauty and uniqueness of the "other's" way, which, like my own, is a product of humanity's cooperative efforts with the creator, is the fruit of the Spirit which allows us to cry from within our hearts: Abba!

The conversion of ethnic and racial divisions into a new unity is truly the work of the Spirit. It is a task of bringing together our gifts of language, cultures, traditions, and history into a new and harmonious unity.

The best image I have for this is what I call the *stewpot* image. Imagine a large kettle filled with all the ingredients needed for a stew: carrots, celery, potatoes, meat, salt, pepper. The stew is cooked by heat, the necessary tension, and in the process of cooking, of becoming, each ingredient is forced to give up something, to die somewhat to itself. The end product is a stew made up of all the parts. No one ingredient ceases to be but each one now exists in a radically new way. Each ingredient has enriched and been enriched by the other.[4]

The "tradition" of religious education, as was mentioned earlier, is the way of the Prophets. The "model" of religious education, then, is the way of *the* Prophet: Jesus. The challenges that face us as a people of God and members of the same crowded village cannot be dealt with by creating new ideologies and writing new laws. Our civil rights acts and emancipation laws have failed to stop discrimination and prejudice because our cultures and prejudices are too deeply engraved in all the fibers of our being.

Our models of change must look deeper into our own hearts and center themselves on the call of the Gospel. What we need most of all is not new laws, but new attitudes of the heart. This call is the radical acceptance of other as "other." It is the call to "love your neighbor" as yourself. This message which appears to be simple and platitudinous is the very core of what Jesus is all about. In fact, the radical acceptance of loving the other as other is the way of God; it is the way of the incarnation: God radically accepting humanity in flesh and blood.

The *kenosis* of God, his emptying of all into the reality of the other, is the radical fundamental chosen acceptance of the humanity of God (Philippians 2:6-11). This is the radical love that exists at the very core of the Gospel message. Having experienced God's love, I can now begin to love others as God loves me! This experience is the conversion of the heart and the birth of a new person. Such a person will see and appreciate self and others and do so in a radically new way—so radical, that it will turn all knowledge and criteria of judgment inside out! It is what John's Gospel (John 12:24) calls the dying to oneself to discover New Life. It is the radical love of neighbor whereby I enter into his/her reality, into his/her worldview, into his/her culture. I live with my neighbor in solidarity, love, and compassion. This in turn leads to "otherness." It is through love that we become the other; it is through becoming the other that we understand them, no longer in a judgmental way, but truly as fellow human beings. It is through this radical love and understanding that we experience this *metanoia*. Precisely because we love, we seek to understand! The mere desire to understand the other will not bring us to understanding or love. Many times trying to understand without loving brings us to a new sense of righteousness. We believe we understand when in fact we do not. It is here in the love that leads to understanding that we discover new attitudes which will be born out of a new experience of the positive value and richness of multicultural living.

We must always keep in mind that Christianity is not an ideology or religious myth but the concrete experience of unlimited love which transcends human boundaries, limitations, or expectations. We speak about it only after we have experienced it. It is foolishness and stupidity to those who have not experienced it and hypocrisy to those who speak about it without living it.

The Hispanic Perspective: Blessings of an Idol Broken

The love for the United States and the patriotic spirit of the Hispanics for this country is certainly beyond question. Our people are proud to be citizens of the United States of America and have certainly proven this in their willingness to serve in the military and give their lives for the sake of this country and the principles for which it stands. But we cannot ignore the oppressive and dehumanizing treatment we have often been subjected to by our fellow countrymen. In the past, many of our people simply tried to assimilate and become "good Americans"—forgetting our language, our customs, and our religion.[5] Today, we are going far beyond the model of assimilation. In our faith in the way of God, we have discovered that simply to assimilate would be a sell out, an insult to our ancestors and a betrayal of our faith.

Our faith has led us to the discovery that precisely because we have suffered much, today we have much to offer in purifying and developing our country so that others will not have to suffer what we have suffered. Furthermore, convinced that God has graced each and every culture with some specific aspects of his goodness and that no one people has an exclusivity on God's gifts, we see ourselves as having much to offer for the human betterment of our country that is desperately needed at this moment of history. There is no denial that we have certainly been enriched by many of the cultural elements of the WASP-American way. For this we are grateful. Yet, there is equally no denial that there is much suffering and unidentified weakness within the WASP-American way that is leading to the ultimate inner destruction of Americanism if it is not critically questioned, purified, and strengthened with new blood.[6]

In our faith, we are convinced that the Hispanics are one of the specific groups among several others which at this moment of history have much to offer towards a significant phase in the build-up of God's Kingdom among us. We are well aware that many see our presence in the United States as a threat and even a curse. They wish we would go away, although some of us were already here long before some of these lands were taken over by the United States. We are a significant part of the United States, we are here to stay, and, much more than that, we are here to take a significant part in the building of the United States of tomorrow, which must start today. We have much to learn, but we equally have much to contribute.

For the Hispanic, life is basically a gift.[7] It is to be lived to the fullest because it is a gift from God who gives life. Life is gradually unfolding. The people accept the totality of life, both joy and suffering, for to live is to know conflict and to experience the tension of being pulled in different directions by many forces. Life is a gift from God, and from this belief everything else follows and develops. The Hispanic people are profoundly religious in the sense of living out a personal relationship with their God who is the source of life and to whom they return.

This conviction is found in the poorest of the poor in Latin America. Although materially they may have almost nothing, they will express an appreciation for life. *Tenemos vida*. Life is a beautiful gift. Fundamental happiness comes with being.

I. The Family

This conviction that life is a gift has a strong existential basis. It is not simply a philosophical acceptance or a truth that has been read in the catechism. The people have come to this appreciation through the strong sense of *la familia*, the family. This concept of the family as the basis of all society existed in the pre-Columbian cultures.

For the Hispanic of today, the family remains the basis of society. It is in the family that one finds the meaning of life, and it is here that the Hispano finds himself realized; therefore he will have a family. For many reasons, the Spanish-speaking may be having smaller families today, but they will never accept the concept of zero population growth. The husband and wife will continue to have children, for to do so is part of life's essence.

The Mexican American family will always find room for one more; hospitality is part of the tradition of *la familia*. Though the family may have very little to give, what they do have will be divided among family and visitors, for this is part of life.

The concept of family includes more than just the mother, father, and children. When Mexican Americans speak about family, their concept goes beyond these immediate bounds to include the extended family. The family includes all the relatives, *los parientes*, anyone who is in any way related has a place in the home. The "American Way," which has broken down the extended family to the nuclear family, has not yet destroyed this concept.

The Spanish system of relatives includes more than just blood relatives. A system of in-laws exists, for in a marriage a full relationship of both families is established. Relationships include not only mothers-in-law (*suegras*) and fathers-in-law (*suegros*), but aunts (*tías*), uncles (*tíos*), and even cousins-in-law (*los primos políticos*). Since the entire family usually comes together only at marriages and funerals, an understandable confusion arises about who is related to whom. All these relatives begin to form part of the larger family.

Los ancianos, the elderly, are another part of the family. An *anciano* is one who has advanced in wisdom and understanding. Thus the *abuelitos*, the grandparents, are *ancianos* for they have advanced far in wisdom and knowledge, and they have much to offer. The Spanish-speaking have a deep veneration for the elderly; the *ancianos* are not looked upon as a burden, although physically they might be, but as a personal blessing upon the home in which they live. They bring the wisdom of the family, of the *tradición* (tradition), of the *costumbres* (customs), of all those things that are an important part of the heritage of a people.

The *ancianos* have maintained the tradition of oral history. The Hispanics in this country and in Latin America have not had, for the most part, the opportunity for formal education. Therefore the *abuelitos* have kept the stories and traditions alive, passing them on from old to young. They can quote dates, figures, names, and incidents from the time of their grandparents and before; they are living history and have a marvelous wealth of knowledge about the past.

This is not the entire family relationship. Another aspect is the *compadres*. In English they are called godparents, but in Spanish they are called *com-padres,* the co-parents of the children. This idea of *compradazgo* is a deeply held tradition in the Spanish-speaking community. The complete origins of how the early missioners were able to instill this notion so strongly in the people is not known. Often the obligation of godparents is spoken of in the church, but in the Latino community this seems to be almost an innate idea.

Two aspects of the *padrino* are important. One is the spiritual relationship that it forms between the parents and those who are asked to be co-parents of the child. Relatives are inherited, and that cannot be changed. A person is born into a family and may like them or hate them, but *padrinos* are freely chosen and they freely accept the relationship. The *padrinos* are related in something which is much deeper than blood—the spirit. It is through the spirit that people become co-parents and enter into a profound relationship. A strong bond exists between the two families; a second strong bond also is formed between the child who is baptized and his *padrinos* (godparents). Most children will tell you spontaneously who their *padrinos* are. They may not know the names of their aunts and uncles, but they will know their *padrinos*, because it is part of the duty of the godparents to provide for the child throughout life, especially at Christmas, Epiphany, birthdays, and graduations. The child loves the *padrino* because he is an extra father, who brings him special gifts at special times. Therefore sometimes the *padrino* is chosen not because of the spiritual bond but because of the financial status of the friends who will be able to provide for the child.

The *compadres* become a very intimate part of the family because of the freely chosen and freely accepted spiritual relationship. The greatest compliment a family can pay to someone is to ask them to be the *compadres* or *padrinos* of their child.

These are some aspects of *la familia*. Together they are a reflection of the Hispanic concept of life as a gift, and together these relationships make up the *barrios*. Today, when people speak of the *barrio*, they usually refer to a slum area, but *barrio* is not necessarily a bad word. A *barrio* could be a slum area, but basically it is a geographical one in which all of these relationships constitute the community. All the people are interrelated through *compradazgo, viejitos*, and intermarriage. In the *barrio*, even in the poorest areas, children grow up with a certain security because they are wanted and cared for by the adults of the *barrio*; because of the personal concern, a certain security and beauty exist in the midst of poverty, an idea of living community. In large urban centers today much of this no longer appears, but the traditions continue in the rural areas. Thus, the home truly becomes the first and most important school of human relationships. In the *familia* the art of human dynamics is taught through the many cultural dynamics of everyday life.

II. Suffering and Death

As part of the totality of life, suffering is accepted by the Latin American people. It is seen as a way of final happiness. To accept life is to accept death, for death is the supreme moment of life. In their vocabulary Latinos will even play with death. They will laugh and joke about death and do not mind giving their lives for an ideal they believe in, because they know they will not die. They live on not just in memory, but in *la memoria*, which has a much richer meaning than the English word. *La memoria* is a dynamic force through which the person continues to be alive. The person lives on in *la memoria*; thus, death is not the end, but the passage into the fullness of life. To die is to live forever in *la memoria* of those who stay behind, in communion with those who have gone before, in communion with the cosmos, and in communion with the giver and source of life, God. Death is sometimes hard and painful, but it is not the pain of failure, only the pain of separation for a new birth.

III. Time

Because they accept all limitations, Hispanics accept time. Many people have misunderstood this concept of *mañana*. It is not laziness as outsiders have often seen it. To watch the farm workers in the fields or to see the labor of a carpenter or worker is to know that Hispanics are not lazy. They are willing to do the hardest and often most dangerous jobs.

A realistic acceptance of limitations exists, so that even though one does one's best, no one person will be able to do it all. If Jesus himself, the Son of God, did not finish the work of salvation in three years, much less will another finish it. Perhaps it could be said that the Latin American people take themselves so seriously that they take themselves lightly. Persons who do not take themselves seriously enough are the ones who take themselves too seriously; they confuse themselves with God and end up destroying themselves by self-imposed guilt about not being God. The truly serious person accepts limitations with the realization that not all will be accomplished. One is to live to the fullest today, and tomorrow will take care of tomorrow, for tomorrow exists only in the mind. The question, "Why do today what can wait until tomorrow?" is not a sign of laziness but a metaphysical understanding and acceptance of one's nature as a limited creature.

The Hispanic is futuristic in an eschatological sense, living an eschatology already begun here and now. Eternity is the everlasting *now*; there is no need to rush. The realistic acceptance of fundamental limitations in space and time as expressed in the attitude of *mañana* is the source of great peace for Hispanics but of great tensions for the non-Hispanics.

Paul Tillich calls the fear of accepting the limitation of time one of the greatest sources of suffering for North Atlantic people. They feel that everything must be accomplished today by five o'clock, and they will work hard and save so that they may enjoy themselves tomorrow, in retirement, doing then all that they have been saving money for. While the Latino lives in the futuristic eschatology which has already begun today, the North American generally lives in the hope of a pragmatic eschatology that will begin in retirement.

IV. Prophetic-Festive

Life for the Hispanic has always been a struggle for justice because oppressive injustice has been our daily way of life. The concrete struggles as exemplified by César Chávez, Dolores Huerta, Archbishop Oscar Romero, the four martyred women of El Salvador, and many others, are the prophetic roads we have been traveling to Jerusalem.

Through it all we continue to celebrate. We celebrate because we have a sense of the tragic, accepting the many forces of life and yet realizing we live in the ultimate happiness which has already begun. Through our celebrations, we are able to affirm our Christian hope: hope against all human hope. We celebrate the end which is already the beginning. This prophetic way is the basis of our *fiesta*.

Hispanics do not allow themselves to be swallowed up by the many tensions and problems, the moments of sickness and death that are part of life, but rise above them in celebration. This is why *fiesta* is such a symbol of the Hispanic world. The Hispanic sees the world in movement; we view the many difficulties and yet know that we are on the road to the final end which has already begun. Already we are partakers of the ultimate victory. The Hispanic accepts life realistically but works toward the future and celebrates the gift of life in *fiesta*. The Hispanic cannot be understood without understanding *fiesta*. The world cannot be entered until the world of *fiesta* is entered. It is not an escape from the world of problems but a bringing of the whole day into the celebration of life as a gift. This *fiesta* is the celebration of God's unlimited and transforming love, for there can be no *fiesta* without bringing God into it.[8]

Conclusion

The task of religious education is to take the stuff of everyday life and reread it through the eyes of the Gospel. In doing this we unveil the real, concrete, historical, and cultural roots of sin in our society and announce the alternatives of the Gospel.

It is not the task of religious education simply to make people comfortable, falling prey to Marx's evaluation of religion. Giving people a superficial good feeling with a few religious terms is not the way of Jesus.

Religious education leads the people into a new way of seeing—with the eyes of the Gospel—thus being in a new way. It creates new attitudes and releases a new spirit. It leads people to see the other, the cultural other, with the heart and thus understand with the mind. When this takes place we cease to see cultural differences as threats and begin to see them as gifts. We begin to see the threat of the other as an invitation to die to ghettoism so that we may resurrect to a greater life. This dying relativizes one's own unsuspected cultural absolutes which had functioned as idols blocking the way to a greater life.[9] We do not cease to be who we are, but we are who we are in a radically new way. The segregating and limiting barriers of the human City of Man are destroyed as a more universal and cosmopolitan society—the City of God—emerges wherein each person and each culture is recognized as the glory of God.[10] Finally, nowhere will this awakening to the other be more richly experienced than in the festive celebrations, those key moments of each cultural group. It is there that we experience one another and otherness at its deepest level. These celebrations, in the midst of chaos, slavery, death, and division, are where we celebrate and experience the presence of God, incarnate and one with us, journeying to the heavenly Jerusalem where differences will be celebrated while divisions will be annihilated for we will all truly experience the innermost unity of the one family of God.

Notes

[1]The good and the bad aspects of this foundational image are beyond the scope of this paper to discuss. However, I am convinced that in a functional way of speaking, "Americanism" as unquestioned patriotism has functioned as the fundamental religious conviction of this land— everything else being of secondary importance. For some interesting readings on this point, consult: Alexis de Tocqueville, *De la Democratie en Amerique*, ed. Phillips Bradley (New York: A. A. Knopf, 1989); Elise Marienstras, *Les Mythes Fondateurs de la Nation Americaine* (Paris: Maspero, 1976); Robert Michaelsen, "Americanization: Sacred or Profane Phenomenon?" *New Theology* 9, ed. Martin E. Marty and Dean G. Peerman (New York: MacMillan, 1964).

[2]Andrew M. Greeley, *An Ugly Little Secret: Anti-Catholicism in North America* (Kansas City: Sheed, Andrews and McNeel, 1977); *The American Catholic* (New York: Basic Books, 1976).

[3]Martin E. Marty, *Righteous Empire* (New York: Dial Press, 1976).

[4]For an excellent and very precise presentation of the various models of diversity in the U.S., consult: Andrew M. Greeley, "The Persistence of Diversity," *The Antioch Review* 39 (Spring 1981): 141-155.

[5]Virgil Elizondo, *Christianity and Culture: An Introduction to Pastoral Theology and Ministry for the Bicultural Community* (Huntington, IN: Our Sunday Visitor, 1975) especially chapter 7; and *Mestizaje: The Dialectic of Cultural Birth and the Gospel* (San Antonio: Mexican American Cultural Center Press, 1978), especially part II.

[6]Ervin Laszio, "A Real 'New Foundation,' " *Newsweek* (19 February 1979): 13.

[7]Most of the following section is taken from the author's work, *Christianity and Culture*, chapter 8.

[8]*Mestizaje*, chapter 9.

[9]For a brief study of the universalizing process of Christianity, consult this author's work "Culture, Church and," *New Catholic Encyclopedia*, vol. 17 (New York: McGraw Hill, 1979) 168-169.

[10]Irenaeus, *Adversus Haereses*, III 20, 1-3.

3. Cultural Pluralism and the Catechism

(1994)

Virgilio Elizondo

I begin with a personal note. I come to you first of all as a fellow catechist who has taught every level of catechesis from pre-school to university. I have been professionally involved in catechetics since the mid-1960s when I participated in the International Study Week of Catechetics at the East Asian Pastoral Institute and the Medellín Catechetical Study Week, and have continued to be involved in catechetics since then in various ways.

I also come to you as a pastor of a very active parish who is learning that the more local we are, the more universal we become. We televise a Sunday liturgy to the entire nation. It is a very Mexican celebration. Yet the appeal of this mass is far beyond the Hispanics of the United States. Our growing audience (millions each week) includes peoples of all ethnic backgrounds and even of other denominations. We are also discovering that the more traditional we are, the more contemporary we become. This is the very paradox of church: local yet universal, traditional yet contemporary. The church is not an either/or, but the mystery of the unity of the past with the present, the particular with the absolute, and the finite with the infinite.

Finally, I come to you with the experience of the last twenty years of pioneering inter-cultural ministry through the work of the Mexican American Cultural Center in San Antonio. We are discovering more and more that ethnic, cultural, and racial diversity is not a curse to be avoided or a problem to be solved, but a challenge for the rehabilitation of God's broken and wounded humanity. It is in fact the great challenge and opportunity for the build-up of a radically new human community such as the world has never known. Either we work toward this new community, or we all face the danger of ethnic annihilation together. I look to the *Catechism of the Catholic Church* as potentially a great tool to help us in the build-up of this new inter-cultural and pluri-cultural community.

Those who were expecting a world catechism that would be the same for everyone everywhere in the globe, one that simply needs to be translated into the local languages, simplified and illustrated, will find the new Catechism a terrific disappointment. Whereas everyone is invited to read it, the *Catechism of the Catholic Church* (*CCC*) is primarily a guide book for bishops and catechetical leaders to serve them as a reference point in their ministry of expounding and clarifying the Christian mysteries. It is like the grammar book—not the grammar that will create an artificial and unnatural language, but one that has been carefully dis-

72

cerned and systematized out of the people's living language of faith. One might also say that the *CCC* is like the dictionary—nobody goes to the dictionary to study literature, but it helps to clarify and bring out the exact meaning of the stories and adventures of literature. Native speakers can be quite fluent in their language before studying the grammar but the grammar nonetheless enriches and guides their use of the language. The message is not in the dictionary or the grammar but in the literature. So, the Catechism might well be described as the grammar and dictionary of the living faith language and culture of the Catholic faithful in their living tradition of nearly two thousand years. The great challenge for local catechetical teams will be to produce catechisms that will be both grammatically correct and as substantially exciting as a good novel—in message, stories, illustrations, style, ordering. The more that this is so, the more that each catechism will be at one and the same time very particular and very universal, faithful to the local people for whom it is composed and faithful to what the Catholic Church teaches for all.

John Paul II states in the apostolic constitution *Fidei depositum* that this *Catechism of the Catholic Church* is the product of the various consultations throughout the entire church over a period of several years. It represents and pulls together the collective wisdom of the past and the present. The process, though not perfect and to everyone's satisfaction, made it possible for a good sample of the *sensus fidelium* to emerge. The *CCC* collates and presents what has become most basic across the centuries and yet it itself does not tire in pointing to the one indispensable and unchanging basis of faith and unity: the Lordship of the crucified Jesus of Nazareth.

My assignment is to look at the *CCC* from the perspective of cultural pluralism. After a preliminary sketch of the notion of diversity, I shall proceed in two sections: (1) textual highlights of the Catechism that explicitly bring out the necessity of diversity in various areas of the church's life, and (2) our challenge for the future, or "where do we go from here?" It is a fascinating, daunting, and exciting task. The innermost questions of culture and religion are among the deepest, most devastating, and most ancient questions plaguing today's world. They appear as the greatest obstacles to peace and unity among peoples. Yet these very same questions and historical tensions equally present the greatest potential for a new world vision and structure wherein diversity will not be seen as a curse to be eliminated, but a blessing to be assumed and appreciated. Because the church is in the world, the world's questions and its struggles are the questions and struggles of the church. To balance diverse religious expression and unity of faith is one of the most intriguing and fascinating challenges for today's global and local church.

Preliminary Observations on Cultural Pluralism

Cultural pluralism is not several cultures simply living next to each other and tolerating one another (at best). It is not one dominant and normative culture that allows the folkloric and subalternate presence of others—especially those that it cannot avoid or keep out. It is not every group simply doing its own thing.

Cultural pluralism is the modern-day phenomenon of several cultures/races co-existing together in the same geographical space and participating actively in the same political/economic state and even in the same religious assemblies. This is the reality of countries like the United States, France, England, Australia, and several others. Various peoples are becoming part of the whole without giving up the essential elements of their ancestral cultural/religious identity. For this to take place without introducing new divisions, it is necessary to relativize certain elements of each culture while sharpening the innermost spirit that can mobilize the various peoples/cultures/races into "one people"—one people of God. Given the multicultural reality of the United States, this will be a very special and unique challenge to the church of our country.

Today, the right to be oneself, that is, "to be other," is being recognized as a fundamental human right. Culturally speaking, there is no human group—ethnic, civic, or religious—that can hold claim to being the absolute and normative model for all others. Everyone is being called to a new humility and to a new awareness of how much we can learn from one another. Today we are seeking to build paradigms on the "both/and" model, which seeks to harmonize differences for the betterment of everyone. Differences can be seen more in terms of complementarity than by way of opposition. This makes of every other and their otherness a potential friend, collaborator, and source of enrichment.

Purpose and Intent of the *CCC*

The *Catechism of the Catholic Church* is definitely not intended to be a universal catechism in the sense that one catechetical text will serve the needs of every place in the world for all time. In *Fidei depositum*, Pope John Paul II emphasizes twice that the Catechism is intended as a *reference text* for the *catechism and compendia* that are *to be composed* (not translated!) in the *diverse countries*. He goes on to state that it is not intended to replace local catechisms but rather to encourage and help redaction of local catechisms, which are aware of diverse situations and cultures while guarding unity of faith and fidelity to Catholic doctrine. (The emphases are my own.)

In its very opening statements the *CCC* states clearly that it is "destined to serve as a point of reference for the elaboration of catechisms or compendia in diverse countries" (Section 11). It does not say that it is simply to be translated and used with all peoples everywhere. It invites anyone who is interested to read it, but the document is primarily intended for bishops and those responsible for catechetics:

Let no one imagine that only one kind of souls are confined to their care and hence are to teach all the faithful in the same way . . . The words should be carefully chosen according to the spirit and intelligence of the audience (24).

We might say that the *Catechism of the Catholic Church* is to be like the skeleton that is to be thoroughly enfleshed in each local church.[1] Since it refers to itself as a reference point, we might well liken it to the architectural principles elaborated by the magisterium after having listened carefully to the people of God. These principles are needed for the creative architect to produce the blue-print—considering the local terrain, climate, history, and present reality. This will be the task of the catechetical team of the local (regional) church. The publishers will be the builders, while the local pastors and catechists will be the construction workers that will build up the local edifice of God's kingdom in this specific locality and in this precise moment of time (the challenge of the local pastors and catechists). The diversity of the local churches, with their traditions, liturgies, catechisms, spiritualities, and theologies, reflect an earthly image of the Father's house in which there are many mansions (not utility apartments that look all the same and boring), but no division whatsoever.

Diversity: Gift or Curse

The diversity of peoples is a fact of life in our contemporary world. Diversity and similarity of individuals, families, groups, nations, and races is the obvious fact of human existence. All humanity is one, but there are no two individuals—even identical twins—who are exactly the same in everything. Because we are human and in order to be human, we seek to socialize. From our earliest beginnings, we seek the company of those we recognize as our own and are afraid of the unknown other—a baby cries spontaneously when an unknown person approaches and presents a potential danger. We are comfortable with our own, but threatened by the other to the degree that our defense mechanisms are alerted as the other approaches. Even if the stranger is appealing to us, we are still uncomfortable and defensive because of his/her otherness. In ordinary life, the other is first perceived as danger rather than as friend. This is true whether at the level of individuals, families, classes, nations, or races. This deep human instinct is reinforced by the religious beliefs that inform the deepest levels of the human psyche—both personal and collective.

Even though migrations and the mixing of peoples (*mestizaje*) have taken place since time immemorial, cultural identity has frequently been intimately associated with the race, geographical place, and historical pilgrimage of a people. In many ways, the "nation" was "the people," that is, the cultural synthesis of the various forces that had led the people to be who they are here and now in this time and space. The collective soul of the people has been gradually formulated and expressed through the customs, foods, language, values, artistic forms, and religious expression of the people. Others who today come into this space and time are foreigners and immigrants.

Today, the world of nations is changing very rapidly. Twenty-six nationalities make up one small village in northern France, and their children are all growing up "French" and "other" at the same time. The children of the Spanish migrant workers in France and in England are growing up "French-Spanish" or "English-Spanish," the children of the Ethiopians in Italy are growing up "Italian-Ethiopian," the children of the Japanese in Brazil are truly Brazilian-Japanese, and we could go on *ad infinitum*. Migrations and the mixture of peoples are taking place throughout the globe, and even though they might live in ethnic ghettos for a while, a newness begins to emerge in the children. Nowhere is this taking place more rapidly than in the United States. We are truly a multi-ethnic and multi-racial nation. We are a people of many peoples. We struggle with many unresolved problems of linguistics, racism, and ethnicity, yet our ongoing challenge is to grow even stronger as a united people. The future of the United States is in the diversity of its peoples; its curse is special interest groups that subvert the common good for the sake of their own profit and gain.

An even more astounding development is the growing awareness within the church of the positive values of all religions. We are becoming more aware of the great variety of religions in the world and of the great variety of religious expressions and teachings within each religious group. Religions should not be out to eliminate one another but to enrich one another. This has certainly been my personal experience—the more I learn about other religions, the more I deepen and expand the appreciation of my own Christian Catholic tradition. And even our own Latin (Roman) Catholicism is certainly not monolithic. There is great variety and diversity even within a given diocese, parish, or religious community.

Highlights of the *CCC*

The *Catechism of the Catholic Church* is to be implemented within the context of the living faith, that is, within the historical and cultural reality of the people. The church in its great tradition has fostered diversity much more than conformity and in so doing has brought about the great unity of the Spirit that started at Pentecost. Historically, to the degree that the church becomes defensive and tries to impose uniformity from on high, it ends up bringing about the very opposite of what it intends: division.[2] The Gospels themselves are a good example of a pluriform catechetical text; we have only one Jesus of Nazareth, but there are four diverse accounts of his life and ministry. The entire *CCC* emphasizes the enriching role of diversity and insists on the elaboration of texts for diverse countries. We could add that, given the actual situation of most of the Catholic countries of the West, and especially the United States, not only will there be different catechisms for different countries, but quite diverse catechisms within a given country, and even more so, a genuine pluriformity within each of the diverse catechisms. This is the social reality of these countries, and this is the reality out of which the church must reach out in its catechesis. Here are some especially important texts in the *CCC*.

Foundational Image of God's Intent and Humanity's Evil

The great diversity of the peoples as created by God (Gen. 10) stands in complete contrast to sinful humanity's empires of uniformity (Gen. 11). In the second creation (after the deluge), God blessed Noah and told him to multiply and fill the earth (Gen. 9). God made a covenant with Noah. The sign of that covenant was the rainbow—the beauty of unity in diversity from beginning to end. The result of that blessing (Gen. 10) was the great diversity of families, peoples, languages, and nations that filled the earth. Each one in its uniqueness radiated a portion of God's glory, but no one nation alone revealed the fullness of God's glory. God did this, according to the *CCC*, to keep any one nation from becoming too proud, thus thinking that it was self-sufficient and without need of God or of others. Diversity of peoples is the creator's great gift, and their harmonious unity is the creator's great glory. Paragraphs 337, 341, and 361 elaborate on the positive value and beauty of diversity as created and intended by God.

Paragraph 57 brings out that sinful human beings will choose a totally different type of unity than the one intended by God. As in the beginning, humanity constantly prefers its own way to God's. In Genesis 11, humanity wants to meet God in its own way by building a city with a tower: an image of one uniform and totalitarian way of life for everyone. Thus one people's way of life will appear as God's own way, and this people will set themselves up against all others. They will not just be different, but superior. Once people set themselves up as the exclusive image of the values, the beauty, and the greatness of God, they make of themselves an idol! Sinful humanity now becomes united "only in its perverse ambition to forge its own unity as in the tower of Babel" (57)—a forced and idolatrous uniformity for everyone. This is the great evil of the world—to set ourselves up as the measure of good and evil for all others! We become normative and judgmental. In this sinful condition, even in trying to do good for others, we often end up destroying their inner soul. As any nation can easily become an idol, so can any local church when it sets itself up as the norm for all others.

Unconsciously and certainly not maliciously, the Euro-North American church has functioned in this way in relation to the local churches of the rest of the world. Since Vatican II, things have started to change, but it is not easy to change an unquestioned practice of centuries. A rediscovery of the tradition of the church is helping to bring this about. However, the temptation will always be there to make of our own cultural, national, or ecclesial expression the idol that will become the norm for all others.

"There is no single aspect of the Christian message that is not in part an answer to the question of evil" (309). We have to unveil the specific manifestations of evil in our society. The false sense of superiority and righteousness of some cultures and some churches that justifies multi-faceted racism, sexism, classism, ethnocentrism, ecclesio-centrism, religio-centrism, and other forms of human degradation and marginalization is the great evil of today's world. It is this righteous sense of superiority that has enabled so-called Christians and a civilization that called itself Christian[3] to conquer entire peoples, steal their lands, enslave their people, exploit their natural resources, underpay their workers, and destroy entire ways of life that were sacred to the peoples of the land. Those defined as "unwanted/untouchable" by the dominant groups are still kept out of the structures of responsibility and opportunity on a wholesale basis—even out of the priesthood and religious life. This great evil still persists and often goes unquestioned and unchallenged by the catechists and theologians of the more powerful Christian churches. The entire Christian message must be understood and proclaimed as radically opposing this evil, which continues to cause so much pain and misery to the masses of the world. This evil denies the fundamental dignity of the human person in his/her historical and cultural reality.

Beginning of New Creation: Son of God Becomes Human Flesh

The very particular and historically and culturally conditioned Jesus of Nazareth becomes the universal savior of humanity. The section on the Son of God (426ff) brings out clearly what is repeated in various ways throughout the document, that Jesus of Nazareth is the heart of all catechesis. Without question, this entire section places Jesus among the poor, the lowly, the marginalized and the ridiculed of society—"the king of glory rides on a donkey" (559). The glory of God's own Son "is hidden in the weakness of the new-born baby" (563). When he was born, people had no room for him or his parents. Throughout his life he associated with the public sinners (social outcasts) and untouchables of his own people. In the end, his sufferings "took their historical and concrete form in the fact that he was rejected and handed over" (572). From his conception to his death on the cross, Jesus is without doubt "the stone rejected by the builders of this world" (Acts 4:11).

Yet, precisely out of the evil of marginalization and rejection, the marginal Jesus of Nazareth dares to live and proclaim a new human alternative: the reign of God who is love unlimited and who invites us to a life of love, forgiveness, fellowship, and self-sacrifice for the sake of others. This love will destroy all barriers that keep people apart, whether they are racial, sexual, ethnic, religious, or moral, and will heal the wounds of those whom society has humiliated, disregarded, ignored, judged as "public sinners," and unwanted except when they need to be enslaved and exploited (544).

The table fellowship of Jesus to which all are welcomed is the very particular, real, and concrete beginning of the new divine alternative to humanity's multiple divisions. The holiness of Jesus comes through in the fact that, like his Father, he welcomes everyone without exception—especially the most disliked and unwanted of society and religion. Everyone is invited not just to follow him, but to become a body and blood member of his family! For this, he will give his own body and blood so that the cosmic body will no longer be ripped apart by our human arrogance and the divisions caused by it.

It is important to note the privileged role of the poor and the outcasts of Jesus' own culture and religion. These people continue to have a privileged role in every culture that receives Christianity. The dominant culture must be questioned and challenged from their perspective (1676). The marginal of the dominant culture are the first ones to hear and receive the word and through their popular piety and rites truly make it their own. It is among them that God's new alternative for society begins.

The Holy Spirit and the Church

Disciples. The people of God assembling together throughout the world (752) is the fruit of the Spirit. The church is sent to make disciples within all nations

(767), that is, to enable persons to see themselves and others in a radically new way: as accepted, respected, and loved by God. God's accepting love heals the deep wounds of segregation and rejection. The disciple is one who breaks through the dehumanizing prejudices and sees the beauty, dignity, and truth of oneself and the others as God sees us: all children of the same God, all equal members of the same family. The disciple does not abandon the heritage or religious expression of his/her ancestors, but begins to live it in a new way.

Discipleship affirms the local culture while destroying its prejudices and fears of others. That is precisely why the church is such a complex reality (771): it is the mystery of the intimate unity with God of all peoples and therefore the intimate unity of the human race, of all the peoples of all nations, races, and languages. Thus the church is both the instrumental beginning of that unity and the great sign of the ultimate unity that is yet to be accomplished (775). The original covenant with Noah is brought to perfection: not just coexistence of nations, but a new loving fellowship.

While all nations/cultures are invited to become disciples, "God does not belong to any one nation or people" (782). By consequence, we can say that God does not belong to any one local church of a given country. No one local church exhausts the mystery of God, and no local church is superior to or better than the others. Each one has a legitimate and beautiful uniqueness while being united with all the others in the one Spirit that allows us all to confess that the crucified Jesus of Nazareth is the Lord. The Holy Father "presides over the whole assembly of charity and protects legitimate differences, while at the same time such differences do not hinder unity but rather contribute to it" (*Lumen Gentium* 13).

The Universality of the Church. In view of the evil of the world, what makes us "a holy nation" (803; 1 Peter 2:9) is precisely our refusal to reject anyone and our openness to the otherness of the other. The reason for this is the very foundation of the church: the Holy Trinity, which is the ultimate source of God's life—unity in diversity (814). Because of this, the very catholicity of the church, its innermost universality, which exists at the core of every local church, is precisely its ability to take root in any of the cultures of the world (835). This inner attitude of being big enough to be able to take in anyone and everyone is the universal life and spirit of the church.

This is precisely why any effort to impose a superficial or even intellectual uniformity is such an incredible assault on the most beautiful aspect of the church: its innermost catholicity. It is this spirit of a positive prejudice in favor of the otherness of the others that distinguishes the church universally. Its desire to discover and appreciate the positive elements of other peoples and other religions is a result of its universal love of God's very diverse creation. The universality of the church does not erase differences nor bring about a uniform humanity. In the power of the one Spirit of unlimited love, the particular (without ceasing to be particular) now has universal implications in that it welcomes others universally. This is the one universal and universalizing element of the church—not that it is the same everywhere and at all times, but that it now has a big enough heart and mind to love everyone as they are!

The Particularity of the Universal.[4] In Christian language, the word "church" is used for the liturgical assembly, the local community, and the universal community of believers. These three meanings are inseparable. The church is the people of God assembled and realized throughout the world. It exists in the local communities and is realized as a liturgical community, especially in the Eucharist (752). The *CCC* goes on to state: "The great richness of their diversity is not opposed to the unity of the church" (814). The healthy tension between the particular historical-cultural ecclesial expression and the universal tradition of the church will enhance the unity of the Spirit, which is so totally different and opposed to the idolatrous uniformity of the dominant of this world.

The church is the sacrament of Christ, and sacraments are "signs perceptible by the senses" (1070). We know that the signs are perceived quite differently by different cultures. That is why in the celebration (liturgy) and explanation (catechesis) of the Christian mystery, so much careful attention has to be placed on the local history and culture. The creative composition of local catechisms that utilize the language, wisdom, and iconography of the people and that are attentive to the particular needs and problematic of the area is a fundamental task of the local church (1075). This implies much more creative elaboration than a mere translation of the Catechism. As the Synod on Catechesis of 1977 points out:

> The real incarnation of the faith through catechesis involves not just the process of giving but also that of receiving. This means that not only must there be a process by which the faith transforms and purifies culture, but there also has to be a process by which the very faith itself has to be rethought and reinterpreted . . . In this sense, cultures themselves must discharge the function of hermeneutic criterion in regard to the faith.[5]

The local catechism is to become one of the chief tools of the ongoing inculturation of the church, thus allowing the life and tradition of the church to become incarnate in this particular people. Catechesis and culture are intimately and mutually interdependent within the process of the growth and maturation of the local church.

> Good theology is culturally and historically transcending only by its fidelity to its own particularity. Good catechisms are good by their fidelity to the same paradox of transcendence through the common confession rendered in distinct ways for distinct cultures. No one needs to become European to join "the world." No one should be expected to become European to join their narrative, their culture, their particularity to Jesus Christ and his culture-transcending (but not ignoring) church.[6]

The liturgy cannot just be taken from one place to the other. It has to be enhanced by "the cultural richness belonging to God's people who are celebrating." There has to be a "harmony of signs" (1158). Hence the music, the words, the artistic decorations, the bodily motions and postures must be congruent with local variations. Without becoming just another festival of the people, the liturgy must be in tune with a people's natural way of celebrating and their style must be incorporated creatively into the liturgy so that it is truly a liturgy of the people. Different moments of the liturgy will have different emphases for different peoples. For example, in the Eastern Churches, all of Holy Week is celebrated as "the great week" (1169). This is similar to our Latin American tradition of celebrating in a very special way *la semana mayor*. The celebration of Easter (1169) on different dates by the great traditions of the church is not just a mistake of the calendar, but has diverse historical/theological reasons behind it.[7] Liturgists have heart attacks with the Mexican Catholics, for whom the feast of Our Lady of Guadalupe is of far greater historical/liturgical importance than a Sunday of Advent, but the people consider the liturgists to be totally irreverent and ignorant of the salvation history of the Mexican people when they cannot recognize this fact.

The authentic inculturation of liturgical celebration is much deeper and implies much more than just singing in the local language and using local material for the vestments. It implies a deep respect and willingness to accompany the people's faith pilgrimage with the full liturgical celebration of the special events that have marked their life and that form part of their collective memory. Catechetics needs to help in the creation of the local tradition of living faith. These local and particular liturgical customs develop as the faith tradition of the church gradually dialogues with the local culture and traditions of the people. In this process, there will be a mutual interpretation and enrichment of both the tradition and the new developing local tradition. The cultural diversity of liturgical celebration that will emerge is a great source of enrichment that will continue to deepen, enlarge, and expand the innermost catholicity of the church (1203-1206).

Book II, Section 2.4 of the Catechism is entitled "Other Liturgical Celebrations." The title itself is quite fascinating because it places sacramentals and the popular faith among the liturgical celebrations of the church. The very title gives a new understanding of the relationship between sacraments, sacramentals, and popular expressions of faith. We have been accustomed to thinking of the sacraments as "the real thing" and the rest as something we could just as easily do without. But the Catechism appears to reject this notion in favor of greater complementarity.

The sections on sacramentals and popular piety are most important. This is probably the area through which inculturation takes place in the most natural and effective way. The reason for this is that "sacramentals respond to the needs of the culture and history of the particular regions and time" (1668) and they arise from the priesthood of the baptized (1669). This means that they arise out of the genius and needs of the people of faith, who are impelled by the Spirit to express and celebrate their Christian faith in ways that are totally natural to them. Since the people are not encumbered with the many studies that unfortunately remove the professional minister from the ordinary faithful, their expressions of faith can more easily come from the collective heart and mind of the people of God in this particular region. From the perspective of authentic inculturation, I would dare to say that these are the purest expressions of the faith in the local church. I am not saying that they are perfect, but definitely that they are neither false nor inferior to the liturgical forms that are all too often still imposed by outsiders on the particular local church. In these celebrations, everyone participates equally—laity and clergy, men and women, theologians and the simple faithful.

The Catechism makes its own the richest section of the *Puebla Conclusions* of 1979 in the area of popular piety (1674), designating the popular piety of the people as the chief criterion for discerning whether the Gospel is being served or not:

> For the common people this wisdom (of popular religion) is also a principle of discernment and an evangelical instinct through which they spontaneously sense when the Gospel is served in the church and when it is emptied of its content and stifled by other interests.[8]

The section on "Life in the Spirit" (beginning in 1699) brings up more questions that can only be answered adequately in the local cultural setting. The notions of good/evil, right conscience, truth, obligation, law, etc. all have very different connotations in different cultures and historical situations. This is also true of the entire section on the Ten Commandments. Which interpretations are cultural, having to do with the western assumptions of the individual right to private property versus the collective ownership of this portion of the earth by a particular tribe or nation? Many such questions will come up and can only be answered by the moralists of the local church. Other aspects of morality, because of particular circumstances, will have more urgency and importance in some regions than in others. This is an excellent place for each group to develop a listing of the particular "cultural sins" that are destructive of this local people. For example, in the United States, I would consider upward mobility without limits one of the deepest idols and cultural sins, often accompanied by an extreme individualism that is not concerned with the common good, the poor, and the foreigner. Each human group has its own cultural sins that are destructive of life and of human dignity. These must be faced honestly by local catechisms.

The final section of the *CCC* (2587ff) deals with prayer. Prayer forms vary with local history and culture—an example of this is the Psalms themselves. Inspired songs and dances come out of the deepest spiritual recesses of a people. The Native and African Americans have marvelous forms of prayer that can certainly enrich all of us. One form of prayer should not be imposed on the others, but a variety of forms can enrich everyone. For many of my people at San Fernando Cathedral, the lighting of a simple vigil light comes through as a truly mystical experience. Many of our old *viejitas* are masters of contemplation and mysticism. We have so much to learn from them. For a very good example of this, I suggest a careful reading of Victor Villaseñor's classic book, *Rain of Gold*.[9] The home altars of our Mexican poor are true temples of the divine indwelling in the home and should be studied and fostered as an excellent prayer form for today's world.

Because prayer is the language of intimacy, each church is called to propose to its faithful, according to its historical, social, and cultural context, the language of prayer (2663). Yet, despite all the very legitimate differences among us, and even contradictions (2791ff), we dare to say together "Our Father." This prayer, uttered together, opens us to God's love for all God's children—no matter how different they might be, whether they are believers or not—and develops within us a love and concern for all people anywhere: those closest to us and those farthest away.

What Has to Be Done?

The particular challenge for the church in the United States is both fascinating and scary. Our greatest challenge is not the cultural but the inter-cultural and multicultural. Even though the Euro-American culture has dominated throughout much of U.S. history and has functioned as the norm for "a good Christian person," today there is no homogeneous culture of the United States, but a mosaic of cultures with a common spirit. We might say that all the cultures of the world are included within the contemporary culture of the United States. Educators, public health officials, advertisers, social workers, politicians, and many others are becoming increasingly aware of this challenge. This is both problematic and exciting. It is this reality that must come through in any catechetical text of the United States.

It should be noted that we are not alone in this search for healthy unity amid the diversity within the United States, but we as church should be at the forefront of these efforts. Precisely because of our biblical faith, we should be a visionary church that is ahead of society and not behind it in these present-day struggles. How can we accomplish this?

Much has already been done and should be continued. Catechetical efforts in the United States have been outstanding, and the various publishing houses with their teams of theologians, catechists, and liturgists are to be commended for their efforts and risks; they should be encouraged to continue their exploratory efforts. The *CCC* can serve as a reference point to see if anything essential is missing from the totality of our catechetical programs, but it should not be seen as a negative criticism or, worse yet, a reason to halt the marvelous catechetical movement within the United States. But even the best of materials can be improved and become more complete by a careful critique in the light of the *CCC* and the historical-cultural reality of the people for whom the materials are intended.

Catechetics in the United States can learn a lot from the multicultural efforts of educators, advertisers, and multinational corporations. Our present-day catechetical collections can be greatly improved by including more testimonial stories from our Native Americans, African Americans, Mexican Americans, and other groups. The faith struggles of the minorities of the United States can certainly enrich our whole U.S. family of faith.

Recognize with enthusiasm that the United States is a multicultural local church. Within the multicultural fabric of our country and church, five very distinct groups with particular histories stand out: (1) the Native Americans, with their own rich variety of customs and traditions; (2) the Europeans, who first immigrated and established the basis of the dominant WASP culture of the United States; (3) the African Americans, who were torn out of Africa and brought here to serve as slaves; they became Christian in their own ways and, especially in the independent churches, are an excellent example of authentic inculturation; (4) the Mestizo/Mulatto Hispanics—especially the Mexican Americans and Puerto Ricans, who were colonized as the United States expanded its borders in the 1840s and the 1890s, respectively; (5) Asian Americans and other immigrant groups, more or less easily accepted to the degree they resemble the WASP model.

Today there is an urgent need for centers of concerned listening, research, and creative suggestions as to how we can best create a truly inclusive church in the United States. The stories of the different ethnic groups need to be heard, their cultural expressions appreciated, their prayer forms and religious expressions respected, their special needs acknowledged, and their music, art, and iconography encouraged. The different groups do not want to be judged by some "superior church group" but want to be acknowledged and appreciated as integral parts of the total U.S. church. The findings of these centers could be most valuable for the production of local catechetical and liturgical materials that are faithful to the demands of the *CCC*. The Mexican American Cultural Center in San Antonio has been doing this for the Mexican Americans, and after twenty years we feel that we are just beginning to make a serious start.

In the United States we cannot ignore the strong weight of the dominant and righteous WASP culture with its racism and ethnocentrism. Special emphasis must be made throughout the catechetical texts to attack every notion that consciously or unconsciously promotes white western culture as superior and normative for all others. The Catechism attacks this as the idolatry of nations (782, 803, 2112, 2317); this is still one of the great cultural sins of the dominant culture of the United States and thus of the U.S. Catholic Church. We must become clearly aware of this and counter it in every way possible.

Special attention to issues of social justice. Precisely because of the power and wealth of the United States, special emphasis must be made throughout every U.S. catechism to point out the multiple faces and causes of poverty and misery both within the United States and in other countries. The teachings on social justice of our popes must come through every level of the catechetical process. This is not an addendum to the doctrinal teachings of our church, but an integral part of it—carefully tied in to the creedal, sacramental, and moral life of Christians. Questions of just wages, worker compensation, accessibility of medical care, ecology, ownership, care of the elderly, treatment of immigrants, sale of arms to poor neighborhoods and countries, waste disposal, exploitation of natural resources, etc. must be included throughout. For the Catechism, charity is necessary but not enough. Christians must work to change the international economic structures that cause so much poverty and misery.

Pluriform catechesis and liturgy better reflects the richness of God's people. Whereas a specific catechism might be useful for a particular group at a particular moment, it is my impression that what most of the diverse groups are asking for is not separate and distinct catechisms. This in effect would foster division and segregation. What we want is to be significantly included throughout any of the texts that are developed for the United States—not to appear as an appendix, but as an integral part of the text. This is why every authentic catechetical text must be pluriform; otherwise, it will foster segregation by leaving out the traditionally "unwanted" of our society. For example, the same catechism could describe different baptismal, wedding, and funeral customs associated with the same sacrament, such as the integral role of *padrinos* in the Hispanic culture. They are all legitimate celebrations of one and the same sacrament. Also, besides the official holy days of the universal church, a section could include some of the special days of other groups, such as Our Lady of Guadalupe and *Día de los Muertos* (Day of the Dead) for Mexicans and *San Roque* for Italians. A beautiful section could present some of the various Christmas traditions. The students should be encouraged to speak about each other's feasts and celebrate them together. In the celebration of a common feast, we experience ourselves to be a united people.

I suggest the preparation of a simple catechetical/liturgical hymnal that could include several of the most popular and traditional songs of each group. A simple cassette could accompany the booklet and children could gradually learn one another's songs. Religious music is a very important element of the particular religious tradition of each people. It is a way of maintaining communion with the ancestors, which is very important to many groups, and of furthering a joyful fellowship among the diverse cultural traditions. The inter-cultural church should be festive and joyful so that it may be a foretaste and sign of the fullness of God's reign.

People enjoy feasts, and the attendance of Jesus at feasts is evident throughout the Gospels. Parishes should celebrate the particular feasts of the people of the parish (e. g., Our Lady of Guadalupe for Mexicans) with all the trimmings of that culture, while inviting the entire parish to participate. On the other hand, when the universal feasts are celebrated, such as Christmas or Easter, linguistic and cultural elements of the various cultures represented in the parish should be included.

Furthermore, given the multi-religious reality of the United States and the very positive approach the *CCC* takes to "other religions" (843), it would be exciting to include some of the key feasts of Jews, Muslims, Native American religions, and others. These could be presented as giving us other insights into the mystery of God, which could certainly enrich our own since no one expression can exhaust all the possibilities (42). This could be a new and very exciting section— presenting the other great religions not as something false and to be fought against, but as other elements of the ultimate mystery of God. This does not mean that we as Christian Catholics do not have the truth, but it does liberate us from the arrogance of thinking that we alone have it all.

No one catechetical text will respond to all the needs of the United States. Hence we need to encourage a variety of texts. This will not be divisive, but enriching.

We are beginning a fascinating moment of planetary communication. I hope and pray that our church may help to bring about a new paradigm of human existence: the reign of the God who watches over all the peoples of the world and who wants us to live in harmony and not in destructive fights and wars. To the degree that we can celebrate our unity in our diversity, we will have something truly new to offer today's divided world. Catechesis and the Catechism, as crucial and important as they are for the life and growth of the faithful, are nevertheless of secondary importance, for they presuppose an effective evangelization through which the whole life and teachings of the crucified and risen Jesus of Nazareth have been accepted by the people, making Jesus the Lord of our life. Catechesis presupposes and builds upon evangelization and conversion. Since the popes, synods, and recent statements of our own U.S. bishops have been calling for a renewed evangelization as the primary and urgent necessity of the entire church at this moment of history, we can surmise that the best of our catechisms and catechesis will be ineffective if Jesus Christ has not been proclaimed and confessed. The church's immediate priority is the most basic presentations, which lead the people to a personal knowledge of Jesus of Nazareth as the fullness of the incarnation of God's eternal Word.

Notes

[1]Between the "local church" as a diocese and the universal communion of churches, the documents of Vatican II (*Ad Gentes* and *Lumen Gentium*) refer to what I would call a regional communion of churches, that is, those local churches that find a natural unity because of a common language, cultural heritage, and historical journey. However, the case of a local church composed of peoples from various other local churches is something totally new for the church. This is the case in the United States.

[2]Jean Marie Tillard, "Theological Pluralism and the Mystery of the Church," in Virgil Elizondo, Claude Geffré, and Gustavo Gutiérrez, eds., *Different Theologies, Common Responsibility: Babel or Pentecost?* (Edinburgh: T. & T. Clark, 1984).

[3]Term used by Pope John Paul II in Senegal on February 22, 1992, in referring to the European civilizations that took an active role in the slave trade that deported forty million Africans and forced them into slavery.

[4]Joseph A. Komonchak quotes extensively from Cardinal Ratzinger's statement bringing out that the one church is only realized in the many local churches. "The Authority of the Catechism," in Berard L. Marthaler, ed., *Introducing the Catechism of the Catholic Church* (New York: Paulist Press, 1994) 18-31.

[5]1977 Synod of Bishops, no. 5.

[6]David Tracy, "World Church or World Catechism: The Problem of Eurocentrism," in Johann-Baptist Metz and Edward Schillebeeckx, eds., *World Culture or Inculturation?* (Edinburgh: T & T Clark, 1989) 36.

[7]Tillard, "Theological Pluralism and the Mystery of the Church" 63.

[8]CELAM, Third General Conference (Puebla, 1979) n. 448; Paul VI, *Evangelii Nuntuandi*, n. 48; *Catechism of the Catholic Church*, n. 1676.

[9]Victor Villaseñor, *Rain of Gold* (Laurel Trade Paperback, 1976).

4. Benevolent Tolerance or Humble Reverence?

A Vision for Multicultural Religious Education

(1997)

Virgilio Elizondo

At the very core of a true multicultural religious education program is the original New Testament story of the Christian movement: how the slaves, the disenfranchised, the low merchants, the widows, the unemployed, the immigrants, and the socially downcast found a new and exciting alternative to social life that the world had not imagined possible. In the new community, everyone was accepted with reverence and respect. If the Lord had emptied himself of all social status for them, then they were to do the same for one another. It was the excitement of this new way of life that attracted everyone—even the rich, the righteous, and the mighty. The joyful simplicity of Christians was contagious. Yet it was dangerous, because it dared to transgress all borders for the sake of a new unity.

The Originality of the Christian Movement

To best appreciate the challenge and the grace-filled possibilities of multicultural religious education, we need to rediscover and make our own the liberating and life-giving *originality* of the Christian movement. It offered to all peoples, no matter where they came from, a new family name: Christian. It offered equally to everyone, no matter what their race or nationality, a new, common bloodstream: the blood of Jesus. It flowed through everyone who joined, producing one close-knit unity: the body of the Lord! Thus the body and blood of Jesus, broken and spilled for the sake of humanity, now rehabilitated a broken humanity divided and crushed by the human blood that produces everyone's fundamental earthly identity. Peoples of diverse backgrounds, histories, and heritages could now begin to share in the common story and heritage of Jesus and the biblical heritage of their ancestors in the faith. This new story would not destroy the histories of peoples, but would bring them into a new common space and time. The kingdom of God was now available to everyone.

Christianity produced a new human being who was totally different from the world's nationalities, not by transforming the basic nationality but by transforming the limitations of national identities. The early Christians were considered atheists because they refused to recognize the national gods of any nation. Christians had only one God who was truly creator and parent of all. They were respectful of civic authority but refused to accept it as absolute, for they had only one absolute—the unconditional love of God for all human beings regardless of their national or racial identity.

Hence, the Christian identity was the hyphenated identity: Jewish-Christian, Greek-Christian, Roman-Christian. Their identities as Christians made them open to the otherness of others as truly brothers and sisters, all children of the same parent God. The refreshing originality of Christianity is that it transgressed all barriers of separation and division, whether rooted in blood or sacred traditions.

Historical Christianity as Divisive

The Cultural Reality of the United States

Despite the unity in diversity evident among the earliest Christians, historical Christianity has often served more as a basis of exclusion than of welcome. Multiculturalism is rather new in U.S. churches and in society today, yet it is an unquestioned fact of life. Some see it as the new life of the future while others see it as destructive of all unity—civic, social, and religious. Regardless of how it is understood, multiculturalism is a growing fact of life in the United States. Today as a church we attempt to break new ground in our understanding of the many aspects and implications of multiculturalism.

The Emergence of a Racist and Segregating Christianity

The U.S. churches are finally coming to grips with the original sin of the great European (and later American) evangelizing efforts that accompanied conquering and colonizing European expansion that began in the fifteenth century. Very simply put, white Europeans saw themselves as godly people while judging all others and their ways as demonic: we the saved, and they the damned; we the masters, and they the servants or slaves; we the true and beautiful human beings, and they the false and ugly human beings; we the possessors and guardians of truth, and they who are enslaved by error.

The white Christian invaders had no doubts about the divine righteousness of their invasion, conquest, and colonization of other people. They never questioned their own superiority. Western culture itself became the great idol of our churches. All had to conform or be cast out. It is the pseudo-divine status of white Western culture that is finally being revealed as the false idol that must be destroyed. It is not that Western culture needs to be destroyed, but its pseudo-divine status that allows it to continue functioning as the unquestioned normative culture and religious expression for all others.

Western theologians still tend to see the Western churches as "the church," while viewing the churches of other people of the world as "local churches." Western tradition is regarded as "Tradition," while everything else is regarded as local tradition. Western theologies are regarded simply as theology, while the theologies and methodologies of other cultures are regarded as ethnic or particular theologies. The West still keeps to itself the right to be the exclusive ecclesial master of the world and guards this right carefully through its universities and publications.

There is no doubt that in the past, and to a large degree today, most of our churches have been monochurches: monolingual, monocultural, and monoracial. Uniformity and conformity in all things have been the unquestioned norms of acceptance and belonging. These unquestioned norms allowed white churches of the past to justify and legitimize slavery and segregation. In effect, the churches implicitly sacralized fear, dislike, and hatred of others. Separate churches were built to keep diverse people worshipping separately. It has often been observed that eleven o'clock on Sunday mornings is the most segregated hour in America, and that the more churchgoing people are, the more prejudiced they seem to be.

It is out of this scandalous reality of the past that today we are seeking to bring about a new church with a truly multicultural face and heart.

A Graced Opportunity

The undeniable increase in racial and ethnic diversity in the United States poses many potential problems, yet greater than the problems are the opportunities to create something new and life-giving on the face of the earth. More and more religious educators attempt to facilitate a Christian response to the graced opportunities of our multicultural society. However, to promote the emergence of a real multicultural religious experience, we must go from a benevolent tolerance of the otherness of the others to a sincere reverence of others in their otherness.

Before we can embark on a multicultural religious education that is not merely a benevolent tolerance stemming from guilt feelings about the past, we need to undergo a deep cultural conversion from our previously unquestioned Western paradigm of truth itself—that all truth, whether personal, cultural, technical, natural, or religious, is one, absolute, and complete and therefore can be known in terms of either/or: true or false, good or bad, beautiful or ugly. For such a transformation to take place we must all die a bit to our collective self-righteousness so that we may be more willing to listen and learn from the others. As communication between persons, cultures, and nations increases, we are becoming aware that it is not possible to reduce truth to one expression. No one has an absolute and exclusive monopoly on truth. We have much to offer one another, if only we can have the humility to accept it.

A Puzzle Paradigm vs. a Pyramid Paradigm

Ultimate and absolute truth is like a massive puzzle. Each cultural expression of truth, together with its religious expression, is like a large piece of the complete puzzle of God and humanity. But no one piece alone gives us the complete picture. A more complete picture of the true, the good, and the beautiful comes through when all the pieces are together in their proper interconnectedness. Yet the fullness of the mystery of God and of humanity will still lie beyond our human understanding. This alone is the glory of God—no one piece dominating or controlling the others, but all joined together and giving meaning, life, and beauty to one another. This is different from the pyramid paradigm in which one builds on the others to eventually get to the top. In the puzzle all pieces are of equal importance. Only when they are joined together does the whole make sense. This model does not ask who is the best or the most important. It asks how each one fits into the rest for the benefit of everyone.

Multicultural religious education presupposes a truly multicultural church, or at least a church that is striving to be multicultural. But how does Christian multiculturalism come about? How do we build churches that welcome all people as they are, not to the degree that they become like the dominant group of the congregation? Do our churches welcome the diversity of God's humanity? Do we merely tolerate diversity, or do we reject it completely?

The ultimate success or failure of a truly multicultural religious education program depends on the personality of the local congregation, the person of the religious educator, and the total environment of the church—its people, ministers, decorations, music, church order, and celebrations. It is not just a question of the right materials and the right pedagogical methods, but a totally new attitude about church, ourselves, and others, a new attitude about the way we see and value the otherness of other persons and peoples. In a word, we must decide if we are going to be a tower of Babel or a Pentecost assembly of believers.

Multicultural Christianity as Unifying

My experience at San Fernando Cathedral, an active Mexican parish in San Antonio since 1731, has been an enriching one. Even though our basic identity is very Mexican, we work hard at welcoming others. We have not found this to be divisive in any way. On the contrary, it continues to be very enriching. Last Pentecost Sunday we celebrated our worship service in several languages and had the active participation of thirty-three ethnic groups. It was a great experience of the power of Christ bringing us together in ways no human power is capable of doing. The multicultural experience is not easy, but it is certainly exciting and enriching.

In my experience, a truly multicultural congregation emerges through three phases, or moments—not necessarily one before the other. The three moments are confession, conversion, and construction. But I suspect the first and foremost question is, Does the congregation really want to be a multicultural Christian family? Does it really want to be something new on the face of the earth? Or does it just want to be nice and add new ethnics to its already existing congregation? Does the congregation want continuity with just a bit more color and foreign accents? Or does it really want to be a community of all God's children?

Confession: Naming and Claiming the Sin

The Sin of Dogmatic Ethnocentrism. All of our churches in the United States came out of the great European colonizing enterprise that started in 1492. The church of that period, because of the Reformation and Counter-Reformation, emphasized dogma and looked at any type of difference as heretical and divisive. This emphasis also dogmatized the cultural and racial ideas of the emerging dominant nations of Europe. "White" and "Western civilization" thus became the dogmatically correct image of the dignified, beautiful, and authentic human being. All others would be looked upon as undignified, ugly (except for the young women of the conquered who often appeared to the conquerors as more exotic than their own women), and subhuman.

The Catholic and Protestant churches accepted without question the assumption that white Europeans, especially the Anglo-Saxons in North America, were the superior race which had been divinely chosen to be normative of the only true humanity possible or desirable by people in their right minds. Everyone else was considered inferior, heathen, and at best underdeveloped! The benevolent looked on the others as children who needed the loving care and discipline of the white Europeans. The ruthless looked on the others as mere beasts of burden. In many ways, this is still the case today.

Europeans and their American descendants fortified their sense of cultural superiority with the religious conviction that they belonged to the one and only true religion. Throughout history they had fought bloody battles among themselves as to which was the dogmatically correct version of this one true religion, but they never questioned that European Christianity was the one salvation for all the peoples of the world. Of course, "Christianity" meant their own particular understanding of it: Catholic, Lutheran, Methodist, Baptist, and so on.

It was this dogmatic certainty intermingled with the European sense of superiority and the European's need for cheap labor that "in good conscience" and with the blessings of religious authorities produced such an incredibly racist and segregated American continent. European immigrants did not hesitate to set up their own churches where they could experience salvation while exploiting and murdering the Natives, the imported Africans, and the conquered Mexicans, without any qualms of conscience.

It is true that some church voices protested loudly, and it is true that church movements have been a part of the force that has attempted to bring about change. But in general, the churches sanctified the white, neo-European culture of the Americas and thus sanctioned contempt for people of other races, cultures, and languages.

For a truly multicultural community to emerge, all are called to recognize their specific cultural sinfulness so that they may repent, receive God's forgiveness, and begin to create a new way of relating with each other.

The Sin of Arrogant Pride. White Western Christians need to convert from their sins of arrogance and pride. Their righteous sense of superiority has blinded them to their own inadequacies and sinfulness and has kept them from appreciating the treasures God has bestowed on the peoples of the other races and cultures of the world. This unclaimed sin of arrogant and self-righteous pride still allows them to see themselves as human while seeing the others as "cultural groups" or "ethnics."

There is a deep and unquestioned Western conviction, bolstered by financial, technological, and military superiority, that the West alone knows the truth, the way, and the life. All others either live in ignorance or at best possess only small bits and pieces of the truth. The minorities might be accepted and enjoyed "folklorically," but the West thinks that it alone knows the right way of life for all who want to be correctly human.

The confession of our cultural arrogance will be the beginning of the liberation from the current ethnocentrism that impels us to demand that others conform to our image and likeness. A collective recognition of our limited view of reality, of humanity, and of God will be the beginning of a new enrichment and source of life. It will be the beginning of a new life that, at the present moment, is impossible to imagine.

The Sin of Humiliating Shame. On the other hand, those who have been marginated, brutalized, abused, segregated, put down, ridiculed, or merely tolerated need also to recognize their sin: the sense of inferiority that some come to believe and accept. The victimizer's ultimate triumph is to get the victims to accept the blame for their situation of misery. The sin of the victimized is to accept this as true, resulting in a loss of dignity and self-worth. Attitudes of docility, embarrassment of color or heritage, and the many negative and self-destructive feelings grow out of the inner sense of shame at being who one is.

Even oppressed people who do not believe in their supposed inferiority are forced to live the consequences of inferiority, marginalization, and subservience. This is very painful. It is humiliating and it destroys the inner soul of the person and of a people. The sin of accepting assigned inferiority leads to a distrust of one's own, a disgust with one's culture and language, and a devastating break with the ways of one's ancestors.

Without confession of our cultural singleness, we will at best tolerate one another. We will never enter into a true fellowship among equals, a true family spirit that embraces all as children of the one God. We need to be willing and ready to name and confess our sin so that we may move on to conversion—that is, to a real *metanoia* whereby we will turn our innermost attitudes of life in a radically different direction.

Conversion to the Way of Jesus

Jesus surprised and astounded everyone, rich and poor, sinful and saintly, accepted and rejected, by portraying a totally new vision of the human and the sacred in the very simple and ordinary way in which he related with people and with God in his everyday life. He invited us to share in this new reality that will truly revolutionize our own vision of ourselves, of others, and of God.

Jesus invites us to see ourselves and others in a radically new way through the prism of God's unconditional love for everyone. Through God's love we move from our typical judgmental and conditional tolerance and acceptance of others to the spontaneous joy of discovering our unsuspected sisters and brothers, each one revealing a bit of God's glory. Everyone is invited to convert from pride or shame to a grateful and humble acceptance of who we are and who the other is. This will lead us from either total rejection or benevolent tolerance to a truly humble reverence for one another and an appreciation for the giftedness of each person, nation, and race.

Jesus: The True Image of the Human and of God. The dominant groups of Jesus' day perceived him as an outcast. Being Jewish, he belonged to people who were rejected culturally by the powerful Romans. Being from Galilee, he was from a region scorned socially by Jewish officials in Jerusalem, who frequently viewed their coreligionists from Galilee as unknowledgeable and lax in the practice of their faith. And to make things even more interesting, there were rumors about his dubious parentage and scandals about his friendships with prostitutes and public sinners. Thus did the sacred unseen and untouchable God become visible and touchable in the socially, culturally, and religiously rejected Jesus of Nazareth!

In the very social-cultural-religious human being that God became, Jesus revealed to us the mystery hidden by humanity's sinfulness since the origins of sin itself: that every human being is of infinite dignity, unmeasurable worth, and unique beauty. In its sinfulness, the world constantly creates categories of unworthiness, untouchability, and inferiority, while at the same time creating artificial and often unnatural categories of beauty, importance, dignity, and worth. These sinful categories begin to define the truth of the human and of the divine while in effect hiding (or perverting) the ultimate truth of God and destroying any possibility of human authenticity. Since the escalation of sin (described in Genesis 3-11), this has become the way of the world—the way of men and women throughout history. This was the way Peter was thinking when he wanted a glorious Messiah. This is the way we think when we want only socially acceptable members of the right color and ethnicity in our congregations. But this is not God's way! God creates and loves all of God's children alike.

These human classifications are the sin that brings about the distortion and blindness of the world. In Jesus, God became the nothing of the world so that through Jesus—with him and in him—all might be liberated from their own false notions about themselves and others, and thus come to appreciate people for what they truly are: children of God. There is nothing Jesus condemns more than hypocrisy. Sinful people he deals with compassionately; hypocrites he has no stomach for. People who give in to the world's struggles for superiority, honor, artificial beauty, and the like, lose themselves to the world and are destructive of self and of others.

The New Image of Self and Others. All are invited to convert—to think and feel in a radically new way so as to belong to God's own family. The rich and mighty are invited to give up their wealth and power while the poor and lowly are assured that they will be uplifted and will receive their fill.[1] In other words, those who have considered themselves superior are invited to think less of themselves. The righteous are invited to recognize their sinfulness, and those whom society deems unwanted "public sinners" are invited to become aware of their fundamental worth. Those who think of themselves as trash or as nothing are invited to recognize their strength and independence. Thus all are invited to a change of heart and mind. Through baptism we die to the old self to be reborn with the heart and mind of Jesus. We truly become a new creation within the old creation, and thus we are reborn to a new tension. The great difference is that now we know that ultimate triumph is assured and nobody can take it away from us. Hence we can live in peace even within the context of the tensions and uncertainties of the new life of grace.

It is in the very radical acceptance of our personal and collective mystery of giftedness/lack, wealth/poverty, blessing/curse, health/sickness, understanding/ blindness, saintliness/sinfulness, truth/ambiguity, knowledge/ignorance, that we become truly human. It is in the recognition of our innermost existential poverty as persons, as cultures, and as races that we begin truly to appreciate and welcome the wealth of others. It is in this radical acceptance of God's love for us as we are that we receive the courage to accept ourselves as we are and truly rejoice in the acceptance of others as they are, not as we would like them to be.

Division Because of Unity. In the Gospels, the same Jesus who prays "that all may be one"[2] tells us that he has come to bring about division.[3] These statements seem to contradict each other. Yet in practice it is quite obvious what Jesus is speaking about. Precisely because all are invited in an equal way, those who have usually enjoyed status and privilege will not want to come, not because they are not invited, but precisely because now everyone is invited, especially those considered to be unworthy, unwanted, and untouchable. When the club is made available to everyone, those who took pride in belonging to the exclusive, private club will not want to belong to the new one! In the process of working for the unity of the kingdom, we can expect the scandal, criticism, and persecution of those committed to the empires and sacred institutions of this world. The great paradox is that the call to unity so frequently leads to bitter division!

Construction of New Church Bodies

Each local congregation could easily become like a laboratory specimen of the new creation—and is it not in the cell that new life begins? Prayerful insight, patient trust, and a spirit of welcome are the seeds from which the new creation is born, whether at the congregational level or within the dynamics of multicultural religious education.

Prayerful Insight. Because the unity of the church is not one of men and women but of the Spirit, the work of multicultural unity must begin with sincere prayer that God may enlighten and strengthen us to go beyond our own fears and limitations. It is not through the conclusions reached by rational discourse but by the insight revealed through sincere and prolonged prayer that the new church will be built. Without prayer that truly opens up our minds and hearts to the unconditional love of God in all its consequences, even reading Scripture can simply confirm our distorted notions without giving us insight.

Prayer will bring about a new vision of vision itself, a new understanding of understanding itself, and a new truth regarding the reality of truth. Prayer leads us from narrow tunnel vision to a panoramic one, from isolated to more integrated understanding, and from partial to more complete truth. This does not relativize truth; it amplifies it! This is far more objective than the subjective conviction of one cultural group or another.

Patient Trust. The new multicultural fellowship will not come about overnight. It will take patience with ourselves and with others. We are embarking on something new and deeply personal, yet of planetary implications and consequence. It will not be easy. Even when we are committed to doing it, we will not always know just how to bring it about. Cultural misunderstanding is steeped in fear and misunderstanding. Sometimes signals, gestures, or words will be misinterpreted. Insult will be taken when none is intended, and rejection will be easily experienced.

Trust cannot be mandated. It builds up gradually but can be destroyed in an instant. There is no simple pedagogy for building trust. It takes a lot of love, self-giving, and the willingness to hurt with another and to see and feel in ways we are not accustomed to. It comes about through a lot of careful listening, especially to the silence and absence of those who are marginal or newcomers.

It will take time to build up the trust and confidence that people need to truly be themselves. Everyone has to be able to give up a bit of self to receive much from the others. But in the process of giving and receiving, a new and profound commonality will gradually emerge. In this process, all can truly become one body without anyone having to become like all the others simply in order to belong.

The more each one experiences the willingness of each member to die a bit to self for the sake of others, the more this love will become the new commonality and source of unity for the group. The source of unity will no longer be the racial color, the language, the ethnicity, the social class, the sex or sexual orientation, or even precise religious expression, but the love that allows each one to transgress the taboos that separate us. The new language will be that of *agape*, which finds ways of communicating through any and all the languages of humanity.

A Welcoming and Inclusive Home. To be truly multicultural, a local congregation must visibly reflect the various peoples making up the congregation in every aspect of church life. The very physical surroundings should put us in contact with the places of origin of the various members: pictures, decorations, maps, furniture, and signs in the various languages represented. Efforts should be made to help the members pronounce each other's names correctly. Simple greetings can be learned in one another's languages.

People should be invited to share their personal stories—where they came from, what they left behind, why they came, the struggles it took to get here, how they are getting adjusted, what they miss. Some, like many of our Mexican Americans and Native Americans, never left home but were made foreigners in their own lands. Others might have forgotten the migrations of their previous generations. The story of each one is important. It is by means of personal stories that we break through the stereotypes and begin to know persons as Juan, Mary, Karl, Nindu, Sun Ai, Yong Ting Jin. Through the stories we begin to interconnect on a very personal level.

Religious education activities should explore the various diverse and legitimate religious expressions of our one faith. People can experience the excitement of discovering how each expression enriches the ongoing incarnation of our faith. We need to appreciate the ancestral rites of our Asian Christians, the ancestral traditions of our African Christians, the Mestizo Christian traditions of our Latin American Christians. They include such beautiful customs as the Day of the Dead (which is actually the day of the living), *La Virgen* (which is not understood by North American Catholics or Latin American Protestants), and the crucified Jesus as *el Señor del Poder*; they also include the community dance and meal rituals of our Native Americans, the icons of Eastern European Christianity, the written alphabetic word for Western Christians, the role of the image-painted word for Christians of hieroglyphic cultures.

We must go even further. As Christians, we should lead the way in seeking to truly understand and appreciate all others. If in our minds and hearts we are secure in our own religious conviction, we do not have to be defensive or apprehensive in the face of others. Only one who is insecure will seek to discredit others. Hence, we should present and study the other great religions of the world, not asking whether they are true or false or even if they are a preparation for Christianity, but simply trying to appreciate them as they are. To see the beauty and truth of the others does not deny our own! In fact, it can even strengthen our own and help us to appreciate it more. I have found out in recent years that the more I appreciate the other great religious traditions of the world, the more I come to appreciate and love my own, not because I think we in our faith are better or superior to others, but simply because I have come to a greater awareness of who we are in relation to the others. We need to go beyond the sacralized divisions of the past so that we can become one very diverse and beautiful human family before we destroy one another in the name of the God we confess.

Festive Christianity as Proclamation

The early Christians made many converts through their new life of joy and simplicity. Many of the people Christians encountered had a great deal materially and socially and yet were bored and disillusioned with life. The Christians disregarded social rank and status and were happy because they welcomed everyone alike! All could partake of the table together—master and slave, citizen and foreigner. No matter what their role or status in society might be, within the Christian community they were truly of equal status because here they were brothers and sisters. It was not long before the Christian group was headed by a slave as successor of Peter—Pope Calixtus.[4]

Christians came together not to argue, defend, or try to impose, but simply to sing songs of joy, to tell about the memory of Jesus, to see how they could help one another, and to celebrate their new ritual, the breaking of the bread. In the breaking and sharing of the bread they transgressed the taboos and celebrated what was now begun in them but would only be fully achieved at the end of time—the ultimate unity of humanity. Our multicultural congregations can be the luminous and glorious rainbow whose worship foreshadows the banquet of the eschatological end, anticipating here and now God's ultimate triumph over the divisions of humanity.

Notes

[1] Luke 1:52-54.

[2] John 17:11.

[3] Luke 12:51.

[4] Calixtus I, also known as Callistus, became pope in 218. He was born a slave and died a Christian martyr in 223.

PART TWO

Popular Religion

INTRODUCTORY ESSAYS

Pasión y respeto

Elizondo's Contribution to the Study of Popular Catholicism

Orlando O. Espín

During my last year of college (over thirty years ago!), I was involved in CCD work at a local parish in Miami. The pastor recommended that I attend the religious education congress being held at a major hotel in Miami Beach—it would, he suggested, help me become a better catechist. I went, and there I met Virgilio Elizondo for the first time. That chance meeting in time led me down the path to the theological study of popular Catholicism. I vividly recall that several things impressed me about Virgilio Elizondo at that first meeting: his *passion and respect for the Latino/a people's religion*, his extraordinary *pastoral sensitivity*, and the fact that he was a *U.S. Latino* theologian.

As the years passed, Elizondo and I have had the opportunity to meet at many other formal and informal gatherings and to work together on a number of projects. My first impressions of him have been confirmed many times; and I have learned much from his writings and from conversations with him throughout the last three decades. Indeed, when years ago I had to decide to enter the field of professional theology, his advice carried great weight: given the dearth of Latino/a theologians in the United States, plus the increasing demographic and pastoral impact of our people on the American Catholic Church—and the myriad theoretical and practical consequences that flow from these two facts—it was imperative that more U.S. Latino/as become theologians, not to imitate European Americans, but in order to create a new theological method coherent with and derived from the faith of our people.

Elizondo's passion and respect for Latino/a popular religion have consistently led him to focus much of his written work on the Mexican and Mexican American devotion to Our Lady of Guadalupe; and his concern for a Latino/a theological method underlies his reflections on *mestizaje* and intercultural dialogue. Indeed, today it is simply impossible to study or write Latino/a theology without relying on Elizondo's foundational intuitions and elaborations on popular Catholicism and on *mestizaje*. In this article I want very briefly to focus on two of his contributions, which have become indispensable to the *theological* study of popular Catholicism: (1) the establishment of the field of popular Catholicism itself as a discipline within theology, and (2) the role of cultural interpretation within that discipline.

Establishing the Study of Popular Catholicism as a Discipline within Theology

Virgilio Elizondo's pastoral sensitivity and acumen led him to value and respect popular Catholicism.[1] He has always been well aware of the latter's limitations, however—he knows that discernment and catechesis are also necessary. But popular Catholicism's shortcomings have not diminished, in Elizondo's mind, the respect due to the people's religion. He has consistently regarded popular religion as a privileged means of evangelization and the people's faith as authentically Christian. It is impossible to read the articles included in this section, as well as his several books on Guadalupe, and not be impressed by his relentless passion and respect for the people's religion and its symbols.

Elizondo's passion and respect taught him to defend the faith of the people. And defense, in turn, became explanation and justification. It is at that point that he argues for the *theological* study of popular Catholicism.[2] This is no disinterested proposal. Its pastoral intent is very evident: to study theologically the faith of the people is not for the academic benefit of the theologian. The people must be the main beneficiaries, because theology must always be at the service of the faith of concrete Christian communities.[3] In conversations and lectures throughout the country, Elizondo repeated the challenge and the project: theologians had to take popular Catholicism seriously into account, within the theological disciplines, because this is how real people believe and how they ground their lives.

Most U.S. Latino/a Catholic theologians today consider popular Catholicism as an obvious source and locus not only for Latino/a theologizing, but for all (Catholic) theology.[4] Following Elizondo's earlier suggestions, Latino/a theologians began the process of creating a new theological method from the heart of our people's faith and culture. Professor Sixto García and I coauthored the first several texts to examine methodologically what Catholic theology might "look like" if popular Catholicism were seriously incorporated as source and locus.[5] García and I worked on a theology of Providence, for example, as a first exercise of the new methodological approach.[6] The ever growing bibliography of U.S. Latino/a theology, by an equally growing number of scholars, indicates that Elizondo's original proposal was heeded and his challenge engaged.

But why is popular Catholicism so important for the church? Why should anyone in theology pay serious attention to it and, therefore, to Elizondo's suggestion that it be methodologically incorporated into theological reflection?

Popular Catholicism could be defined in many ways.[7] For our purposes here, let me briefly describe it as *a legitimate manner of being Catholic* (arguably, the manner typical of the vast majority of Catholics throughout the world, and certainly of most U.S. Latino/a Catholics). It does not subvert what might be considered "official" Catholicism, although it has historically acted as corrective of "officially" held views. Popular Catholicism is a complex of beliefs, ethical expectations, religious experiences, and rituals that have been and continue to be created by the people in response to Christian tradition. Popular Catholicism preserves (and witnesses to) necessary dimensions of the Catholic tradition. Popular Catholicism, therefore, is memory, witness, prophecy, and experience. It too is a socialization of the experience of the divine.

The church's tradition has historically expressed itself through other means beyond and beside the fixed biblical text. One of these means has been and is popular Catholicism. There is plenty of evidence to support the view that popular Catholicism, of one kind or another, has been in existence since at least the postapostolic church (and some might claim, not without reasonable arguments and evidence, that even the apostolic generation had created its own brand [or brands] of popular Catholicism). In theology, one need not prove that some of today's official dogmas were yesterday's popular beliefs.

Some theologians or historians might say that the *sensus fidelium* or the *depositum fidei*, or perhaps some other apparent constant in the history of dogmas, can explain the transformation of popularly held beliefs into the church's officially defined dogmas. Such explanation can indeed be offered, but it cannot be easily substantiated. The data would in fact indicate that popular Catholicism was the mine from which the magisterium extracted some of the defined dogmas, but it too would show that on some occasions popular Catholicism held on to and proposed beliefs that the magisterium (at the time) officially and actively opposed—please recall the ancient trinitarian and christological controversies and the indispensable contributions of popular Catholicism to what later came to be regarded as orthodox doctrines. In other words, the universe of popular religious beliefs and practices, fashioned by the people somehow to "supplement" or "correct" official Christianity, has been (and still is) a vehicle through which truth can be and is communicated in the church—a vehicle through which God speaks! A proper understanding of tradition cannot ignore this role of popular Catholicism (nor can studies on popular Catholicism disregard this very important function of the people's faith life).

Popular Catholicism, however, has not only been a vehicle for potentially defined dogmas. It has been (and still is) a means of communicating nondefined doctrine—which might or might not coincide with the magisterium's positions. Popular Catholicism plays a significant role in preserving the people's discerning *sensus fidei* (which relates not only to the doctrinal but also to the "praxical"), as well as a *crítica* of official teachings and practices. I want to emphasize that this role of critic of official teachings and practices should be understood not in the manner of subversion but in the manner of prophecy.

Popular Catholicism has also been (and still is) an important means through which people are evangelized. The faith has been preserved among many because of popular Catholicism's evangelizing and "supplementary" roles. If tradition can be seen as the historical continuation and/or prolongation of the Christian experience and faith, and if it can also be understood as the development, application, and interpretation of the contents of the biblical text (without forgetting that the church, to whom tradition belongs and whose bearer it is, is broader than the magisterium), then popular Catholicism, by its roles and functions, is certainly an important (and arguably necessary) vehicle of tradition.

If one understands popular Catholicism and tradition, and the relationship between them, then one can easily see the immense importance that the study of popular Catholicism has for *all* theology. When confronted with the role that popular Catholicism has in the U.S. Latino/a context, its importance becomes so central that it would be meaningless to attempt to theologize in the Latino/a context while disregarding popular Catholicism.

Latino/a Christianity exists thanks to the evangelizing role of popular Catholicism. Without popular Catholicism, the historical neglect to which Latino/as have been submitted in this country by church and society, along with the constant pressure to "assimilate" and the unfortunate racist tendencies among some in North American society and the church, would have long ago done away with Catholicism among Latino/as and with Latino/a culture in general.

The Catholic faith of the Latino/a people has been one of the key elements in the preservation of culture, and vice versa. The relationship between faith and cultural identity (and all that the latter implies) cannot be overly stressed in the Latino/a context. Catholicism has been a matrix of Latino/a culture, and this is of utmost importance for theology.

When we speak of Catholicism in relation to Latino/a culture, however, we are not simply or mainly referring to the institutionalized version most frequent among Anglos. In the Latino/a context Catholicism is mostly (though obviously not exclusively) "popular Catholicism," in other words, the version born of popular Catholicism and handed down through generations by the laity more than by the ordained ministers of the church. This way of being Catholic has always thought of itself as being the true faith of Christians, as being just as "Catholic" as the clergy's version (to the point that, in many Latino/a cultural communities, the two visions are distinguished precisely as "the clergy's" and "ours").

If the two visions of tradition were *synoptically* compared (i. e., placed side by side), it is my contention that differences will be found in the symbolic, cultural, and analogic spheres and, consequently, in liturgical expressions, in doctrinal emphases and understandings, and in prioritizing ethical expectations. I do not believe, however, that significant differences will be found in the *essential* elements of the faith (*if one keeps in mind the role that culture plays in always contextualizing the faith and every expression of it*). In other words, when careful examination is made of the "official" and "popular" traditions, the two will be found to be foundationally the same, *though culturally and symbolically expressed in different manners*, and with doctrinal and praxical emphases that deeply reveal the socio-historical, cultural realities and interests of the holders of either vision of the tradition. I further believe that it is these socio-historical realities and interests that ultimately create much of the distinction between these two strands of the one Christian tradition.

Elizondo's pastoral intuition, his passion and respect for the people's religion, and his call to reflect on the faith of our people have indeed opened an immense new discipline within theology. But, as can be expected, new questions have consequently arisen. When confronted with the reality of Latino/as, with the cultural matrix role of Catholicism, and with the (not always public) distinctions between the "popular" and the "official" Catholic visions of tradition, Latino/a theologians face a serious set of challenges and urgent questions. First of all, Latino/a theologians are members of the official church that has alienated (and continues to alienate) so many Latino/as in this country. This can be a drawback: for whom and for whose ideological and social interests do theologians speak? Who benefits socio-historically, in fact, from their theology? Second, Latino/a theologians share (consciously or not, by ecclesiastical and academic recognition and by professional training) in the vision of tradition that is presented as "official" to Latino/as and which Latino/a popular tradition does not easily accept as *solely* valid. Which tradition must the theologian be faithful to? Can a theology, as we know it, be made that excludes either vision of tradition? Can a theology be made that combines the two visions, and if so, how can this be done, what are the criteria, without "colonizing" either vision? Would the result radically alter theology as we know it? Many in the new generation of Latino/a theologians are attempting to respond to these (and many other) questions; Elizondo's original proposal (i. e., that theology take seriously the faith of the Latino/a people) has clearly begun to bear fruit.

Cultural Interpretation of Popular Catholicism

In his many studies on *mestizaje* and on Guadalupe, Elizondo has frequently emphasized the methodological and hermeneutic importance of culture and contextualization.[8] Referring to the Guadalupan devotion, Elizondo reminds us that "studying it through the mariological practices and theologies of the West will lead to misunderstanding and error. Such a process would impose a meaning that would not correspond to the true meaning which it has for the people."[9] This insight is equally applicable to the study of any other aspect of popular Catholicism, and indeed to everything in theology.

It seems impossible today to study popular Catholicism within the theological disciplines without delving into culture and contextualization and into many other subjects related to these themes. Elizondo has always been aware of this and has consequently reflected on cultural issues from the earliest stages of his theological career.[10]

Virgilio Elizondo has always known and been proud of his cultural roots and of his people's struggles. His *mexicanidad* is the front for much of his theological reflection. And among the several elements that may be said to shape and define his *mexicanidad*, few stand out more clearly than his devotion to Our Lady of Guadalupe. His frequent return to the Guadalupan devotion is not just for the sake of further theoretical development of earlier insights—the *Virgen de Guadalupe* is a key component of Elizondo's human and Christian existence, experientially and theologically. And yet, every one of his writings on Guadalupe is grounded in cultural interpretation.[11] His study of this symbol of Mexican and Mexican American popular Catholicism is always an interpretive study, contextualized in the history and social reality of the people. Indeed, and once again, Elizondo's passion and respect for his people's religion has nourished his extensive theological and pastoral bibliography on the *Virgen*.

The way Elizondo reflects on Guadalupe implies a certain method.[12] If I may be forgiven an extremely oversimplified synthesis of his approach to Guadalupe (and, by extension, to his study of other elements within Latino/a popular Catholicism), it might be said that Elizondo always begins with the historical contextualization of the two cultures (Nahua and Iberian) that gave birth to the *Virgen de Guadalupe* as the *mestizo/a* symbol par excellence. His method usually proceeds by then examining the context of conquest within which the opposing Nahua and Iberian cultures clashed and *mestizaje* violently commenced. Guadalupe is then presented as a creative synthesis of the new *mestizaje* (a new human reality which resulted from such painful birth) that represents the New World's current reality, and as the preeminent inculturated symbol of Christianity in the Americas. And finally, his method leads to an interpretive reflection on the meaning of the past and Guadalupe for the men and women of the present.

The "Galilee principle,"[13] which Elizondo proposed in his christologically inspired *Galilean Journey*, is operative in his Guadalupan studies too. Synthesis, *mestizaje*, and inculturation—these seem to be three axes of Elizondo's interpretive reflection. These three axes ultimately address, interpret, and result from suffering human reality, so much part of the U.S. Latino/a experience, namely: from struggle, confrontation, and oppression will come, by God's choice and grace, a new shared life of hope and community. In Elizondo's work, Guadalupe is the great symbol of this "paschal" transition in the Americas, synthesizing the former opposites in a new *mestizaje* that expresses its reality in equally new cultural forms.

But there is more. Whenever Elizondo examines culture or history, or when he contextualizes Guadalupe within culture and history, the purpose is not the gathering of "facts," although he does this too. His approach to culture, especially, is intentionally "interpretive"—by this I mean that Elizondo seeks in the Nahua, Iberian, Mexican, and Mexican American cultural milieu those elements that may *explain* how and why his people understood the gospel, and how and why they persevered in the faith despite so many challenges and so much suffering. His is no cultural or historical research for the sake of "pure" knowledge, and not even for mere historical explanation; rather, his interest is explicitly present, particular, and pastoral. Elizondo's cultural and historical research wants to discover why and how his people believe as they do and live as they do, in order pastorally to accompany them as they speak and affirm their own identity. Once again, Elizondo's passion and respect for the faith of the people guide his approach and intent.

Elizondo's method became more explicit in the work of other Latino/a theologians. The new theological generation has expanded, corroborated, elaborated, and at times perhaps moved beyond Elizondo's original insights on the need for cultural interpretation of popular Catholicism. No one claims to be merely *repeating* what Elizondo said; but it is evident that most contemporary U.S. Latino/a theologians have built their work on the foundations laid down by Elizondo.

Pastoral sensitivity, coupled with his deep respect and passion for the people's religion, has guided Virgilio Elizondo's study of popular Catholicism. No one can expect a single theologian's work to say, examine, and explain everything within a given field of research or learning. No matter how creative and brilliant, no theologian knows all there is to know about any given subject. Perhaps some might have wished Elizondo to have written on other topics, or to have dealt with different aspects of the subjects he actually studied, or perhaps to have delved deeper into this or that issue, or to have been more explicit in one or another point. Virgilio Elizondo has not said or written all that could have been said or written on popular Catholicism; and perhaps he should have dwelled more on some subjects which he has only treated tangentially. Nonetheless, his contribution to the theological study of popular Catholicism has been immense—indeed, the discipline, among American Catholic theologians (and not just Latino/a ones), owes its very existence to him! Elizondo's greatest impact on the future of Catholic theology in the Americas rests on his insistence that the faith of the people be taken seriously as source and locus of theology. His approach to popular Catholicism—cultural and historical analyses—has proven to be the methodological foundation for his theological discipline. This is more than sufficient reason to honor him!

Notes

[1]Elizondo's respect for the people's religion is evident from his earliest writings, not only as a topic for discussion but also as passion. His earlier work clearly shows that popular Catholicism already acts as source for his theological reflection. See, for example: "Biblical Pedagogy of Evangelization," *American Ecclesiastical Review* 168 (1974): 526-543; "Religious Education for Mexican Americans" 58-61 above; *Religious Practices of the Mexican American and Catechesis* (San Antonio: Mexican American Cultural Center Press, 1974); *Christianity and Culture: An Introduction to Pastoral Theology and Ministry for the Bicultural Community* (Huntington, IN: Our Sunday Visitor, 1975); and especially his doctoral dissertation *Métissage: Violence culturelle, annonce de l'évangile. La dimension interculturelle de l'évangélisation,* 3 vols. (Paris: Institut Catholique, 1978; published in English as *Mestizaje: The Dialectic of Cultural Birth and the Gospel* [San Antonio: Mexican American Cultural Center Press, 1978]).

[2]This turn from defense to explanation is evident in *Mestizaje: The Dialectic of Cultural Birth and the Gospel,* and especially in his *Christianity and Culture.*

[3]See the previous note, and also his "Conditions and Criteria for Authentic Intercultural Theological Dialogue," in V. Elizondo, C. Geffré and G. Gutiérrez, eds., *Different Theologies, Common Responsibility* (Edinburgh: T & T Clark, 1984) 18-24, where he sets down criteria for authenticating theological reflection.

[4]The current bibliography is so vast that it is impossible to include it all in a single note. The following are just a few examples: O. Espín, *The Faith of the People: Theological Reflections on Popular Catholicism* (Maryknoll, NY: Orbis, 1997); R. Goizueta, *Caminemos con Jesús: Toward a Hispanic/Latino Theology of Accompaniment* (Maryknoll, NY: Orbis, 1995); J. Rodríguez, *Our Lady of Guadalupe: Faith and Empowerment among Mexican American Women* (Austin: University of Texas Press, 1994); A. M. Isasi-Díaz and Y. Tarango, *Hispanic Women: Prophetic Voice in the Church* (San Francisco: Harper & Row, 1988); besides other books and numerous scholarly articles by R. Goizueta, J. Rodríguez, García-Rivera, M. Díaz, S. García, O. Espín, A. Bañuelas, M. P. Aquino, etc. A fine collection of articles on systematic theology, most of which

refer to popular Catholicism as source and locus of theologizing, may also be found in: O. Espín and M. Díaz, eds., *From the Heart of Our People: Latino/a Explorations in Systematic Theology* (Maryknoll, NY: Orbis, 1999).

[5]These papers were presented at two consecutive conventions of the Catholic Theological Society of America: "Sources of Hispanic Theology," at the CTSA Forty-Third Annual Convention (Toronto) in 1988; and "Toward a Hispanic-American Theology," at the CTSA Forty-Second Annual Convention (Philadelphia) in 1987. The texts may be found in the CTSA *Proceedings* for the respective years.

[6]"Lilies of the Field: A Hispanic Theology of Providence and Human Responsibility," in *Proceedings of the Catholic Theological Society of America* 44 (1989): 70-90.

[7]For the remainder of this section, see my *The Faith of the People* for supporting bibliography. See also the arguments and bibliography included in my article, "An Exploration into the Theology of Grace and Sin," in: O. Espín and M. Díaz, eds., *From the Heart of Our People,* and M. P. Aquino's article, "Theological Method in U.S. Latino/a Theology," in the same collection. See, further, R. Goizueta's *Caminemos con Jesús.*

[8]I am specifically thinking of his three articles included in this section, as well as his *Christianity and Culture*; *Mestizaje: The Dialectic of Cultural Birth and the Gospel*; *La Morenita: Evangelizer of the Americas* (San Antonio: Mexican American Cultural Center Press, 1980); *Guadalupe: Mother of the New Creation* (Maryknoll, NY: Orbis, 1997); *Galilean Journey: The Mexican-American Promise* (Maryknoll, NY: Orbis, 1983); and his article, "*Mestizaje* as a Locus of Theological Reflection," 159-175 below.

[9]Virgilio Elizondo, "Mary and the Poor: A Model of Evangelizing Ecumenism," in Hans Küng and Jürgen Moltmann, eds., *Mary in the Churches* (New York: Seabury, 1983) 59.

[10]See the bibliography included in note 1.

[11]This is so evident from Elizondo's writings that there is no need to refer the reader to particular books or articles. As samples, however, see the foundational chapters in his *The Future Is Mestizo: Life Where Cultures Meet* (Bloomington, IN: Meyer-Stone, 1988), as well as the pertinent sections in *Galilean Journey.*

[12] The method I merely synthesize in this brief paragraph may be found, *in extenso*, for example, in *La Morenita* and *Guadalupe: Mother of the New Creation*. The Guadalupe article in this section also illuminates Elizondo's approach.

[13]The principle reads as follows: What human beings reject, God chooses as his very own. Elizondo, *Galilean Journey* 91.

The Common Womb of the Americas

Virgilio Elizondo's Theological Reflection on Our Lady of Guadalupe

Jeanette Rodriguez

Virgilio Elizondo articulates his reflection on Our Lady of Guadalupe with sensitivity and passion fueled by the communal experiences he grew up with in San Antonio, Texas. He describes a childhood memory of visiting the Guadalupe Basilica in the following way:

> As we gradually walked toward the luminous image, she appeared to be coming toward us, as if she were descending to greet each one of us personally. Through the darkness we walked towards the light, the warmth, and the beauty of La Virgen Morena. We could not stop; the crowd simply moved us on. We were never pushed or shoved; we all simply walked in deep mystical union with one another. We were in the rhythmic movement of the universe—indeed, at this moment we were in contact with the very source of life and movement.[1]

This childhood memory reflects the experience of thousands upon thousands of Guadalupe devotees in the Americas. In a variety of his works, Elizondo reveals his growing realization of how extraordinary this story and its impact is in the context of salvation history. He contends, "I do not know of any other event since Pentecost that has had such a revolutionary, profound, lasting, far reaching, healing, and liberating impact on Christianity."[2] If one follows the numerous articles that he has written on Our Lady of Guadalupe[3] as well as his books *La Morenita* and *Guadalupe: Mother of the New Creation*, one witnesses an evolution of his understanding regarding the Guadalupe event. He begins by describing his affective bond toward Guadalupe that grew from his neighborhood formation and goes on to identify her as foundational to Mexican identity and Mexican Catholicism. He integrates his intuition and experience with a more systemic understanding of her significant theological contribution. This theological unfolding recognizes Guadalupe as "mother" and as the evangelizer of the church and the Americas, as one who is the protector and liberator of the poor. More recently Elizondo's development of her message has led him to proclaim her as "the beginning of a new creation, the mother of a new humanity, and the manifestation of the femininity of God."[4] In many ways, Virgilio's work reflects those values and vision of the cosmos deeply imbedded in the indigenous psyche.

Although there are many doubts about her origins and various positions regarding the historical validity of the tradition, her impact on and living presence among the devotees of the Americas is beyond doubt or refutation. My own work on Our Lady of Guadalupe and her impact on Mexican American women would not have been written if not for *Madre del Sol* (Mother of the Sun), a trilingual play in English, Spanish, and Nahuatl performed at the Mexican American Cultural Center in San Antonio during 1982. This is where I first met Father Virgilio Elizondo, founder and first president of the Mexican American Cultural Center and the premier Chicano theologian in the United States. My own work has drawn from and builds upon his original, creative contribution.

Virgilio was the first Latino theologian to identify and unpack the notion of *mestizaje*. Historically, *mestizaje* referred to the biological mingling of Spanish and Indian blood. Today, words that come to mind in relationship to this concept are conquest and resistance, borderlands, born and/or raised in the United States. Other concepts emerge: struggle for integrity, anger, pain, economically and politically marginalized, multiple identities. The *mestizo/mestiza* is in a constant position of having to define him- or herself in the context of a society that has ignored or kept him/her invisible. In addition to not having a place, the *mestizo/mestiza* must struggle to balance among a variety of intrapsychic, interpersonal, and cultural matters. Here is one description of what it is like to cross between cultures: "Indigenous like corn, the *mestiza* is a product of crossbreeding, designed for preservation under a variety of conditions. Like an ear of corn—a female seed-bearing organ—the *mestiza* is tenacious, tightly wrapped in the husks of her culture. Like kernels she clings to the cob; with thick stalks and strong brace roots, she holds tight to the earth—she will survive the crossroads."[5]

Although *mestizos* cross back and forth between these dual identities, they sometimes feel so terribly unaccepted—orphaned. Some do not identify with Anglo-American cultural values and some do not identify with Mexican cultural values. Mexican Americans are a synthesis of these two cultures with varying degrees of acculturation, and with that synthesis comes conflict. One woman told me how it feels for her: "Sometimes the Latina in me doesn't understand or is in contradiction to the Anglo-educated side of me. Sometimes I feel like one cancels out the other. And I feel like nothing."[6] Mexican Americans have been raised within a culture and a church which have never taught Mexican American literature, history, customs, traditions, or foods. We have had to study about everyone else but never about ourselves. We now need to take that time to study ourselves and our origins because "history is not merely the record of the past but the life source of the present and the hidden energy of the new future."[7]

Virgil's second contribution is the unpacking of the Guadalupe narrative that releases its liberating message and hope for a new humanity. "Guadalupe is definitely a very popular devotion. But behind this devotion lies also a new image and understanding of reality, of truth, of humanity, and of God."[8] This notion of a new image of reality, which includes a new way of perceiving truth, of understanding the human and how God is revealed, is one of Virgilio's greatest contributions. Despite the historical context out of which Guadalupe appeared, with all its violence, conquest, and shame, Virgilio has a wonderful way of seeping through that pain and horror. He does not sanitize or deny, but seeps through it and finds hope and the potential for creating something new. In Guadalupe he is able to see a way of transforming the harshness of that reality into an ever-life-pulsing belief that God is still present and can make anew.

The third point I wish to emphasize is Virgilio's ability to bridge two protagonist cultures by identifying the source of conflict (which is still experienced today) and offering a solution for reconciliation. Our cultural background, which includes sociological, psychological, political, and economic dimensions, impacts our personal theological orientation. In his work, Virgilio begins by sharing the story of his life, the story of his own faith journey in the world. It is a faith journey in a world constituted within a political, socioeconomic context. He begins his reflections on the devotion to Our Lady of Guadalupe with that same pedagogy. He examines the historical context out of which the apparition of Guadalupe emerges. For Virgilio, the story of Our Lady of Guadalupe really begins in 1492. He contends that for Europe, it was the beginning of some totally new opportunities for fame, wealth, adventure, and conquest. For the church, it was an opportunity to start over, to build a new church that would truly reflect the gospel and move away from the many abuses committed in the churches of Europe. For the natives of the Americas, the experience was quite different. There was a beginning, but this was the beginning of an invasion. This was the beginning of an encounter with an unknown type of humanity. It was the beginning of hard labor and humiliation, sickness, enslavement, death, and the abandonment of their gods.[9]

The Spanish takeover of the Aztec empire was facilitated by a number of factors. First, there was a certain unrest among the Nahuatl population, dominated by the Aztec people. The Aztecs were the dominant indigenous military group and had developed an aristocracy. They were hated and feared by the subordinate groups, many of whom felt that the Aztec's obsession with human sacrifice had totally perverted the religion.[10] Whether the Spaniards were gods or humans, they presented the potential for liberation from this.[11]

A second factor was that the beginning of the conquest coincided with the ancient Nahuatl predictions that their civilization had lived its time and would come to an end.[12] This "end" was predicted to come about with the return of the god Quetzalcoatl. To the Nahuatl, it was more than a coincidence that these Christians should also come from the east, the direction from which Quetzalcoatl had predicted he would arrive, in exactly the same year he had set for his return.[13] They remembered the word of Quetzalcoatl, who had promised to return; since tradition held that he was a large man with blue eyes and blond hair, the Spaniard Cortés certainly fit the description.

Miguel León-Portilla summarizes in detail the good and bad omens that are said to have foretold the arrival of the Spaniards, such as a comet sighted in the skies, an unexplained burst of flames in the temple of Huitzilopochtli, and the damage to another temple by a bolt of lightning.[14] The Aztec leader Moctezuma II addressed Cortés, greeting him as Quetzalcoatl, and welcomed him back to his throne.[15] Thus Quetzalcoatl had returned to redeem the various groups from the captivity of the Aztecs, who had perverted his religion.[16] This anticipated hope was soon turned into a devastating "encounter."

In addition to deaths caused by warfare, forced labor, brutality, military force, and subjugation, many died from epidemic disease: "The diseases brought to Mexico by Europeans wiped out whole towns. These diseases manifested themselves in the form of smallpox, typhoid, measles, typhoid fever, and diphtheria epidemics. Because they were isolated from the rest of the world and the Indians had developed no resistance at all . . . certain Calpullis lost 80% of their people through disease."[17]

The Spaniards' technical superiority, combined with Spain's policy of expansionism as well as their evangelical zeal and conviction that the conquest was ordained and supported by *their* God,[18] brought about brutal violence and the takeover of the economic, political, religious, and social institutions of the indigenous people.[19] Given this brutality and the conquest mentality of the sixteenth-century Spaniards, one would be inclined almost to take sides. But Virgil doesn't do that. He acknowledges that

> each civilization produced its own language, philosophies, artistic works, sophisticated crafts, and complex religion. Each had its unique ways of approaching truth, expressing beauty, and communicating with ultimate reality. Each was guided by different value systems, different systems of logic, different anthropologies, and different mythologies. Europeans had known of the great mysterious differences between themselves and the people of some other great continents, but they had not even suspected the existence of the continents they ran into in the beginning of 1492. Here they encountered not only an unsuspecting continent, but a different humanity.[20]

Virgil's work continues to describe, not judge, the differences between these two groups, so that one might understand the source of the conflicts.

Virgil pierces the foundational depths of the issue, the question of what it means to be human. For the Western Europeans, to be fully human one had to be Christian and perceive oneself as rationally superior to all of creation. The indigenous, on the other hand, saw the human being as a creature whose existence depended on their interconnection with all life. The difference between the European anthropology of rationality and the indigenous anthropology of creatureliness was the source of an "anthropological clash."[21] Virgil does not leave the issue here, however. Rather, he challenges us to remember the Phoenix who rises from the ashes. For out of the ashes of the conquest emerges Guadalupe.

The narrative of Guadalupe, passed on to us in the *Nican mopohua*, is the indigenous account of "the real new beginnings of the Americas."[22] Guadalupe's significance is that she responds to the deepest instincts of the Mexican psyche; her iconography contains symbols the indigenous encountered, understood, and honored. The titles Guadalupe used to introduce herself in the official account of the *Nican mopohua*—Mother of the God of Truth, the Mother of the Giver of Life, the Mother of the creator, the Mother of the One who makes the sun and the earth, the Mother of the One who is near—coincide with the names given the ancient Mexican gods.[23] The five names of the gods were well known to the Nahuatl. Guadalupe stated who she was and where she came from, utilizing what the

Nahuatls understood to be the operative essence as well as the cosmological and historical dimensions of their gods. Affectively, the woman who speaks touches the deepest beliefs and longings of the human heart: the desire and need to be seen, heard, understood, accepted, embraced, and loved. Guadalupe represents even more than compassion, relief, and a means of reconciliation between different groups of people. By identifying herself as "Mother of the true God through whom one lives," she connects herself with the supreme creative power, that is, the creative and creating presence. She is a symbol of a new creation, a new people.[24]

For Mexican Americans today, Our Lady of Guadalupe is a symbol of religio-cultural identity. For a brutally conquered people, she restores their dignity, their humanity, and their place in history. Virgilio contends that only a divine intervention could have turned around the devastation caused by the conquest. She "who comes from the region of light on the wings of an eagle" restores dignity and life to a people who were dead.[25]

To appreciate the significance of Our Lady of Guadalupe, it is crucial to understand the context in which she is recognized: popular religion. Popular religion—that is, how religion is lived and experienced by the majority of a people—contributes to our understanding of Our Lady of Guadalupe.[26]

When I speak of Catholicism in relationship to the Mexican American culture, I am not referring to the institutionalized version of Catholicism, but to popular Catholicism, handed down through generations by the laity more than by the ordained clergy. Although Hispanic popular religion has its historical roots in sixteenth-century Catholicism, it has evolved a life of its own that captures the identity, values, and inspirations of the people in a way that I believe official religion has ignored.

From the point of view of the institutional church, popular religion has not been seen as equally Catholic, but as primitive and backward, even childlike. But popular religion is a hybrid which continues to exist because, for the poor and marginalized, it is a source of power, dignity, and acceptance not found in the institutional church. Popular religion is not celebrated by a few, but by the majority of the people. It is an expression of faith which has survived over a considerable period with roots in the historical beginnings of Hispanic culture. Above all, popular religion is active, dynamic, lived, and has as its purpose to move believers and enable them to live their beliefs. This includes the people's expression of their own history, both personal and cultural. This lived and articulated history is foundational in the human-divine drama. God's cause (the poor) must be the cause of humanity; God's actions for the cause of the poor are the actions that humanity must realize.[27] Only through our action on behalf of justice can we elevate our consciousness regarding God's immanent presence in the human condition.

In the narrative, Guadalupe is God's action on the side of the poor, as is Juan Diego. In his encounter with the religious powers of the time, Juan Diego is the protagonist, representing all who are marginalized. Similarly, Mexican Americans today are the poor; Guadalupe comes and stands among them to reflect who they are—mothers, fathers, men, women, children, *morenos, mestizos*—and gives them a place in a world that negates them.

Virgilio also emphasized Guadalupe's ability to give people a place in a world that has rejected them. He transforms the negative concepts and attitudes of *mestizaje* into a powerful transformation—a new creation. This is yet another one of his great contributions. Virgilio's work also illuminates a way of knowing, a way of being, a way of understanding that is reflective of pre-Columbian thinking. This way of thinking and knowing and understanding is one that is determined by, motivated by, and lived in the heart. For Virgilio, "the heart is the active and dynamic center of the person; it is the symbolic place of ultimate understanding and certitude. Truth resides in the heart."[28]

Pre-Columbian Nahuatl philosophical thought as expressed by philosopher León-Portilla is "an aesthetic conception of the universe; to know the truth is to understand the hidden meanings of things through flower and song *(flor y canto)*."[29] This refers to a more intuitive and heart-oriented way of understanding and interpreting reality.

"Flower and Song" is an example of *disfrasismo*, used in the Nahuatl language to connote a complementary union of two words or symbols to express one meaning. The phrase *flor y canto* is a metaphor which expresses a worldview many of us inherit. The Nahuatls believed that only through *flor y canto* could truth be grasped. Truth intuited through poetry derives from a particular kind of knowledge. It is a knowledge that is the consequence of being in touch with your own inner experience as lived out communally. This truth is mediated through the cultural constructs of the community as understood through the individual. In the Nahuatl worldview, the concept of the individual is manifested through *rostro y corazón*, face and heart.

Understanding the language and the affectivity of the heart is paramount to this worldview. This concept of the individual *rostro y corazón*—pursuing the mysteries of life through *flor y canto*—reflects the emphasis on the intuitive nature of thinking in Nahuatl philosophy. It is not a Western European understanding in that it does not emphasize rationality, but rather is dynamic, open, creative, and searching. Both paradigms are legitimate, though incomplete if taken alone.

In the early years, I remember Virgilio's presentations always having the impulse of reconciliation. Despite the brutal history of our ancestors, he believed that the only way to go beyond either a simplistic or an arrogant stance was to transcend the notion of defeat/victory, oppressor/oppressed, and to see the beginning of the Americas for what it was. As Virgilio puts it, this beginning was "the long and painful birth of the new person—a new human individual, community, civilization, religion, and race."[30]

From this position of rebirth and new creation, Virgilio proceeds to reflect on the impact of the encounter and the ultimate contributions of this new creation. Guadalupe marks the beginning of a human/divine communication in the Americas. This symmetry between the human and the divine was a core element in Nahuatl cosmology. The Guadalupe narrative is a poem about revelation expressed through Nahuatl theo-poetics in which literary elements like words and images must be in balance. Virgilio's theological reflection illuminates his desire for balance and harmony, as evidenced in his contextual treatment of sixteenth-century Spaniards and Indians. He explores the "cosmo vision" and values of both the sixteenth-century Spaniard and the Nahuatl. He sets the stage by explaining that neither group ever suspected the existence of the other. Each group had produced its own civilization with its own philosophies, artistic expressions, language, complex religion, and ultimately its own unique way of grasping truth. Virgilio moves on to compare and contrast the Jewish and Christian tradition with that of the Native Americans. He credits and affirms both groups as having established glorious temples and cities, that of Tenochtitlan and Jerusalem. Both groups were at one time a nomadic people. Both groups saw themselves as God's chosen people. In their struggles and wanderings, both the Israelites and Aztecs forgot their own honorable beginnings. They had forgotten their own wanderings—their orphanhood—and oppressed not only others, but their own.[31]

Virgilio moves from the collective to the intimate in the personal encounter between Juan Diego and Guadalupe. He states that in many ways Juan Diego and Mary of Nazareth were also similar. Both were puzzled that a divine communication would be brought to them. Both were asked to participate and collaborate with the divine. Virgilio compares the beautiful singing of the birds in the Guadalupe narrative to the angel Gabriel's calling, "Rejoice highly favored." Like Mary of Nazareth, Juan Diego is invited into God's plan for humanity. Both are humble, both do not feel worthy, and both surrender to the will of the divine.[32]

The site where Our Lady of Guadalupe appeared is Tepeyac, the ancient site of Tonantzin, the mother goddess of the Aztecs. Through her, Mt. Tepeyac takes its place among the famous mountains of God's saving history. It is the "Mt. Sinai of the Americas," states Virgilio. "Like Mt. Sinai, it is here on Mt. Tepeyac that God gives a law. This time, it is the law of love, compassion, and defense for the people."[33]

Virgilio grounds his understanding of the Guadalupe narrative, emphasizing the historical communal context and the role of the protagonist—Juan Diego; he is ever mindful to set this narrative within the larger Christian traditions reflecting salvation history. He compares Guadalupe with Jesus and even with the early Christian community, describing this story as a blossoming of Christian faith, as a means of promoting the way of Jesus, of being the catalyst for repentance and conversion. Interestingly enough, this notion of conversion is modified according to the group that is being addressed. For example, "Jesus calls us to repent for the sinful (righteous and judgmental) way of viewing human beings and human groups and to convert to a new way of seeing ourselves."[34] Jesus' call for repentance from the downtrodden, the poor, the rejected, is a change of heart in terms of their own feelings of worthlessness or inferiority. He calls them "to recognize themselves for what they truly are: dignified children of God with unlimited potential for doing good."[35] Virgilio contends that through this process of conversion, through the way of Jesus, those who had no place in the world, who were rejected for being poor or slaves or servants, ignorant or sick, were no longer ashamed of who they were. This fellowship created by and through the love of and for Jesus gave this community a new identity and status that transcended "the previous identity struggles and dehumanizing divisions between men and women."[36]

In a similar way, Guadalupe in her message declares that she is there to share her love, her compassion, her hope, and her defense. She is very clear about the people to whom she is speaking: "To you, to all of you, to all the inhabitants of this land." She does not place any conditions on this gift except the following: "To those of you who call upon me, love me, and trust me, I will hear your sorrows, your pains, and your lamentations and I will respond."[37] Virgilio asserts that Guadalupe is "in effect speaking about the reign of God that was the core of the life and message of Jesus. Guadalupe is thus a good Nahuatl translation of New Testament reality of the reign of God as revealed by Jesus."[38] In his later work, Virgilio moves from a focus on Guadalupe as a mother embracing her orphans to a much more christological interpretation. "The innermost core of the message, even though la Virgen never mentions it as such, is what she carries within her womb: the new source and center of the new humanity that is about to be born."[39] He further moves from highlighting her as a Marian image to saying in his 1997 book, *Guadalupe: Mother of the New Creation*, that she is

> not just another Marian apparition. . . . Guadalupe has to do with the very core of the Gospel itself. It is nothing less than an original American Gospel, a narrative of a birth/resurrection experience at the very beginning of the crucifixion of the Natives, the Africans, and their mestizo and mulatto children.[40]

Notes

[1]Virgilio Elizondo, *Guadalupe: Mother of the New Creation* (Maryknoll, NY: Orbis, 1997) x.
[2]Ibid. xi.
[3]Virgilio Elizondo, "Our Lady of Guadalupe as a Cultural Symbol" 118-125 below; Elizondo, *La Morenita: Evangelizer of the Americas* (San Antonio: Mexican American Cultural Center Press, 1980).
[4]*Guadalupe: Mother of the New Creation* xi.
[5]Gloria Anzaldúa, *Borderlands* (San Francisco: Aunt Lute Book Company, 1987) 78-81.
[6]Interview with Christina, one of the many Latinas across the country whom I interviewed regarding cultural identity. Berkeley, California, 1984.
[7]Virgilio Elizondo, *The Future Is Mestizo: Life Where Cultures Meet* (Bloomington, IN: Meyer Stone, 1988) 39.
[8]*Guadalupe: Mother of the New Creation* xii.
[9]Ibid. xiii.
[10]Virgilio Elizondo, *Mestizaje: The Dialectic of Cultural Birth and the Gospel*, 3 vols. (San Antonio: Mexican American Cultural Center Press, 1978).
[11]Alfredo Mirandé and Evangelina Enríquez, *La Chicana: The Mexican American Woman* (Chicago: University of Chicago Press, 1979) 5.
[12]Virgilio Elizondo, "The Christian Identity and Mission of the Catholic Hispanic in the U.S." Paper presented to the National Conference of Catholic Bishops, Chicago, April 30, 1980. See the bibliography at the end of this volume for published versions of this paper.
[13]Adelaida R. Del Castillo, "Malintzin Tenépal: A Preliminary Look into a New Perspective," in *Essays on la Mujer*, ed. Rosaura Sánchez and Rosa Martínez Cruz (Los Angeles: University of California, Chicano Studies Center Publications) 133.
[14]Miguel León-Portilla, *The Broken Spears: The Aztec Account of the Conquest of Mexico* (Boston: Beacon Press, 1962) 4-5.
[15]Michael C. Meyer and William Sherman, *The Course of Mexican History*, (3d ed., New York: Oxford University Press, 1987) 113.
[16]*Mestizaje: The Dialectic of Cultural Birth and the Gospel* 95.

[17]James Diego Vigil, *From Indians to Chicanos* (Prospect Heights: Waveland Press, 1980) 75.

[18]León-Portilla, *The Broken Spears: The Aztec Account of the Conquest of Mexico* 6-7.

[19]Jeanette Rodriguez, *Our Lady of Guadalupe: Faith and Empowerment among Mexican-American Women*, foreword by Virgilio Elizondo (Austin: University of Texas Press, 1994) 2-3.

[20]*Guadalupe: Mother of the New Creation* xiv.

[21]Ibid. xv.

[22]Ibid. xviii.

[23]See Rodriguez, *Our Lady of Guadalupe* 8, 17, 40; and Elizondo, *Guadalupe: Mother of the New Creation*.

[24]Jeanette Rodriguez-Holguin, "God Is Always Pregnant," in *The Divine Mosaic: Women's Images of the Sacred Power*, ed. Theresa King (St. Paul: YES International Publishers, 1994) 118.

[25]Rodriguez, *Our Lady of Guadalupe* 47.

[26]Robert Schreiter, *Constructing Local Theologies* (Maryknoll, NY: Orbis Books, 1985) 122.

[27]Clodomiro L. Siller-Acuña, "Anotaciones y comentarios al Nican Mopohua," *Estudios Indígenas* 8 (March 1981).

[28]*Guadalupe: Mother of the New Creation* 7.

[29]Miguel León-Portilla, *Aztec Thought and Culture: A Study of the Ancient Nahuatl Mind* (Norman, OK: University of Oklahoma Press, 1963) 182.

[30]Virgilio Elizondo, "The New Humanity of the Americas" 272-277 below.

[31]*Guadalupe: Mother of the New Creation* 26-27.

[32]Ibid. 37.

[33]Ibid. 47.

[34]Ibid. 82.

[35]Ibid. 81.

[36]Ibid. 101.

[37]Paraphrase, *Nican Mopohua*.

[38]*Guadalupe: Mother of the New Creation* 129.

[39]Ibid. 128.

[40]Ibid. 134.

ESSAYS BY VIRGILIO ELIZONDO

5. Our Lady of Guadalupe as a Cultural Symbol

(1977)

Virgilio Elizondo

Nowadays we realize that religious symbols which the theologian has labeled as "popular" religion and has looked upon as a species of pagan practice do not have to be rejected, but reinterpreted. In past decades the tendency of rational theology was to consider symbols as fantasies, to underline their ambiguity, and therefore to speak of them only in negative terms. This leads to an opposition between the religion of the people, which is not looked upon as true faith, and faith in Christ, which appears as the religion of the intellectual elite. A closer view of reality leads to a different understanding.[1] Even to the theologian, popular devotion appears ambiguous; nevertheless, it is the way the people relate to the God of Jesus. Therefore, from the pastoral as well as from the theological point of view, we have to try to answer the following question: What is the meaning of popular symbols and how do they function in relation to the Gospel? In this article I will try to clarify the problem by considering one of the most important living symbols of the Catholicism of the Americas: Our Lady of Guadalupe.

If Our Lady of Guadalupe had not appeared, the collective struggles of the Mexican people to find meaning in their chaotic existence would have created her. The cultural clash[2] of sixteenth-century Spain and Mexico was reconciled in the brown Lady of Tepeyac[3] in a way no other symbol can rival. In her the new *mestizo*[4] race, born of the violent encounter between Europe and indigenous America, finds its meaning, uniqueness, and unity. Guadalupe is the key to understanding the Christianity of the New World[5] and the Christian consciousness of the Mexicans and the Mexican Americans of the United States.

Historical Context of the Apparition

To appreciate the profound meaning of Guadalupe it is important to know the historical setting at the time of the apparition. Suddenly an exterior force, the white men of Europe, intruded on the closely knit and well-developed system of time-space relationships of the pre-Columbian civilizations.[6] Neither had ever heard of the other, nor had any suspicion that the other group existed. Western historiographers have studied the conquest from the justifying viewpoint of the European colonizers, but there is another perspective, that of the conquered. With the conquest, the world of the indigenous peoples of Mexico had, in effect, come to an end. The final battles in 1521 were not just a victory in warfare, but the end of a civilization. At first, some tribes welcomed the Spaniards and joined them in the hope of being liberated from Aztec domination. Only after the conquest did they discover that the defeat of the Aztecs was in effect the defeat of all the natives of their land.[7] This painful calvary of the Mexican people began when Cortez landed on Good Friday, April 22, 1519. It ended with the final battle on August 13, 1521. It was a military as well as a theological overthrow, for their capital had been conquered, their women violated, their temples destroyed, and their gods defeated.

We cannot allow the cruelty of the conquest to keep us from appreciating the heroic efforts of the early missioners. Their writings indicated that it was their intention to found a new Christianity more in conformity with the Gospel, not simply a continuation of that in Europe. They had been carefully prepared by the universities of Spain. Immediate efforts were made to evangelize the native Mexicans. The lifestyle of the missioners, austere poverty and simplicity, was in stark contrast to that of the conquistadors. Attempts were made to become one with the people and to preach the Gospel in their own language and through their customs and traditions. Yet the missioners were limited by the socio-religious circumstances of their time. Dialogue was severely limited, since neither side understood the other. The Spaniards judged the Mexican world from within the categories of their own Spanish world vision. Iberian communication was based on philosophical and theological abstractions and direct, precise speech. The missioners were convinced that truth in itself was sufficient to bring rational persons to conversion. They were not aware of the totally different way of communicating truth, especially divine truth, which the native Mexicans believed could only be adequately communicated through flower and song.[8] Even the best of the missioners could not penetrate the living temple of the Mexican consciousness.

This was also the time of the first *audiencia* of Guzmán which was noted for its corruption and abuses of the Indians. During this period the church was in constant conflict with the civil authorities because of these authorities' excessive avarice, corruption, and cruel treatment of the natives. The friars were good men who gradually won the love and respect of the common people. However, the religious convictions of generations would not give way easily, especially those of a people who firmly believed that the traditions of their ancestors were the way of the gods. As the friars tried to convert the wise men of the Indians by well-prepared theological exposition, the Indians discovered that the friars were in effect trying to eliminate the religion of their ancestors. The shock of human sacrifices led many of the missioners to see everything else in the native religion as diabolical, whereas the shock of the Spaniards' disregard for life by killing in war kept the Indians from seeing anything good or authentic in the conquerors' religion.

This mutual scandal made communication difficult.[9] Furthermore, the painful memory of the conquest and new hardships imposed upon the Indians made listening to a "religion of love" difficult. Efforts to communicate remained at the level of words, but never seemed to penetrate to the level of the symbols of the people, which contained the inner meanings of their world vision. For the Indians these attempts at conversion by total rupture with the ways of their ancestors were a deeper form of violence than the physical conquest itself. Christianity had in some fashion been brought over, but it had not yet been implanted. The Indians and missionaries heard each other's words but interpretation was at a standstill. Many heroic efforts were made, but little fruit had been produced. The missionaries continued in prayer and self-sacrifice to ask for the ability to communicate the Gospel.

The Apparitions and Their Meaning

In 1531, ten years after the conquest, an event happened whose origins are clouded in mystery, yet its effects have been monumental and continuous. Early documentation about what happened does not exist, yet the massive effect which the appearance of Our Lady of Guadalupe had and continues to have on the Mexican people cannot be denied. The meaning of the happening has been recorded throughout the years in the collective memory of the people. Whatever happened in 1531 is not past history but continues to live, to grow in meaning, and to influence the lives of millions today.

According to the legend, as Juan Diego, a Christianized Indian of common status, was going from his home in the *barriada* near Tepeyac, he heard beautiful music. As he approached the source of the music, a lady appeared to him. Speaking in Nahuatl, the language of the conquered, she commanded Juan Diego to go to the palace of the bishop of Mexico at Tlateloco and to tell him that the Virgin Mary, "Mother of the true God through whom one lives," wanted a temple to be built at Tepeyac so that in it she "can show and give forth all my love, compassion, help, and defense to all the inhabitants of this land . . . to hear their lamentations and remedy their miseries, pain, and sufferings." After two unsuccessful attempts to convince the bishop of the Lady's authenticity, the Virgin wrought a miracle. She sent Juan Diego to pick roses in a place where only desert plants existed. Then she arranged the roses in his cloak and sent him to the bishop with the sign he had demanded. As Juan Diego unfolded his cloak in the presence of the bishop, the roses fell to the ground and the image of the Virgin appeared on his cloak.

The Mexican people came to life again because of Guadalupe. Their response was a spontaneous explosion of pilgrimages, festivals, and conversions to the religion of the Virgin. Out of the meaningless and chaotic existence of the post-conquest years, a new meaning erupted. The immediate response of the church ranged from silence to condemnation. Early sources indicated that the missionaries, at least those who were writing, were convinced that it was an invention of the Indians and an attempt to re-establish their previous religion. Yet gradually the church accepted the apparition of Guadalupe as the Virgin Mary, Mother of God.

In 1754 Pope Benedict XIV officially recognized the Guadalupe tradition by bringing it into the official liturgy of the church.[10]

To understand the response of Juan Diego and the Mexican people it is necessary to view the event not through western categories of thought but through the system of communication of the Nahuatls of that time. What for the Spanish was an aberration for the conquered and dying Mexican nation was the rebirth of a new civilization. The details of the image conveyed a profound meaning to the Indian peoples. In reading the legend, the first striking detail is that Juan Diego heard beautiful music, which alone was enough to establish the heavenly origin of the Lady. For the Indians, music was the medium of divine communication. The Lady appeared on the sacred hill of Tepeyac, one of the four principal sacrificial sites in Mesoamerica. It was the sanctuary of Tonantzin, the Indian virgin mother of the gods. The dress was a pale red, the color of the spilled blood of sacrifices and the color of Huitzilopochtli, the god who gave and preserved life. Indian blood had been spilled on Mexican soil and fertilized mother earth and now something new came forth. Red was also the color for the East, the direction from which the sun arose victorious after it had died for the night. The predominant color of the portrait is the blue-green of the mantle, which was the royal color of the Indian gods. It was also the color of Ometéotl, the origin of all natural forces. In the color psychology of the native world, blue-green stood at the center of the cross of opposing forces and signified the force unifying the opposing tensions at work in the world. One of the prophetic omens which the native wise men interpreted as a sign of the end of their civilization was the appearance, ten years before the conquest, of a large body of stars in the sky. The stars had been one of the signs of the end, and now the stars on her mantle announced the beginning of a new era. Being supported by heavenly creatures could have meant two, not necessarily contradictory, things. First, she came on her own and, therefore, was not brought over by the Spaniards. Second, the Indians saw each period of time as supported by a god. This was recorded by a symbol representing the era being carried by a lesser creature. The Lady carried by heavenly creatures marked the appearance of a new era. She wore the black band of maternity around her waist, the sign that she was with child. This child was her offering to the New World. The Lady was greater than the greatest in the native pantheon because she hid the sun but did not extinguish it. Thus she was more powerful than the sun god, their principal deity. The Lady was also greater than their moon god, for she stood upon the moon, yet did not crush it. However, great as this Lady was, she was not a goddess. She wore no mask as the Indian gods did, and her vibrant, compassionate face in itself told anyone who looked upon it that she was the compassionate mother.

The fullness of the apparition developed with the Lady's request for a temple. In the Indian hieroglyphic recordings of the conquest, a burning, destroyed temple was the sign of the end of their civilization and way of life. Therefore, the request for the temple was not just for a building where her image could be venerated, but for a new way of life. It would express continuity with their past and yet radically transcend that past. One civilization had indeed ended, but now another one was erupting out of their own mother soil.

Not only did the Lady leave a powerful message in the image, but the credentials she chose to present herself to the New World were equally startling. For the bishop, the roses from the desert were a startling phenomenon; for the Indians, they were the sign of a new life. Flowers and music to them were the supreme way of communication through which the presence of the invisible, all-powerful God could be expressed. As the apparition had begun with music, giving it an atmosphere of the divine, it reached its peak with flowers, the sign of life beyond life, the sign that beyond human suffering and death there was something greater-than-life in the dwelling place of the wonderful giver of life.[11]

The narration as it exists today does not appear to be historical, at least in the western scientific understanding of the word. It is not based on objective, verifiable, written documentation. However, it is a historical narrative to the people who have recorded their past through this specific literary genre.[12] Furthermore, popular religion has often been too easily labeled by outsiders, especially sociologists and theologians of the dominant groups, as alienating and superstitious. Popular piety is not necessarily and of itself alienating; in fact, for a defeated, conquered, and colonized people, it serves as a final resistance against the way of the powerful. Popular religion becomes alienating when agents of religion use it to legitimize and maintain the *status quo*. However, it becomes liberating when used as a source of unity and strength in the struggle for dignity and subsequent change against the powerful of society. It is the collective voice of the dominated people crying out: "We will not be eliminated; we will live on! We have been conquered, but we will not be destroyed." In the first stages, it gives meaning to an otherwise meaningless existence and thus a reason for living. As the triumphant group has its way of recording history, so those who have been silenced by subjugation have their interpretation of the past. Their accounts exist in an even deeper way. For the defeated and powerless, history is recorded and lived in the collective memory of the people: their songs, dances, poetry, art, legends, and popular religion. For the powerful, history is only a written record, whereas for the defeated, history is life, for it is the memory that keeps telling them that things are not as they ought to be. This memory cannot be destroyed or opposed by the powerful because they do not understand it. Accordingly it is not surprising that in the history of Mexico there is no place for the Tepeyac tradition. Guadalupe, the most persistent influence in Mexico, is found only in the folklore and popular religious practices of the masses.

At the time of the apparition, the Spanish were building churches over the ruins of the Aztec temples. The past grandeur and power of Tenochtitlán-Tlatelolco (the original name of present-day Mexico City) was being transformed into the glory of New Spain. Juan Diego dared to go to the center of power and with supernatural authority (as the Lady commanded) demanded that the powerful should change their plans and build a temple—a symbol of a new way of life—not within the grandeur of the city, in accordance with the plans of Spain, but within the *barriada* of Tepeyac in accordance with the desires of the people. The hero of the story is a simple conquered Indian from the *barriada* who is a symbol of the poor and oppressed refusing to be destroyed by the dominant group. This story's purpose was to convert the bishop, the symbol of the new Spanish power group, and to turn the attention of the conquering group from amassing wealth and power to the periphery of society where the people continued to live in poverty and misery.

The narration is only a wrapping for the continuing struggle of the masses for survival and liberation from the imposition of the ways of the powerful, a struggle which has been going on for nearly five hundred years. Through unceasing struggle, a dynamic tradition has emerged from the primitive story. This tradition has come to stand for the dignity, identity, unity, personal and collective emancipation, and the liberation movements of the Mexican people. Miguel Hidalgo fought for Mexican independence under the banner of Our Lady of Guadalupe. Emiliano Zapata led his agrarian reform under her protection. César Chávez battled against one of the most powerful economic blocks in the United States under the banner of Our Lady of Guadalupe and succeeded in his struggle for justice against all human odds. This tradition was relegated to the area of fable or legend not because it was lacking in historical veracity, but precisely because its living historical veracity cannot be fully accepted by the powerful political, economic, educational, sociological, or religious elite of any moment of history. The full truth of Tepeyac is the obvious disturbing truth of the millions of poor, powerless, peripheral oppressed of our society. Guadalupe's significance is the voice of the masses calling upon the elite to leave their economic, social, political, and religious thrones of pseudo-security and work with them—within the *movimientos de la base*—in transforming society into a more human place for everyone.

It was through the presence of Our Lady of Guadalupe that the possibility of cultural dialogue began. The missioners' activity had won a basis of authentic understanding, bringing to a climax their work of pre-evangelization. As at Bethlehem when the Son of God became man in Jesus and began the overthrow of the power of the Roman Empire, at Tepeyac Christ entered the soil of the Americas and began to reverse the European domination of the people in those lands. Tepeyac marks the beginning of the reconquest and the birth of Mexican Christianity.

It is from within the poor that the process of conversion is begun. The poor become the heralds of a new humanity. This critical challenge of our compassionate and liberating mother to the powerful of any moment and place in the Americas continues today; it is the dynamic voice and power of the poor and oppressed of the Americas groaning and travailing for a more human existence. Her presence is not a pacifier but an energizer which gives meaning, dignity, and hope to the peripheral and suffering people of today's societies. Her presence is the new power of the powerless to triumph over the violence of the powerful. In her, differences are assumed and the cathartic process of the cultural-religious encounter of Europe-America begins, but it has a long way to go. Nevertheless, it has begun and is in process. This is the continuing miracle of Guadalupe—the mother—queen of the Americas. Now, the dream of the early missionaries, a new church and a New World, has definitely begun. The new people of the land would now be the *mestizo* people—*la raza*—and the new Christianity would be neither the cultural expression of Iberian Catholicism nor the mere continuation of the pre-Cortez religions of indigenous America, but a new cultural expression of Christianity in the Americas.

Today, theologians cannot afford to ignore the function and meaning of popular religion for the popular masses.[13] A theologian's task is not the canonization or rejection of the religious symbols of the people, but a continuous reinterpretation of them in relation to the whole Gospel. In this way popular religion will not be alienating but will help to lead people to a deeper knowledge of the saving God. It will not be alienating or enslaving, but salvific and liberating. Popular religion which is regenerated (not eliminated) by the Gospel becomes the invincible and efficacious power of the powerless in their struggle for liberation.[14]

For millions of Mexicans and Mexican Americans of the United States, Our Lady of Guadalupe is the temple in whom and through whom Christ's saving presence is continually incarnated in the soil of the Americas and it is through her mediation that:

He shows strength with his arm.
He scatters the proud in the imagination of their hearts.
He puts down the mighty from their thrones,
and exalts the oppressed.
He fills the hungry with good things,
and the rich he sends away empty handed.
(Luke 1:51-52)

Notes

[1]For an excellent exposition of this point in relation to the popular religion of Mexico see Jean Meyer, *La Cristiada* (Mexico: Siglo Veintiuno Editores, 1974) 316-323.

[2]"Culture" is used here as all those solutions that a group finds in order to survive its natural and social situation. It is the complete world vision—norms, values, and rituals—of a group. Spain and Mexico had very highly developed cultures at the time of the clash.

[3]*Tepeyac* is the hill north of Mexico City where the sanctuary of Tonantzin (which means our Mother)—the female aspect of the deity—was located. It was one of the most sacred pilgrimage sites of the Americas. Bernardino de Sahagún, *Historia general de las cosas de Nueva España* (Mexico, written in mid-1500s) 3:352.

[4]*Mestizo* is the Spanish word for a person who is born from parents of different races. In contemporary Latin America it is acquiring a positive meaning and the arrival of Columbus is celebrated as the day of *la raza* (the race), meaning the new race formed of Europe and Native America. There is no English translation of this concept as the English word "half-breed" (a social rather than a biological term) is very derogatory and would have a completely different meaning.

[5]For the first twelve missioners who came to Mexico, "New World" was a theological term indicating the place where the new Christianity was now to emerge. It would not be simply a continuation of the Christianity of Europe, but a new, evangelical Christianity. Silvio Arturo Zavala, *Recuerdo de Vasco de Quiroga* (Mexico: Editorial Porrua, 1965); Jacques Lafaye, *Quetzalcoatl et Guadalupe* (Paris: Gallimard, 1974) 52-67.

[6]Some of the Native American cultures were very well developed and in many ways superior to those of the Europe of the sixteenth century. For a good description of this, see: Miguel León-Portilla, *Aztec Thought and Culture* (Norman, OK: University of Oklahoma Press, 1963) esp. 134-176.

[7]Octavio Paz, *The Labyrinth of Solitude* (New York: Penguin, 1961) 93-96.

[8]León-Portilla, *Aztec Thought and Culture* 74-79.

[9]Jacques Soustelle, *La Vie quotidienne des Aztèques à la veille de la conquête espagnole* (Paris: Hachette 1955).

[10]For a good description of the development of the Guadalupe tradition, see Lafaye, *Quetzalcoatl et Guadalupe* 281-396.

[11]León-Portilla, *Aztec Thought and Culture* 102.

[12]For a good example of a scholar who has been able to penetrate the historical consciousness alive in the folklore of the people, see: Nathan Wachtel, *La Vision des vainçus* (Paris: Gallimard, 1971); Rodolfo Acuña, *Occupied America* (New York: Harper & Row, 1981).

[13]Pope Paul VI, *Evangelii Nuntiandi* (8 December 1975), sections 48 (on popular piety) and 63 (on adaptation and fidelity in expression). See also Meyer, *La Cristiada* 307, which brings out the false way that North American and European missioners have judged Mexican Catholicism.

[14]Meyer, *La Cristiada* 275-323.

6. Popular Religion as Support of Identity

(1986)

Virgilio Elizondo

Introduction

The Mexican American is one who through birth or acquired nationality is a *citizen of the United States while maintaining a deep Mexican heritage.* Today there are approximately 14,300,000 Mexican Americans in the United States and the number continues to increase daily. It is a highly complex socio-cultural group that is quite at home in the United States without ever fully assimilating the United States way of life. It is neither fully North American nor fully Latin American. It lived in its present-day geographical setting long before the United States migrated west and took over the Mexican territories. One of the key factors in the group identity, cohesiveness, and continuity of the group is the persistence of its religious symbolism which we will explore briefly in this presentation.

Function of Religious Symbols

The popular expressions of the faith *function in totally different ways for various peoples depending on their history and socio-cultural status.* For the dominant culture, the popular expressions of the faith will serve to legitimize their way of life as God's true way for humanity. They will tranquilize the moral conscience and blind people from seeing the injustices which exist in daily life. For a colonized/oppressed/dominated group, they are the ultimate resistance to the attempts of the dominant culture to destroy them as a distinct group either through annihilation or through absorption and total assimilation. They will maintain alive the sense of injustice to which the people are subjected in their daily lives.

By popular expressions of the faith I do not refer to the private or individual devotions of a few people but to the *ensemble of beliefs, rituals, ceremonies, devotions, and prayers which are commonly practiced by the people at large.* It is my contention, which is beyond the scope of this paper to develop but which will be its point of departure, that those expressions of the faith which are celebrated voluntarily by the majority of the people, transmitted from generation to generation by the people themselves, and which go on with the church, without it, or even in spite of it, express the *deepest identity of the people.* They are the ultimate

126

foundation of the people's innermost being and the common expression of the collective soul of the people. They are supremely meaningful for the people who celebrate them and meaningless to the outsider. To the people whose very life-source they are, no explanation is necessary, but to the casual or scientific specta-tor no explanation will ever express or communicate their true and full meaning. Without them, there might be associations of individuals bound together by com-mon interest (e. g., the corporation, the State, etc.), but there will never be the experience of being a people.

It is within the context of the tradition of the group that one experiences both a sense of *selfhood* and a sense of *belonging*. Furthermore, it is within the tradition that one remains in contact both with one's beginnings through the genealogies and the stories of origins and with one's ultimate end. We are born into them and within them we discover our full and ultimate being. I might enjoy and admire other traditions very much, but I will never be fully at home within them. No matter how much I get into them, I will always have a sense of being other.

From the very beginning, Christianity presented a very unique way of univer-salizing peoples without destroying their localized identity. People would neither have to disappear through assimilation nor be segregated as inferior. The Chris-tian message interwove with the local religious traditions so as to give the people a deeper sense of local identity (a sense of rootedness) while at the same time breaking down the psycho-sociological barriers that kept nationalities separate and apart from each other so as to allow for a truly universal fellowship (a sense of universality). In other words, it *affirmed rootedness while destroying ghettoishness*. Christianity changed people and cultures not by destroying them, but by reinterpreting their core rituals and myths through the foundational ritual and myth of Christianity. Thus, now a Jew could still be a faithful Jew and yet belong fully to the new universal fellowship and equally a Greek or a Roman could still be fully Greek or Roman and equally belong to the new universal group.

Religious Traditions of the Americas

The beginning of the Americas introduces *two radically distinct image/myth representations* of the Christian tradition. The United States *was born as a secu-lar enterprise* with a deep sense of religious mission. The native religions were eliminated and totally supplanted by a new type of religion: Puritan moralism, Presbyterian righteousness, and Methodist social consciousness coupled with deism and the spirit of rugged individualism to provide a sound basis for the new nation-alism which would function as the core religion of the land. It was *quite different in Latin America* where the religion of the old world clashed with those of the new, and in their efforts to uproot the native religions, Iberian Catholics found themselves totally assumed into them. Iberian Catholicism with its emphasis on clerical rituals and the divinely established monarchical nature of all society con-quered physically but itself *was absorbed by the pre-Columbian spiritualism* with its emphasis on the harmonious unity of opposing tensions: male and female, suffering and happiness, self-annihilation and transcendence, individual and group, sacred and profane. In the secular-based culture of the United States, it is the one who succeeds materially who appears to be the upright and righteous person—the good and saintly. In the pre-Columbian/Iberian-Catholic *mestizo*-based culture of Mexico, it is the one who can endure all the opposing tensions of life and not lose his or her interior harmony who appears to be the upright and righteous one.

With the great western expansion of the United States in the 1800s, *fifty percent of northern Mexico was conquered* and taken over by the United States. The Mexicans living in that vast region spanning a territory of over 3500 kilometers from California to Texas suddenly became aliens in their own land—foreigners who never left home. Their entire way of life was despised. The Mexican *mestizo* was abhorred as a mongrel who was good only for cheap labor. Efforts were instituted to *suppress everything Mexican: customs, language, and Mexican Catholicism*. The fair-skinned, blond Mexicans who remained had the choice of assimilating totally to the white, Anglo-Saxon Protestant culture of the United States or being ostracized as an inferior human being. The dark-skinned had no choice! They were marked as an inferior race destined to be the servants of the white master race.

Today, social unrest and dire poverty force many people from Mexico to move to the former Mexican territories which politically are part of the United States. Newcomers are harassed by the immigration services of the United States as illegal intruders—a curious irony since it was the United States which originally entered this region illegally and stole it from Mexico. Yet the descendants of the original settlers of this region plus those who have immigrated continue to feel at home, to resist efforts of destruction through assimilation, and to celebrate their legitimacy as a people.

Mexican American Religious Symbols

The Mexican Americans living in that vast borderland between the United States and Mexico have *not only survived* as a unique people but *have even maintained good mental health* despite the countless insults and put-downs suffered throughout their history and even in the present moment of time.[1] Anyone who has suffered such a long history of segregation, degradation, and exploitation should be a mental wreck.[2] Yet despite their ongoing suffering, not only are the numbers increasing, but in general they are prospering, joyful, and healthy thanks to the profound faith of the people as lived and expressed through the common religious practices of the group. I could explore many of them,[3] but I will limit myself to what I consider to be the *three sets of related core expressions* which mark the ultimate ground, the perimeters and the final aspirations of the Mexican American people: *Guadalupe/Baptism; dust/water; crucifixion/the "dead" ones*. They are the symbols in which the apparently destructive forces of life are assumed, transcended, and united. In them, we experience the ultimate meaning and destiny of our life pilgrimage.

There is no greater and more persistent symbol of Mexican and Mexican American identity than devotion to Our Lady of Guadalupe. Thousands visit her home at Tepeyac each day and she keeps reappearing daily throughout the Americas in the spontaneous prayers and artistic expressions of the people. In her, the people experience acceptance, dignity, love, and protection. They dare to affirm life even when all others deny them life. Since her apparition she has been the flag of all the great movements of independence, betterment, and liberty.

Were it not for Our Lady of Guadalupe[4] there would be no Mexican or Mexican American people today. The great Mexican nations had been defeated by the Spanish invasion which came to a violent and bloody climax in 1521. The native peoples who had not been killed no longer wanted to live. Everything of value to them, including their gods, had been destroyed. Nothing was worth living for. With this colossal catastrophe their entire past became irrelevant. New diseases appeared and, together with the trauma of the collective death-wish of the people, the native population decreased enormously.

It was *in the brown Virgin of Guadalupe that Mexicanity was born* and through her that the people have survived and developed. At the very moment when the pre-Columbian world had come to a drastic end, a totally unsuspected irruption took place in 1531 when, in the ancient site of the goddess Tonantzin, a *mestizo* woman appeared to announce a new era for "all the inhabitants of this land." Guadalupe provided the spark which allowed the people to arise out of the realm of death like the rising phoenix arising out of the ashes of the past—not just a return to the past but the emergence of a spectacular newness.[5] In sharp contrast to the total rupture with the past which was initiated by the conquest-evangelization enterprise, Guadalupe provided the necessary *sense of continuity* which is basic to human existence. Since the apparition took place at Tepeyac, the long-venerated site of the goddess Tonantzin, it put people in direct contact with their ancient past and in communion with their own foundational mythology. It validated their ancestry while initiating them into something new. The missioners said their ancestors had been wrong and that the diabolical past had to be totally eradicated. But the lady who introduced herself as the mother of the true God was now appearing among them and asking that a *temple* be built on this sacred site. Out of their own past and in close continuity with it, something truly sacred was now emerging.

Furthermore, she was giving meaning to the present moment in several ways for she was promising them love, defense, and protection. At a time when the people had experienced the abandonment of their gods, the mother of the true God was now offering them her personal intervention. At a time when new racial and ethnic divisions were emerging, she was offering the basis of a new unity as the mother of all the inhabitants of the land. At a time when the natives were being instructed and told what to do by the Spaniards, she chose a low-class Indian to be her trusted messenger who was to instruct the Spaniards through the person of the bishop and tell them what to do.

Finally, she initiated and proclaimed the new era which was now beginning. Over her womb is the Aztec glyph for the center of the universe. Thus she carries the force to gradually build up a civilization which will be neither a simple restoration of the past nor simply New Spain, but the beginning of something new. For the Indian world, the sign of flowers she provided as a sign of her authenticity was the sign which guaranteed that the new life would truly flourish.

Thus in Guadalupe, the *ancient beginnings connect with the present moment and point to what is yet to come!* The broken pieces of their ancient numinous world are now repieced in a totally new way. Out of the chaos, a new world of ultimate meaning is now emerging. The phoenix had truly come forth not just as a powerful new life, but also as the *numinosum* which would allow them to once again experience the awe and reverence of the sacred—not a sacred which was foreign and opposed to them, but one which ultimately legitimized them in their innermost being—both collectively as a people and individually as persons.

The second great religious expression is the baptism of infants. Our Lady of Guadalupe had sent the Indian Juan Diego to the church. The Indian world immediately started to go to church and ask for baptism. Yet, they were no longer being uprooted totally from their ancient ways in order to enter into the church. They were entering as they were—with their customs, their rituals, their songs, their dances, and their pilgrimages. The old Franciscan missioners feared this greatly. Many thought it was a devil's trick to subvert their missionary efforts. But the people kept on coming. They were truly building the new temple the Lady had requested: the living temple of Mexican Christians. It is through baptism that every newborn Mexican enters personally into the temple requested by the Lady. Through baptism the child becomes part of the continuum and is guaranteed life despite the social forces against life. The community claims the child as its very own and with pride presents it to the entire people. In the group, the child will receive great affirmation and tenderness. This will give the child a profound sense of existential security. He/she will be able to affirm selfhood despite the put-downs and insults of society: they will dare to be who they are—and they will be who they are with a great sense of pride!

The ashes of the beginning of Lent are a curious and mysterious religious expression of the Mexican tradition which finds its full socio-religious meaning when coupled with the holy water which is blessed during the Easter Vigil. For people who have been forced to become foreigners in their own land, who have been driven from their properties, and who have been pushed around by the powerful in the way the mighty wind blows the dust around, ashes, as a moment of the continuum of the pilgrimage of life, become most powerful. They mark the radical acceptance of the moment—actually there is no choice. But this is not the end, for the people do not only come for ashes. Throughout the year they come for *holy water* to sprinkle upon themselves, their children, their homes—everything. They are very aware that our entire world yearns and travails in pain awaiting to be redeemed—a redemption which in Christ has indeed begun but whose rehabilitating effects are yet to take effect in our world of present-day injustices. The sprinkling with the waters of the Easter Vigil is a constant call for the *regeneration of all of creation.* The dust which is sprinkled with the water will be turned into fertile earth and produce in great abundance. As in the reception of ashes there is an acceptance, so too in the sprinkling of holy water there is an unquestioned affirmation: the ashes will again become earth; the dust-people will become the fertile earth and the earth will once again be ours. The *dust-water binomial* symbolizes the great suffering of an uprooted people who refuse to give in to despair but live in the unquestioned hope of the new life that is sure to come.

The final set of religious celebrations which express the core identity of the Mexican American people is the crucifixion, which is celebrated on Good Friday, and the dead, whose day is celebrated on November 2. For a people who have consistently been subjected to injustice, cruelty, and early death, the image of the crucified is the supreme symbol of life despite the multiple daily threats of death. If there was something good and redemptive in the unjust condemnation and crucifixion of the God-man, then, as senseless and useless as our suffering appears to be, there must be something of ultimate goodness and transcendent value in it. We don't understand it, but in Jesus the God-man who suffered for our salvation, we affirm it and in this very affirmation receive the power to endure it without it destroying us. *Even if we are killed, we cannot be destroyed.* This is the curious irony of our celebrations of the dead: they appear to be dead, but they are not really dead! For they live not only in God but in our hearts and in our memory. Those whom the world thinks are dead—those who have been killed by society— defy death and are alive in us. In our celebrations of memory, their presence is keenly experienced. Thus what is celebrated as the day of the dead is in effect the celebration of life—a life which not even death can destroy. Society might take our lands away, marginate us, and even kill us, but it cannot destroy us. For we live on in the generations to come and in them we continue to be alive.

Conclusion

The *conquest of ancient Mexico by Spain in 1521* and then the *conquest of northern Mexico by the United States in the 1840s* forced the native population and their succeeding generations into a split and meaningless existence. It was a mortal collective catastrophe of gigantic death-bearing consequences. Yet the people have survived as a people through the *emergence of new religious symbols* and the reinterpretation of old ones which have connected the past with the present and projected into the future. The core religious expressions as celebrated and transmitted by the people are the unifying symbols in which the opposing forces of life are brought together into a harmonious tension so as to give the people who participate in them the experience of *wholeness*. In them and through them, opposites are brought together and push toward a resolution and the people who celebrate them experience an overcoming of the split. Where formerly there was opposition, now there is reconciliation and, even greater yet, synthesis. This is precisely what gives joy and meaning to life, indeed makes life possible in any meaningful sense regardless of the situation. It is in the celebration of these festivals of being and memory that the people live on as a people.

Notes

[1] Rodolfo Acuña, *Occupied America* (New York: Harper & Row, 1981).
[2] Roberto Jiménez, "Social Changes/Emotional Health," *Medical Gazette of South Texas* 7 No. 25 (June 1985).
[3] For a greater discussion of other religious symbols, consult my previous works: *Christianity*

and Culture (1975), *La Morenita: Evangelizer of the Americas* (1980), and *Galilean Journey: The Mexican-American Promise* (1983).

[4]For other aspects of Guadalupe, consult my previous articles "Our Lady of Guadalupe as a Cultural Symbol" 118-125 above; "Mary and the Poor: A Model of Evangelising Ecumenism," in Hans Küng and Jürgen Moltmann, eds., *Mary in the Churches* (New York: Seabury, 1983) 59-65.

[5]Jacques Ruffie, *De la biologie à la culture* (Paris: Flammarion, 1976) 247-251.

7. Pastoral Opportunities of Pilgrimages

(1996)

Virgilio Elizondo

Pilgrimage is one of the oldest physical-spiritual exercises of humanity and of our Christian tradition. It can certainly have many different meanings and functions for different persons, yet the phenomenon of pilgrimage appears as a constant in humanity regardless of the many changes in the human condition. In speaking to a convocation of pilgrimage directors in 1980, John Paul II stated: "You have in your hands a key to the religious future of our times."

Pilgrimages are not the essence of Christian faith, but they can definitely be privileged moments in everyone's personal journey of faith, as well as fascinating adventures full of unsuspected experiences. One does not have to go on a geographical pilgrimage to grow in the faith, but a true pilgrimage can certainly help to advance one's personal faith-journey to the fullness of life. An authentic pilgrimage will be a privileged time and space for discovery, discernment, healing, and illumination. The church has a marvelous opportunity for helping to make these deeply personal moments of life's journey even more fruitful than they would be without the presence of the church. People want to go on pilgrimage. How can the church be of genuine service in the pilgrim's quest?

Because people come in great numbers and the majority of them come in a spirit of searching, repentance, gratitude, and openness to divine favor, pilgrimage sites become privileged places of evangelization and pastoral ministry. Throughout the pilgrimage, the church will have many opportunities of evangelizing through hospitality, conversation, and various forms of pastoral ministry. The pilgrimage itself is as important as the experience at the sacred site, or maybe even more important. One cannot rush a pilgrimage and expect to obtain its beneficial effects. A sufficient length of time is crucial to an authentic experience of pilgrimage. Sweat, struggle, fatigue, and even blistered feet could well be important elements of a pilgrimage.

On the pilgrimage route and during the extended time spent at the sacred site, one has the opportunity, like Jesus with the disciples on the road to Emmaus, to converse freely with strangers about what is happening in one's life, society, and the world, to discuss openly what is in one's heart, and to reflect on the meaning of the scriptures in the light of the events of life. In the word of the stranger who is simply a fellow traveler, we can easily hear the most precious "word of God" that we will ever hear in our lives. No one programs, directs, or manipulates their conversation, so all are given to the guidance of the Spirit. This is invitational, story-sharing, and dialogical evangelization at its best! It is not marked by proselytistic, moralistic, or doctrinal jargon, but the incarnational language of life, the story-telling language of the Gospel. It is in this very context that we, the pilgrims, become "word of God" to one another without even realizing it. At the very moment it is happening we may not think of it as "word of God," but in reflection, some very ordinary phrases, words, images, and insights will definitely emerge as God's word to me at this particular moment of my life.

The pastoral ministry of the church in regard to pilgrimages might be divided into three areas.

Preparation for the Pilgrimage

One of the core images of the church used by Vatican II and called forth frequently by the third eucharistic prayer is that of the pilgrim church. The very pilgrimage itself reflects and is a living experience of the innermost reality of the church. Hence it would be good if parishes, dioceses, religious, seminaries, and universities would encourage their people to go on pilgrimage some time in their lives. But it should be clear from the beginning that "pilgrimage" is not just a religious term for modern-day tourism.

The preparation for the pilgrimage should not be merely on the material level, but even more so on the spiritual one. Regardless of the immediate reason why a person decides to go on a pilgrimage, the pilgrim should be helped to look forward to the entire process as a privileged time in his/her life—a time of unsuspected and uncontrolled life-giving surprises. The pilgrimage should be a fabulous journey of discovery—of self, others, other cultures, nature, and God. It will be a time of inner freedom from daily affairs and pressures which will allow the sojourner to see, hear, remember, comprehend, and talk about aspects of life which have previously remained unnoticed. Those going on the pilgrimage must be ready to leave behind their business, professional, and family concerns—no faxes, e-mail, or telephone calls. It is crucial to "let oneself go" in order to be disposed to the action of God during the pilgrimage.

In the context of spiritual freedom from ordinary concerns, one can more easily come to grips with both the shadow and the luminous sides of one's life and accept, respect, and love oneself as one truly is. We should not go on the pilgrimage with well-defined expectations, but rather with an open mind and heart to discover and obtain insight and favors that are beyond the control of any earthly authority. It is in the spirit of total openness and surrender to the wisdom and power of divine love that the fullest benefits of the pilgrimage will be obtained. The spirituality of pilgrimage, that is, the spirituality of the inner freedom that comes through distance and detachment, is fundamental for a truly successful pilgrimage.

Prayer is always answered, but not always in the way we think. It is true that many people go on a pilgrimage seeking a special favor, especially a physical cure, and there is nothing wrong with this, as it is evident that it is not the magic of any one place but the faith of the pilgrim which brings about healing. As Jesus often stated: "Your faith has healed you." As God has manifested very special and visible favors in certain places on earth, it is obvious that going to such a place can certainly intensify the faith of the pilgrim, the faith which can move mountains and restore life. Miracles do take place, many more than we dare to suspect, but quite often the greater number of miracles do not bring the physical healing of a person, but the inner healing of the entire person who through the process of the pilgrimage discovers a new life. Often the healing which comes through a new vision and appreciation of life results in an insight obtained during the pilgrimage. I have had many testimonies of such experiences.

Pastoral Ministry during the Pilgrimage

Pastoral Ministry among Those Who Embark on Pilgrimage on Their Own

Whereas many people go on pilgrimage in groups, some choose to start on pilgrimage alone. Yet in the very process of the journey, others will be met and new friendships will be formed. Whether one is on a pilgrimage to a sanctuary, a monastery, a mountain, the desert, or some other special place, the church can be of assistance whenever possible by providing welcome and hospitality to the pilgrims. In the old days of the great medieval pilgrimages, this was very well organized. Today, it would be most helpful if the well-known pilgrimage sites could inform people about the hostels and rest-stations that are especially dedicated to the reception of pilgrims. Just finding lodging in a hotel is not the same as staying in a place with fellow pilgrims. At each rest-station, pilgrims should have the opportunity of resting, eating, praying, contemplating, and meeting fellow travelers who accompany them on at least a portion of the journey. Each new experience of fellowship will be like a foretaste of the ultimate fellowship at the end of time.

Pilgrimages Organized by the Church (Parish or Diocesan)

The pilgrimage is a process embracing different stages which include the spiritual preparation of the pilgrims before departure, a trip of sufficient time and distance, a considerable stay at the sacred site, and active participation in the various activities of the sacred site. People often go on pilgrimage because they are seeking something which they sense is missing in their lives. Life on today's electronic super-highways of instant information and change makes less and less sense. What do we do with all the information at our disposal? The ultimate questions of meaning and purpose become more and more urgent. Whether people live a life of plenty or of poverty, whether they are super-educated or illiterate, they sense that something essential is missing in today's world, and the ordinary institutions of religion and education do not seem to have adequate responses. Their ordinary church services and university courses do not seem to satisfy the deepest questions and yearnings of their heart. The ancient tradition of pilgrimage emerges as an inviting possibility of illumination.

Pilgrimage should not be just a religious term for pious tourism, as is often the case today. You cannot just visit the site, buy souvenirs, send postcards, attend mass, and leave! A pilgrimage is not just another trip. It cannot be rushed, and the very rhythm of the pilgrimage should be totally different from the ordinary rhythm of life. Just as some activities will be most helpful, a time for "holy idleness" will also be necessary for one to come into contact and communion with one's true self. It is a time of personal freedom, a time away from home, friends, and relatives, a time to discover different places, customs, languages, persons, and human situations; it is a time of discernment and illumination, and it is a privileged time of hearing the word of God which throughout the pilgrimage will come in many diverse forms, experiences, and persons. At a time when our personal calendars seem to be ever more charged and crowded with many pressing yet ultimately insignificant affairs, the "time away" will be a sacred journey into the depths of one's self, society, and God's creation and equally a journey beyond the limits of one's ordinary vision and concerns. It is a journey both to the very innermost depths of one's being and to the outermost limits of all existence—to inner space and to outer space.

A pilgrimage can be a unique experience of the separation and intimacy which are two of the deepest yearnings of the human heart—often in conflict with each other, yet both yearning for fulfillment. Intimacy needs the space of separation in order to grow, appreciate, mature, and deepen the relationship with others, while separation needs the bonds of intimacy so that it will not lead to depressing loneliness and spiritual death. If there is to be a true pilgrimage, sufficient time should be devoted to allow for separation from the ordinary routine of life so as to have plenty of time to spend with oneself apart from the others; yet there should also be sufficient time to spend with the others: visiting, singing, searching, joking, eating together, relaxing and equally fasting together, praying, contemplating, listening to the cries and testimonies, hearing the stories of this particular site and why it is a privileged manifestation of the sacred, listening to the word of God, and celebrating especially the sacraments of reconciliation and Eucharist. Reconciliation is a moment when distance and closeness meet as one breaks with the past and embraces a new spiritual reality of communion with God, neighbors, and the cosmos; this new reality is celebrated in the Eucharist.

In the very separation from the ordinary persons and engagements of everyday life, it is possible to discover a new and deeper level of intimacy with one's inner self—something which is often missing in life and which keeps us from entering into true intimacy even with the ones we love the most. If we cannot be intimate with our inner self, we will not be able to enter into truly intimate relations with others. The newly experienced sense of intimacy within myself will allow me, upon my return home, to enter into new levels of intimacy with the very persons whom I love but had been growing distant from. The positive experience of separation during the pilgrimage can be the very passage into new forms and levels of intimacy when I return home.

The pilgrimage is not a time for a doctrinal or moralistic catechesis, but rather a time for the catechesis of the heart which will come through new profoundly human experiences of friendships, relationships, wonder, gratitude, peace, and joy. The pilgrimage is not so much a solution to life's problems or an answer to life's questions as an illuminative and liberating initiation into the mysterious journey of life. This experience of the living word of God as it is seen, experienced, and heard through these various sources will help the pilgrim to re-image his/her own life in the true image and likeness of God. Through this re-imaging of oneself, one can gradually discern the sacred meaning and purpose of one's life, and of one's people. Our own historical journey with all its joys and tragedies, successes and failures, convictions and doubts, vice and virtue thus becomes the sacred journey that life truly is. This is not a time for apologies or regrets any more than it is a time for boasting, bragging, or argumentation, but a time for discovering the closeness within the distance, the timelessness within the timeliness, the unlimited within the limits of place and time, the sacred within the human, the divine within the ordinary, and the eternal within the temporal. It is a time of coming to grips with the mysterious complexities of life which will never be resolved but which can be accepted, assumed, transcended, and celebrated in a totally new way, that is, in the total submission to the divine will which, far from being a dehumanizing surrender, is the beginning of communion with the infinite and with the infinite possibilities of life. This transforming illumination could well be the greatest miracle of the pilgrimage.

The Bible itself is the best example of how every single aspect of life—the heroic and the scandalous, the weak and the strong, the virtuous and the sinful—becomes an integral fiber in the mosaic of God's revelation. Meditating on the scriptures in the light of the footsteps of my own trail can certainly lead to an illumination of the mind and the heart that will transform me from within. This illumination takes place not through some sort of thunder and lightning from heaven, but in the very sharing with others throughout the pilgrimage. Through the process, the clarifying light of God's grace gradually comes through, removes the cataracts of the soul, and allows me to see in the totally unsuspected ways of God!

Seriousness is not opposed to happiness and prayerfulness is not opposed to joyfulness. Fun ought not be alien to pilgrimages, since they should be a foretaste of the unending happiness of heaven. Humor and laughter are two of God's greatest gifts to humanity. Through the struggles and sacrifices of the pilgrimage, joyfulness and light-heartedness should equally shine forth. A dull and laughless pilgrimage would not be a Christian one, any more than one that is mere fun and games with no time for reflection, prayer, repentance, insight, transformation, and contemplation. The balance of seriousness and fun will make for a true pilgrimage. The total experience of the pilgrimage can help each participant to become more human by coming closer to God, other human beings, and other cultural and linguistic expressions of humanity.

Pastoral Ministry at the Sacred Site

Everything about the sacred site should help the pilgrim to achieve a true moment of passage—passage from previous concerns, idolatrous convictions, and limited viewpoints to a new and deeper understanding and appreciation of life in all its mysterious complexities. Arrival at the pilgrimage site is best initiated by a gathering mass in which the pilgrims can be welcomed and introduced into the spirit and possibilities of the place. Ample opportunities should be provided so that the pilgrims can participate in the various celebrations of the faith. The entire complex of the sacred site is important with its natural terrain, its walking paths, reflection spaces, devotional sites, and central unifying shrine. The pilgrims should be encouraged to see and appreciate the natural terrain—whether beautiful mountains, desolate land, the great plains, or whatever it may be—which is the very first revelation of God's presence, beauty, and goodness. The very architecture, lay-out of the buildings, art-work, and decorations can lead one to a great appreciation of the creative works of men and women who are made in the image of the creative God. But precisely because the pilgrimage site is a place of gathering together totally diverse persons from all backgrounds and walks of life, persons who are complete strangers to one another and even people who would never gather together at home, it can be a graced opportunity for becoming aware of other persons and their human situation—the handicapped, the infirm, the refugees, the "untouchables" of any society, and many others. In discovering ourselves to be in community with others, even total strangers, we experience the ultimate reality of the church as the people of a God who has no boundaries and is open to everyone without exception. There should be ample opportunities for the pilgrims to meet one another and have good fraternal experiences among strangers. This will be a "mini" but powerful experience that illuminates the dynamics of church-building. The pilgrimage experience which is seen and lived can expand and deepen our appreciation of the church itself.

During medieval times, great plays were often organized for the education and edification of pilgrims. Often the porticos of the churches were adorned with the various scenes from the Bible so as to instruct the faithful. This same spirit can be carried out today through the use of modern media: videos, photos, and multimedia exhibits. Scenes of the last judgment of Matthew can be correlated with scenes which bring out the plight of the poor, the abandoned, the imprisoned, and the starving of this world. Because people come with a predisposition to meet others, the exhibitions of the pilgrimage site can help the pilgrims to come into contact with the others from home or from other nations who might not be immediately obvious: the sickly, the dirty, the undernourished, the crippled, the homeless, the abandoned children or elderly, and everyone whom the ordinary world keeps well hidden; all of these "invisibles" could be made present and visible. Everything should help pilgrims to develop a deeper sensitivity to their sisters and brothers in need.

Within this context of encounter, there should be plenty of opportunities for silence and reflection; meaningful devotions, especially the Way of the Cross; sacramental reconciliation with compassionate confessors for those who want truly to cleanse themselves and make a new beginning; and good liturgies with good singing and preaching that truly speaks to the quest of the pilgrims. The departing Eucharist should be the true highlight of the pilgrimage and not just a ritual which appears as a necessary but uninspiring moment of the process. It should bring the process to a climax and send the pilgrims forth with a renewed and even restored sense of faith, hope, and apostolic zeal. No one should leave for home as they departed from home! The end of the pilgrimage mass should be a true missionary mandate for those who have been transformed and given new life through the process of the pilgrimage.

Pilgrimages do not replace the ordinary ministries of the church, but they can certainly be privileged experiences which can be sources of new life both for the individual faithful and for the church itself. Precisely because they are not necessary or mandated, they can be moments of spiritual freedom enabling great marvels to take place in the lives of men and women. When the church accompanies the pilgrims in the proper way, our ministry can serve as a catalyst to the many wonders which God will bring about.

PART THREE

Mestizaje and a Galilean
Christology

INTRODUCTORY ESSAYS

A *Mestizo* Theology

Jacques Audinet

Years ago, a young man came to my office in Paris and told me, "I would like to write my doctoral dissertation on *mestizaje*." As I listened to him, I wondered if such a study was even possible.

For doctoral dissertations I usually accepted the topic a candidate proposed, but this time I pondered the objections that could be made to such a choice. First of all, *mestizaje* is not a traditional theological theme. As far as I knew at the time, there was not one reference, one book, not even a single theological passage written on the subject. In theology, as in other disciplines, *mestizaje* was at best a marginal topic, if not nonexistent. It had nothing to do with the grandiose deployment of God's design from creation to parousia which is usually considered the domain of theology.

Of course, the 1960s and 1970s were a time when many theologians began to approach theology in a different way. It was the time of the Council, a time of new awareness, creativity, and daring. Theology was no longer envisioned as merely a commentary on the sources, but as an attempt to formulate the traditional message in a new way that addressed the contemporary age and adapted to present modes of thinking. Theologians recognized that in order to know God you have to know the human person and in order to gain a hearing you have to speak the common language of human beings. New topics began to arise in theology, such as a theology of "work" (Chenu), a theology of "terrestrial realities" (Tiberghien), and even a theology of "science." The most famous theological development was surely "liberation theology." All these theological breakthroughs followed a similar pattern: they began with a specific human reality (e. g., work, family, political conflict) and tried to relate it to the word of God as received in revelation. And in order to do this, theologians endeavored to articulate concepts that were as significant at the human level as they were at the theological level. In the process they dealt with key questions about the life of society and the life of the church and engaged intellectual sources that were known and acclaimed in the wider scholarly world.

The subject of *mestizaje* did not have such a wealth of intellectual sources. I had known Virgil for several years and we had spoken a lot about Mexico. Thanks to my friend Francisco Aguilera, I had visited Mexico several times. There were many good books on Mexican history and Mexican anthropology. Most of them, however, were dedicated to the ancient Mexicans, the Aztecs and other groups who occupied those lands at the time of the *conquista*. In addition, there were some good works on Mexican life today, especially on the psychology of the contemporary Mexican.

But the people Virgil wanted to address were neither the ancient Mexicans nor the contemporary citizens of the Mexican Republic. Rather, he focused his gaze on a very specific group: the people of the border, the people of what is now the Southwest United States, *"el pueblo de la frontera," "el pueblo Chicano," "mi pueblo."*

Virgil's interest in people of Mexican origin in the Southwest posed yet another difficulty. For many academicians and other observers of the contemporary scene, the people Virgil wanted to speak about did not even exist. Scholars vaguely knew that there were some problems at the southern border of the United States, but for many North Americans those "problems" were perceived negatively: they were associated with illegal immigration. A common response was to ignore the "illegals" and let the police and immigration authorities do their job. While traveling to the eastern United States, I heard the question: "But what are you going to do with those Indians down there?" Many Mexican Americans themselves were neither knowledgeable about nor proud of their origins. Some tried to hide their identity, working hard to help their children become "good American citizens" and even forbidding them to speak Spanish. The word *mestizaje* has no equivalent in English and was not used in daily conversation to name one's own identity. Of course, in some ways, things were beginning to change. Thanks to the activism of leaders like César Chávez and Dolores Huerta, along with the works of some historians and novelists, even people outside the United States began to recognize the *mestizos* of the borderlands. But was there enough information on them to write a doctoral dissertation?

The human sciences provided little material, since the notion of *mestizaje* is not a scientific concept. Furthermore, in the human sciences the analysis of the social situation was not usually in terms of cultural encounter, but in terms of political functional analysis, such as the examination of groups, conflicts, and integration. At that time, such questions and approaches were dominant in fields like sociology.

At the committee meeting to discuss Virgil's thesis proposal, the great theologian M. D. Chenu, who was a member of the dissertation board, wondered aloud: "Will all this last?" By this he meant the specific identity of the Mexican American people. "What you say about the Mexican American, a small group in a vast country, will this not disappear and be engulfed by the powerful 'melting pot' which is the United States? Surely the new culture of the media and consumerism will absorb all the cultural differences and level all ethnic groups into one." Even Chenu, with his wide knowledge and acute perception, was in doubt about the validity of the project and its relevance for the contemporary situation. But the young Virgil Elizondo insisted: he wanted to write his doctoral dissertation on *mestizaje*. So the dissertation committee decided to let him go and explore the possibilities for a theology of *mestizaje*.

Twenty years later, we have the answer. Nobody except a prophet could have foreseen it. The project was not only valid, but unquestionably relevant and valuable. Who could have known that this theology would have such a wide-ranging impact when Virgil began to work on it more than two decades ago? In order to pursue his task, he had to (1) define the field and (2) find a method in order to (3) produce a theology of *mestizaje*. This is exactly what he has accomplished, as his dissertation and many subsequent books and articles demonstrate. Let us briefly consider these three points from the work of Virgil. They illuminate both the newness of his thinking and the way he situates himself in the theological field.

The scope of his work is the destiny of a specific people: the Mexican Americans of the Southwest United States. These people exist and, despite the assimilationist pressures that surround them, they have a future as a group with a distinct heritage and identity. There is no doubt about that. How did Virgil come to be so prophetic about the future of his people? His natural optimism is not a sufficient explanation. The concept of *mestizaje* itself is an important part of the answer, especially the way he chose to emphasize it and let it guide the development of his work. Significantly, for Virgil, *mestizaje* does not name an object but a process, the process by which a culture has to die in order to survive. Like every human reality, like human beings themselves, cultures are born to die. The experience of Mexico-Tlatelolco remains in human history the paradigmatic witness of this possibility. Through the suffering of conquest and cultural death, something new was born. *No fue victoria ni derrota, pero el dolorozo comienzo del México mestizo de hoy*, "Neither a defeat nor a victory, but the painful birth of a new people" (inscription from the Plaza de las Tres Culturas).

The concept of cultural survival is a key issue in the contemporary world. Today, cultures are obliged to meet. Often they threaten each other, with the strongest cultures dominating the weaker ones. Many conflicts, wars, and political revolutions arise from a clash of cultures. "To be recognized as who we are" is a frequent motto for many minority groups in the present situation. But in order to survive a culture has to be transformed. There is no survival without transformation. This is the reason why the process of transformation, which is also a process of survival, is essential to understanding contemporary cultures and their dynamic interplay.

The concepts Virgil uses to examine *mestizo* culture, specifically Mexican American culture, help him to show how that culture survived and continues to thrive today. His concepts of *multiple mestizaje* (a people twice mestisized), *multiple memory* (the dynamic mixing of the European, the indigenous, the African, and the North American), and *violence* (a people twice violated) reveal that cultural encounters usually entail some form of violence. These concepts therefore illuminate that such violence can be part of a survival process. This is the price for *identity, a new identity.*

The events of the Spanish *conquista* some five centuries ago remain as a light in the dark for Virgil. Somehow the experience of *mestizaje* is the continuation, the reenactment of those founding events. And speaking of double *mestizaje* dramatizes even more the ongoing significance of the *conquista* for Mexican Americans today.

For Virgil, the destruction of Mexico was not only a local event, one episode of history among others, destined to be forgotten from historical memory. Rather, it is an event of "cosmic importance," to echo the words of the famous Mexican thinker José Vasconcelos. I don't say that I accept all aspects of Vasconcelos, but there is one point which is extremely significant for the rest of the world. It is the fact that in Mexico West and East met and the most violent culture of the West— the Spanish—met the most violent culture of the East—the Aztecs. The violent Catholicism of the Spaniards mixed with the violent culture of the Aztecs, which had taken its origins from the Asian branch of humanity. In Mexico the two branches of humanity met for the first time in history, giving this encounter a cosmic character and a cosmic significance. The price was high because the encounter was terribly destructive, but that high price enabled the emergence of a new identity.

Virgil's choice to explore human experience from the perspective of *mestizaje* gave his doctoral work an openness and a wideness that has no equivalent. His work is not only the analysis of a particular culture but, through this particular culture, an astounding exploration of humanity. He does not engage in a purely scientific analysis, whether functional or structural, of a particular human group, but transcends the characteristics of that group to seek out our common destiny as human beings. Of course, his work nonetheless uses the best available material, including an insightful survey and fascinating historical research. But his intuition, I should say his vision, led him beyond mere positive data to a wider analysis of his people, their destiny, their mission, and their significance for other human groups. All this coalesced in the imaginative title "Galilean Journey." Or to say all this in a different way, using the semiotic language of Virgil's protégé Alex García-Rivera, the little tiles of the analysis were shaped into a larger design.[1] Some people are more attentive to the "little tiles." Virgil, although always interested in the concrete aspects of the situation, is also intrigued by the larger design.

Why? Because he has the conviction, the intuition—I don't know what is the most accurate word—that the experience of his people is unique. Some would go so far as to say there is something messianic or prophetic in his way of looking at reality. In any event, he holds the strong conviction that the Kingdom of God does not emerge through the thoughts of theologians, as grandiose as they are, but abides in the life of the people. This conviction led to his groundbreaking work at San Fernando Cathedral and his focused theological attention to popular devotions.

Virgil's unwavering commitment to a theology rooted in the faith of his people is the reason why, for him, what is usually labeled as "religious" is first and foremost "human." There is no separation, no opposition. Pilgrimages, devotion to the Blessed Virgin, and religious celebrations are central events in the life of the people. They don't belong to a separate religious realm apart from human reality. Rather, they are an integral part of the people's daily life, their situation, their sufferings, and their hopes. This is the reason why they have to be considered as a primary source for a theology that flows from the life of the people.

The best example of this is probably Virgil's recent book on Our Lady of Guadalupe.[2] In order to understand the meaning of Guadalupe's appearances to Juan Diego, Virgil examines the narrative and the symbols associated with the

Guadalupe story, both within their historical context and the context of contemporary life. In other words, Virgil's work on Guadalupe shows that there is no understanding of religion without an anthropological understanding of the human situation. Virgil makes a strong case for this insight in his article "*Mestizaje* as a Locus of Theological Reflection."[3] He contends that the starting point of theology is not in the past, nor in the texts of theologians, but in the life of the people here and now. From this vantage point, the ever new significance of revelation for humanity arises. The reality of Christianity lies in the daily lived experience of ordinary people. And the role of the theologian is to name that experience and express its fruitfulness and significance.

But what significance? The experience of the people is a Christian experience; since the *conquista* the people, *mi pueblo*, has been explicitly associated with Christianity. This leads to an important question: What is the link between the experience of the people here and now and the experience of the people in the Bible?

This link is not an ethical link. The usual manner of approaching this question is to relate the present situation to the central statements of the Bible (or of church doctrine) on a given topic. Confronted with contemporary experience, theologians or other church leaders relate a pertinent point of doctrine or faith to this present experience. The presupposition is that the rich tradition already has the answer to today's questions. Those answers have to be reformulated, better explained in contemporary language, but all the answers are already available. This method of establishing a link between the present situation and the Bible, which some deem as "ethical," is frequent in theology, preaching, and catechesis. Here is not the place to analyze and criticize this way of approaching theology and ministry. The danger, however, is obvious: the message of revelation appears as external to the present situation of human beings. It appears as an "ideology" superimposed on the reality of human life. And little by little it becomes empty and irrelevant.

That is not the way Virgil proceeds. Rather, he takes a symbolic approach, connecting the founding events of his culture with the founding events of Christianity. That is the deep meaning of his choice of exploring Jesus' identity as a Galilean from Nazareth. In modern times, the theme of Nazareth has been developed as a reflection on the "hidden life of Jesus" as opposed to his active life. It belonged to "spirituality" but was not part of theological thinking. There was a "spirituality" of Nazareth. There was not a "theology" of Nazareth.

Virgil created a theology of Nazareth. As I see it, this theme interweaves with other core themes in his thinking, such as the border, the poor, women, the suffering. And his purpose is not primarily to develop spiritual attitudes, but to uncover meaning in a specific situation: the situation of his people and, ultimately, the situation of humanity at large. The figure of Jesus of Nazareth, which is so traditional in Spanish-speaking countries, takes on a new meaning. He is not only the suffering Jesus whose life and agony move us, but the borderlands reject who shows us the way to pass through all the obstacles of life. With a keen sense of the Christian tradition, Virgil bypasses the borders of groups, languages, and styles of life and opens new ways. In the process, he envisions the mysteries of Incarnation and Redemption in a new light. He also frequently articulates the theme of the *new humanity* as the ultimate end of *mestizaje*. It is not a closed end, but an open and mysterious one. We cannot know it in its fullness. Virgil's writings on these themes are at the same time new and original and yet very traditional. In this sense also his theology is a "*mestizo* theology," crisscrossing the borders of intellectual fields.

As was previously mentioned, Virgil often begins his writings with an analysis of the situation of his people and from there moves to a larger vision. He probes the same themes at different levels, all corresponding to the main aspects of the Mexican American experience today, in history, in relation to humanity at large, and in relation to the design of God. This way of proceeding enables him to speak from the specific perspective of his people while relating to the larger experience of humanity. Many of his books and articles illuminate this basic structure in his thought. The topics are specific to the Mexican American experience: the border, the transgression of the border, the role of the poor, the place of women. More than any other theme, however, he examines *mestizaje*: the fractured identity of the *mestizo* person, the suffering of rejection, the hope of a new and universal identity. But all these themes, though specific to Mexican American culture and people, are, at the same time, basic and universal themes that correspond to contemporary questions. Twenty years ago nobody was speaking of the border or of *mestizo* identity in those terms. Today, immigration, displaced persons, and wars have made these themes a common preoccupation in many countries around the globe.

This point is important. Anthropologically, it shows how the work of Virgil has been and remains prophetic. Long before anyone else, he raised the key questions that must be addressed in today's multicultural societies. More and more, societies from every continent are confronted with displaced persons, immigrant groups, and "illegals" arriving in their territories. Too often the coexistence of these groups leads to confrontation and violence. Segregation, "ethnic purification," racial lynching, and rapes are daily realities in some parts of Europe as well as in Africa, Asia, and the Americas. Tragically, the laws of democratic nations are frequently all but powerless against such behaviors. A multicultural society is a beautiful project, but in many places it still remains impossible because of obstacles which are not only economical but rooted in the archaic fears of the "others" and of their differences. Virgil's analysis of *mestizaje* illuminates these fears. Moreover, his presentation of the Mexican American experience invites us to go beyond those fears toward a new humanity.

While clearly significant in human terms, this point is also important theologically. At first glance, a theology related to one particular group, dedicated to only a single people, appears to betray the key dimension of Christianity, which is universalism. Such a theology could easily become a new particular messianism, sacralizing one group and forgetting that salvation is for all. It could become—as has so often happened in history and still occurs today—a political messianism with the inevitable consequences of domination and exclusions. But Virgil does not sacralize his people. Rather, he tries to understand them, to uncover the meaning of their life today. Far from isolating his people or encouraging them to disparage others, he enables them to discover the self-knowledge that is their only means of survival and to offer their unique contribution to humanity.

In conclusion, let us underline two significant insights. First, Virgil gives us an example of what a practical theology can be. In addition to other approaches, such as a theology of the sources or a theology comprised of commentaries on the tradition, today a practical approach to theology is absolutely essential. Contemporary human beings tend to define themselves more by what they do than by who they are. Contemporary thinking, especially in the human sciences, pays more attention to human action than to human essence. A practical theology tries to deal with such a praxis-oriented approach. Emphasizing the process of *mestizaje* as the key concept of his theological thinking, Virgil opens new possibilities for the understanding of revelation. For more than thirty years his work has shown the fruitfulness of this approach.

Second, Virgil's theology and pastoral praxis clearly demonstrate the validity of the cultural approach. In the present situation of humanity, more and more peoples and governments are realizing that economics and politics are not enough to solve the problems of human beings. The future does not depend solely upon a better economic organization or a better political collaboration. It depends on the capability of people to coexist, to survive together on the same planet earth. Samuel P. Huntington warns us about the deadly effects of a war of cultures.[4] He is right, if cultures are conceived as fixed elements. In that case, their survival depends on their rigidity. But Virgil shows us that cultures are *mestizo* and that their survival depends on their acceptance of *mestizaje*. Therefore, the conflict of the future is not between cultures, but within each culture, between those who accept *mestizaje* and those who reject it in the name of power, tradition, or purity. In that sense, what is happening at the southern border of the United States is meaningful for the rest of the world. And, as Virgil's work so clearly exemplifies, the Mexican American experience is also meaningful for the future of the Christian adventure.

Notes

[1]Alex García-Rivera, *St. Martin de Porres: The "Little Stories" and the Semiotics of Culture*, with a foreword by Virgil Elizondo and an introduction by Robert J. Schreiter (Maryknoll, NY: Orbis, 1995).

[2]Virgil Elizondo. *Guadalupe: Mother of the New Creation* (Maryknoll, NY: Orbis, 1997).

[3]Virgil Elizondo, "Le Mestissage comme lieu theologique," *Spiritus* 24 (December 1983): 349-375, trans. as *"Mestizaje* as a Locus of Theological Reflection" 159-175 below.

[4]Samuel P. Huntington, *The Clash of Civilizations and the Remaking of the World Order* (New York: Simon and Schuster, 1996).

A Christology for a Global Church

Roberto S. Goizueta

At the dawn of a new millennium, the principal challenge confronting the Christian world is that represented by the globalization of the Christian faith. As Christianity becomes increasingly a third-world religion, shaped by the worldviews and cultures of those regions in which the Christian faith is experiencing its greatest growth, the future of the church will not be determined by ecclesial and theological movements in Europe. For, unlike the "globalization" effected through violence and conquest, this new historical reality is taking root in and being nurtured by local churches and grassroots communities. The face of this global church is marked not so much by colonization as by immigration. This global Christianity finds its cradle not in the great cathedrals of Paris and Cologne but in the poor neighborhoods of Lima, Manila, and San Antonio.

It is here, in these neighborhoods, that Virgilio Elizondo has lived, labored, and articulated a new theological vision. Above all, it is here that he has looked for and encountered Jesus Christ. And in so doing, Elizondo has revealed for us all the *mestizo* face of that Christ—and the *mestizo* face of the church. Beyond the Christ of the kings and princes, beyond the Christ of the theologians and philosophers, beyond the Christ of the clerics and bishops, is the Christ of Juan Diego. This Christ is found not primarily in Jerusalem but in Galilee. Theologians and scripture scholars have only begun to appreciate the significance of this central insight. And even as scripture scholars give increasing attention to Jesus' Galilean identity as essential to understanding his life, mission, and theological import, the groundbreaking character of Elizondo's work in this area remains unappreciated. Indeed, the recent, highly acclaimed findings of scholars (see, for example, the citations below) who have provided brilliant analyses of Galilean life in the first century and underscored the central importance of Jesus' Galilean identity in the Gospels corroborate the insights that Virgilio Elizondo presented in his doctoral thesis nearly a quarter-century ago. As Christians strive to understand the meaning of Jesus Christ in the context of the new, global Christianity, we would do well to retrieve the christological insights developed by Elizondo—the "*mestizo* Jesus" he discovered—in the light of the Galilean research recently undertaken by archeologists and scripture scholars.

The Border as *Locus Theologicus*

Virgilio Elizondo's christology is profoundly marked by the reality of the border as *locus theologicus*, the *mestizo* reality of the borderland as a truly sacramental reality. For him, the border is not only a place *in which* he is located, or *from which* he comes; the border is *who* he is as a *mestizo*, a person—like all Latino/as, whose very identity and reality is "in between."

As a Christian pastor and theologian, Elizondo asks how the God of Jesus Christ may be encountered on the border. If the border is not merely a geographical category but is, more profoundly, an epistemological and anthropological category defining a *human* reality, a human community, is it possible to encounter God in the midst of that reality, that community? If so, how and where? In articulating an answer to these questions, Elizondo sets forth the outlines of a christology for a global church, a christology for the twenty-first century.

At the same time, however, we must ask how the dominant culture's understanding of that border and the Latino/a understanding of the border may influence our reading of the border as a *locus theologicus*. Thus, before examining Elizondo's understanding of Jesus Christ, we must consider how that understanding presupposes and demands a transvaluation of "the border" as this reality is interpreted by the dominant culture.

We should note at the outset, therefore, that Elizondo's notion of *mestizaje* affirms a Latino/a perception of the border rooted in the distinctive history of Latin America itself. The difference between North American and Latin American perceptions of "the border" is observed by Justo González:

> [I]n the north it was possible and convenient to push back the native inhabitants rather than to conquer and subdue them. What northern colonialists wanted was land [rather than slave labor]. The original inhabitants were a hindrance. So, instead of subjugating the Indians, they set about to push them off their lands, and eventually to exterminate them. If the myth in the Spanish colonies was that the Indians were like children who needed someone to govern them, the myth in the English colonies was that the Indians were nonpeople; they didn't exist, their lands were a vacuum. In north Georgia, in the middle of Cherokee County, there is a monument to a white man who was, so the monument says, "the first man to settle in these parts." And this, in a county that is still called "Cherokee"! This contrast in the colonizing process led to a "border" mentality in Mexico and much of Latin America, and a "frontier" mentality in the United States. Because the Spanish colonizers were forced to live with the original inhabitants of the land, a *mestizo* population and culture developed. . . In contrast, in the lands to the north, the process and the myth were of a constantly moving frontier, pushing back the native inhabitants of the land, interacting with them as little as possible. There was civilization this side of the frontier; and a void at the other side. The West was to be "won." The western line, the frontier, was seen as the growing edge; but it was expected to produce growth by mere expansion rather than by interaction.[1]

In the North, the border is perceived as moving in only one direction, outward; in the South, the border is perceived as allowing for movement in both directions. In the North, any movement back across the border is thus perceived as "an incursion of the forces of evil and backwardness into the realm of light and progress."[2]

The dominant culture in the United States promulgates a clear image of the border: on this side, civilization—on the other side, savagery. Thus, the border, which was initially established through conquest and expansion, must now be preserved through a systematic process of exclusion, without which our "civilization" is itself threatened. "The quest for human purity," contends Virgilio Elizondo, "defines boundaries and very quickly excludes those who have been the product of territorial transgression. There seems to be an inner fear that the children of territorial transgression pose the deepest threat to the existence of the group and to the survival of its purity."[3]

The border, however, can be conceived and valorized differently. The Latin American experience of *mestizaje* embodies—at least implicitly—another understanding of the border:

A border is the place at which two realities, two worldviews, two cultures, meet and interact . . . at the border growth takes place by encounter, by mutual enrichment. A true border, a true place of encounter, is by nature permeable. It is not like medieval armor, but rather like skin. Our skin does set a limit to where our body begins and where it ends. Our skin also sets certain limits to our give-and-take with our environment, keeping out certain germs, helping us to select that in our environment which we are ready to absorb. But if we ever close up our skin, we die.[4]

The *mestizo* experience affirms the possibility that divisive and exclusive borders can also allow for mutually enriching interaction. If the drive to conquer others and expand the border outward has legitimated rape and murder, the *mestizo* children of that violent encounter are living witnesses to a hope and life that are born even in the midst of despair and death. The border is not only a cemetery but a seedbed; not only a Calvary but a manger.

Mestizo Jesus: God Chooses What the World Rejects

In the Gospels, the borderland and its inhabitants take on theological significance. It is no mere coincidence that, in the Synoptic accounts, Jesus comes from Nazareth, in Galilee, meets his end in Jerusalem, and, finally, returns to Galilee, where he appears to the apostles after his resurrection (Mark 14:28; Matt. 26:32; 28:7, 10, 16).

The theological significance ascribed to the Galilean borderland is rooted in the history, geography, and culture of the region. As Elizondo notes, Galilee "was an outer region, far from the center of Judaism in Jerusalem of Judea and a crossroads of the great caravan routes of the world. It was a region of mixed peoples and languages."[5] Contiguous with non-Jewish territories and geographically distant from Jerusalem, Galilee was often viewed by first-century Jews as "a Jewish enclave in the midst of 'unfriendly' gentile seas."[6] "The area as a whole," writes Richard Horsley, "was a frontier between the great empires in their historical struggles."[7] The Roman administrative cities of Sepphoris and Tiberias were centers of Hellenistic-Roman culture. Consequently, Jewish worship in these cities was "dramatically affected by the influences of Hellenistic-Roman culture and political domination."[8] "It is possible, perhaps even likely," argues Horsley, "that some Jews considered themselves faithful even while they utilized what would be classified as pagan or Greco-Roman symbols as a matter of course in their everyday lives."[9] Their religio-cultural diversity, together with their economic wealth, made the Galilean urban centers objects of resentment and opposition throughout the Galilean countryside, where village life among the peasantry was "guided by Israelite customs and traditions."[10]

Yet even the Jewish traditions of the peasants were different from those practiced in Jerusalem:

> Galilee was heir in some form to the traditions of the Northern Kingdom . . .
> Torah was important, as was circumcision in Galilean society, but not the
> written and oral Torah as interpreted by the Judean and Jerusalem retainer
> class and enforced where they could by the Temple aristocracy. Rather
> Galilee was home to popular legal and wisdom traditions . . . Galilee was also
> ambivalent about Jerusalem, the Temple, the priestly aristocracy, temple dues
> and tithes.[11]

In short, as Richard Horsley argues, Galilean Jewish practices could be described as a kind of popular religion:

> The distinction anthropologists often make between the "great tradition" and
> the "little traditions" may be of some help in formulating the issues. A
> "society" may develop cultural traditions at two levels: the traditions of origin
> and customary practice continue as a popular tradition cultivated orally in the
> villages, while specialists codify those same traditions in a standardized and
> centralized form as an official tradition, which is cultivated orally but perhaps
> also reduced to written form. Something like this distinction between official
> tradition and popular tradition may help explain the situation in Galilee as
> seen both in sources from the first century C.E. and in early rabbinic
> literature.[12]

The history of Galilee as a land under contention and a political crossroads resulted in the emergence of popular religious practices which reflected that multicultural history:

> The bulk of the Galilean population, . . . while not Judean, would likely have
> been other descendants of former Israelites. While sharing certain common
> Israelite traditions with the Judeans, they would have had traditions of their
> own and distinctive versions of the shared Israelite traditions. Yet it is also
> inherently unlikely that all Galileans in late second-temple times were
> descendants of former Israelites . . . Thus at least some of those living in
> Galilee must have been non-Israelites, ethnically or in cultural heritage . . .

> Within the same village, Israelites and Gentiles lived in adjacent houses or
> shared the same courtyard, . . . or perhaps even shared a house or oven . . . A
> great variety of cooperation between Israelite and gentile peasants took place
> on a regular basis . . . [13]

In the Gospels, this social, political, cultural, religious, and geographical reality
takes on soteriological significance as the place that defines the very character of
the Christian revelation, for the Good News is incarnated in the person of Jesus
Christ, Jesus the Galilean. And this is the central, groundbreaking insight that
Virgilio Elizondo has made available to us. As he notes, "the overwhelming originality of Christianity is the basic belief of our faith that not only did the Son of
God become a *human being*, but he became *Jesus of Nazareth* . . . Jesus was not
simply a Jew, he was a Galilean Jew; throughout his life he and his disciples were
identified as Galileans."[14] Consequently, argues Elizondo, any christology that
claims to be rooted in the Gospels—and that takes seriously the Christian doctrine of the Incarnation—must take as its starting point the *historical-theological
particularity* of Jesus Christ. That particularity, including his racio-cultural dis-
tinctiveness as a Galilean Jew, is not merely accidental to the Christian *kerygma*;
it is at the very heart of the *kerygma*.

In order to understand the Good News, insists Elizondo, we must understand
the soteriological *value* (or, rather, anti-value) of Galilee, especially its villages,
such as Nazareth. Like so many human societies throughout history, the ruling
elites in Jesus' world attached a moral and indeed theological value to the racial-
cultural differences of the Galileans:

> In Galilee the Jews were looked down upon and despised by the others as they
> were in the rest of the world. They were considered to be stubborn, backward,
> superstitious, clannish, and all the negative stereotypes one could think of.
> Furthermore, the Jews of Judea looked down upon the Galilean Jews, for they
> considered them ignorant of the law and the rules of the temple, contaminated
> in many ways by their daily contacts with pagans, and not capable of speaking
> correct Greek, for their language was being corrupted by admixture with the
> other languages of the region. In short, their own Jewish relatives regarded
> them as inferior and impure. Because of their mixture with others, they were
> marginated by their own people.[15]

Galilee and its inhabitants symbolized backwardness, ignorance, poverty, discon-
tent, rebellion, and, above all, religious and racial-cultural impurity:

> Scripturally speaking, Galilee does not appear important in the unfolding
> drama of salvation and, culturally speaking, at the time of Jesus, it was
> rejected and despised by the Judean Jews because of the racial mixture of the
> area and its distance from the temple in Jerusalem. For the Jews of Jerusalem,
> Galilean was almost synonymous with fool! . . . The Galilean Jews appear to
> have been despised by all and, because of the mixture of cultures of the area,
> they were especially despised by the superiority-complexed Jerusalem Jews.

Could anything good come out of such an impure, mixed-up, and rebellious area?[16]

The answer to this question is what Elizondo calls the "Galilee Principle," God chooses "what is low and despised in the world" (1 Cor. 1:28):

> The apparent non-importance and rejection of Galilee are the very bases for its all-important role in the historic eruption of God's saving plan for humanity. The human scandal of God's way does not begin with the cross, but with the historico-cultural incarnation of his Son in Galilee . . . That God has chosen to become a Galilean underscores the great paradox of the incarnation, in which God becomes the despised and lowly of the world. In becoming a Galilean, God becomes the fool of the world for the sake of the world's salvation. What the world rejects, God chooses as his very own.[17]

The Jewish establishment in Jerusalem could not conceive that God's Word would be revealed among the "impure" people of the borderland: "Search and you will see that no prophet is to rise from Galilee" (John 7:52). Yet it is precisely in the very midst of a *mestizo* people, among "savages" and "barbarians," that God takes on human flesh: "Culturally and linguistically speaking, Jesus was certainly a *mestizo* between Judaism and the other cultures that flourished throughout Galilee. And we know from the early Jewish charges that tried to discredit Jesus that he was even accused of being the bastard son of a Roman soldier named Pantera, which could also be a colloquial term for simply meaning 'a Roman,' which could have made of him a biological *mestizo* as well."[18]

Moreover, it is precisely in the midst of those racial-cultural outcasts that the resurrected Christ, the now-glorified Witness to God's power and love, will be encountered: "he has risen from the dead, and behold, he is going before you to Galilee; there you will see him" (Matt. 28:7). Just as the ministry and mission that define Jesus Christ as Son of God had begun in the villages and countryside of Galilee, so will that ministry and mission find their eschatological fulfillment in Galilee: "there you will see him." Jesus's ministry will end where it began; it is in Galilee that his disciples will see the resurrected Jesus. The chosen place of God's self-revelation is there where Israelites and Gentiles live side by side, where Jewish religious practices incorporate Hellenistic influences, where popular Judaism remains outside the control of Jerusalem's "official" Judaism. The *mestizo* culture of the borderland is the privileged locus of God's self-revelation. God becomes incarnate in a *mestizo*, a Galilean, who is crucified in Jerusalem, is raised from the dead, and, now in glorified form, returns to the Galilean borderland, where his disciples are gathered and the new *ekklesia* is born: "The point of bringing out all this is to appreciate the human beginnings of God's mission. God becomes not just a human being, but the marginated, the shamed, and rejected of the world. He comes to initiate a new human unity, but the all-important starting point is among the most segregated and impure of the world. Among those whom the world has thrown out, God will begin the way to final unity."[19]

Jesus Christ in the New Millennium:
The Significance of Elizondo's Contributions to Christology

If Virgilio Elizondo's retrieval of Latino/a popular religion and the historical experience of *mestizaje* have already made an impact on Catholic theology (most notably, as the foundation for the development of a U.S. Latino/a Catholic theology), the prophetic significance of his christological insights has yet to be fully appreciated. Yet it is precisely in his christology that Elizondo most forcefully brings his Latino Catholic perspective to bear on the larger Catholic Christian intellectual tradition. Moreover, in a world in which the most vital Christian communities are living alongside and in the midst of other religions and in which, therefore, Christians are becoming increasingly aware of the inescapable fact of religious and cultural pluralism, Elizondo's *mestizo* christology has important implications for the possibility of living as Christians in a profoundly pluralistic global context.

The central question posed to Christians by this context is: How can we affirm the truth of our faith while, simultaneously, affirming the value and desirability of pluralism? The dilemma is aptly explained by David Tracy:

> In a culture of pluralism must each religious tradition finally either dissolve into some lowest common denominator or accept a marginal existence as one interesting but purely private option? Neither alternative is acceptable to anyone seriously committed to the truth of any major religious tradition. The need is to form a new and inevitably complex theological strategy that will avoid privatism by articulating the genuine claims of religion to truth. For those in any religious tradition who reject pluralism, such a complex strategy will be deemed unnecessary. Rather the truth of one's own monism can be restated over and over again in the hope that this messy pluralism will one day go away . . . For those like the present author who accept pluralism as a fundamental enrichment of the human condition, hope must lie elsewhere. But where? A simple affirmation of pluralism can mask a repressive tolerance where all is allowed because nothing is finally taken seriously. Or pluralism can offer a genial confusion. To affirm pluralism responsibly must include an affirmation of truth and public criteria for that affirmation.[20]

Virgilio Elizondo's *mestizo* christology suggests a way out of this dilemma by locating the roots of an authentic pluralism, an authentic *mestizaje*, at the heart of the Christian truth itself, that is, by identifying the "way, truth, and life" that is Jesus Christ with the affirmation of human otherness and difference. Thus, the very possibility of affirming and believing in Jesus Christ demands an affirmation of and belief in the reality of human diversity. Pluralism is neither threatening nor irrelevant to the Christian truth; rather, it is the very essence of that truth. Thus, Elizondo's christological insights call us to embrace human diversity and pluralism while, at the same time, insisting on the truth embodied in the person of

Jesus Christ. The former is not in conflict with but, rather, implied in the latter.

The alternatives provided to us by the dominant culture, dogmatism or relativism, are false alternatives, neither one of which will serve Christians as we strive to live in and make sense of a genuinely pluralistic, global Christian community. Only an option that affirms the intrinsic connection between a commitment to truth and a commitment to pluralism can offer a way out of the dilemma. By reminding us that the truth of the Christian faith is found in a person, Jesus Christ, who was and is himself a *mestizo*, Virgilio Elizondo has offered us such a way.

Moreover, suggests Elizondo, the privileged place where that truth is encountered is among those peoples "on the other side" of the border, among the inhabitants of the borderland. The birthplace of a truly global church will not be the traditional centers of privilege, which have historically identified globalization with conquest. Rather, the birthplace of the global church of the twenty-first century will be among the victims of conquest themselves, among those "mixed breeds" whose very faces bear witness to both the violent consequences of a globalization that identifies inclusivity with conquest and, paradoxically, the richness of the *mestizo* culture and people that are the offspring of that conquest. In the person of Jesus Christ, who comes from and, resurrected, returns to Galilee, the *mestizo* victim is revealed as the sacrament of God's reign, the witness to a truly global *ekklesia*.

Notes

[1]Justo González, *Santa Biblia: The Bible Through Hispanic Eyes* (Nashville: Abingdon, 1996) 85-86.

[2]Ibid. 86. This view of national borders is painfully and blatantly evident, for example, in the ideology underlying the North American Free Trade Agreement and California's Propositions 187 and 209, as well as the 1996 Welfare Reform Act that denies welfare benefits to documented immigrants and their children. That ideology accords a freedom of movement to financial capital which it simultaneously denies to human beings. The "natural" right of capital ("market forces," the "law" of supply and demand, "free" trade) to expand into new global markets must be affirmed as absolute and inviolable, while the right of labor (i. e., human beings) to do so must be artificially restricted.

[3]Virgilio Elizondo, *The Future Is Mestizo: Life Where Cultures Meet* (Bloomington, IN: Meyer Stone, 1988) 80.

[4]González, *Santa Biblia* 86-87.

[5]Virgilio Elizondo, "*Mestizaje* as a Locus of Theological Reflection" 168 below.

[6]Douglas Edwards, "The Socio-Economic and Cultural Ethos of the Lower Galilee in the First Century: Implications for the Nascent Jesus Movement," in *The Galilee in Late Antiquity*, ed. Lee I. Levine (New York: Jewish Theological Seminary of America, 1992) 54.

[7]Richard A. Horsley, *Galilee: History, Politics, People* (Valley Forge, PA: Trinity Press International, 1995) 241.

[8]Richard A. Horsley, *Archaeology, History, and Society in Galilee: The Social Context of Jesus and the Rabbis* (Valley Forge, PA: Trinity Press International, 1996) 55.

[9]Ibid. 63.

[10]Ibid. 122.

[11]Jonathan Draper, "Jesus and the Renewal of Local Community in Galilee: Challenge to a Communitarian Christology," *Journal of Theology for Southern Africa* 87 (June 1994): 35-36.

[12]Horsley, *Archaeology, History, and Society in Galilee* 173.

[13]Horsley, *Galilee: History, Politics, People* 243-244.

[14]Virgilio Elizondo, *Galilean Journey: The Mexican-American Promise* (Maryknoll, NY: Orbis, 1983) 49.

[15]Elizondo, *"Mestizaje* as a Locus of Theological Reflection" 168 below.

[16]Elizondo, *Galilean Journey* 53.

[17]Ibid.

[18]Elizondo, *"Mestizaje* as a Locus of Theological Reflection" 168 below.

[19]Ibid. 168-169.

[20]David Tracy, *The Analogical Imagination: Christian Theology and the Culture of Pluralism* (New York: Crossroad, 1981) xi.

ESSAYS BY VIRGILIO ELIZONDO

8. *Mestizaje* as a Locus of Theological Reflection

(1983)

Virgilio Elizondo

The Hispanic Catholics of the United States have experienced a long history of neglect and oppression not only by society at large, but by the very church that is supposed to be our mother. We had somewhat been ministered to but we had never been invited to be active ministers in our own church. The church was so foreign to us that many felt that priests came only from Ireland or Spain, but it was unthinkable that we would become a priest or a religious.

Quite often we were scolded because we were not sure what the foreign missioners expected us to be as measured by the standards of the Catholicism in their place of origin. But hardly ever were we confirmed in our faith and helped to grow and develop in our pilgrimage of faith. Yet it was the deep faith and simple home practices of our *abuelitas* and *abuelitos* (grandparents) that sustained us in the faith and maintained us loyal to the Catholic tradition.

Church institutions had been so oppressive to us that when the Chicano movement started in the 1960s, the leaders often told priests and religious who tried to join them to get lost. They felt that the only way to help Hispanics get ahead was to get rid of Catholicism. It was painful to hear their insults, but as painful as their accusations were, we had to admit that they were true—if not totally, at least 95 percent of what they were saying against the church was correct. The church had kept us out and had by its silence approved the ongoing exploitation and oppression of Hispanics.

The Chicano movement gave inspiration to the Chicano clergy and later on to all the Hispanic clergy in this country. We began to organize and to work for change within our own church. It was quickly evident that it was not sufficient simply to use Spanish in the liturgy, create our own music, and get more people involved in the work of the church. Much more was needed. We needed both practical know-how so that we could make the structures of our society work in favor of our people and we needed to have a new knowledge about ourselves, our social situation, and our religious beliefs. Until now, others had been telling us who we were. Nobody had bothered to ask us "Who are you?" Until now, all kinds of experts had studied us, but no one had even sought to enter into conversation with us so that they might truly understand who we see ourselves to be. This was the very root of our oppression. We were not allowed to be who we were. We were never allowed to simply say: "I am."

It was at this moment of the struggle that we met Gustavo Gutiérrez and became aware of his method of doing theology. It was God-sent! He was conceptualizing and expressing perfectly what we felt had to be done but had no idea of how to do it or even that we were on the right track. From the documents of Vatican II and our own experience of exclusion, we pretty well sensed what had to be done, but it was not yet clear. Reading Gustavo's work was like turning on the light switch.

The first thing we learned from Gustavo was that theology is important and we cannot leave it to the theologians alone—and much less to theologians who are foreigners. Theology cannot be imported. Neither can it be developed in isolation from the believing and practicing community. It is a joint enterprise of the believing community, which is seeking the meaning of its faith and the direction of its journey of hope lived in the context of charity. Great theologies were coming out of other parts of the world, but no one could do our theologizing for us. We had both the privilege and the responsibility! What follows is an attempt to do our own interpretation of our Christian existence.

The Human Situation of Mexican Americans

The ancestors of today's Mexican Americans have been living in the present-day United States since the early 1600s. Our group did not cross the border to come to the United States; rather the United States expanded its borders and we found ourselves to be a part of the United States. Since the early beginnings, many generations have crossed the Rio Grande to come over to the other side of family lands. Yet we have always been treated as foreigners in our own countryside—exiles who never felt at home. The Mexican Americans are a people twice conquered, twice colonized, and twice mestisized. This is our socio-historical reality!

Mestizaje: *Undefined Identity and Consequent Margination*

Mestizaje is simply the mixture of human groups of different makeup determining the color and shape of the eyes, skin pigmentation, and makeup of the bone structure. It is the most common phenomenon in the evolution of the human species. Scientists state that there are few, if any, truly "pure" human groups left in the world and they are the weakest, because their genetic pool has been gradually drained. Through mixture, new human groups emerge and the genetic makeup is strengthened. Biologically speaking, *mestizaje* appears to be quite easy and natural, but culturally it is usually feared and threatening. It is so feared that laws and taboos try to prevent it from taking place, for it appears as the ultimate threat to the survival of the species itself.

Mestizaje could certainly come in various ways, but it is a fact of history that massive *mestizaje* giving rise to a new people usually takes place through conquest and colonization. This has certainly been the case of the Mexican and the Mexican American *mestizaje*. The first one came through the Spanish conquest of Mexico beginning in 1519, and the second one started with the Anglo-American invasion of the Mexican northwest beginning in the 1830s. The French biologist Ruffie states that, since the birth of Europe thirty-five thousand years ago when the invading Cro-Magnons mated with the native Neanderthals, no other event of similar magnitude had taken place until the birth of European Mexico some five hundred years ago. I would add that a similar event of equal magnitude is presently taking place in the southwest of the United States—an area larger than Western Europe and populated by several million persons.

Conquest comes through military force and is motivated by economic reasons. Yet, once it has taken place, conquest is totalitarian. It imposes not only the institutions of the powerful, but also a new worldview in conflict with the existing one. This imposition disrupts the worldview of the conquered in such a way that nothing makes sense anymore. In many ways, the ideas, the logic, the wisdom, the art, the customs, the language, and even the religion of the powerful are forced into the life of the conquered. Although the conquered try to resist, the ways and worldview of the powerful begin to penetrate their minds so that, even if political and economic independence come about, the native culture can never simply return to its pre-conquest ways.

Yet there is not only the obvious violence of the physical conquest, but the deeper violence of the disruption and attempts to destroy the conquered's inner worldview, which gives cohesion and meaning to existence. The conquered's fundamental core religious symbols provide the ultimate root of the group's identity because they mediate the absolute. They are the final tangible expressions of the absolute. There is nothing beyond them that can put us in contact with God. They are the ultimate justification of the worldview of the group and the force that cements all the elements of the life of the group into a cohesive, meaningful, and tangible world order. When such symbols are discredited or destroyed, nothing makes sense anymore. The worldview moves from order to chaos, from significant mystery to meaningless confusion.

Hence, the ushering in of new religious symbols, especially when they are symbols of the dominant group, are in effect the ultimate conquest. In a nonviolent way, missioners were the agents of a deeper violence. They attempted to destroy that which even the physical violence of the conquerors could not touch—the soul of the native people. In spite of the missionary's conscious opposition to the cruel and bloody ways of the conquistador, the nonviolent introduction of religious symbols of the Spanish immigrant in effect affirmed and justified the way of the powerful, and discredited and tried to destroy the way of the powerless. This same process has taken place with the predominantly Irish-German clergy and religious who have ministered to Mexican American Catholics.

The most devastating thing about the conquest is that it established a relationship so concrete and so permanent that it took on the nature of a metaphysical reality. In many ways, it determines the behavior and the characteristics of the members of each group. It even influences theological reflection as the members of the conquistador group will appeal to scripture and theology to explain and legitimate the relationship. In his classic book *The Righteous Empire*, Martin Marty gives an excellent exposition of how theology and biblical studies can be used to legitimize oppression. The powerful now establish their own version of truth as objective truth for everyone and impose it through their various means of power.

The image of the conquistador as "superior" and of the conquered as "inferior" will be imposed and interiorized by all the media of communications: dress, food, manners, language, modes of thinking, art, music, bodily gestures, mannerisms, entertainment, and all the institutions of society, such as the family, economics, school system, politics, and church, and most of all the religious imagery and mythology. It is now the gods of the powerful who preside over the new world order. The totalitarian image that colonizing Europe established and implanted in the colonized peoples as the universal model for everyone continues to have a determining influence around the world. This "normative image" of Western civilization continues to be reinforced and projected through television and movies, books, periodicals, universities, and the European/United States-controlled religions. Only the white Western way appears as the truly human way of life; all others continue to be relegated to an inferior status. This is not necessarily a conscious effort, but it takes place all the time.

Yet, in spite of the difficult situation of inequality, the very seeds for the destruction of this dichotomy of colonizer-superior vs. colonized-inferior are physically implanted by the conquistador himself. Through his very bodily intercourse with the women of the conquered group, a new biological-cultural race is born, a race that will be both conquistador and conquered, superior and inferior, at one and the same time: he or she will be a real blood sister/brother of both, without being exclusively either. Furthermore, because the mother is the fundamental transmitter of deep cultural traits, it is the culture of the conquered that will gradually triumph over the culture of the conquistador in providing the dominant and deepest personality characteristics of the new group.

Mestizos are born out of two histories and in them begins a new history. The symbolic and mental structures of both histories begin to intermingle so that out of the new story which begins in the *mestizo* new meanings, myths, and symbols will equally emerge. They will be meaningful to the *mestizo* as the firstborn of a new creation, but will remain incomprehensible to persons who try to understand them through the meanings, mythologies, and symbols of either of the previous histories alone. Yet from birth to maturity, there is a long period of painful search.

The deepest suffering of the *mestizo* comes from what we might call an "unfinished" identity or, better yet, an undefined one. One of the core needs of human beings is the existential knowledge that regardless of who I am socially or morally, I am. The knowledge of fundamental belonging—that is, to be French, American, Mexican, English—is in the present world order one of the deepest needs of persons. When this need is met, it is not even thought about as a need; but when it is missing, it is so confusing and painful that we find it difficult to even conceptualize it or speak about it. We strive "to be like" but we are not sure just which one we should be like. As Mexican Americans, we strive to find our belonging in Mexico or in the United States—only to discover that we are considered foreign by both. Our Spanish is too Anglicized for the Mexicans and our English is too Mexicanized for the Anglos.

In the case of Mexico, it was the *mestizo* image of Our Lady of Guadalupe that provided the beginning of the new socio-cultural synthesis. It was not merely an apparition, but the perfect synthesis of the religious iconography of the Iberian peoples with that of native Mexicans into one coherent image. This marks the cultural birth of a new people. Both the parents and the child now have one common symbol of ultimate belonging. For the first time, they can begin to say "we are." As the physical birth of Mexicans had come through conquest, cultural birth came through the new image. It is only after the apparition that those who had wanted to die now wanted to live and to celebrate life. In and through Our Lady, new meanings, myths, and symbols will begin to emerge that will be truly representative and characteristic of Mexico.

Struggles for Accepting and Belonging

In the first stages of the struggle to belong, the *mestizo* will try desperately to become like the dominant group, for only its members appear to be fully civilized and human. This struggle includes every aspect of life, because the whole world structure of the dominant will have been assimilated and made normative for human existence. It equally involves a violent rejection of the way of the conquered, because that now appears to be inferior. Only the scholars of the dominant group will appear as credible, only their universities as prestigious, their language as civilized, their medical practices as scientific, and their religion as true religion. The dominated will sometimes attempt to keep some of their original folklore, but, in every other way, they try to become like the dominant.

Some of the well-intentioned and kind members of the dominant group will help the brighter and more promising ones (according to their own standard of judgment) to better themselves by "becoming like us." They will privilege them with scholarships to the best universities in Europe or the United States and help them to learn the European or American way of life and language.

Some of the marginated will make it into the world of the dominant society, only to discover that they will never be allowed to belong fully, and furthermore that down deep inside they are still somewhat "other." Yet it is this very pain of not being able to belong fully that also marks the beginning of a new search.

In the first stages of the search, the ones who choose not to join the struggle to become like the dominant ones will tend to reject the world of the dominant in a total way: absolutely nothing good can come of it. They will not only reject it but will hate it passionately. The only way to treat the dominant ones is to get rid of them. They are the ones who are guilty not only of the individual sin of homicide, but of the collective sin of ethnocide.

Throughout all these struggles, there is something radically new beginning to emerge. Even though the seeds are planted from the very beginning and biologically this new life begins from the very start, it will take time for cultural identity to emerge as a distinct identity of its own. This new identity does not try to become like someone else, but it struggles to form its own unique individuality. It accepts from both parent cultures without seeking to be a replica of either. It is like the maturing child who no longer tries to be like the mother or like the father, nor to simply reject both of them, but is simply himself or herself. Through the pains and frustrations of trying to be what we are not, the uniqueness of our own proper identity begins to emerge. It is an exciting moment of the process and usually the most creative state in the life of the group.

It is at this moment that the quest to know ourselves begins to emerge in a serious way. In the beginning, knowledge of ourselves will be confused because we see ourselves through a type of double image—that is, through the eyes of the two parent groups. As the group develops, its own proper image will begin to emerge and it will be easier to study ourselves more critically. It is this new and more clearly defined self-image of who we are as Mexican Americans that is presently beginning to take shape. As usual, it is the poets, the artists, and the musicians who are beginning to point and to sing and to suggest the new identity. It is now the critical thinkers who are coming in and beginning to deepen, conceptualize, verbalize, and communicate the reality of our identity. And it is only now that for the first time we begin to ask ourselves about our Christian identity, about our church, and about our religion. What does it really mean? Who are we as Mexican American Christians?

The Human Situation: Divisions and Collective Self-Protection

When one looks at the history of humanity, wars, divisions, and family fights appear more natural than do peace, unity, and harmony. This is evident from the global level down to the family cell. It appears more natural for brothers and sisters to fight one another than to love one another. We struggle to protect ourselves against each other and to conquer others before they conquer us. We prepare for peace by preparing for war. Only violent means appear to help us control or curb violence. Might makes right because power establishes its views as objective truth so as to justify its own position of privilege. The survival of the fittest appears to be the first law of individuals and of society—the survival of the powerful at the cost of the weak.

From this struggle for survival at the cost of others, certain anthropologico-sociological characteristics and behavioral laws appear. The members of the dominant group in power see themselves as pure, superior, dignified, well-developed, beautiful, and civilized. They see themselves as the model for all others. They see their natural greatness as the source of their great achievements. Even the least among them consider themselves superior to the best of the dominated group.

On the other hand, they look upon the conquered and colonized as impure, inferior, undignified, underdeveloped, ugly, uncivilized, conservative, backward. Their ways are considered childish and their wisdom is looked upon as superstition. Because might is subconsciously assumed to be right, everything about the weak is considered to be wrong and unworthy of being considered human. The conquered are told that they must forget their backward ways if they are to advance and become human. Acculturation to the ways of the dominant, in every respect whatsoever, is equated with human development and liberation.

Even the best among the dominant group find it very difficult to truly accept the other as other: to enjoy their foods, learn from their wisdom, speak their language, dress in their styles, appreciate their art and their music, interpret life through their philosophies, live in their ways, even worship through their forms of cult. Even though many go out, even heroically, to be of service to the poor and the oppressed, and really love them, there is still an inner fear and rejection of their otherness. The way of the powerful as the normative human way for all persons is so deeply ingrained that it takes a dying to oneself to break through the cultural enslavements that keep the dominant from appreciating the inner beauty, the values, the worth, and the dignity of the ways of the conquered.

Because of the image imposed upon them about themselves, some of the conquered will begin to think of themselves as inferior and good for nothing. This develops a type of domesticated, happy-go-lucky, subservient attitude in relation to the dominant. It is a very dehumanizing existence, but the powerless have no choice—either conform to the status assigned by the powerful or be eliminated physically. Law and order work in favor of the rich against the poor. Whereas the rich tend to be considered innocent until proven guilty, the poor are usually considered guilty until proven innocent. They are blamed for all the problems of society and are considered to be the source of all evil and crime. Thus, the very victims of the institutionalized violence of power are labeled by the establishment as the causes of this violence! The powerful can define the image and status of the oppressed as "guilty of all evil" and force them to live accordingly. The poor and the oppressed thus serve as scapegoats for the crimes of the establishment, which can continue to think of itself as pure and immaculate. However, as long as the traditions of the oppressed continue, especially their deepest religious traditions, they may be forced to live as dirt, but they cannot be forced to perceive themselves as such. Through their traditions, perfectly understood by them but incomprehensible to foreigners, they continue to perceive themselves as they truly are: free human beings with full human dignity who, although dominated through external powers, nevertheless remain free and independent in the innermost core of their being.

The in-group will defend tradition, law, and order because its members are the privileged ones of the establishment. National and personal security will be among the top priorities of this group as it strives to maintain the status quo. For the powerful, tradition protects their position of privilege; for the powerless, their own traditions are the ultimate rejection of the status quo of the dominant—their bodies might be dominated but not their souls.

Tradition functions in a diametrically opposed way for the powerful and for the powerless. For the powerless, tradition is the affirmation of inner freedom, independence, and self-worth. It is the power for the radical transformation of the existing order. For the moment, it might appear as a tranquilizer, but we should not underestimate its power in keeping a people alive as a people. As long as their traditions are alive, they are assured of life and ultimate liberation. If their traditions disappear, they will no longer have to work for integral liberation because they will have ceased to exist as a people.

In attempting to analyze the dynamics between the oppressor in-group and the oppressed out-group, three constants seem to function as anthropological laws of human behavior.

First, when one studies the human story across the ages, the tendency of group inclusion/exclusion—that is, to protect our own by keeping others out—appears to be one of the most consistent and fundamental anthropological laws of nature. Dominant groups will struggle to curtail outside influences in a multiplicity of ways, and weaker or dominated ones will likewise fear and resist any type of intrusion. The purity of the group must be maintained. Human barriers of race, class, language, family name, education, economic status, social position, and religion are regularly used as signals to distinguish "our own" from "the others."

The second tendency that appears as an anthropological law of nature is: others can be used and enjoyed, but a social distance must be maintained. Deep friendships might develop and even strong love relationships, but the social barriers are so deeply interiorized and assimilated that they are very difficult to do away with. There are not just laws that keep peoples apart, but also sustain the relationship of superior-inferior that is established, projected, transmitted, assimilated, and even sacralized by religion. This keeps persons from truly appreciating each other as fully equal and from seeing the true human dignity of one another. Even the best among the dominant group tend to see and treat the others as inferior and "different." We can even do good things for the lesser others, but they remain lesser. They can be exploited legitimately, because the culture and the laws of the dominant sanction the superior-inferior relationship. This gives the "master" the right and the obligation to use and "protect" the lesser ones.

This law of social distance is probably the hardest one to break through, because it is not only enforced by external laws and the economic-political mechanisms of the land, it is also interiorized in a number of ways. For example, in ordinary commercials we see blacks waiting on whites, but I have never seen a commercial with a white serving a black. Blacks, but never racially mixed families, appear in commercials. Brown skins do not even appear at all. Social barriers of separability are drilled into a people through all the media of communication and education. Even religious education material and religious images in our churches exhibit a definite racial preference, thus indirectly telling the others that they cannot be reflected in the sacred.

Finally, the third constant that appears as an anthropological law of nature is: anyone who threatens to destroy or annul the barriers of separation will be an outcast—an impure untouchable who must be eliminated.

As should be evident by now, *mestizaje* is feared by established groups because it is the deepest threat to all the humanly made barriers of separation that consecrate oppression and exploitation. It is a threat to the security of ultimate human belonging—that is, to the inherited national/cultural identity that clearly and ultimately defines who I am to myself and to the world. It is even a deeper threat to established societies because the *mestizo* cannot be named with clarity and precision. So much is in the mystery of a name! I am comfortable when I can name you for, in many ways, it indicates that I am somewhat in control of the situation. I may not like what I know, but at least I have the comfort of knowing what it is. But there is a nervousness when I do not know who you are—your name and your cultural nationality are so important, for they tell me who you are personally and fundamentally. They give me your immediate and ultimate human identity.

Because of their hyphenated identity, *mestizos* cannot be named adequately by either group's categories of analysis. They do not fit into the single-history set of norms for testing and identifying persons. This is threatening to both groups—we can name them and even study them, but they cannot name us or even figure out how to really study us. It is threatening for anyone to be in the presence of one who knows us very well, even in our innermost being, but we do not know who they are. To be an outside-insider, as the *mestizo* is, is to have both intimacy and objective distance at one and the same time. Insofar as we are in Mexico, we are outside the United States; but insofar as we are in the United States, we are distant from Mexico. As such we can see and appreciate the aspects of both, aspects which neither sees of themselves or each other. In this very in-out existence lies the potential for our creativity: to pool the cultural genes and the chromosomes of both so as to create a new being!

The potential for newness will not be actualized automatically. The *mestizo* can simply become like one of the parent groups and continue to do unto others as they have done unto us. However, they can equally, although with more hidden difficulties than anyone suspects, choose to live out the radical meaning of their new being. This is exciting but difficult because, even though the dominant way may be rejected totally and explicitly, subconsciously the oppressed will strive to become like the oppressor, for they have already assimilated many of the dominant group's characteristics. Will the group simply obtain power and acceptance by reverting to the ways of the parent group or will they initiate new life? That is the key question.

As a Mexican American Christian, I am convinced that the full potential of *mestizaje* will be actualized only in and through the way of the Lord, which brings order out of chaos and new life out of death. It is in the Lord's way that the salvific and liberating role of our *mestizo* humanity finds its ultimate identity, meaning, direction, and challenge.

The Concrete Historical Meaning of God's Saving Way

The Human Identity of the Savior

The racial-cultural identity of a person is the very first and immediate revelation of who one is. We all have stereotype prejudices about certain colors, accents, languages, features, regions, and religions. There is a natural tendency to categorize persons according to our stereotypes of them and to prejudge them as to their human worth and potential even before they have said or done anything. Looks are all-important and they are the first revelation, according to the standards of the world, of the person's worth and dignity. Persons from the outer regions of any country are usually looked down upon as rustics, whereas those from urban centers look upon themselves as sophisticated.

What was the racial-cultural identity of Jesus? What did others think of when they first saw or heard of him, before they even heard him speak or saw his actions? These are all-important questions, for we know from the New Testament itself that it is in the human face and heart of Jesus that God has been self-revealed to us. It is through the full humanity of Jesus that God has allowed us to see God in a human way.

There is no doubt that, during his lifetime, Jesus was regularly known as a Galilean, that most of his disciples were from Galilee, and that most of the things we remember best of his activity took place in Galilee. There is no doubt that Galilee plays a key role in the life and mission of Jesus as presented in the Gospels.

The full human signification of the *kenosis* of the Son of God becomes evident when we look at the image of Galilee in Jesus' time. First of all, if it had not been for Jesus, Galilee would probably remain an unknown region of the world. Jerusalem, Greece, and Rome were all important with or without Jesus, but not Galilee. It was an outer region, far from the center of Judaism in Jerusalem of Judea and a crossroads of the great caravan routes of the world. It was a region of mixed peoples and languages. In Galilee the Jews were looked down upon and despised by the others as they were in the rest of the world. They were considered to be stubborn, backward, superstitious, clannish, and all the negative stereotypes one could think of. Furthermore, the Jews of Judea looked down upon the Galilean Jews, for they considered them ignorant of the law and the rules of the temple, contaminated in many ways by their daily contacts with pagans, and not capable of speaking correct Greek, for their language was being corrupted by admixture with the other languages of the region. In short, their own Jewish relatives regarded them as inferior and impure. Because of their mixture with others, they were marginated by their own people. There were no doubts about the cultural *mestizaje* that was taking place and, knowing the ordinary situation of human beings, a certain amount of biological *mestizaje* was equally taking place. Culturally and linguistically speaking, Jesus was certainly a *mestizo* between Judaism and the other cultures that flourished throughout Galilee. And we know from the early Jewish charges that tried to discredit Jesus that he was even accused of being the bastard son of a Roman soldier named Pantera, which could also be a colloquial term simply meaning "a Roman," which could have made of him a biological *mestizo* as well. I am, of course, in no way denying or even questioning that Jesus was conceived by the Holy Spirit. What I am saying is that in his human appearance, as viewed by those who knew him only in a worldly way and not through the eyes of faith, he certainly appeared to be of mixed origins. The New Testament itself gives clear evidence that nothing good was expected to come out of Galilee.

The point of bringing out all this is to appreciate the human beginnings of God's mission. God becomes not just a human being, but the marginated, shamed, and rejected of the world. He comes to initiate a new human unity, but the all-important starting point is among the most segregated and impure of the world. Among those whom the world has thrown out, God will begin the way to final unity. It is among those whom the world labels as "impure" that a new criterion for real purity will emerge.

Although the world expected nothing good to come out of Galilee, God chose it to be the starting point of God's human presence among us. The principle behind the cultural image of the Galilean identity is that God chooses what the world rejects. What is marginal to the world is central to God. It is through those whom the world has made nothing that God will reduce to nothing the power and wisdom of the world. It is through the poor and non-persons of the world that God continues to reveal God's face and heart in a human way and among them—the Galilees and Galileans of today—salvation continues to begin for all the peoples of the world.

The Cultural Function of His Mission

The mission of Jesus is not some sort of esoteric or aesthetic truth. He comes to live out and proclaim the supreme truth about humanity, which will have immediate and long-term implications in everyday life and in the history of humanity. Those who hear his word and are converted to his way will see themselves and will equally see all others in a radically new way. This new image of self and others will allow everyone to relate with each other as never before.

Because of his concrete human identity, Jesus had personally suffered the pains of margination and dehumanizing insults. He was concerned with the pains of hunger, sickness, bad reputation, rejection, shame, class struggles, loneliness, and all the real sufferings of humanity. His concern was not abstract, but real and immediate. He spoke with the Samaritan woman, ate with the rich, the tax collectors, and sinners alike. He did not feel repelled by the leper; he enjoyed the company of women and little children. Jesus was truly at home with everyone and it is evident that everyone felt at home with him. This is nowhere more evident than in his ability to enjoy himself in table fellowship with everyone without exception.

Out of the cultural suffering of rejection, Jesus offers a new understanding of the kingdom. He did not come to restore the kingdom of David for the Jewish people but to initiate the reign of God who is the Father of everyone. The innermost identity of Jesus was his life of intimacy with God-Father. It is this living relationship with the absolute that cuts through and relativizes all human images of importance or non-importance, be they dignified or undignified. When we know the ultimate origins of a person—that he is really the son of the king—the superficial appearances are no longer important. It is the ultimate origins and name of a person that give us his or her true worth. It is precisely this intimacy with God-Father which is the basis of the innermost identity of Jesus. It is not the labels that the world places on persons that count, but one's own innermost identity and image of oneself as reflective of the likeness of God.

By discovering that God is our Father we begin to see everything in a new way. No longer will I see others as superior or inferior to me, but as brothers and sisters of the same Father. In this realization is the basis for a totally new value system for humanity. In fidelity to God, Jesus refuses to conform to any human law or tradition that will dehumanize and make appear as inferior any human being whatsoever. The truth of Jesus will upset humankind's criteria of judgment. Because one is, one is a child of God. But precisely because everyone can now belong, those who have set up and guarded the multiple barriers of separation will not only refuse the invitation but will discredit the new way and try to prevent it from coming into existence. This allows them to enjoy the privileges of being "in" at the cost of keeping the so-called inferior ones "out."

But it is not sufficient to invite the rejected into the kingdom. It is not sufficient to tell the exploited and marginated of society that they are truly free human beings who are equal to all others. One must go to the roots of the human mechanisms, both to the external and the internal structures of society, to make known the segregating and dehumanizing evil that has been institutionalized and is now hidden in the various structures of the group. Jesus makes known that he must go to Jerusalem, where the sufferings of his people are highlighted. Truth in the service of love must bring out clearly the evil hidden in human structures, evil which passes as good. Such confusion allows the evils of power to appear as the good of society, while the sufferings of the marginated appear as the cause of all evil. Criminals appear as good; victims appear as criminals. This is the ongoing confusion of Babel, which continues to mask and confuse both the evil and the good of the world.

Jesus appears in the New Testament as the aggressive prophet of nonviolent love who refuses to endorse the violence of the structures and remains faithful to the tradition of the God of his people, of the God who sees the suffering, who hears the cries of affliction, and who wills to save. He questions the human traditions that oppress or destroy a people. Jesus must go to Jerusalem, because that is the center of institutionalized power. When he arrives he goes to the very core of Judaism: the temple. In Jerusalem we see Jesus who does not hesitate to question the very legitimacy of the structures that were enslaving the masses of the people. The house of the God of compassion and justice had become the place that now legitimized and covered up the evil ways of the establishment. The same story is found in all human institutions. We need institutions in order to live in an orderly and peaceful way. Yet, all institutions have the tendency to become self-serving to the benefit of those in control. They are set up to serve persons, but persons end up serving them. It is this very tendency to absolutize that must be confronted and made known.

As institutions, customs, and traditions become absolutized, they function as the idols of the group. Whether we call them God or not, they function as the real gods of the group. To question them is the same as questioning God. And when we challenge them, we will be accused of blasphemy. Yet to the degree that these ways dehumanize or reject any human being, they must be questioned in the name of God. But Jesus does not confront the power of the world with a power of the same order. He does not give in to the ways of humanity. He confronts the power of the world and human violence with a power of an entirely different order: the power of unlimited love which will not engage in violence to eliminate violence.

The nonviolent way of Jesus worked in a diametrically opposed way to the nonviolent way of the missioners of the power countries. First of all, he begins by assuming the way, the language, and the worldview of Galileans—the non-persons of the world. The all-powerful God, in becoming a Galilean, converts to become the marginated, the rejected, and the non-person of the world. Second, he not only denounces the accepted practices of the powerful, as good missioners often do, but, unlike the average traditional missioner, he even denounces and desacralizes their ultimate authority as enshrined in their religious symbols, for it is the religious symbols of the powerful that ultimately legitimize their way as God's way. Third, the radical difference between the missionary activity of Jesus and that of missioners who are culturally and nationally members of the powerful countries is apparent in the response of officials.

Official Judaism condemned Jesus and got rid of him. His accusers disowned him to the Romans because he questioned their ultimate authority and the ultimate legitimacy of their structures. The officials of mission-sending countries support and reinforce the missionary endeavor because it in effect affirms and perpetuates the legitimacy of their own world order. In supporting the missions, they affirm their own ultimate authority and the divine legitimacy of their ways. Let me be clear on this point: this is not necessarily done in an intentional or malicious way. In fact, I would say that quite often it is done with the best of intentions; however, the final result remains the same. The Spanish missioners did not hesitate to chastise openly and consistently the crimes and abuses of the conquest; however, they legitimized the way of the conquerors by affirming their ultimate symbol as superior and true in relation to the captured peoples' symbols of ultimate reality.

The way of Jesus to Jerusalem and the cross is the challenging task of those who are on the margins of society. Their temptation will always be to become simply the powerful themselves, as even the disciples wanted to do. But the challenge is to be willing to die so that a new way will truly be ushered in. The authorities kill Jesus but they cannot destroy him. He remains faithful to his way to the very end. He came to reject every type of human rejection and, even when all appear to have rejected him, even his God, he rejects no one. He dies in perfect communion with his people and his God. He came to tear down barriers of separation and, no matter what humans tried to do to stop him, they were not able to break him down. As he lived his life in communion with everyone—so he died. All had rejected him, but he rejects no one.

God's love in and through Jesus triumphs over all the divisive hatreds and consequent violence of humanity. Jesus passes through death to life. In resurrecting him, God rejects the rejection of humanity, destroys all the charges of illegitimacy, and demolishes the idolized structures. In the resurrection, God ratified the entire way and message of Jesus. It is from the resurrection that the entire way of Jesus and every aspect of his life takes on a liberating and salvific signification.

It is in the resurrection that the new life initiated and offered to everyone by Jesus is now fully and definitively present. No human power will be able to destroy it or slow it down. Jesus is the firstborn of the new creation, and in his followers a new human group now begins. It is definitely a new human alternative now present in the history of humanity.

First of all, those who had nothing to offer now have the best thing to offer to everyone: new life. It is the rejected and marginated Galileans who receive the Spirit and, without ceasing to be Galileans, now see themselves in a new way as they begin to initiate the new humanity. Everyone is invited, but it is the very ones who had been excluded who now do the inviting. It is obvious from the history of the early church how quickly the new way spread to all peoples. It crossed all boundaries of separation. Without ceasing to be who they were culturally, people nevertheless saw themselves in such a new way that the ordinary human barriers were no longer obstacles to the new fellowship.

It is equally evident that the crossing of cultural boundaries was not easy, for each group had its own unsuspected idols, yet the miracle is that it took place. Cultural-national groups which had been totally separated, now can come together—no longer Jew or gentile, master or slave, male or female, but all one in Christ. They continued to be who they were, but they lived their nationality and religion in a radically new way. Their identity was affirmed but their exclusiveness was destroyed. This openness led them to discover new values and criteria of judgment: from competition to cooperation, from divisions to unity, from strangers to a common family, from a superior or inferior status to common friends and all children of the same Father.

The radical all-inclusive way of Christianity started among the rejected and lowly of society. This is the starting point. In the Spirit, they struggle to build new human alternatives so that others will not have to suffer what they have had to suffer. It is they who first hear the invitation to the new universal family of God, and it is the converted poor and suffering of the world who see themselves in a new way, who now go out and invite—by deeds and words—all others into the new society. God continues to begin where humanity would never suspect. Out of the Nazareths and Galilees of today, salvation continues to reach the entire world.

The God-Meaning of Our Mexican American Identity and Mission

"God chose those whom the world considers absurd to shame the wise." (1 Cor. 1:28)

It is in the light of our faith that we discover our ultimate identity as God's chosen people. It is in the very cultural identity of Jesus the Galilean and in his way from Galilee to Jerusalem that the real ultimate meaning of our own cultural identity and mission to society become clear.

For those who ordinarily have a good sense of belonging, the idea of being chosen is nothing special. But for one who has been consistently ignored or rejected, the idea of being noticed, accepted, and especially chosen is not only good news, but new life. For in being chosen, what was nothing now becomes something, and what was dead now comes to life. In the light of the Judeo-Christian tradition, our experience of rejection and margination is converted from human curse to the very sign of divine predilection. It is evident from the scriptures that God chooses the outcasts of the world not exclusively but definitely in a preferential way. Those whom the world ignores, God loves in a special way. But God does not choose the poor and the lowly just to keep them down and make them feel good in their misery. Such an election would be the very opposite of good news and it would truly be the opium to keep the poor quiet and domesticated. God chooses the poor and the marginated of the world to be the agents of the new creation.

The experience of being wanted as one is, of being needed and of being chosen, is a real and profound rebirth. Those who had been made to consider themselves as nothing or as inferior will now begin to appreciate the full stature of human beings. Out of the new self-image, new powers will be released, powers which have always been there but have not been able to surface. Through this experience, the sufferings of the past are healed though not forgotten, and they should not be forgotten. For it is precisely out of the condition of suffering that the people are chosen so as to initiate a new way of life where others will not have to suffer what the poor have suffered in the past. When people forget the experience of suffering, as has happened to many of our immigrant groups in this country, such as the Irish in Boston, then they simply inflict the same insults upon others that had previously been inflicted upon them. The greater the suffering and the more vivid the memory of it, the greater the challenge will be to initiate changes so as to eliminate the root causes of the evils which cause the suffering. It is the wounded healer, the one who has not forgotten the pain of wounds, who can be the greatest healer of society's illnesses.

It is in our very margination from the centers of the various establishments that we live the Galilean identity today. Because we are inside-outsiders, we appreciate more clearly the best of the traditions of both groups, while equally appreciating the worst from the situation of both. It is precisely in this double identity that we in effect have something of unique value to offer both. The very reasons for the margination are the bases of our liberating and salvific potential not only for ourselves but for the others as well. In a privileged way, God is present in the marginated, for distance from the powers of the world is closeness to God. It is consistently in the borderlands regions of human belonging that God begins the new creation. The established centers seek stability, but the borderlands regions can risk to be pioneers. It is the borderlands people who will be the trailblazers of the new societies. "The stone which the builders rejected has become the keystone of the structure. It is the Lord who did this and we find it marvelous to behold" (Matt. 21:42).

"I have chosen you to go and bear much fruit." (John 15:16)

God chooses people not just to make them feel good, but for a mission. "I have chosen you to go and bear much fruit" (John 15:16). To accept God's election is not empty privilege, but a challenging mission. It is a call to be prophetic both in deeds and in words. It is a call to live a new alternative in the world, to invite others into it, and to challenge with the power of truth the structures of the world that keep the new alternative from becoming a reality.

Our Mexican American Christian challenge in the world today is not to become like someone else—Mexicans or Americans—but to combine both into a new way. It is through the very mechanisms of forging a new and more cosmopolitan identity that new life begins to emerge. It must be worked at critically, persistently, and creatively, for the temptation will always be there to become simply one or the other of the previous models. The temptation will always be there to restore the kingdom rather than to usher in the kingdom of God. In our present powerlessness we may think that this is stupid but, in our faith, we know that we must take the risks and begin to initiate new ways of life that will eliminate some of the dehumanizing elements of the present one. We know that we will not eliminate them all, nor will this come about easily and without much effort, organization, and frustration, but nevertheless the efforts must be made to introduce new forms and new institutions that will continue some of the best of the past while eliminating some of the worst. We will not build the perfect society, but we must do our part to at least build a better one. We must begin with the grassroots, but we must equally go to the very roots of the problems.

This is our "divine must"! We, too, must harden our faces and go to Jerusalem. We must go to the established centers of power, whether political, economic, educational, or religious, to confront their sacred idols which prevent them from truly serving all the people. It is the idols of society which function in favor of the rich and the powerful, and against the poor and powerless. It is they which mask the hidden viciousness and manipulations of the wise of the world who find many ways of exploiting the poor and the simple of the world.

We really do not have a choice if we want to be disciples following Jesus on his way to the cross. It is this road from Galilee to Jerusalem which has to be continued if evil is to be destroyed, not with new forms of evil, but with the power of truth in the service of love. We have no choice but to speak the truth which brings to light clearly the evil of the world, knowing full well that the powers of darkness will not stop at anything in order to put out the light.

"Your grief will be turned to joy." (John 16:20)

It is in our fiestas that our legitimate identity and destiny are experienced. They are not just parties; in fact they are the very opposite. They are the joyful, spontaneous, and collective celebrations of what has already begun in us even if it is not recognized by others or verbalized even by ourselves. It is the celebration of the beginning of the ultimate eschatological identity where there will be differences but not division. It is the celebration of what has already begun in germ but is yet to be totally fulfilled. The fiesta is a foretaste and experience, even if for a brief moment, of the ultimate accomplishment. It is a result of who we are and a cause of what is yet to become. For just as it is true that the celebrations of the people can be used to drug the people and keep them in their misery, it is equally true that the fiestas can be used as rallying moments that not only give the people an experience of togetherness, but can also nourish the movements of liberation. In the fiestas, we rise above our daily living experiences of death to experience life beyond death. They are the moments of life that enable us to survive, come together, rally, and begin anew. The spirit not only to survive but to bring about a new existence can be enkindled in the fiestas so as to ignite the people to action.

Fiestas without prophetic action easily degenerate into empty parties, drunken brawls, or the opium to keep the people in their misery. But prophetic action without festive celebration is equally reduced to dehumanizing hardness. Prophecy is the basis of fiesta, but the fiesta is the spirit of prophecy. It is in the combination of the two that the tradition of faith is both kept alive and transmitted to newcomers. It is through the two of them that the God of history who acts on our behalf, on behalf of the poor and the lowly, continues to be present among us, bringing the project of history to completion.

Thus it is precisely through our fiestas that we are kept together as a people. It is through them that we have continued to maintain our identity and sense of belonging. They are the deepest celebrations of our existence—meaningful to those who belong and incomprehensible and folkloric to outsiders. They are the lifeline of our tradition and the life sources of our new existence.

9. Transformation of Borders

Mestizaje and the Future of Humanity

(1998)

Virgilio Elizondo

[Editor's Note: This presentation was a keynote address to the 1997 annual meeting of the College Theology Society.]

Congratulations to the College Theology Society. You certainly chose one of the most important issues for the church, society, and the world at this moment of history and you could not have chosen a better place than San Diego/Tijuana to probe the question of borders. This is an area, like the entire border between the United States and Mexico, that both separates and keeps peoples apart while at the very same time providing the cradle for the growth and development of a new humanity which defies all previous borders of separation. I congratulate you on your prophetic and visionary choice, for at the very moment when the powerful nations of the world are tightening their borders to keep "undesirables" out, you dare to speak about expanding the borders—a courageous choice indeed.

A short time ago, we all rejoiced at the tearing down of the Berlin Wall, but today in the United States, not only are we building an electronic wall to keep Mexicans and Latin Americans out of the United States, we are even militarizing the border as if it were a major war zone. We eagerly want Mexican trade and cheap Mexican labor to produce U.S. goods in our assembly plants—*maquiladoras*—in Mexico but at no cost do we want poor, dark-skinned Mexicans and Latin Americans to enter our country. There is a similar attitude throughout the Western Christian nations of the world: reinforce the borders so as to keep the poor and dark-skinned peoples of the world out.

We send our agents into the poor countries to open new markets for our products, thus exciting them about our "good life," we tease them about our "heavenly" existence of material abundance, we tell them through our products, movies, and publicity how good we have it in the United States. While trying to sell our products and our way of life abroad, we are in effect inviting them to come join us, to come to the source of material bliss. Many of them will risk everything—including their lives—to come to this apparent earthly paradise, maybe not of milk and honey, but certainly of hamburgers and Cokes! But the reality is that we want their money or their cheap labor but not their bodies and their presence among us in our neighborhoods, parishes, and cities.

There is a growing fear seizing the Western world about the perceived invasion

176

of the poor and dark-skinned peoples of the world, which results in a growing anti-immigrant phobia and attempts to seal the borders so that the unwanted do not get in. Furthermore, while many in the Western nations are into zero population growth, the immigrant poor see large families as a divine blessing. Hence their presence continues to grow. The media and the politicians make the immigrant poor and their children appear as the root cause of all the problems ailing our countries. Border patrols are increased and life is made most difficult for those who dare to penetrate the border defenses. How quickly we forget that at one time, our founders were the unwanted poor of Europe. How quickly we forget that we are an immigrant country made great through the untiring efforts of those who dared to emigrate to a new country and carve out a new existence—a greatness which sometimes was the result of hard work and ingenuity, but quite often came about through the enslavement, exploitation, or elimination of others.

When we look at the history of humanity, we quickly discover that throughout history there have been migrations, *mestizajes*, and new identities. As new groups forge their geographical-social identity, they tend to forget their ancient origins. Immigrations, *mestizajes*, and new identities are as old as the planet itself and as natural as life itself but they are feared worse than hell itself. They appear as a threat to one's defined existence and identity, thus borders of all kinds are set up and interiorized so as to protect the perceived "purity" of the group from foreign contamination. Any transgression of these borders (racial, national, religious, class, clan, even family, and others) provokes disgust and even excommunication. The quest for national purity can easily and quickly become a death-bearing idol justifying such horrors as the holocaust and wars of ethnic cleansing. National pride and identity, which is certainly a cherished virtue, can easily turn others into despised enemies who are a threat to the national welfare and existence.

Yet, as I look at our own experience of the Mexican Southwest of the United States—*La Frontera*—I dare to ask: Need the transgression of borders be feared? Could it not be welcomed as the natural way of producing a new humanity, a new pool of biological, cultural, and spiritual genes that will produce an even more human humanity? Is the transgression of borders destruction of life or the birth of new life?

My Personal Experience

My entire lifetime has been one of crossing borders! Sometimes it has been quite painful at the moment of crossing, but in the long run, each border-crossing has been most life giving. I was born and grew up in San Antonio, Texas in the section of the city which might just as well have been Mexico. Our language, our customs, our humor, our religious expression, our foods, our bodily language— everything was Mexico, U.S.A.!

My first border-crossing, and probably my most traumatic one, was when I crossed the street that was the sort of dividing line between Mexican San Antonio and Anglo San Antonio (this has long since disappeared) and went to an English-speaking school. It was my first encounter with "total otherness." I hated school—

I didn't know the language, the customs were strange, and even the way of attending Mass was quite different (it was painful rather than joyful). I became very quiet and reserved. I kept to myself and was afraid to speak because I felt bad when people could not understand my English.

Later on, in yet another Anglo school, a nun took a special interest in me and made all the difference. All of a sudden, I started to like school and my grades improved immensely. The border-crossing started to be fun and exciting. I started to realize that I was not losing, I was gaining. I also, for the first time, started to enjoy, rather than be embarrassed by, this constant border-crossing which allowed me many options, including the ability to get along in two languages rather than just one. High school was even better. I was able to compete with all the other students as true equals regardless of our ethnic backgrounds.

College and early priesthood became times of great questioning: Was I "Mexican" or "U.S. American"? When visiting Mexico, no matter how Mexican I might try to be, someone would remind me that I was a *Pocho*, a United States Mexican; and in the United States, no matter how "American" I tried to be, someone would remind me I was Mexican and of course Mexican in a quite derogatory sense. It seemed like the separation between the United States and Mexico reached to the very depths of our individual and collective soul. The separation seemed irreparable. It seemed that no matter where we were, Mexico or the United States, we had to be constantly apologizing for who we were—too "Gringo" for the Mexicans and too Mexican for the "Americans." It became quite tiresome to be always explaining, defending, clarifying: "No, I am not really fully Mexican . . . No, I am not really just United States." We could easily say, "No, I'm not . . ." but we could never simply say: I am! All this produced a certain type of shame in being who we were, for we had no place we could really call home, where we could really be ourselves. The only being we knew was our non-being and the only place we had was "in-between" Mexico and the United States.

In 1967, Father Francisco Aguilera, a Mexican *mestizo* who was comfortable and proud of both his Spanish and Amerindian ancestry, took me to visit the *Plaza de las Tres Culturas* in Mexico City where the final battles between the Aztecs and the Spaniards took place. In this sacred ground where a colonial church sits upon the ruins of the old pyramid-temples and is surrounded by modern-day apartment houses, there is an inscription which reads:

> *On this site*
> *on the sad night of August 13, 1521*
> *heroically taken by Cortéz*
> *valiantly defended by Cuauhtemoc*
> *it was neither a defeat nor a victory*
> *but the painful birth of the Mestizo people*
> *which is México today.*

We then went to visit Our Lady of Guadalupe. I had been there before, but this was a totally new experience as Father Aguilera explained to me how in and through her, the Iberian soul had united with the ancient Mexican soul to give rise to the *mestizo* soul of Mexico. This was the ongoing miracle of Guadalupe, this is what truly made her the Mother of the Americas, because she had given birth and continues to give birth to the new people of the Americas.

This was the beginning of a real rebirth for me, a coming to grips with the innermost reality of my being and that of my people. I immediately realized that what had appeared as "non-being" was in reality the beginning of new being. The carnal and spiritual borders of identity and belonging had been pierced, the geographical/historical being of "the other" had been penetrated, and a new being had been conceived and born who would be fully both and something new. I quickly reread the Alamo story through the same categories—not of defeat or victory, but of birth—the birth of a people, the birth of a soul, the birth of a spirituality, the birth of a church, and the birth of a religion. I could be proud of my collective grandparents: Iberia and pre-Columbian Mexico, and I could equally be proud of my parents: WASPish United States and *mestizo* Catholic Mexico.

In recent years, I have come to realize that my own quest for identity and belonging is not just limited to my people of the Mexican-United States *Frontera* but that it is the human quest of peoples throughout the world. Having traveled vastly around the world and experienced the quest of growing numbers of peoples like myself, I dare to say that in my very body and soul, I am today's great human quest. As Alex García-Rivera would say, in the little story of one human being is the universal story of humanity. In the *mestizo* peoples of the world, the new identity of the Third Millennium is beginning to emerge and proclaim its presence.

World Experience Today

It is evident to any casual observer that the old, established, geographical-biological-ethnic identities are fading away quickly. Just stay a few minutes in the center of any city or watch major events like the Olympics or the World Cup and you will see that you can no longer identify a country by the color of the skin or the ethnic and racial characteristics of its people.

Today, multiple and massive migrations are taking place in every direction. The poor and formerly colonized peoples of the world are moving to the rich countries which are the homelands of their former colonizers. Their children have no desire to relocate in the "old" country or to continue the lives their parents fled from. Yet, they are still different from the native-born peoples in many ways no matter how much they might like to simply fade in. Intermarriage begins to take place and the children gradually become aware of their "otherness" in relation to the ethnicities of their parents.

The Western colonization of the former centuries prepared the way and opened the doors for today's immigration into the Western countries. Furthermore, as world business looks for new markets enticing poor peoples of the globe to buy into the "Good Life" of the Western world, the peoples take this as an invitation to come to the source of this "good life" and they will strive at all costs to resettle in these countries. The exportation of our products, our entertainment, our way of life, and even our religion is an invitation to come join us. We may not see it or intend it that way, but that is the way it functions. The West continues to project the image of "paradise on earth" to the poor peoples of the world and they will continue to sacrifice and risk whatever is necessary to get themselves and their families here. Many who die in the process are the modern-day martyrs of our world.

Today's cities and towns are rapidly becoming world cities—the entire world is present in each major concentration of peoples. This is just as true of San Diego as it is of Los Angeles, Chicago, New York, London, Madrid, Paris, Rome, and even the small towns of any Western country. As evident as the mixture is, so are the growing racial, ethnic, and religious tensions around the world. So, we ask the crucial question: What humanity do we want for the Third Millennium? A homogeneous society where there will be no differences and everyone will be exactly the same? An ethnic/racial "cleansing" with all its violent consequences? A society of ghettos always living in tension with one another? A fragile coexistence that could easily erupt into violence? Or, do we dare to dream of something new and recognize what is happening right here in *La Frontera* as the beginning of that newness?

The Christian Contribution

At the very core of Christianity is the conviction that a universal human family is truly possible and desirable, one that transcends the blood and ethnic bonds which usually identify us and divide us.

Initial Border-crossing of Jesus Christ

From its very inception, Christianity is about crossing apparently impenetrable borders for the sake of a new unity, the unity of a new source of family belonging. The eternal Christ, the Word of God, crossed the border between the eternal and the temporal, between the divine and the human, to become Jesus of Nazareth. As the New Testament affirms, "Christ, though in the image of God, didn't deem equality with God something to be clung to—but instead became completely empty and took on the image of oppressed humankind: born into the human condition, found in the likeness of a human being" (Phil. 2:6-7). Even stronger, the eternal Word which was God became flesh and dwelt among us. And the very geographical-historical place where this took place was in Galilee, a crossroads of the peoples of the world, a place whose people were considered impure and inferior precisely because here the boundaries of identity and belonging were constantly crossed if for no other reason than for basic survival.

From this region of ongoing mixture, Jesus proclaimed the reign of God for everyone and lived it out in many ways, most especially through his joy of table fellowship with everyone and anyone. Isn't it amazing that what was most shocking and scandalous for all the pure-minded religious people of his time, breaking the barriers of acceptability in the context of a common meal, would become the most sacred and cherished activity of the followers of Jesus? What was contamination and scandalous to the ordinary good, religious, and saintly folks of his time becomes the most sanctifying, edifying, and purifying activity of the new movement of universal and universalizing love.

Out of this context, Jesus asks the crucial question of all his followers: "Who is my mother, my brothers, and my sisters?" (Mark 3:33). It is definitely not those of my own race, ethnicity, nationality, clan, or family, but those who do the will of God which is clearly expressed in the prayer of Jesus: that all may be one! Not that all might be uniformly the same, but that all might love universally. Jesus gave his body and blood for this so that the curtains of sacralized division—be they prejudices, taboos, or national borders—might be destroyed, for nothing can hide the true sacredness of God which is the human person regardless of racial, ethnic, national, or familial identity: "*He opened for us a new way, a living way, through the curtain—that is, through his own body*" (Heb. 10:20). The most sacred and cherished rite of the new group would be the festive family meal—sacred because it dared to exclude no one!

Early Christianity

From its earliest moments, those following the way of Jesus started to transgress the most sacred and absolute borders on behalf of the new way. Jews, Ethiopians, Samaritans soon became family members of the new way. Peter the staunch Galilean Jew went through defilement to enter the house of Cornelius the Roman while Cornelius equally risked derision in welcoming the militant rabble-rouser into his home. In the context of their encounter, previous borders were relativized without either losing their original identity, yet both became more human in the process of entering into one another's world. When Paul confronted Peter on behalf of the Gentiles it was likewise a transgression for the sake of liberation—liberation from boundaries which keep us from appreciating the inner beauty and dignity of the other whom we have feared and even detested.

Without destroying anyone, the new way provided a new spirit through which people could break through whatever borders divided them and become a new race, which is precisely what the earliest Christians were called. Christianity introduced into the world the joy and excitement of the hyphenated existence: you continued being who you were, but now in a radically new way. It did not destroy peoples but it did destroy ghettoishness. It made people aware that precisely because we were all "foreigners" (1 Pet. 2:11) in this world order, with "*no permanent country*" to claim for ourselves exclusively, absolutely, and permanently (Heb. 13:14), our only lasting family and ultimate root of belonging will be in the love for one another which leads us to welcome all who come to us in need. For in the end all things will pass away and only love and hence the family of love will remain (1 Cor. 13:8).

Christianity Today

Although historical Christianity has often sinned and been a source of division and bloodshed, the original Christian spirit of welcoming rather than fearing others is the great contribution which Christianity can contribute to the making of the new human family of the next millennium. If in the past missionaries from the Western world went out to all the known corners of the earth to welcome peoples into the Christian family, today the mission of the church, at least of the Western world, is to receive the foreign poor into our homeland, for in receiving the poor of the world, we are receiving God (Matt. 25:35).

Today's parishes have the marvelous opportunities of becoming the greenhouses wherein the new life of the next millennium will be cultivated and developed. By developing a spirituality of hospitality and welcome, rejoicing with each new-comer, and giving thanks to God for the gifts which each one brings for the better-ment of the entire parish family, each parish can become a microscopic cell of the new humanity which will be inclusive of everyone. New friendships and mar-riages between the children of the old-timers and the newcomers will take place, and their children will enflesh the bodily, cultural, and particular characteristics of both parents, yet they will be something new. If in the worldly *mestizaje* of the past the *mestizo* children were usually ashamed of the "inferior" side of their heritage and tried to deny, hide, and forget it, in the Christian *mestizaje* of the new way, the children will be equally proud of and grateful for all their ancestral traits, shades, and colors. Our Christian tradition, purified of its Eurocentric absolut-ism, is in a privileged position to appreciate and foster the positive evolution of these new identities.

I recently baptized the child of a Nigerian father and an Irish mother born in the United States. I challenged the parents and grandparents to make the child proud of both its African-Nigerian and European-Irish heritage while encourag-ing the child to develop its own synthesis in the context of the U.S. way of life. I also had an Anglo-Jewish-Mexican Catholic wedding where I challenged the Catho-lic to help her Jewish husband become a better Jew while challenging the Jew to help his Catholic wife become an even better Catholic and let their children grow up in a love and respect for both and through the grace of God (not the manipula-tion or pressure of either parent) develop its own new synthesis—faithful to both, yet creating something new! Look at Tiger Woods, the new golf champion who is an Asian, African, North American. The mixture is happening with or without us but we have the graced opportunity of making it something really positive and exciting.

That it is happening, there is no doubt. Yet there is equally no doubt that the fear of others and especially otherness is becoming more and more violent. We want to make the foreign other the culprit for all our national woes. It is precisely here that you the theologians, the writers of insightful articles and books, have the greatest contribution to make. Why not write letters to the editors of your local papers, or Op Ed pieces giving a positive view of immigrants and *mestizaje*? Your professional writings are read by very few and in all honesty, probably influence even less. Yet your faith interpretation of reality communicated through the pub-lic media could easily influence and change the minds of millions! Humanity needs your voice. Someone like Cardinal Roger Mahony of Los Angeles has been a heroic prophet in favor of the rights and dignity of immigrants. You could do likewise. Our Holy Father is constantly calling upon the church to be the voice of the voiceless and powerless in society. You could easily and very effectively be precisely that. The immigrant poor need you to give the wider society an alternate and positive view of immigrants, immigration, foreigners, and *mestizaje*. A prophetic article or letter in the public press in favor of the poor, the marginalized, and the "kept-out" could easily be much more valuable than the best of articles in professional journals or the most award-winning theological books of the theological academy. In the end, it will not be your academic peers who will judge the ultimate value of your work, but the poor of society who will testify on your behalf for having come to their assistance.

Transformation of Borders

Borders normally signify the limits of existence, identity, and belonging— beyond the border you are no longer in Mexico, France, the United States, etc. When you cross the border, you cross from belonging to being a foreigner, an alien, or a visitor—in any case, you become an outsider! But we are discovering a new meaning and function of borderlands as the frontiers of new existence. Just as they have served to separate and keep apart, they can equally be the privileged meeting places of persons and of cultures and thus the birthplace of truly new human beings—biologically and culturally—and the cradles of new cultures, that is, of a new humanity.

Borders will not disappear, differences will not fade away, but they need not divide and keep peoples apart. Rather than being the fences of separation they can well serve as reference points marking regional characteristics that are both appealing and humanizing. They guard against a dull, homogenized society without any differences. Borders should not disappear but neither should they divide and keep people apart. The very nature of our faith can lead us to a creative transformation in the meaning and function of borders. Rather than seeing them as the ultimate dividing line between you and me, between us and them, we can see borders as the privileged meeting places where different persons and peoples will come together to form a new and more inclusive humanity. Rather than viewing them as the ultimate chaos of mixture, impurity, and disorder, we can begin to see them for what they truly are: the cradles of the new humanity. Our sense of universal and universalizing love can transform these potential regions of ethnic and racial violence into the new civilization of love wherein differences will be brought together for the betterment and enrichment of the whole human family.

Every border-crossing relativizes human absolutes and challenges previously unquestioned taboos for the sake of the new family of unlimited love. The borderlands people are often looked down upon as "impure" and despised in various ways by the "purists" of the great centers of identity and belonging—Boston, Paris, Jerusalem, Berlin, Mexico City, Buenos Aires—yet it is in the out of the way frontier places, in the Galilees of today, that a new humanity is in the process of being born. It is here that the boundaries of purity are pierced through and the previously "impure" become the ordinary stock of the new humanity which enfleshes the skin and blood of those who were previously irreconcilable! Jesus went through this when he touched lepers, dined with sinners, and conversed with the Samaritan woman. Peter went through this when he dined with Cornelius, Paul when he went to the Gentiles. This is the way of Christianity—a constant defiance and crossing of borders for the sake of the new human family, for the only one unquestioned absolute is the reign of God's love.

In this new humanity, no one person, culture, religion, or race will be accepted as universal, normative, and ideal for everyone else. Each one has its richness and its limitations, its expressions of grace and of sin, its vision and its blindness, its knowledge and its ignorance, its illumination and its darkness. Each has the need of the others to become more human. Every culture is good but no culture is perfect. Thus difference is not a defect but a richness, for in the very particularity of each human group, its richness and limitations will be revealed. Through every encounter with others, more and more will be revealed of oneself and of the others.

In the very encounters across defined borders, we become a source of revelation to one another for, in the comparison, we can all become more aware both of our own graces and sins as well as those of others and begin to form a new identity, taking from the best of each and hopefully eliminating the bad of each. This is an intriguing and exciting process of both affirmation and purification, of pain and joy, of death and birth, of tears and celebration.

To appreciate this newness in a positive way, one must discover the positive and exciting value of diversity in a spirit of great humility, recognizing that no one person, culture, or region has an exclusive monopoly on the value, meaning, and destiny of human life. Each language has its ability to communicate as well as its limitations. When we are speaking of a variety of cultures, we are speaking about what will often appear as contradictions and ambiguities, for the ordinary and self-evident ways of one culture always appear as odd or even unnatural to the other culture. If one faces differences with the fear of contamination or even a threat to one's identity, these differences will never be understood, appreciated, enjoyed! Once one can make an inner conversion and begin to see differences as positive and exciting—new worlds to be discovered and enjoyed—the diversity, rather than threatening, becomes life-giving and enriching.

Despite the positive potential for the renewal of humanity, every crossing is painful, for we have to let go of the absolute character of the ideas, customs, values, and taboos which were most sacred to us, because what appears as sacred can often be the ultimate barrier that keeps us from appreciating the godliness of others. As painful as this letting go is—for it is nothing less than a dying to one's self—it is equally liberating and joyful, for it is a resurrecting into a new and more human existence. This is the paschal mystery in the world today: in every death to my cultural-historical absolutes, I do not cease being who I am but I become much more of a human being for I become open to the beauty and treasures of the values, customs, traditions, and way of life of others.

The most painful border-crossing is that of *mestizaje*, which allows us to break through the most absolute of all borders at the deepest level of human existence: the body, the blood, and the human spirit! Through *mestizaje*, a new body, a new culture with its language, and even a new form of religious expression comes into existence. It does not destroy its own sources of life—the parent races and cultures—but it brings them together into a new form of human existence.

What I am speaking about is not an academic theory about *mestizaje*, but an honest attempt to explore the great human adventure of the Americas, especially of the great border between North (United States) America and *mestizo* Latin America, between the WASP and the Catholic Mestizo, between the ancient religions, the Protestant, and the Catholic, as it is happening within my own self and within the millions of Mexican Americans who live in the great border between the United States and Latin America. All the barriers are broken through and something truly new begins to emerge.

For the emerging *mestizo* peoples of the world today, the pressing issue is not so much that of multiculturalism or the intercultural/interreligious dialogue which seems to presuppose division and separation, but the searching and probing of truly intercultural human beings who seek to conceptualize, articulate, and communicate the innermost (spirit-soul) and outermost (body-culture) nature of their new identity. This new identity defies even the most sacred barriers of humanity for that which alone is sacred to God: the all-inclusive human family. This is the great difference between the intercultural (religious) dialogue and the intercultural person—the former speaks out of separation, the latter speaks out of unity! Between the two partners of an interracial (cultural or religious) marriage, there will be dialogue, but their child will struggle to conceptualize and articulate his or her own proper identity which is definitely some of each parent, but equally something truly new.

This is happening right here in this city of San Diego where we are meeting for this conference, in my own city of San Antonio, and throughout *la Frontera* of Mexico/United States. Old animosities are evolving into new partnerships and differences which had been feared are now being celebrated. Where does this take place? It's taking place in many places and in many ways, but most of all at the level of the gut and the spirit! Mexican tacos complement the all-American hot dogs at ball games while *mestizo* religious celebrations are becoming the common religious-civic symbols of entire cities.

For us today, *mestizaje* is both a fact and a great challenge. That we are *mestizo*—the proud heirs of great races, cultures, and religions—there is no doubt. What are we to do with this? This is the great question and challenge. How can we combine the most humanizing elements of our parent races and cultures to help form an even more human one with more opportunities for all? This will not take place overnight or even in one generation, but we must begin the process, and indeed we have begun.

Closing Remarks

Today, on the threshold of the Third Millennium, we have before us the possibility of total human annihilation or the beginning of the ultimate human family. A few months ago, it was predicted in the *Journal of Foreign Affairs* that the ultimate and most devastating war would be a religious ethnic war between the civilizations of the planet which would bring humanity to an apocalyptic end. I do not agree. I dare to think that we can make the difference in helping to usher in the ultimate human family wherein no one will be excluded, no one will be shamed, no one will be marginalized; I dare to think that we can expand the table fellowship of Jesus to the universal banquet-fiesta where no one will be excluded from the table of abundance; I dare to think of a planet where people will move freely within the planetary human household; I dare to think of the day when we can all pray together to the God who is greater than our best expressions of God.

Idle dreams? Let me assure you we have begun, in a very small way, but we have begun. Every year on the feast of Thanksgiving, Muslims, Jews, Buddhists, Hindus, Native Americans, Orthodox, Catholics, Protestants, Fundamentalists of all races and backgrounds join at San Fernando Cathedral in San Antonio, Texas to celebrate a foretaste of what we all want to become: the human family. Our desire is to become a human family united as the very diversity which previously divided us and opposed us to one another and which still makes us enemies of each other in many parts of the world. Now, however, in the power of the Spirit, we pray that in our very diversity, we might be a source of enrichment and encouragement to each other and united in harmony by the glory of God! If the second creation after the great flood could start through Noah's Ark, then why cannot the new humanity of the Third Millennium begin through the prayer of religions at San Fernando Cathedral—the oldest cathedral sanctuary of the United States?

PART FOUR

Sin, Forgiveness, and the Experience of God

INTRODUCTORY ESSAYS

Vivir en la gratitud

Elizondo's Contribution to Theological Anthropology

Carlos Mendoza-Álvarez

Life at the Borders

The first time I met Virgilio, he was standing in front of a viceroyal picture by the great painter Cabrera. The painting represented a preaching angel who was announcing new times. With a smile, Virgilio welcomed me with a warm embrace as someone who is used to crossing borders to go out and meet the other. With his unique restless look, he asked me: What are young Mexicans saying about today's Latin American theology? That encounter took place at the University Parish in Mexico City on the occasion of the presentation of a new theological journal, *Anamnesis*. The journal's objective was to enhance the discussion on speaking about God in Latin America by giving the floor to Latin American youth and taking into account the foundational contributions of liberation theology, but with the desire to open up the discussion to the crisis of modernity, a crisis already being felt as a growing avalanche under the names of globalization and exclusion. This took place in 1991.

From that time on, I have always been in personal contact with Virgilio in terms of our common projects: the exchange of works, discussions in Mexico about such problems as inculturation, the theology of Indians, the violence in Chiapas, and the new faces of secularity in the megalopolis of the South. In seeing him and listening to him, I have always been surprised by his fresh outlook on the world, his critical sense in the presence of idols which conceal the living God. But I am especially amazed when I feel his vibrant and personal interest for popular religiosity and, in those gestures and symbols of a poor people, his living the pristine faith expression of the believer who cries out to heaven. I have learned to read these foundational realities of the act of faith in a new light and, above all, with hope.

During a recent trip to Mexico, on the occasion of the Second Conference of the Faculty of Theology of the Pontifical University of Mexico in 1997, Virgilio spoke at length about his personal experience as a believer, especially about the identity crisis he had to face as a Mexican American, that is, as a cultural minority within a racially diverse society that is so powerfully seduced by the American dream. There, ever since his youth, Virgilio learned to practice tolerance and peaceful coexistence among different traditions. He also repeatedly met the signs of exclusion on the basis of cultural plans of domination:

> Through the years, I have learned that my experience of tolerance, fraternity, and communion was the great exception. As a rule, this does not happen in the United States, in other countries, and even less in the world . . . Even though there is a great deal of dialogue about being open to the other, we still have to admit that there is a profound and radical resistance . . . This openness to the other seems impossible for the political, cultural, academic, and religious institutions marked by the worldview of the West. For several centuries, white Western men have considered themselves as the normative models of the universal being . . . From the West, this has also given an interpretation to our Christian religion by regarding it as superior to all others and the basis from which other religions had to be judged.[1]

Yet, in this land of modern illusions, an inhospitable place for outsiders, Mexican Americans learned to live a historical and existential[2] exodus that would lead them to proclaim the *mestizo* God. This is the God who, as in Jesus the Nazarene in Israel, lives itinerancy, experiences borders, and generates an alternate world by his practice of universal love: the reign of God that has come to the people waiting for messianic times.

Therefore, Virgilio's theological thinking is not an invention without roots in his land or apart from his historical path as part of a people in search of their identity. The living God has given marvelous signs to the poor and, in particular, to European/indigenous *mestizos* in the event of Tonantzin-Guadalupe.[3] This event is a sign of hope from the other side of the Spanish conquest and the start of a new America.[4]

According to an Elizondian contextual rereading of this foundational event of *mestizo* identity, God continues to enlighten and to attract the least ones by leading them through the new borderlands that are prevalent in our days of technical and scientific modernity: globalization, the free market, the concentration of wealth, and the exclusion of the growing mass of workers-consumers. From this historical nonplace for the poor and precisely there at the margin of official history, God continues to call God's people to learn to be witnesses of life by creating places of communion and historical solidarity.

Thus, Virgilio is one of the first and most original interpreters of such a mystical and political itinerary for the Latin American people in social and economic exile: an emigrant people at the center of power but kept at the periphery as a sign of contradiction from which God manifests God as the God who removes the nails from crucified peoples.

The Foundational Experience: Gratuitousness

Fourteen years ago, Virgilio wrote: "Sin could kill [Jesus] but it could not destroy the power of unlimited love."[5] The fundamental conviction of Virgilio

Elizondo's narrative theology is the total affirmation of the human being as the living image of God. As a matter of fact, in his various works on theological anthropology, Virgilio tells us about the existential adventure of believers; he relates their experience of gratuitousness in the midst of a conflict that is expressed as historical violence and as vicious circles of victim-executioner, perverted power. Such processes are expressed through the interiorization of personal and collective resentment and the appearance of many faces that are denied the original vocation of the human condition.

In his article on forgiveness and memory, Elizondo situates us at the heart of the existential theology which emerged after the war in the North Atlantic world (Bonhoeffer) but which is read from the perspective of a new cultural context in the light of the original contributions of Gutiérrez's theology of liberation in the Catholic world and of Alves in the Protestant world. Thus, he examines the theological experience of the Mexican American people and its universal meaning from the perspective of their historical particularity.

In this reflection that theologically accompanies the historical journey of this believing people, we can distinguish at least three levels in Elizondo's theological discourse:

(a) The phenomenology of resentment understood as the description of the subjectivity which, at first, takes refuge in the pain caused by the offense. This is a process which turns to physical, psychic, and social self-destruction.

(b) The emergence of God's justice as the key to interpreting and to overcoming the conflict: in the praxis of Jesus of Nazareth, we find the fundamental religious and human attitude which enables us to overcome fratricidal violence through trust in "the power of unlimited love lived out even unto the extreme."[6] This practice of unlimited love introduces us into the divine dimension. It frees us from resentment and from revenge, thanks to the witness and the spirit of Jesus, and it enables us to initiate a new path which is salvation in history.

(c) The start of messianic times appears precisely through the new life generated by this qualitative leap: a leap which goes from the offense done to the innocent to the living memory of the free human being overcome with forgiveness, absence of resentment, and gratuitous love. Thus, Virgilio writes, "The ultimate basis for human relations would no longer be the offenses we commit against one another but the love which is capable of transcending the pain and bitterness of the offenses."[7]

In this sense, the experience of the resurrection—the principle of Christian identity in the world—is primarily rooted in this new and strong empowerment for loving relationships as soon as we existentially unite ourselves with the crucified and risen Jesus *who remains free to love and to proclaim forgiveness.*

The messianic times, which are inaugurated by the eschaton, begin, therefore, with this prophetic memory of the cross by which we confess that Jesus preferred to die rather than to hate; such a hatred would have meant breaking up his loving relationship with others, with the world of creatures, and with his Father. According to this Elizondian reading, we can state that the crucified and risen One becomes the beginning of new human relationships because *believing in Jesus allows us to live like Jesus.* This new humanity appears on the horizon of communities which are subjected to the vanity of the systems of modern exploitation as a sign of contradiction for the powerful and a sign of consolation for the least ones.

Therefore, the soteriology proposed by Elizondo in an incarnational approach assumes two original anthropological dimensions, namely: (a) the overcoming of the fratricidal historical conflict (rereading of *peccatum mundi*) and (b) its significance for human relationships freed from resentment as the beginning of a new creation in gratuitousness (*gratia liberans*). Liberation and glory are, therefore, the revolving points of the soteriological path experienced by the Mexican American people, a path which is described in vivid words by our author.

Evil as Structural Violence

Criticism of Modernity

Elizondo's thinking on the experience of sin and forgiveness, however, is not only centered on the subjective aspect (psychological and theoretical) of the salvation brought by Christ Jesus. The author's prophetic conscience, cultivated in his experience as a believer who forms part of an oppressed people,[8] along with his closeness to European progressive theology and to the Latin American theology of liberation, enabled him to ponder over that other constitutive aspect of theological anthropology: the social (collective, ideological, structural) dimension of evil in which the experience of God takes place as the proclamation of a new world.

The historical consciousness of the people originating on the American continent (also called Indian people) reaches us as an original rereading in the pluricultural context of Elizondo's theology. In the past, in 1492, as today at the beginning of the millennium, the victims of modernity continue to cry out to heaven: "underpaid workers, slaves, exploited migrants, abandoned elderly and sick people, expelled peoples"[9] and so many other victims over whom the techno-scientific civilization is rising.

According to Elizondo, the civilization crisis which the world is experiencing at the end of the millennium is due to the idolatrous subject of modernity which is reflected in the Western models of success, progress, science, and efficiency.[10] The modern ego has destroyed the other (Indians, blacks, migrants) by denying their identity, exploiting and enslaving them for the self-affirmation of the Western hegemonic subject. In this sense, with the Latin American philosophers of liberation[11] of the postmodern era, we can say that Elizondo shares a common trait which is prevalent in the culture of fragmentation: disillusionment in the presence of the emancipation meta-accounts of the North Atlantic West and prophetic criticism in the presence of the idols of modern reason.

Reading in the Spirit of Jesus

Elizondo's approach as a believer brings something of his own, however, the technocrat model did not limit itself to destroying the faces of others in that epic of the modern and enlightened "I." This model has also reached the point of manipulating the idea of God to its own advantage: " 'God' has been recreated to the image and likeness of the dominant culture."[12]

Structural violence is the greatest sign of the sin of a world which creates victims of exclusion: the unemployed, women, Indian people, the unskilled, sexual minorities. These victims of modern reason constitute a major theological locus: God is revealed in the history of the victims in order to change the logic of domination and death that modern idolatries generate. As Virgilio states, "God does not will victimization, but uses the victims to bring salvation to all—victims and victimizers alike."[13]

The radicalness of the *Deus liberans* consists in God's infinite love for humankind that is assumed through the incarnation of the Logos in the history of Jesus the Nazarene. This is true because "God sends his Son to enter into ultimate solidarity with the victims of this world by himself being born a victim—Jewish (world's outcasts), Galilean (despised by the Jews), and son of Mary (of questionable parentage). Jesus lived a constantly victimized life and died a victim."[14]

The lordship of Jesus of Nazareth over the powers of death is, therefore, manifested as a historical power of liberation from situations of exclusion so that history, as a theological locus, is not only read in abstract, deductive, and transcendental terms. It is also read in historical and conflictive terms where God takes the side of the marginalized: the widows, the poor, the orphans, and the aliens of every epoch of history. The Nazarene is master of life in the sense that he enables us to be free from resentment and from the desire for revenge in order to create communion at the heart of human relations of power and violence and, thus, inaugurates the reign of God through the power of the Spirit of the Lord of history.

Elizondo sees the experience of the basic ecclesial communities in Latin America as a hopeful sign of the power of the crucified and risen One in the history of oppression-liberation. It is there that the poor become subjects of their own history. It is there that the God of Jesus and of all the just of history takes on a concrete face which summons us to convert all idols into the only true God. Furthermore, it unites us in the practice of ethical solidarity which generates a new world on the basis of the poor of the earth.

The Attitude of Believers: Eschatological Imagination

The Experience of Believers

Historically situated in the midst of the conflicts of unjust and violent power, the community of believers seeks to construct alternatives of humanization which are eschatological signs of new times. Thus, for example, the social movements of the human rights of blacks (Martin Luther King) and of Hispanics (César Chávez) in the United States during the last decades symbolize the return of the people of God to the margins of history where they mark out new paths in which the "victims took the lead"[15] in transforming society. This is not, however, to repeat the spiral of domination and violence that plagues the world. Instead, with great effort, believers attempt to build up a society of humanism, fellowship, and tolerance which is a historical parable of Jesus' promise of new life. As the Christ of God, he made this promise to those who would follow in his footsteps by believing in him.

In this sense, speaking of Christian eschatology in Elizondian terms inevitably sends us back to the poor's historical struggles for liberation because it is there that God is revealed as God of the people. God sustains them with a providential hand so they may be a living hope, evoking salvation for all, the victims as well as the executioners.

Overcoming historical resentment becomes the beginning of the end time and brings us closer to God's reign, which transfigures our human history: "The resurrected peoples of the Americas are the ones who will usher in the truly new humanity of the Americas. They are the people of hope."[16]

Eschatology and history blend into a salvific[17] becoming that announces a new world from the underside of history, in the here and now of the history of oppression of Latin and Mexican American people.

Human temporality has been overcome by the reign of God. This means that all human realities (and even more realities dealing with creatures) are being transfigured into the dynamism of eternal life, a life that starts from the rescue of the victims of fratricidal violence, which is accomplished in the Passover of Jesus. The Good News is, therefore, the coming of God-with-us as new networks are being woven, networks of new social, political, and cultural relations that promote life in all its forms. This is especially true in terms of life that is denied by mechanisms of injustice and cultural and racial intolerance, as well as by systems of economic and religious exclusion.

The existence of believers is, therefore, a historical narrative of salvation. We are dealing with the same reality which Schillebeeckx[18] called the account by which God is telling his story of love for creation in its most profound dynamism: the love which can do all things in the foundational, creative action that is God.

Eschatological Imagination

The messianic time inaugurated by Jesus of Nazareth has a historical dimension constitutive of the new order willed by God. This dimension provides structure and order for the Elizondian anthropological project which is based on the following fundamental aspects:

(a) Life for Victims

The vocation of the Messiah consists in "rescuing the poor who were crying out" (Ps. 71), as the ancient prophetic tradition of Israel declares in its Davidic messianic model. But the Hebrew and Christian Scriptures also bear witness to the mercy of God's action in the vindication of the just. God does not rescue innocent victims in order to glorify them as new sovereigns and executioners but to bring forth an alternative world on the basis of the actualization of that history which manifests the merciful heart of the holy God, a God who fills his anointed One (Jesus, his people) with the power of his enlivening Spirit.

(b) Forgiveness for Executioners

It is not enough to liberate the poor as if they were just passive recipients. It is also necessary to allow ourselves to be animated by the exuberance of universal love which is manifested in the forgiveness of executioners and in the establishment of networks of relationships transformed by justice and love. We should not forget, however, that Elizondo is not referring to the exaltation of resignation or abnegation in the presence of the power of the oppressor-sinner. Instead, we are dealing with the reversal of the mechanisms of exclusion and violence so that corrupt worlds, fruit of the iniquity of conceited hearts, may be left behind to give way, step by step—thereby opening up history to the living memory that forgives—to a new humanity. This new humanity overcomes resentment and hatred without neglecting to do justice and to ask for some retribution of oppressors for the evil they have done.

(c) Restoration of the New Order

The interpersonal dimension of divine liberation is the third aspect of Virgilio's anthropology. In this sense, the power of the crucified and risen One manifests itself in terms of our ability to give ourselves in relationships with others: "the goodness of persons [is seen in] how they give themselves to others, relate to others."[19] In fact, the meaning of eschatology is the gestation of a new humanity: in the claiming of our own identity (personal and collective) over and above historical oppression, an identity which is expressed in terms of human relationships marked by communion in our differences, in the fraternal sharing of those who know they are eternally loved by their Father in the power of the Spirit of the Son.

This anthropological substratum enables us to set up an interpretation of the church in terms of an eschatological community, situated in conflictive history, where the pacification of the human heart is being accomplished through the practice of justice by following Jesus Christ.

New forms of community are thus emerging as alternatives to an idolatrous society and as authentic theological loci at the heart of modernity and its crises. In this regard, Elizondo is telling us: "The need to be willing to take risks, to let certain cultural expressions of church die, is essential so that new expressions of church may come forth, so that the church will be renewed. We need to believe in the paschal mystery in our religious institutions, our dioceses, and our parishes."[20]

The church is a sign of eschatological salvation as long as it affects historical processes as the people of God journeying toward liberation and glorification. The church's mission is rooted in the power to communicate the grace of Jesus Christ in experiences where historical misfortune has distorted the faces of those who are being crucified. Being a witness of the Passover of the Lord makes the church a prophetic voice that denounces modern and postmodern idolatries (in the world as well as within the church itself) and affectively and effectively consoles the excluded by spreading hope in God's reign which is coming to us.

New Challenges

The Crisis of Modernity

Elizondo's theological works are a living witness to the thinking of a believer who is journeying with his migrant people. By invoking the God of the prophets, the God of Abraham and of Jesus of Nazareth, and the maternal love of the mother of the Lord,[21] Elizondo is summoning us to a process of sociopolitical, cultural, and believing commitment in which we can discover the amazing aspects of God's unfathomable love for little ones.

Besides his insights about the drama of modernity with its sequels of injustice, hunger, and exclusion, in Elizondo's theology we also find new questions which appear on the horizon of a new millennium. We find a critical reading of modernity which gives an account of the good things caused by techno-scientific reason over and beyond the liberal optimism of some North American postmodern people. What they call pragmatic correctives to neoliberalism is an ideology which justifies the logic of capital as an omnipotent value. We need a critical reading of modernity.

With Elizondo, we can go on with the investigation into the causes of the growing abyss between the rich and the poor, the economic mechanisms of the international public debt which is suffocating poor countries, the absence of ethical criteria in the market economy, and so many other structural problems which are weighing heavily on Western societies of a South that is overcome by premodern, modern, and postmodern worlds.

As a matter of fact, modernity is an age of crisis at its very foundations. This calls for a restating of the ethical dimension of the economy. It is precisely here that the reference to faith can contribute new light in terms of the transcendent meaning of human society, actualizing the prophetic word of Jesus Christ and his message of the reign of God as the beginning of the fullness of time.

Toward a Theological and Relational Anthropology

When postconciliar theology took up the questions about God, which emerged with an existential and political undertone, it generated a vast production of writings that attempted to cast the salvific event in the immanence of history and of the human condition. Without a doubt, the contribution of European progressive theologies and Latin American theologies of liberation are two of the most significant fruits of this effort by contemporary theology to make the message of faith in modern times both significant and credible.[22]

Elizondo's thinking was nourished by both currents of ecclesial thought: first, when he was a student in Paris, and later, as a pastor and theologian in Texas. He proclaimed his own word in this theological and social agora. He contributed his reflection to the group Concilium which, in its editorial policy, brought up the challenge of assuming modernity and exclusion as coordinates in order to speak about the living God.

Nevertheless, in the course of the sixties, theological anthropology was laboriously starting to build up its own categories to give an account of the structure of the new life in Christ Jesus, of the mechanisms of finiteness and grace, and also of the real incidence of God's love in human beings. All this is shown in the works of Rahner, Schillebeeckx, and González Faus. The past two decades have seen the emergence of various proposals for a theological and relational anthropology.[23] The guiding line of this discourse is the edification of people in their ecological and relational milieu. This edification is indicated by calling for a new conceptual recipient which tells about the event of the gift of the crucified and risen One in the heart of the relational experience of human beings.

In this context of theological reflection, Elizondo's work is precisely situated in the transition toward new forms of reflection about the fundamental themes of anthropological theology such as grace, sin, and eschatology. The narrative feature of his written works, based on his vast pastoral experience, has been a vibrant theological anamnesis situated in the context of modern frontiers. The pastoral consequences of the road he has traveled have further implications for ecclesiology and the theology of the mystery of God's Trinity.

Ecclesial Places of Diversity

While Elizondo's contribution to contemporary ecclesiology has been evaluated in other essays in this celebrative volume, it is fitting to say that an ecclesial model, with a vast outreach in today's world, is derived from Virgilio's basic anthropological discourse which has been briefly described here.

By its contextual aspect, reflection on the grace of Christ Jesus announces salvation in the histories of people situated in life-death processes, people who are anxious to find liberation and hope, especially for those who are left out of history. The work of the Spirit of the Messiah of God in his people brings forth historical and human processes of liberation from resentment (interpersonal subjectivity) and from oppression (historical objectivity) in such a way that we are re-creating a network of solidarity which is more than an eloquent gesture in catastrophic situations. It is an attitude of loving surrender in the image of the crucified and risen One in whom all things have been renewed since he is "the firstborn of all creation" (cf. Col. 1:12-20).

Consequently, the church actualizes its identity, its sacramental and ethical mission, in the footsteps of the living Lord insofar as it is an efficacious sign of the love of Christ Jesus at the heart of these historical and interpersonal processes. By creating therapeutic communities in the power of the Spirit as authentic ecological niches of realization of human beings in conflictive modern history, the church is "the salt of the earth and the light of the world" for a pluralistic and democratic society on its way to the reorganization of justice for all.

The ecclesial places of diversity arise as a challenge for the actualization of Christ's love in these times of modernity in crisis: *Ecclesia ab Abel*, open to the experience of God for all the just and the innocent of history. These "ecclesial places" find their main locus in the experience of Jesus of Nazareth, the head of the new humankind because of his love which was creative of a new order.

Virgilio Elizondo's theological reflection resonates in the Catholic Church and beyond its boundaries by announcing a new world which is possible thanks to the power of God's love. Elizondo's theology is a critical and narrative word that announces the works and wonders of God's preferential love for the poor and the disinherited of the earth, a love which was fully manifested in the words and works of Jesus of Nazareth, proclaimed by the church as the Messiah and the Son of God.

(Trans. Colette Joly Dees)

Notes

[1]Virgilio Elizondo, "Pluralismo y verdad: espacios de tolerancia, fraternidad y comunión en la sociedad y en la Iglesia," in E. Castillo et al., eds., *Secularidad y cultura contempornea: Desafíos para la teología* (Mexico: UPM, 1998) 81-83.

[2]Virgilio Elizondo, "*Mestizaje* as a Locus of Theological Reflection" 159-175 above.

[3]Virgilio Elizondo, *Guadalupe: Mother of the New Creation* (Maryknoll, NY: Orbis, 1997) 107.

[4]Cf. Virgilio Elizondo, "Pluralismo y verdad: espacios" 88.

[5]Virgilio Elizondo, "I Forgive But I Do Not Forget" 212 below.

[6]Ibid. 211 below.

[7]Ibid. 213 below.

[8]Elizondo, "*Mestizaje* as a Locus of Theological Reflection" 159-175 above.

[9]Virgilio Elizondo, "Evil and the Experience of God" 225 below.

[10]Cf. Virgilio Elizondo, "Unmasking the Idols" 217-224 below.

[11]See especially Enrique Dussel's significant work, *La ética de la liberación en tiempos de la globalización y la exclusión* (Madrid: Sígueme, 1998).

[12]Virgilio Elizondo, "Evil and the Experience of God" 226 below.

[13]Ibid. 227 below.

[14]Ibid.

[15]Ibid. 231 below.

[16]Ibid.

[17]Cf. Gustavo Gutiérrez, *Teología de la liberación. Perspectivas* (Madrid: Sígueme, 1980) 199-226.

[18]Edward Schillebeeckx, *Los hombres. Relato de Díos* (Madrid: Sígueme, 1994) 217-223.

[19]Elizondo, "Unmasking the Idols" 222 below.

[20]Elizondo, "Unmasking the Idols," *SEDOS* 24 (15 May 1992):138 (taken from the transcript of a question and answer session not reprinted in this volume).

[21]Elizondo, *Guadalupe: Mother of the New Creation* 115-136.

[22]See the interesting and crucial confrontation between both theologies in Christian Duquoc, *Liberación y progresismo* (Madrid: Sígueme, 1990).

[23]Cf. Barbara Andrade, *¿Creación? ¿Pecado?* (Mexico: Universidad Iberoamericana, 1992); James Alison, *The Joy of Being Wrong: Original Sin through Easter Eyes* (New York: Crossroad, 1998).

Sin, Forgiveness, and the Experience of God

Justo L. González

Since one of the articles that follows deals with not forgetting, it is essential, as I begin this introductory essay, to remember some of our common course together—Fr. Elizondo's and my own. We met many years ago, as I recall, in connection with the efforts around the Fund for Theological Education, Inc. to provide funding for Hispanics in theological education. This itself is one of the facets of Elizondo's work that must not be forgotten: he has been a mentor to an entire generation, not only of pastors and theologians, but also of musicians, liturgists, and lay leaders. Virgil's writings are a very important part of his work, and to them I shall return shortly; but even more important is the work he has performed as a pastor and as a mentor, encouraging and making it possible for others to study, working with musicians trained in classical and traditional liturgical music so that they may be empowered to produce a music more consonant with the Mexican American milieu, and providing in the Mexican American Cultural Center a place where such explorations, and many others, could take place.

Then I came to know Virgil as a priest and a pastor. Under his leadership, the Cathedral of San Fernando in San Antonio became a place of welcome, not only for his own parishioners, nor only for visiting Catholics, but even for a "separated brother" such as myself—who in San Fernando never felt "separated"! In the eucharistic celebration at San Fernando I truly experienced the presence of Christ.

Finally we became colleagues and our friendship increased. Eventually I asked him to write a foreword to a book of mine and in it he came up with the intriguing and very true notion that while I am a "catholic Protestant," he is a "protestant Catholic." Interestingly, the book for which he wrote the foreword was awarded that year the "Virgilio Elizondo Award" by the Academy of Catholic Hispanic Theologians in the United States (I am not sure whether the book or the foreword got the award, but that is another matter!).

The manner in which the framers of the present volume have arranged the topic with which I am to deal shows a keen insight into Elizondo's theology. They have joined "sin, forgiveness, and the experience of God." Since the volume does not include a separate section on the doctrine of God, this means that the editors have joined subjects that Peter Lombard would have kept apart, discussing one in the first book of his Sentences, and the others in his second and third books. And yet, although this combination might have seemed quite strange to Peter Lombard, and probably also to Thomas Aquinas, it is quite natural when it comes to discussing Elizondo's theology.

As the reader of the essay "Evil and the Experience of God" will readily note, although Elizondo subscribes to the traditional assertions having to do with divine revelation in creation, he insists that God is most clearly revealed where we must come to grips with sin and the need for forgiveness: "it is precisely in contrast to our own vengeance, cruelty, and callousness that the most fascinating tenderness, kindness, and compassion of God becomes most gloriously experienced and revealed."[1] Or, later in the same essay: "God was supremely revealed and experienced at one of the most unreligious and least spiritual moments of human history: the cruel and bloody execution of an innocent victim."[2] For him, the true knowledge of God begins with the experience of forgiveness. It is also there that the true image of God in human beings is manifested.

Yet, this is not a cheap forgiveness. It does not mean that Elizondo undervalues the power of evil, nor its structural, societal, and oppressive nature. This is not the traditional liberal call for a forgiveness that leaves things as they are and allows evil and injustice to continue. The very title of the first of the essays that follow shows this: "I Forgive But I Do Not Forget."

Without repeating what Elizondo has said much better than I could, there are some points in that essay that merit special attention.

First of all, it is important to note that Elizondo does not privatize sin. Nor does he limit his perspective to that of the sinner. On the contrary, he clearly takes the position of the sinned-against. This is not to say he claims that those who have been victims of others have no sin. That is an all too common caricature of any theology that seeks to speak a word of justice on behalf of the sinned-against. What Elizondo is saying is that when Christians—in this case minority, Mexican American Christians—look at sin, they must deal, not only with their own sin, but also with the sin that has been committed against them.

Yet, this is not a matter of vengeance, nor even of venting anger. On the contrary, Elizondo very forcefully argues that vengeance in itself is sinful. He refers to this as "the only way we as humans . . . can wipe out an offense,"[3] meaning that this is the "natural," "sinful" way. But then he moves on to argue that when the sinned-against try to wipe out an offense by offending the offender, they themselves sin, and therefore "the ultimate sinfulness of sin itself and its greatest tragedy is that it converts the victim into a sinner."[4]

Although Elizondo does not pursue the matter further, it is clear that what we have here is a particular understanding of original sin and the manner in which it functions. Indeed, it would be interesting and probably quite productive to follow this line of thought. The sin with which we are all born is, at least in part, the sin imposed on us by the very fact that even before birth we have been oppressed and dehumanized by an entire societal structure which in turn is based on sin and further advances sin. If this is the case, the original sin which we all carry, and from which we cannot be liberated on our own, is not merely a trait we have inherited from our ancestors, a stain from which we must be cleansed, but an actual oppression which in turn forces us to respond with further oppression, vengeance, and resentment.

To forget such a sin committed against us—be it "original" or "actual," societal or individual—is not in truth to be free from it. It is to ignore it while it probably continues functioning. It is to flee from it and therefore in a sense still to be subject to it, determined by it, powerless before it.

Hence the motto "I forgive but I do not forget," which may sound angry and even vindictive, but is in fact the indispensable condition under which true forgiveness can take place.

Shortly after writing this essay, as the quincentennial of the so-called "discovery" of the Western hemisphere approached, Elizondo edited, jointly with Leonardo Boff, an issue of *Concilium* entitled *1492-1992: The Voice of the Victims.*[5] Since Elizondo has written much about *mestizaje*, it is not surprising that Elizondo writes about the atrocities and injustices his Spanish ancestors committed against his Indian ancestors. As *mestizos*, Elizondo and all other Hispanics carry in our veins the blood of both oppressors and oppressed, colonizers and colonized. This we cannot forget, but we must forgive. Were we to forget it, we would forget our own identity. Were we not to forgive it, we would be constantly and perennially at war with ourselves. Therefore, the *mestizo* is particularly well placed to see the need for what Elizondo suggests: to forgive, but without forgetting.

This forgiving without forgetting, which is part of our own being, is then extended to our relations with all who have offended us or sinned against us. Just as we can and must forgive ourselves and our ancestors without forgetting, so can we, and so must we, forgive any who oppress us, but without forgetting!

Those who read these words from a different experience may see them as vindictive. This may be in part the result of not having been forced, within their own being, to forgive without forgetting, as the *mestizo* must do. It may also, however, be due in part to the hope on the part of those who sin against others, and who in so doing gain advantages of any sort, to be forgiven in such a way that the structures of oppression that give them an advantage are not challenged or destroyed.

Therefore, when reading this particular essay I invite the reader not to read vindictiveness into what Fr. Elizondo says, but rather to see in it the author's own painful yet liberating experience of self-forgiveness carried out into a project of forgiveness to all—but a forgiveness that does not forget!

Note then that this forgiveness is truly an act of grace—not grace on the part of the one who forgives, but God's grace allowing us to forgive. In a particularly insightful passage, Elizondo argues that to forgive is to uncreate, to undo what has been done; and since only God can create, only God can uncreate, and only God can ultimately forgive. What we do along these lines, we do in imitation of God and by the grace of God.

This leads to a clear contrast between God's true justice and what humans call "justice." From the merely human standpoint, forgiveness is the opposite of justice. In Elizondo's own words, "to our unjust humanity, the very justice of God appears as the annihilation of justice. And that is just what it is—the annihilation of the 'justice' of the unjust."[6]

Although Elizondo only implies this in passing, one should note that the notion of redemption that develops out of this understanding of God's justice is very different from that of Anselm in *Cur Deus homo*, or that of the more traditional, "orthodox" theories of the atonement. According to Anselm, in order to satisfy God's justice and offended honor, a payment had to be made—an infinite payment, because God's offended honor is infinite and therefore the guilt of the offender is equally infinite. Elizondo, on the other hand, implies that this is a very narrow understanding of God's justice, too much like human justice, and not like the justice we see in Jesus Christ. His statement, "the God of the Bible does not want victims,"[7] brings into question a view of Christ's work of long-standing and wide diffusion in Christian theology and piety. According to that view (which has influenced not only much of Western piety, but also much eucharistic doctrine), Christ is the victim offered in sacrifice for us—either because God's "justice" required such a victim, or because the Devil demanded his ransom.

This justice of Elizondo's God is very different from the justice of an offended medieval lord or a vindictive Puritan God. It is the justice of a God who

> sent his only Son to assume our human condition, to become flesh, to struggle through our temptations to do things our way, yet to remain obedient to God's way of mercy, forgiveness, and unconditional love. Love alone can be the principle of life. Thus the command of the Father was to rehabilitate humanity through the power of unlimited love lived out even unto the extreme. This is exactly what Jesus did.[8]

Thus, the Christian experience of God is both alien and liberating. It is alien, because it comes only from God, and it is the experience of a God whose justice is quite distinct from what we understand by justice. (Is it so distinct that there is not even an analogy? In his stress on the contrast between human and divine justice, Elizondo seems to approach the point at which there is not even an analogy, but only a stark contrast, between the two.) Yet it is also a liberating experience, because one who knows this forgiveness can then be liberated from the cycle of sin, in which the sinned-against must in turn respond in the same coin, and so on ad infinitum. And yet, forgiveness must not mean forgetfulness, for those who forget the sins committed against them are likely to commit the same sins against others. The reason why it is important for the *mestizo* Hispanic people to remember the history of their oppressions, both ancestral and more recent, is precisely to avoid committing the same injustice against others. Here one is reminded of the biblical injunction to the people of Israel not to oppress the alien, on the basis of not forgetting Israel's own oppression:

> You shall not deprive a resident alien or an orphan of justice; you shall not take a widow's garment in pledge. Remember that you were a slave in Egypt and the Lord your God redeemed you from there; therefore I command you to do this . . . When you gather the grapes of your vineyard, do not glean what is left; it shall be for the alien, the orphan, and the widow. Remember that you were a slave in the land of Egypt; therefore I am commanding you to do this. (Deut. 24:17-18, 21-22)

On the positive side, as Elizondo correctly declares, "the painful memories of the offense, healed through faith in Jesus, can be the greatest sources for a very fruitful ministry of reconciliation among today's aching humanity."[9] Again, here one is reminded of the passage from Deuteronomy just quoted, where the commandment to do justice (God's justice) to the alien, the widow, and the orphan is based on the memory of what God has already done for Israel.

Those of us who know Virgil Elizondo personally can attest that what he writes has become true in his life, and also that these lines help us understand much of the unique flavor of his ministry and personality. As he says, "If God forgives, who am I, sinner that I am, to condemn others?"[10]

This understanding of forgiveness is tantamount to conversion. Conversion is not the acceptance of a creed, nor is it merely joining a community of faith. It is not a change of religion. These are indeed connected with conversion; conversion, however, is the acceptance of God's forgiveness in such a way that we are not only convinced that we are forgiven, but also compelled to forgive others. When one is converted to Jesus Christ, one is converted to God's justice, to the way God does justice; one accepts it, not only as the standard by which God will measure one's own life, but also as the standard by which one will seek to measure others (Matt. 7:2). Being converted is not forgetting, but remembering in a way that leads to justice and reconciliation. It is for that reason that Elizondo bluntly states that "the real challenge to humanity is not one of forgetting, but one of converting."[11]

Thus, at the heart of the issue is an evangelistic call: the call to accept the good news of God's forgiveness, and to live out of such good news forgiving and remembering sin and injustice: forgiving as a way to reconciliation, remembering as a way to greater justice.

What results from this is a call for a thorough subversion of the existing order—a subversion so deep that it challenges not only the existing order, but also most of the existing programs of subversion. What Elizondo proposes is that "God is speaking to all of us through the cries of today's suffering servants."[12] Or, using a missionary paradigm, that just as the early missionaries came to these lands to unmask the idols of our native ancestors, so must we now listen to the missionary word of the victims, seeking to unmask our own hidden idols:

In the beginning of the Americas, the missionaries chastised the peoples of the Americas for what they considered to be their idols. It seems to me that today the gift of the suffering Christians of the Third World is to help us recognize those idols that we are convinced are life-giving but which are in effect draining us of life.[13]

Clearly, the destruction of the native gods was the most subversive act that the European colonizers performed in these lands—more subversive than the destruction of armies or the enslaving of millions. The destruction of the gods undermined the very basis of traditional society. Likewise, the destruction of the idols of Western civilization—which is what Fr. Elizondo proposes—would inevitably lead to the subversion of Western society as we know it. This is why we are so resistant to it. This is why we cling to our idols with even more zeal than the natives of these lands held on to theirs. And yet, if there was any measure of truth in the missionaries' claim that these native gods were not life-giving, there is even greater truth in the assertion that our present idols are not life-giving.

Elizondo lists those idols—or at least the most powerful among them. The first is money—the Bible would say Mammon—whose religion Elizondo describes as "the conviction that the more one obtains in life the more one is."[14] Few would argue that this description illuminates one of our most widespread and insidious idolatries. I would add that this religion has come to such a point that in its most prevalent form it bases human worth not merely on how much one obtains, but rather on how much one spends—or, in one of its most damaging versions among the poor and the middle class, on how much one owes! And I would also add that this religion has its own missionary movement in the economic globalization process, which brings more and more of the world into its sphere of influence, with dire consequences for the poor as well as for ancient cultures and traditions that cannot withstand the onslaught of "globalization." Describing how this affects the poor, Elizondo correctly states, "This is not just an economic oppression but an overall, englobing oppression of their way of life, their values, their customs, their heritage, their music, their ways of relating. A whole way of life has been stepped on."[15]

Significantly, Elizondo does not shy away from applying the same criticism to our religious institutions, which have "fallen into profit-making schemes because we want to make our religious institutions bigger and better."[16] In other words, the church itself has bowed before the idol, and it too is a worshipper of Mammon!

The second idol Elizondo seeks to unmask is pleasure, whose religion holds that "pleasure brings happiness." Elizondo challenges us: "We need to question this, to rediscover that suffering is part of happiness, that continued pleasure does not lead to happiness."[17] On this point, he would agree with Søren Kierkegaard that the "aesthetic life"—by which Kierkegaard meant a life lived on the basis of pleasure, even the most sophisticated pleasure, such as classical music—necessarily leads to despair. We must, however, note that the idol of pleasure goes much deeper than sex and fun—the two main examples that Elizondo gives in his article "Unmasking the Idols." The idol of pleasure includes any self-centered form of the very American quest after "self-fulfillment." Indeed, as one looks at North American culture in general, this is probably one of the most widely shared myths holding together an otherwise divided society. The poor child in the ghetto seeks self-fulfillment in a pair of running shoes, while the rich entrepreneur seeks it in building a megacorporation. People argue that they have the "right" to do this or to be that, not on the basis of the service they could offer, but simply and only on the basis of their own need for self-fulfillment. The fallacy in such arguments is not that self-fulfillment is bad or should not be sought, but that self-fulfillment can only be found in love and service to others. As Elizondo says, "happiness is realized only when one gives oneself to something which has meaning."[18] Or, as Jesus said, "Those who find their life will lose it, and those who lose their life for my sake will find it" (Matt. 10:39. Cf. Matt. 16:25; Mark 8:35; Luck. 9:24; 17:33; John 12:25).

Thirdly, Elizondo invites us to unmask the idol of beauty—or, more precisely, "our concept of the beautiful."[19] The problem in this regard is not that we value beauty; it is rather the sort of beauty that our society and culture value. Instead of the outer, superficial, and rather racist notions of beauty that prevail in our culture, "we need to rediscover that authentic, radiating beauty is the goodness of persons, how they give themselves to others, relate to others."[20]

Fourthly, and perhaps most important of all, Elizondo tells us that we must unmask the idol of power. I say that this is probably the most important of all because it touches on our understanding of God in a way that the other idols—money, pleasure, and beauty—do not. Few of us would say that money or pleasure are attributes of God. When we speak of God's beauty, most of us are well aware that this is not the superficial and racist beauty which Elizondo calls an idol. The case with power is different. One of the traditional attributes of God is omnipotence. We constantly sing hymns to God's power. This creates a connection between the divine and the powerful that has a direct bearing on the manner in which we organize society and how we value human beings. If God's very nature is to be powerful, then those who in our society are most powerful are most like God. The result is that society is seen as a hierarchy—or a series of hierarchies—in which those who stand closer to the pinnacle stand closer to God. Since they represent God better than the powerless ever can, any resistance to their authority and power is resistance to the power and authority of God. In short, the powerful God becomes the God of the powerful, for the powerful.

Elizondo tells us that this God is an idol, because the power of God is not like human power. On the contrary, we must learn to find "the real, ultimate power of the saving God in the powerlessness of Jesus of Nazareth. We need to unmask the way we identify the power and glory of God with the power and glory of this world's violence."[21]

At this point one is reminded of Luther's *theologia crucis*, as expressed above all in the Heidelberg Disputation of 1518. There he argues that a person deserves to be called a theologian only if he or she is one "who comprehends the visible and manifest things of God seen through suffering and the cross." Luther then goes on to explain that "true theology and recognition of God are in the crucified Christ," and that

> he who does not know Christ does not know God hidden in suffering. Therefore he prefers works to suffering, glory to the cross, strength to weakness, wisdom to folly, and, in general, good to evil. These are the people whom the apostle calls "enemies of the cross of Christ," for they hate the cross and suffering and love works and the glory of works.[22]

Obviously, in this passage Luther is arguing in part for his doctrine of salvation by faith rather than by works; yet there is here much more than that, and we would miss an important point were we to allow that controversy to obscure the point he is making. This point goes beyond the debated questions of soteriology and is an insight essential to the Christian faith: the power of God is different from human power. The power of God is manifested above all in the cross, in love so profound that it takes suffering upon itself.

It is this different understanding of power that makes Elizondo's proposal subversive. Although he is well aware of the unjust distribution of wealth in the world, and specifically in American society—his article on "Unmasking the Idols" deals most directly with North American culture and society—his proposal is not a mere redistribution of wealth, but a redistribution based on love and on a different understanding of the purpose of life and of the world's resources. Likewise, his antidote for the obvious misuse and abuse of power against the weak and the poor is not a turning of the tables, but a dethroning of the very understanding of power that leads to its abuse. It is this point that many in the dominant culture and in the higher echelons of our social hierarchy often fail to see—or do not wish to see. Elizondo and others like him, while refusing to forget the injustices of the present order, are willing to forgive those who profit from it and even those who promote it.

Forgiving without forgetting thus becomes a revolutionary, subversive program for Christian action in society—a program which subverts not only the existing power structure, but also any other similar power structure seeking to occupy its place. Significantly, the two heroes of the Civil Rights movement that Elizondo eulogizes in one of the articles that follow, Martin Luther King, Jr. and César Chávez, were people who insisted on forgiving without forgetting. Their power was precisely in their holding on to both of these—remembering and forgiving—with unbreakable resolve. By remembering, they called attention to the injustices perpetrated against their people, and against all the poor throughout the world. By forgiving they made it clear that their purpose was not to put themselves in the place of the old masters, but truly to build a world with no masters and no servants.

Certainly, this brought violence on both King and Chávez as well as on their followers. This was not a new violence, but simply the continuation and crystallization of a violence that had always been there. What it certainly did was unmask the violence by bringing it to bear upon those who clearly were themselves not violent. Violence usually justifies itself by claiming that it is necessary in order to "keep down" the expected violence of the oppressed. When, as in the cases of King and Chávez, violence is unable to provoke violence, it is unmasked for what it is: the oppressive, unjustifiable use of force to keep the victim as victim.

It is thus that Elizondo understands the work of Christ on the cross. "It is in the cross that the ultimate victimization of the weak is revealed."[23] "All had offended him, he refused to offend anyone. He refused to allow their offenses to be the basis of his relationship with them. This was the only way of breaking the curse."[24] As a result, in the cross, "the destructive cycle of victimization has finally been broken."[25] Likewise, both King and Chávez refused to be forced by violence into violence, and in so doing deprived the existing violence of any supposed justification.

In his writings, Virgil has recalled his own painful experiences on the way to becoming a Mexican American priest and theologian in the midst of a racist society and church.[26] Those who know him know that there is much from this experience that he would rather forget. We also know that, without forgetting, he has been able to forgive. Therein lies the power of his ministry. In his writings, in his conversation, through his own person and lifestyle, he has constantly shown that the power of the cross is still operative, that violence and injustice can still be unmasked and overcome by love. Let us never forget the lessons he has taught us!

Notes

[1]"Evil and the Experience of God" 225 below.
[2]Ibid. 228 below.
[3]"I Forgive But I Do Not Forget" 209 below.
[4]Ibid. 209-210 below.
[5]London: SCM, 1990.
[6]"I Forgive" 211 below.
[7]"Evil" 227 below.
[8]"I Forgive" 211 below.
[9]Ibid. 215 below.
[10]Ibid.
[11]Ibid.
[12]"Evil" 231 below.
[13]"Unmasking the Idols" 218 below.
[14]Ibid. 219 below.
[15]Ibid. 218 below.
[16]Ibid. 220 below.
[17]Ibid. 221 below.
[18]Ibid.
[19]Ibid.
[20]Ibid. 222 below.
[21]Ibid. 223 below.
[22]Heidelberg Disputation, theses 20-21, in Martin Luther, *Works*, 54 vols, ed. Helmut T. Lehmann, trans. Harold J. Grimm (St. Louis, MO: Concordia Publishing House, 1955-1958) vol. 31: 52-53.
[23]"Evil" 228 below.
[24]"I Forgive" 212 below.
[25]"Evil" 228 below.
[26]*The Future Is Mestizo: Life Where Cultures Meet* (Bloomington, IN: Meyer Stone, 1988); "Hispanic Theology and Popular Piety: From Interreligious Encounter to a New Ecumenism" 278-291 below.

ESSAYS BY VIRGILIO ELIZONDO

10. I Forgive But I Do Not Forget

(1986)

Virgilio Elizondo

Introduction

I grew up with the typical slogan of the United States, "Forgive and forget," and without question I assumed that forgiving was equivalent to forgetting and vice-versa. Yet forgetting was never easy and it often seemed that the more I wanted to forget, the more the memory of the past injury persisted. The hurt was still there. Had I not forgiven because I could not forget? Often new experiences of guilt accompanied the inability to forget—feeling guilty about not being able to forgive because I had not forgotten.

The first time I visited Paris, I went to the monument of the deportation of the French who had died in German concentration camps. When I first read the main inscription over the door, I was horrified! "Let us forgive but never let us forget." It was so totally contrary to everything that I had ever considered Christian. As this shocking idea kept turning in my mind, the thought came to me how Jesus had never asked us to forget yet the central message of his words and life was the forgiveness of one another. But was it possible to forgive without forgetting? All of a sudden I realized that the real virtue came in forgiving precisely while re-membering. Yet, if I could forget, I would not have to forgive—it would not even be necessary. On the other hand, remembering only too well the offense, I could forgive with all my heart. That is the very point of forgiveness. For to forgive is not to forget but to be liberated from the inner anger, resentment, and quest for vengeance that consumes every fiber of my being.

The Offender as Lord and Master of My Life

In this world where sin, confusion, and perversion continue to reign in so many unsuspected ways and through so many masks of righteousness, justice, law, and order, the biblical assessment of humanity continues to be quite true: "There is no one who is righteous, no one who is wise or who worships God. All have turned away from God; they have all gone wrong; no one does what is right, not even one. Their words are full of deadly deceit . . . they are quick to hurt and kill: they leave ruin and destruction wherever they go. They have not known the path of peace, nor have they learned reverence of God" (Rom. 3:10-18). There seems to be no way out, for even in our quest for justice and reconciliation we often seek violence to avenge the debts or injuries inflicted upon us. The criminal has to be punished! The crime has to be avenged! The hurt honor has to be restored by bringing the other to his/her knees. It seems that only a violent punishment can compensate for a violent crime.

So often the only way we as humans think we can wipe out an offense is by offending the offender. If I have been offended, I continue to rage until the offender has received what I think he or she deserves. But even when the offender has received punishment, peace and tranquillity are not yet forthcoming. The memory of the offense is still the source of anguish and turmoil. I still experience the bitterness or at least some disappointment. The resentment and the anger continue to rage within me. Frequently I will take it out on others without even realizing what I am doing.

The greatest damage of an offense—often greater than the offense itself—is that it destroys my freedom to be me, for I will find myself involuntarily dominated by the inner rage and resentment—a type of spiritual poison which permeates throughout all my being—which will be a subconscious but very powerful influence in most of my life. Often I will become irritable and insulting, difficult to get along with, and even malicious. I do not even recognize my own self. I begin even to hate my new self. I was not that way before, but I cannot help the feelings within me. I hate the offender for what he/she has done to me but in the very hatred of the other I allow them to become the lord and master of my life. Their life will become one of the dominant forces controlling my entire life. What is God waiting for? Why doesn't God hurry up and punish them?

Can the Jews forget the Holocaust? Can the Japanese forget Nagasaki and Hiroshima? Can the prisoners of war forget the German concentration camps? Can the Native Americans forget the European invasion, conquest, genocide, and domination? Can the Blacks of the Americas forget their generations of enslavement?

Can the child forget the beatings by his/her alcoholic parent? Can a spouse forget the infidelity of the other spouse? Can a friend forget the betrayal of a friend? Can a student forget the ridiculing of a teacher? Can a worker forget the dehumanizing insults of a supervisor? No matter how much one wants, no one can uncreate the past. What has happened has happened. We have to live with it; we have to cope with it; we cannot undo it; we can never completely wipe it out.

The deeper the hurt, the greater the controlling influence of the aftermath. It comes to the point when, as the scriptures say: "I cannot even understand my own actions. I do not do what I want to do but what I hate" (Rom. 7:15). Depression, anxiety, feelings of anger mixed with feelings of unworthiness and inferiority become part of my daily existence. Counseling, hard work, vacations, rest, medicine, group therapy—it all helps but nothing seems to restore my inner freedom, self-acceptance, and peace. Must I simply adjust to living my life in misery, dominated by the very person who offended me?

The ultimate sinfulness of sin itself and its greatest tragedy is that it converts the victim into a sinner. The offended feels in the very entrails of his/her being the need to demand payment in kind. It seems that the damage done by sin can only be repaired by sinning against the one who sinned, except that the action taken against the offender appears as necessary according to the demands of justice. The culprit must be punished—must receive what he/she deserves. The sin must be avenged and, in avenging it, the victim now becomes the sinner for he/she has repaid an evil action in kind! Thus not only has one sinned, but the reaction has made a sinner out of the victim.

The great tragedy is that this type of retaliation simply contributes to the growth and development of the expanding spiral of violence. Furthermore, the scars made to the heart, the memory, and the very soul of the hurt person are themselves a type of spiritual cancer which will simply eat away at the life of the victims. This causes them to be what they do not want to be—grouchy, cantankerous, with-drawn—and to do what they would otherwise not even think of doing—deceit, aggressiveness, jealousy, anger. "What a wretched person I am! Who can free me from this body under the power of death?" (Rom. 7:24). Humanly speaking, there seems to be no way out of the misery created by human beings.

Left to ourselves, repaying offense with offense, we would surely destroy our-selves for even when we have punished the offender, we are still cursed with the memory of the offense which brings out feelings of anger and disgust. Once of-fended, it seems that I will never really regain the peace, tranquillity, and compo-sure which existed before. Even when avenged, the cancer of the wounded heart is not healed but continues to eat away at the very life of the victim. Alone, we do not seem capable of rehabilitating ourselves. We appear condemned to misery for the rest of our lives; worst of all, we pass it on to successive generations in such ways that these types of retaliatory attitudes and actions become part of the historically developed functional nature of humanity. This mind-set becomes so deeply ingrained in our humanly developed ways of life that it not only appears and functions as natu-ral but even as demanded by divine righteousness.[1] Retaliation appears as a demand of nature and non-retaliation appears as weakness, cowardice, and even failure. We learn so well from previous generations and interiorize so deeply what we have re-ceived, that now the very heart demands retaliation as the only way it will be healed.

No wonder that some Jewish leaders said Jesus was blaspheming when he for-gave sins: humanly speaking, true and unconditioned forgiveness seems beyond our natural possibilities or even the deepest demands of the heart. For to forgive is to wipe out the offense. To forgive means to uncreate, but as only God can create out of nothing only God can return to nothing what has already come into exist-ence. So it is only God who can uncreate, it is only God who can truly forgive. Thus for men and women it seems that retribution is the only way to appease the pain created by the offense, yet retribution will never be full rehabilitation.

The Only True Lord and Master of Life

God created humanity. Humanity is the child of God. We are the product of God's genius and goodness. In the mystery of God's plan, God created us weak, limited, and imperfect and yet very good. Even as we have deformed ourselves, the God of infinite love does not forsake us. "God so loved the world that he gave his only begotten son, so that everyone who believes in him may not die but have everlasting life" (John 3:16). A mother loves her child all the more precisely because the child's sickly condition calls forth the loving and caring protection of the mother; it is even more so with God. The parent does not love the sickness, but because the sick child needs the help and assistance all the more, the parent is spontaneously pulled toward the child in need.

"Can a mother forget her infant, be without tenderness for the child of her womb? Even if she forgets, I will never forget you" (Isa. 49:15). Who can better understand God's unending and solicitous desire for the well-being of God's own children than a loving mother? Even when the child has committed all kinds of atrocities and has to be punished, the mother still wills not the destruction but the straightening up and well being of the child. Even when the child has gone to extremes, the loving mother who has tendered the child in her very womb knows beyond all the critical evidence that the child is good. The mother is not ignorant of the facts but she does possess that transrational knowledge of the heart that can pierce through all the external evidence and see the ultimate identity of the erring child— "I know that in spite of all things, my child is good." And the mother is absolutely right! The child is good!

The child might have committed all kinds of wrong-doings—even the worst imaginable. But the child, as a creation of God, is essentially good. The loving mother, despite all the condemning evidence, is right. And if the loving parent could give his/her life so that the sickly child could be rehabilitated and live, it is highly probable that the parent would give his/her life for the life of the child.

It is precisely this image which the Bible uses for God; God's mercy for erring humanity is portrayed from beginning to end as a mother's trembling womb. God's loving mercy is so great, especially in contrast to humanity's pressing quest for revenge and restitution, that it will even appear as unnatural. Even, I would dare say, unjust! According to the norms of justice of a sinful humanity that repays crime with crime, the justice of God who repays sin with loving forgiveness appears as totally unjust. God's justice appears as irrational according to the law of the talion. This law has become so deeply engraved in the hearts of sinful humanity—and all of us have been conceived in sin, born into sin, and contributed to our own sinfulness—that it appears as the ordinary way of civilized society. To our unjust humanity, the very justice of God appears as the annihilation of justice. And that is just what it is—the annihilation of the "justice" of the unjust.

Because the very law of society reproduced and propagated sin, vengeance, violence, and retaliation, the only way to prevent humanity from self-destructing was for God to become human and in his very self begin a new creation—a new humanity. So God sent his only Son to assume our human condition, to become flesh, to struggle through our temptations to do things our way, yet to remain obedient to God's way of mercy, forgiveness, and unconditional love. Love alone can be the principle of life. Thus the command of the Father was to rehabilitate humanity through the power of unlimited love lived out even unto the extreme. This is exactly what Jesus did.

Jesus remained obedient to God even when his people demanded his death. He remained obedient even when the people chose a recognized criminal over him and through his very silence won the release and liberty of the condemned (Luke 23:18-25) just as he had foretold at the very beginning of his public mission (Luke 4:18). He remained obedient even when his very closest friends left him and ran away. He was obedient even when it cost him his life on the cross. Yet throughout all this, he uttered not a curse, not a complaint, not one word demanding justice. All had betrayed him, yet he died with the words of forgiveness. He had been tempted, but he had triumphed. Sin had not been able to force him to sin! Even when all sinned against him, he remained steadfast in loving everyone. All had offended him, he refused to offend anyone. He refused to allow their offenses to be the basis of his relationship with them. This was the only way of breaking the curse which had crept into human history and which had become the ordinary and natural way of dealing with one another. "Father, forgive them for they know not what they do" (Luke 23:34): he finished with absolute confidence in God a mission which by all human standards appears to have been a colossal failure. "Father, into your hands I commend my spirit" (Luke 23:46).

In its justice, humanity had judged him, condemned him, sentenced him, and killed him. But it could not destroy him. Sin could kill but it could not destroy the power of unlimited love. In refusing to demand payment for the offenses committed against him, Jesus breaks definitively with the curse of humanity: offense for offense, crime for crime, insult for insult with the growing crescendo of evil continuing to destroy both individuals and society, both offender and offended alike. Jesus did not deny the offenses of humanity, but he denied the offenses the power to dictate and dominate the lives of others. By freely dying on the cross without a word of protest, Jesus breaks the curse and initiates the only true way to life. God raised him from the dead and confirmed his way as THE WAY—as the one and only way—if humanity is to be delivered from death unto life. Mercy and forgiveness are the only way to put a blunt end to the cancerous spread of sin and violence. There is no other way. Thus in his blood we were finally purified of the poison demanding that we repay sin with sin. In him the growing vicious cycle of life unto death was finally broken and we would now be able to make a new beginning.

From Enslavement to Freedom

Humanly speaking, as was stated in part 1 of this essay, once we have been offended, it is really impossible to escape the enslavement of vengeance leading me to "do the evil that I do not want to do" (Rom. 7:19). Even when I mask it over with rationalizations of justice and understanding, I cannot get away from an inner need to demand satisfaction. Yet this old self doomed to retaliation and even death has come to an end: "We know that our old being has been put to death with Christ in his cross, in order that the power of the sinful self might be destroyed, so that we might no longer be slaves of sin" (Rom. 6:6). Jesus broke the cycle of offense for offense. In this he initiated radical new possibilities for the human person, for human relations, and for society at large. The ultimate basis for human relations would no longer be the offenses we commit against one another but the love which is capable of transcending the pain and bitterness of the offenses.

If the law had been needed in order to curb and control our sinful inclinations, which even appeared as our natural ways, now the new life of love as the basis of all relations would certainly replace the law. As Augustine said, "Love God and do what you please." For the law is only necessary where sin and offenses abound but the law becomes superfluous and even ridiculous where love abounds. As the law had limited human destructiveness, grace would now open the way for new and unsuspected possibilities of the human spirit.

Total forgiveness seems so impossible for us because the memory of the offense keeps haunting us and urging us to demand payment. Thus the all important question becomes: Do we continue on our own human way of seeking retaliation for an offense only to find ourselves becoming new offenders? Or do we dare to believe in Jesus and be set free (Rom. 3:24-28)? It is this conversion from what has become our natural way to the way of Jesus that will enable us to forgive as only a God can forgive—without limit. To believe in Jesus is to trust him and have complete confidence in his way.

Everyone has sinned, but by the sacrificial death of Jesus, our wounded self has been rehabilitated. Our broken self has been put right with God, with others, and even with our own selves. We have been forgiven without any merit of our own. While we were still sinners, Christ died for us (Rom. 5:6). Jesus gave up his life rather than give in to offending us because we had offended him. At the cross he certainly remembered our offenses.

It was our very sinfulness that had demanded his crucifixion. But he will not be dominated by the fleshly demands for revenge. He remains free to love and proclaim forgiveness. He now makes it possible for us to do likewise. "He has brought us by faith into this experience of God's grace, in which we now live" (Rom. 5:2).

The way of Jesus seemed so absurd to a humanity for whom revenge and retaliation had become a natural way of life. People *believed in* what they considered justice and thought their desires were the demands of a just God who seemed to demand such actions. God seemed to demand what sinful humanity had constructed as just. Because Jesus forgave and taught us to forgive one another as God forgives us, the religious officials claimed he was blaspheming and even said he was possessed by the chief of demons (Mark 3:22; John 10:19-20); his own family thought he had lost his mind (Mark 3:21); the ordinary people thought he was altogether too much (Mark 6:3). Would we not have to admit that for most people, and I would dare say for many good Christians and church leaders, this is still the same reaction—we still feel that Jesus is just too much? The church grants sacramental absolution quite easily but often I wonder whether the very ones pronouncing the absolution have themselves fully accepted that the penitent is fully reconciled to God and to the community and that the offense has been wiped out. We still find it much easier to *believe in our own human ways than to believe in Jesus.*

To believe in someone is not just the weak belief that takes place when one is not sure about something. You believe something about someone when you are not sure. But belief in a person is not opposed to knowledge of the person. It is precisely when we know someone well and have confidence in the person that we *believe* in that person. When I know a doctor very well, and have full confidence in the abilities of the doctor, I find it easy to put my complete trust in him/her and do whatever I am told so as to regain my health. What I am told to do may appear as most unnatural, but because I have confidence in the abilities of the physician, I freely choose to do what I am told because I *believe in* the competence of the doctor.

To believe in Jesus is the beginning of our rehabilitation. It is through my faith in Jesus that I am redeemed from the death traps of our ordinary ways. For to believe in Jesus is to make his way our own and to follow in his footsteps, even when my flesh—my natural inclinations[2]—pull in the opposite direction. The more we believe in Jesus, the more that his very life becomes our own life and "If Christ lives in you, the Spirit of life is for you" (Rom. 8:9). This spirit crushes our sinful inclinations to revenge and vengeance. It is this spirit that brings about, not just an adjustment in the self, but a total rebirth into new life. "The Spirit of God makes you God's children and by the Spirit's power we can cry out to God: 'Abba, my Father' " (Rom. 8:15). It is this new life—the life of God's own life within us—that allows us to go beyond our natural inclinations. In Christ, former values and needs are reversed: "For those things which I used to consider as gain, I have now reappraised as loss in the light of Christ." (Phil. 3:7). And the true justice of God now reigns in place of the justice of an unjust humanity: "The justice I possess is that which comes through faith in Christ. It has its origin in God and is based on faith" (Phil. 3:9).

It is the belief in Jesus that regenerates us. It transformed Paul from the zealous persecutor of those who disagreed with him to the untiring apostle of God's unlimited and universal love for all men and women. Even when he was persecuted, beaten, jailed, and insulted, he continued to live and proclaim God's love and forgiveness. Stephen died, like Jesus, with the words of forgiveness for his assassins. The early martyrs went to their death not shouting curses or demanding justice but singing praises to the God of life. In all these cases, a new peacefulness had taken over. There was no burning desire for revenge and no righteous instinct crying for justice. Now, even if they were insulted, maligned, and killed, they could no longer be destroyed. When following our natural ways, even if we were not killed, we were often destroyed by our own inner feelings and gut emotions of anger, anxiety, hurt, disillusion, and disgust. We were condemned to a living death. But now there is a total reversal. Nothing can destroy the inner peace and tranquillity of someone whose heart has been transformed from stone to love.

Thus in forgiveness, it is not a question of forgetting the injuries or ignoring the hurt. In fact it is not even good to forget because if we forget, we might easily repeat the same offenses ourselves and if we are not aware of the hurt, we could easily be ignorant of the incredible hurt that we are able to inflict upon others, even without realizing it. Remembering can be a great teacher and even a source of growth and development in our abilities to be sensitive to others. Hurts transformed by love can be the greatest source of compassion for the hurts of others. The painful memories of the offense, healed through faith in Jesus, can be the greatest sources for a very fruitful ministry of reconciliation among today's aching humanity.

The real challenge to humanity is not one of forgetting, but one of converting. It is in converting to the way of God through our encounter and subsequent faith in Jesus that we make the radical and definitive break with the natural ways of justice and begin to enjoy the justice of God, which in this life repays curse with blessing, injury with pardon, theft with gift, insult with praises, and offense with forgiveness. "To be controlled by human nature results in death; to be controlled by the Spirit results in life and peace" (Rom. 8:6). A new "natural law" begins to function and thus we no longer do what we are urged to do by the pull and pressure of our human customs and traditions but what we are empowered to do by the Spirit. It is not for us to judge or punish, for in the end it will be God who alone knows the secrets of the heart and who will dispense the true justice of the final judgment.

Forgiveness is love surpassing righteousness and divine mercy transcending human justice. Jesus freely accepted death rather than break his loving relationship with others—friends or enemies. Even though the cowardly actions of the apostles on the first Good Friday certainly merited his disgust and at least a good scolding, Jesus does not allow the betraying action of his followers to be the basis of his relationship with them. His love transcends the demands of the human yearnings of the fleshly heart. The first act of the Risen Lord is to go to the apostles not to scold them or demand apologies, but to offer them total and unconditional shalom. Jesus will not allow their bad and stupid actions to be the basis of his loving relationship with them.

Belief in Jesus enables us to live as Jesus lived. When offended, although we are hurting, belief in Jesus and his way allows us to withdraw our disapproval of the offense, even though we have no doubt that it is warranted. We can do this willingly because we do not wish to make the offense the basis of the relationship between us. This does not mean that we approve or ignore the evil that has been done, but simply that we refuse to make the offensive action the basis of our relationship. Forgiveness is not understanding, nor forgetting, nor ignoring. It is an act of generosity which deliberately overlooks what has been done in order to remove the obstacle to our friendship and love. Jesus does not allow the merits or demerits of my life to be the basis of his stance toward me.

Forgiveness is not a consequence of justice, but an outflow of divine generosity toward us which is now alive in us. If God forgives, who am I, sinner that I am, to condemn others? The spontaneous sign that I have truly accepted God's forgiveness is that I will be able to forgive others as God has forgiven me. It is in the very forgiveness of others that I truly interiorize and make my very own God's forgiveness of me! In forgiving others, I ratify and make my own God's generous offer of universal forgiveness. Now I too can forgive as only a God can forgive! Thus it is in forgiving that I am divinized: to err is human, to forgive divine!

In this way I die to the old self that cries out for understanding and restitution.

The old demands of the fleshly heart decrease as the new life of the Spirit begins to take hold, grow, and mature within me. The more I am "grasped" by Christ, the more I will experience the fruits of the Spirit.

Forgiveness will never be easy, for the demands of the natural self will continue to be strong and nag us in many different ways. Yet it is certainly possible and even joyful and peace-producing when we dare to believe in Jesus and trust in his ways. By any human standard his ways will often appear to be senseless and unjust, yet they are the only way to break the destructive cycle of the offender who creates another offender out of the very person they injure. To the degree that we trust our own ways rather than the ways of God, we will go on destroying ourselves and one another. The only way is to put our full confidence in the way of the Lord.

When we dare to trust the divine physician and accept his prescription, we will find ourselves restored to the fullness of human health and even when we die, we will die in peace and sleep the sleep of the just. For those who firmly believe in Jesus, "the Spirit produces love, joy, peace, patience, kindness, goodness, faithfulness, humility, and self-control. There is no law against such things as these" (Gal. 5:22).

It is in converting to the way of the Lord that we can truly forgive while fully remembering the hurts of the past. It is in converting to the way of the Lord that the hurts of the past will be healed while not being forgotten, that the anxieties will be replaced by peacefulness, and the pains of the past will be converted into joy.

Notes

[1] Henceforth in this essay, whenever I use the expression "natural" I do not refer to the true nature of man/woman as created by God, but more to that which through generations of repetition, custom, and tradition has become so ordinary that now it appears and functions as natural. It is so deeply ingrained in us that it appears to be part of our very own flesh and bone. It is in this way that *The Good News for Modern Man* version of the Bible translates *sarx*: the way in which humanity apart from God tends to reason, judge, and act.

[2] I refer here to Paul's *sarx*-inclinations that have become so ingrained in my whole being that they appear to be part of my very flesh. My whole flesh pulls in that direction.

11. Unmasking the Idols

(1992)

Virgilio Elizondo

I would like to begin this talk by quoting from the introduction to the issue of *Concilium, 1492-1992: The Voice of the Victims*. In editing this issue Leonardo Boff and I tried to give a voice to those who suffered the consequences of what happened during the 500 years since the beginning of what we call today "The Americas."

October 12, 1492 was the beginning of a long and bloody Good Friday for Latin America and the Caribbean. It is still Good Friday and there is no sign of Easter Day. The dominant accounts were written from the ships which came to conquer and not by the victims waiting on the shore who suffered the effects of the domination. The victims cry out and their suffering challenges us. This whole issue of *Concilium* will try to be faithful to these protests.

In the first place they denounce the historical and social injustice of the process of colonization and Christianization. They condemn the devastation brought about by the colonizers: "Alas, we were saddened because they came. They came to make our flowers wither so that only their flower might live," wrote the Maya prophet in *Chilam Balam de Chumayel*. And he continues, with more charges against the Christians: "Sadness was brought among us, Christianity was brought among us. This was the beginning of our distress, the beginning of our slavery."

The invasion brought about the biggest genocide in human history affecting around 90% of the population. Of the 22 million Aztecs in 1519, when Hernán Cortéz entered Mexico, there were only a million left in 1600. The survivors are crucified peoples, enduring worse abuses than the Jews in Egypt and Babylon and the Christians under the Roman emperors, as was said many times by bishops who defended the Indians.

We are Christians, we have received the Gospel, we believe in the power of the Gospel to transform and to give life in ways that we often do not begin to imagine. We believe and profess the transforming power of the Paschal mystery. But for the indigenous peoples of the "New World" the Good News was Sad News. Today the Good News is that the poor are no longer remaining silent. They are crying out for life. Their cry is not something passive; it is a demand, it is a challenge. Which one of us stands unmoved at the cry of a baby, the call for attention, for recognition, the call to do something?

The Good News today is that the poor are not remaining silent. They are not simply suffering in isolation and hidden away. They are crying out and being recognized as victims of a system which amounts to the oppression of people who are not the white people of this world. This is not just an economic oppression but an overall, englobing oppression of their way of life, their values, their customs, their heritage, their music, their ways of relating. A whole way of life has been stepped on.

These people are not crying out for revenge but for the life of themselves and others. Not once while I worked with the poor in the Third World have I heard anyone calling for revenge. Restitution yes!—but restitution is not revenge. No one has said: We have to get even. What they said was: Out of our poverty we have to offer new life to everyone.

This is the Good News. The poor are receiving the Gospel in ways they have not been hearing it for 500 years. The great councils of Medellín and Puebla and the U.S. Bishops' letter on the economy are being recognized by those in authority and they are joining their voices to the cry of the poor. It is no longer just the voices of the poor alone, but those who have a place in society that are being heard.

I was deeply moved by the statements of Pope John Paul on February 22, 1992 in Senegal, when he went to the place from which the slaves of black Africa had been deported. Incredible as the statistics seem, 40 million Africans were uprooted and sent to work as slaves in other countries against their will. This robbed that continent of so many potential intellectuals and leaders. Standing on the very site where they were gathered before being sent to the Americas the Pope said: "I have come here to listen to the cry of centuries." He added his powerful voice to that cry. He has raised it before in Brazil, in Peru, and with the aborigines in Australia. But here in this painfully sacred site he said he had come to listen to the cry of centuries, a cry about injustice, the tragedy of a civilization that called itself Christian. Not only have we been involved in the slave-trade that made many of our countries rich, but we dare to call ourselves Christians today and yet we are still involved in forms of enslaving men and women around the world.

The poor today, I am convinced, call us to conversion. Is this the new evangelization, called for by the Pope, new in methodology and new in content? In the beginning of the Americas, the missionaries chastised the peoples of the Americas for what they considered to be their idols. It seems to me that today the gift of the suffering Christians of the Third World is to help us recognize those idols that we are convinced are life-giving but which are in effect draining us of life.

The Great Idols

Who is considered to be a good, beautiful, honorable human being in our society today? Who are the secular saints and heroes whom we look upon as the models of humanity? Who are the young people of our society striving to become?

What are those false idols which we in the West have created and worship, having eyes that see not, and ears that hear not? Are we worshipping the image and likeness of gods that we have created or are we open to being redeemed in the image and likeness of the God who created us, the God we meet in Jesus?

The First Idol: Money

The first idol I would like to identify is the conviction that the more one obtains in life the more one is. One of the unquestioned convictions in our society is that the fundamental human worth of a person is measured in terms of what the person has obtained. That person is worth a lot, we say. Look at their car! Look at their clothes! Look at their homes! People measure human worth by possessions.

Whatever we have is linked to upward mobility. It seems to me that we are at a moment when we have to question the limits above which upward mobility is no longer good but destructive. Are there limits in upward mobility beyond which one becomes a public sinner and a social criminal? In the United States more and more people are unemployed, factories are being closed, and entire families suffer. I read in the *Wall Street Journal* the listing of the top ten salaried CEOs in the country. The first person on the list makes a salary of 92 million dollars per year. When people are unemployed, when some are destitute and starving, when more and more are having less, and fewer are having more and more, should we not ask what quantity of possessions make someone a public sinner?

We have to question this in our catechesis. We owe it to our people to tell them the truth. God has given the world for all God's people. Creation is beautiful. If some people work hard they should have the right to own their home and their land. On the other hand, some have so much when others do not have the minimum! Latin America is not poor. Latin America is rich! The scandal is there are so many poor people there. Have we ever questioned beyond what limits the possession of this world's goods is a public sin? One of the principles of the old moral theology was that if someone has more than they need, and another does not have the minimum needed to survive, the one who has nothing has the right to go in and take what they need. We need to look at this basic reality in our moral theology.

Reading the incredible scandal stories in the newspapers one has the impression that everybody is out to make more money, no matter how they make it. A few months ago I read about an insurance scandal. The company was hiring very handsome, likable young men, the kind that any elderly woman would want to have as a grandchild. They would go to visit retirement homes and visit with elderly women and offer to sell them an insurance policy. Almost all bought a policy. The young men were insuring the elderly women in their 60s, 70s, and 80s for pregnancy risks. It was totally immoral but perfectly legal. Many such schemes are going on right now throughout the world. Balloon loans are made to people who buy homes. Suddenly the mortgage triples and they cannot pay it. The principle is to make a quick profit. It does not make any difference how you make it.

Another scandal emerged recently at the corporate level. It is too expensive to get rid of contaminated waste products in the First World so we send them to the

Third World. Not only are we devastating the natural resources of the Third World, we are now making it a dumping ground for the contaminated trash that we find too expensive to decontaminate and take care of in our own land.

I remember how scandalized I was when I read several years ago that in an effort to "clean Brazil" of indigenous peoples, contaminated clothing was sent there from hospitals in the First World. Native people wore the clothing, contracted disease, and died. That was in the 1930s. But we are doing the same thing today; we are sending waste products there. We are testing drugs in the Third World, selling drugs and pharmaceuticals that are totally prohibited in the First World. The Third World has no controls; they are being used as human laboratories for profit making. Upward mobility? Make money? Profits for the country? We are fumigating crops in the United States while those who are picking the crops are in the fields, and their children are dying early of cancer. The reason remains the same—the profit motive. Is that the supreme value?

We, too, as religious persons have to question ourselves. How often have we fallen into profit-making schemes because we want to make our religious institutions bigger and better? How often have we used manipulative fund-raising and maybe overused a mission in Africa or in Latin America to raise money and make our own congregations or institutions bigger and better? We fall too easily into believing that we need what is bigger and better.

We also need to question the sports heroes, the singers, and the entertainers who are making mega dollars by the support of poor people. Why should our sports figures make millions of dollars from poor people who go to see them play and not in turn subsidize sports so that the poor can play? Why do singers horde the money they make instead of building music schools in the poor districts, the urban districts, where children can learn music?

We have to challenge the rich, to ask whether having more makes one really better or whether having more makes one more satanic. We have to call it what it is in order to deal with it. It is the poor who are calling us to believe that in giving and sharing one receives the truth of the Gospel.

Come to our Cathedral of San Fernando in San Antonio, Texas. You will find a church of poor people. The liturgies have life, have real authentic joy because people are not playing games. They are giving to each other what little they have. It is in giving and not in taking that one becomes fully human. We need to recapture and share this fundamental truth of the Gospel.

The Second Idol: Pleasure

The second idol that I would like to explore with you is the conviction that pleasure brings happiness. Ours is a pleasure-seeking society. We are attracted to anything that will give us pleasure. Even with the current AIDS epidemic the majority of the population is not questioning its views on sex. They are simply saying that you have to be careful. People are not even questioning the fact that sex and drugs are destroying their individual families. Why do they look to sex and drugs for pleasure? The response is: Well, I was feeling down. I needed a pick-up. I felt rejected. I needed something to make me feel good.

High school students drop out of school. Why? I didn't like it. It wasn't fun. I wasn't enjoying it. The conviction is that if I am not enjoying it, it is not good. I have talked to couples who are thinking of divorcing. They have no serious reasons. The only reason is that they do not enjoy themselves anymore. The principle is that only pleasure brings happiness and, therefore, they have to be constantly entertained. This affects sports, music, school, church. Notice how often in our world people give as a reason, "I do not enjoy it."

What is happening? There is an increase of suicides. I remember many years ago being told that in counseling if a young child tells you that he or she is going to commit suicide not to worry because they are not going to do it. It is different now. I recently received a cable from the parents of a young man. They had gone to a prayer meeting and when they returned home they found their son had hanged himself. He left a note saying that he was not enjoying life!—so why continue it?

The level of depression in our First World is incredible. I hear this from professional people in high positions. People simply give up. There is anxiety because they cannot have a good time. We need to question this, to rediscover that suffering is part of happiness, that continued pleasure does not lead to happiness.

There is a profound fundamental truth that we need to deal with—that happiness is realized only when one gives oneself to something which has meaning. This is the whole notion of service in the Gospel, the call to serve even in the smallest of things. Sacrifice for the sake of others leads to happiness. We must unmask the notion that pleasure brings happiness, that if you just enjoy what you are doing you will live happily ever after.

The Third Idol: Beauty

The third idol that we need to question is our concept of the beautiful. Who is considered a beautiful human being today? Just reflect on the advertisements that you see on television or in magazines. Look at what is projected as the image of the desirable human being. The image of the beautiful person that we in the First World are projecting as normative, carries with it the message that if you are not this type of person you are not okay.

We project as beautiful the white, Aryan type. Look at the features. Those who fit the norm are tall, slim, not too old, not too young, well-built; they have perfect teeth, a perfect nose, perfect ears, perfect hair, perfect feet, the right smell, the right clothing. How we are regulating beauty!

There is much concern about diets. It is very important to discover the proper diet. I am not against dieting but think about the extremes. More and more people suffer from anorexia. Children in grade school go through traumatic experiences because they are too fat and others make fun of them. People spend hours exercising, dieting, not relating to their children, not relating to each other, not visiting, not having time to listen or to be aware.

Plastic surgeons today make more and more money remaking noses, chins, cheeks, and breasts. People are afraid of the human being that God has made them to be. We do not dare look at ourselves in the mirror, without our toupee, our false teeth, our false arm, or whatever. We are afraid to say: "You know, God, you really outdid yourself when you made me the natural beauty that you made me!" When was the last time you thanked God for being the beautiful person you are? And just like you are?

All of us worry—and children to an incredible degree. If they are not white their trauma is unbelievable. A brown-skinned co-student of mine from New Mexico recently told us something he had never admitted before. He used to wear long sleeves in his childhood because less of his skin would show! In the bathroom, he would spend hours rubbing himself with pumice stone trying to get "the dirt" out of his skin because he was brown.

What are we telling people? Poor children in San Antonio cannot afford braces for their teeth but are told that if they do not have perfect teeth they are not beautiful human beings. When my little kids at the cathedral come up to Communion a lot of them have teeth all over the place! Their parents cannot afford braces, but on the north side of San Antonio there is hardly a single kid without braces.

So the poor cannot afford to make themselves beautiful. Their added anxiety is that they have to accept the fact that society considers them ugly. No one wants to be ugly. Beauty has been literally reduced to externals—size, shape, clothes, jewelry. Only those that can afford it can be beautiful. All others are relegated to the world of the silent suffering of ugliness.

A girl I was working with tried to commit suicide recently. She comes from a small, very racist town. Her mother headed a one-parent family and had to work very hard to keep the family together. She did not have time to take care of herself. She was overweight, not because she ate too much, but because she could not afford the proper diet. The girl had a school invitation for her mother to attend parent-teacher meetings but she did not want her to go. She was embarrassed because her mother was dark-skinned, heavy, and did not dress properly. She was not as good-looking as the other mothers. In time she began to think she herself would become just as "bad"-looking as her mother. Because of the pressures of beauty pageants in school and dressing right this young girl, a junior in high school, tried to commit suicide. Do not underestimate the suffering of people and the pain when beauty is only seen as external.

We have to rediscover the inner beauty of the human being. This has to be the subject of our catechesis, our preaching, and our teaching—the inner beauty of each and every human being because each person radiates the beauty of God.

We need to rediscover that authentic, radiating beauty is the goodness of persons, how they give themselves to others, relate to others. At Communion in the Mass I love to see the beautiful callused hands of someone who has worked hard to bring up a family. I love to see the wrinkled faces of elderly Mexicans who have withstood the summers and the winters of life.

"One to one" relationship is rare among the poor. They do not have time for it. People do not teach them; people do not listen to them; people do not instruct them or take time just to be with them. To be with someone is to appreciate their beauty and dignity and worth. Today we must teach the truth of the beauty of the whole person, otherwise we will keep on trying to make ourselves more beautiful in ways that in effect destroy us.

The Fourth Idol: Power

The final idol I would like to unmask is that of violent power. It is seen as the source of honor and glory.

I was recently at a Third World theologians' meeting in Nairobi, Kenya. Dr. Mofokeng, a theologian from South Africa, mentioned how in his early days he had rejected Christianity. He felt so antagonistic when he heard hymns and songs of the type "all honor and praise and glory to thee, Redeemer King," for the very people who were oppressing him, denying him his existence and putting him in jail were justifying themselves through this Christ of glory and power. He came to a moment when he even cursed Christ, because this Christ appeared to be justifying his own oppression and that of his people. It was in jail that he started to read the simple Gospel stories. It was there, he said, he discovered power and glory on his own—not the triumphalistic power that appeared to justify worldly power—but the real, ultimate power of the saving God in the powerlessness of Jesus of Nazareth. We need to unmask the way we identify the power and glory of God with the power and glory of this world's violence.

We are developing more and more effective weapons of war. Third World countries are given loans to acquire "weapons of defense"! The glorification of violence is destroying us. Our people are interiorizing the idea that the normal response to a stressful situation is violence.

In the United States, domestic violence has reached its highest level. Statistically speaking, the most dangerous place for a woman to be at night, the place where she is the most likely to be beaten up and hurt, is not in a bar, the street, or a dance hall, but at home with her husband.

Violence in our schools is phenomenal. The latest statistics seem to indicate that many children now take guns to class at some time—not play weapons but real guns. We have interiorized the understanding that the normal response to a stress situation is to kill. It happens at the domestic level, at the level of sexual differences, at the level of war games, and at the level of international politics. When we are threatened—send in the army!

I was personally horrified at the U.S. reaction to the 1991 Iraq crisis. I do not know what it was like in Europe but our people sat there, watching television and cheering as if the war were a game. No one asked how many were being killed nor about the suffering. We still have not been told how many were killed or buried alive. It was "a very clean war" from our perspective and we looked upon it as another video war game. Where are the heroes in this? Look at our movies and the glorification of ugly, destructive violence. The image given is that the more violent you are the more human you are.

We need to question the new world order that we are entering. So often the mind-set is that if you do not like something—attack! The great heroes—Gandhi, Martin Luther King, Jr., Archbishop Romero, Ita Ford, Jean Donovan, Dorothy

Kazel, Maura Clarke, the Jesuit martyrs in Salvador with their house staff—all worked for peace in different ways. And they were all killed.

I recall a priest, a classmate of mine who was killed some years ago in Guatemala because he was labeled as subversive. He was teaching people how to farm and how to read and write. This was not acceptable to the forces of law and order in Guatemala and so he was killed.

I recall a statement made by Archbishop Romero: "My love for my people is greater than my fear of death." When he was asked whether he should have guards to protect him, he said: "No! No, if God wants me to have the ultimate privilege of being a martyr, that will be God's praise, but my love for my people is all I have."

There are prophets like Dom Helder Camara and Dom Pedro Casaldáliga today in Brazil. There is the great Latin American theologian Gustavo Gutiérrez, a man who has known suffering in the most incredible ways. He speaks always about the God of life, about the Paschal mystery, and about finding new ways to eliminate violence. This is not the way of a world which prepares for peace by preparing for war! This is the way of Jesus. Our world today needs prophets of peace to unmask the fragility and the falsity of the myth that weapons of war will lead us to peace.

Conclusion

Today we are at a moment when it is precisely the struggles of the poor that call us to new ways of community, new ways of bettering our lives, so that we do not fall into the trap of choosing destructive idols. We need to recall those who received the Gospel in painful ways 500 years ago. We need to discover the power of the Beatitudes anew.

> Happy are you poor, the Kingdom of God is yours;
> Happy are you who are hungry now, you will be filled;
> Happy are you who weep now, you shall laugh;
> Happy are you when people hate you, reject you, insult
> you and say that you are evil because of me. Be glad when that
> happens and dance for joy because a great reward is kept for you
> in heaven. For their ancestors did the very same thing to the
> prophets;
> But how terrible for you who are rich now, you have had
> your easy life;
> How terrible for you who are full now, you will go hungry;
> How terrible for you who laugh now, you will mourn and
> weep;
> How terrible when all people speak well of you. Their
> ancestors said the very same things about the false prophets. (Luke 6:20-26)

12. Evil and the Experience of God

(1993)

Virgilio Elizondo

Introduction

The greatness and beauty of God is certainly revealed throughout all the marvels of creation. Yet given the actual condition of humanity's destructive sinfulness, which is often camouflaged as the good, the beautiful, and virtuous, it is precisely in contrast to our own vengeance, cruelty, and callousness that the most fascinating tenderness, kindness, and compassion of God becomes most gloriously experienced and revealed. In the difference, the uniqueness becomes all the more evident.

Evil in the World

Whether we look at history or at the contemporary situation, the human condition is one of overwhelming evil. In some cases evil is immediately evident: wars, police brutality such as in Los Angeles or South Africa, private armies to kill the street kids in Brazil, the killings of the Mafia in Italy, the neo-Nazi movements beginning in Germany, the Sendero Luminoso's senseless killings in Peru, today's ethnic wars in the former Yugoslavia, the gang violence erupting throughout the United States, or any other kind of violent destruction and killings which continue escalating throughout the world.

Yet there is a deeper, more prevailing, and even more hypocritical kind of evil which in many ways is even worse because the ones who perpetuate it and whose lives depend on it do not perceive it as evil. In fact, they perceive it as good, reasonable, righteous, and even natural. I am speaking about the institutionalized evil of the socio-economic structures of our contemporary world which started to be built in 1492 and are becoming ever more destructive of much of the world population in 1992 through the "New World Order."[1] At the very basis of our great modern civilizations one finds the blood of the victims through which the civilization was built and continues to be sustained today—underpaid workers, slaves, exploited migrants, abandoned elderly and sick people, expelled peoples, slum dwellers, countries from whom raw materials are stolen, and the like.

Western civilization has certainly led the world in great scientific and technological advances; great strides have been made in forming democratic governments which try to safeguard the basic freedoms of humanity; medical breakthroughs have been miraculous; Western missioners have certainly done heroic works among the poor of the world; and the level of living of the average Westerner has come a long way since 1492. These are but some of the positive advancements, but we need to ask ourselves, "at what cost?"[2]

Assuming that the Western models of progress and success are correct (and I do not think they are), we still have to ask how universally applicable they truly are. Since every human being wants to succeed, these success models can be true only if they are within the reach of all. Can these models of human success be truly available to everyone? If not, they will be more destructive than life-giving, leading to more corruption, crime, and violence than to true happiness.

It is in the very process of trying to succeed—to become someone rich and special—that we begin to manipulate, exploit, enslave, and even murder others in order to obtain our goals and fulfill our desires. But because we have an innate desire of the heart to be good persons, we begin to justify and mask our crimes by turning our victims into inferior, unworthy, uncivilized heathens whose only worthwhile purpose in life is to serve their "natural" masters. This thought will permeate and dominate all the structure of the human heart and of society in general. The victimization of the weaker others will thus appear as a great virtue for the sake of civilization and the glory of God.

In these civilizations, the rich and the powerful will appear as the great heroes to be admired and imitated and as mirror images of the divinity, while the poor and the weak will appear as lesser human beings who can easily be ignored, used, abused, and discarded without any great concern. They are easily expendable. There appears to be no problem in exploiting them and even enslaving them, for their purpose in life, their glory, and their dignity come about only in serving the rich and powerful—their only value is to serve the great ones of society.

In these circumstances, religion more often hides the real face and heart of God than revealing them; for "God" has been recreated to the image and likeness of the dominant culture. God blesses the armies going off to battle, anoints the war leaders, and sanctions the law and order of the group as an extension of God's own ordering of the universe. The enemies of the dominant will appear as the heathens who oppose God. The ultimate argument of the Franciscan missioners to the Indian leaders of Mexico was that they had to admit the Spanish religion was the true one because the Christian God had overpowered their Gods in battle and had sent the Spanish to chastise them for their sins.

This is not to say that there will not be good and charitable persons within this society, but the strong ethnic and racial centrism of their own dominant group will blind those who seek to do good to the basic and fundamental goodness of those who are different. The only way truly to help "those poor and wretched folks" will be by helping them to assume our apparently good and holy ways of life. Thus in seeking to convert the natives to the "true religion" of the victimizers, the well-intentioned missioners will in effect be helping the victims to be victimizers themselves!

The most unfortunate aspect of this victimization is that the victims learn from the victimizers what appears to be the only true way of life possible. The only way to be fully alive is to be like the rich and powerful. They set the stage and their ways begin to appear as the reasonable and natural ways of being good, beautiful, and fully human. This interiorization perpetuates and expands the way of violence as the only way possible for human success. In this world, there seems to be no way out of the escalating cycle of destructive violence and victimization.

When did all this begin? According to the Bible, it began with the very beginning of humanity and each generation will add to the evil it has learned. There appears to be no way out of this vicious cycle of destruction.

God's Struggles against Evil

God's saving entry into human affairs seeks to break with the way of victimization and violence. God wants a good life for all, but not at the cost of any. The God of the Bible does not want victims! God stops Abraham from sacrificing his son, leads the slaves out of Egypt, and will go to the point of allowing his own Son to offer his life in sacrifice rather than victimizing anyone. These are privileged moments of the biblical experience of God.

The Bible begins by affirming the origins of all human beings—we are all descendants of Adam and Eve who were created in the image and likeness of God and are therefore of intrinsic beauty and infinite worth. But Adam and Eve went their own way, Cain killed his brother, and all generations will learn and develop the ways of the first ones! God's creation has gone sour! This corruption has become so ingrained in the inner depths of the human spirit—both collective and personal—that even God will not easily cleanse his people of their false ideas about life: God takes the people out of Egypt much more easily than he can take Egypt's way of life out of their minds and hearts.

But God, being the loving parent that God is, will not let creation destroy itself. The main focus of the entire biblical adventure is God's identification with and concern for the oppressed victims. In the Exodus, God hears the cries of God's people, sees their suffering, and determines to come and save them; during the glorious days of the Israelite kingdom, God speaks through the prophets in favor of the widows, the orphans, and the foreigners who are being exploited by their very own! In the exile God comforts the people living in a foreign land and offers them hope. In the poems of the suffering servant in the prophet Isaiah, it is not God who afflicts the servant, but God who speaks through him, through the excluded and despised other, to offer hope to all others. God does not will victimization, but uses the victims to bring salvation to all—victims and victimizers alike. It is the victim who is God's instrument of ultimate triumph![3] But it is evident from the failures of the Old Testament drama that it was not enough for God to enter into solidarity with the victims of society as a concerned outsider.

Human beings are of such infinite worth that God sends his Son to enter into ultimate solidarity with the victims of this world by himself being born a victim— Jewish (world's outcasts), Galilean (despised by the Jews), and son of Mary (of questionable parentage). Jesus lived a constantly victimized life and died a victim.[4] The core of the revelation of Jesus is that he refuses to accept the image of a good and successful human being from any of the victimizers of his society—

religious, spiritual, economic, political, or revolutionary. Unlike us, he will never seek to follow the way of his victimizers; he refuses to idealize their goals or try to become like them in any way. In this way, he demonstrates complete freedom, even though tempted, from the repetitive cycles of violence and victimization and ends up disappointing everyone—even his disciples. He was altogether "too much" (Matt 13:57).

Jesus introduces a radically refreshing and liberating image of the authentic human being: I am who am! It does not matter who my parents are, my social or economic status, my nationality or race. If God, the all-powerful creator and absolute master of the universe, is my Father, then no humanly created category of identification can erase or hide my ultimate and only truly real identity. My ultimate status and identity come not from human beings, but from God.

Because I am, I am of infinite worth, unique beauty, and sacred dignity! This was the supreme truth that the world's cultures of dominance and victimization could not stand to have revealed, for it demolished and demonstrated clearly the fallacy of their rationalizations and justifications which legitimized their power claims over weak and defenseless human beings.

This revelation makes of Jesus an intolerable rabble-rouser—one who subverts the masses. This is why he must die, for he is disturbing the very foundations—sociological, cultural, and religious—of human groups based on dehumanizing differentiation and segregation. Jesus was born a victim, was a victim of false accusations throughout his life, and died a victim condemned by false accusations. Yet he refused to give in to victimization! He offered salvation to all—victims and victimizers alike—because he refused to imitate the humanly accepted patterns of victimization and invited us to do the same! Free to be without having to destroy anyone! That is the ultimate liberation.

It is in the cross that the ultimate victimization of the weak is revealed: "They all cried out, 'Crucify him,'" while the ultimate loving and saving power of God is equally revealed through the crucified victim: "Father, forgive them, for they know not what they do." Incredible as it sounds, the evil of human beings allows the ultimate glory of God to become manifest and, in so doing, the destructive cycle of victimization has finally been broken.

God was supremely revealed and experienced at one of the most unreligious and least spiritual moments of human history: the cruel and bloody execution of an innocent victim. The nakedness of the victim Jesus dying on the cross revealed in its most stark form the unlimited love and compassion of God who allows his Son to be sacrificed rather than allowing others to be victimized. Through this love, violence and destructiveness have been conquered without destroying the very persons who have sought to perpetuate victimization. They, too, will be offered new life without resorting to the victimization of others. Now we can all be free together!

Yet, in the here and now, sin still reigns in persons and civilizations. Precisely because of our own gospel tradition, it is even more evident in our own Western Christian civilization. One of the greatest lessons we learned from our first Spanish missioners was not to be afraid of calling the demons of our own society by name.[5]

America's (United States') Sinfulness and God's Glory

Let me begin by saying that the foundation of the United States is unique and original. It was built by the outcasts of Europe who truly wanted to begin something new. They wanted to get away from the despotic monarchies of Europe and to create "God's new Israel." In effect, they rejected victimization. In this new land, in this new covenant community, all persons would have a voice and a vote. Their ideals and foundations were certainly correct and earth-shaking. Something truly new was erupting into the history of humanity—a new nation based on the best of biblical and humanistic dreams and ideals of liberty and justice.

This new nation has certainly been the promised land for many from all nations who have come here to forget their past and create a new beginning. Everyone is born equal and has the same opportunities to get ahead in this world—at least this is what we like to believe about ourselves. But we who are not part of the white dominant group of the United States know the actual truth of the situation to be quite different.

The foundation stones were correct, but the building was falsified for it was not really open to all the peoples of the world, only those whom the original inhabitants (northern Europeans) considered to be fully human—like themselves. The natives were not only systematically excluded, but their extermination was biblically justified by identifying them with the Canaanites of old whom the People of God had been ordered to exterminate so that they could take over the Promised Land. Hence, it became a virtue to cleanse the land of the heathen natives!

Africans were brought in as slaves and their enslavement was also biblically justified by identifying them with the cursed children of Canaan (Gen. 10) who were condemned by God to be the slaves of the white peoples for all eternity. Their animal-like transportation, in the process of which many died, their inhuman treatment on the plantations, and their condemnation to a totally inferior status never seemed to have bothered the consciences among the majority of the Christian population.

Finally, in the "manifest destiny" dreams of the young and expanding nation in the 1830s, there were no qualms of conscience about sending agents into the Mexican state of Texas to sow the seeds of discord so as to separate Texas from Mexico, and later about starting the unjust war with Mexico in order to take over fifty percent of the Mexican nation. From that moment on, the captured Mexican *mestizo* became the despised opposite of the good, beautiful, and respectable human person from the WASP nation of the north. When slavery was eliminated, the poor, defenseless, and uneducated Mexicans became a good substitute for the former slaves. Ways were formulated to keep them uneducated so that they could continue being good, quiet, servile workers.

Thus liberty and justice for all really meant for the white, Anglo-Saxon Protestants of the new nation. White Catholics were tolerated but not trusted. Unfortunately, victimization was rejected, but only partially. Ethno-racial centrism, coupled with the insatiable profit motive, has become the real basis of the new American enterprise. It quickly based itself on the age-old structure of the victimization of the weaker other, for the profit and gain of the powerful.

The United States is certainly a marvelous experiment in democracy and opportunity, but in truthfulness we must also be aware of its limitations and deficiencies precisely in faithfulness to the original dream: that a new nation could exist where no one would be victimized for there would be true liberty and justice for all! There are many good, religious, and conscientious persons. Volunteerism and charitable works abound. Many people and corporations truly seek to do good and eradicate misery. Yet our cultural structures prevent us from going to the very roots of the victimization and violence which are required to nourish and fulfill our acquired desires and appetites. We want to do good but are afraid that it might cost us things and ideas that we do not want to give up.

I had many beautiful and exciting religious experiences throughout the Americas, especially in my own United States. I have been at civic ceremonies when the God of our nation has been proclaimed and praised. I have been in our churches wherein our God has been hailed and venerated with great music, sermons, and pageantry. I have been with the pope wherein our own Catholic experience of God has been truly exuberant. Yet none have been as powerful as the two which I would like to share with you.

The first one was the Civil Rights movement led by Dr. Martin Luther King, Jr. The Black victims of racism took the lead, others awakened and followed. It was a nonviolent protest which refused to tolerate any longer the racial discrimination so widely accepted throughout the United States. Certainly slavery had been brought to an end, but segregation reigned throughout the United States, and the churches were not excluded. There was violent opposition to demand that segregation end at all levels of society, but the nonviolent power grew all the stronger. Scripture readings, sermons, chants like "We shall overcome," marches, tears, and fears all served to bring Blacks, Whites, and Browns together in a common crusade for liberty and justice. Many sincere Whites became aware of the ugliness of the hidden racism in our country. In the marches, no one cared whether one's partners were Black, Hispanic, or White; Christian, Jewish, or atheist; Baptist, Catholic, or anything else. We were all together and there was no doubt whatsoever that God was with us leading us on to the liberation of the oppressed victims. Civil Rights was not about asking for favors, it was simply demanding justice in the name of the creator, in the very name of the founding principles of our country. It was one of the greatest spiritual crusades of our nation.

The other great experience of God came through the farm worker movement led by César Chávez and Dolores Huerta, especially in California and Texas. The poor Mexicans in the United States had never been allowed the protection of labor laws. In effect, unions and labor legislation kept saying: Mexican (and other) farm workers do not count in the United States. Migrant workers were constantly brought in from Mexico as needed and then sent back to keep the local farm workers from unionizing.

These *campesinos* were forced to work under the most brutal and dehumanizing circumstances—under the scorching sun, constantly stooped down to pick the crops, without toilets or water. Even worse, often the crops were fumigated with dangerous chemicals while the workers and their babies were in the fields. They were paid less than the minimum wage for seasonal work and received no workers' benefits whatsoever. I am sure that the slaves in Egypt did not have it any worse than our poor farm workers.

César Chávez, a poor farm worker himself, called for nonviolent crusades. The Mexican victims took the lead. People throughout the country were asked to boycott the buying of grapes and lettuce. All the big landowners and labor unions were against them. Many tried to discredit them and even threatened them in many ways. It is said that when the grape boycott was really beginning to take effect across the country, the dietitians at the Pentagon decided that grapes were very good for the soldiers in Asia so eight pounds of grapes per soldier per day were sent to Asia! It was like David against Goliath.

César Chávez dared to reveal the hideous and unjust structures which were kept in place to assure the success of a few at the cost of sacrificing the many on the altars of the crop-picking fields. The human sacrifices continued but they had been nicely and politely camouflaged and hidden. America could enjoy its good fruits and vegetables without having to think about the body and blood sacrifices that were required to get the food onto the tables. Yet the campaign continued and brought some moderate changes. It still continues while the opposition grows more grotesque each day.

All the powers conspired to destroy the defenseless movement of the victimized farm workers. On the other hand, the more the resistance grew, the more men and women of all backgrounds and religious persuasions started to join the crusade. As in the Civil Rights movement, there were Jews, Christians, and others; Protestants and Catholics; religious and laity; Whites, Asians, Blacks, and Browns. No one had any problem marching behind the banner of Our Lady of Guadalupe for she was the traditional protectress of the Mexican poor and their banner in their struggles for justice. We sang religious songs and prayed the rosary. We were together and united and the more we were threatened, the more we knew God was with us. Marching with the farm workers was a re-walking of the way of the cross. Those who took part, regardless of their religious persuasion, knew they had truly experienced God present among us.

The Civil Rights movements and the farm worker movement have brought us into solidarity with the other suffering victims of the Americas in their struggles for new life. They are beginning to see themselves as the suffering servant. It is not God's will to bruise them. As in the Exodus, God is present in the struggles of the oppressed "nobodies" against the unjust oppression of Pharaoh, and the gods of the empire are powerless against the God who hears the cries of the poor. As in the crucifixion, God speaks absolute truth from the position and through the lips of the crucified ones whom God will resurrect. The resurrected peoples of the Americas are the ones who will usher in the truly new humanity of the Americas. They are the people of hope.[6]

These movements are not asking for revolutions, but for the conversion of all: of the poor from their passive and silent suffering, of the dominant from their arrogance and blindness. The call of our society's victims is like the call of Jesus to the rich young man. God is speaking to all of us through the cries of today's suffering servants—will we listen?

The experience of the God of life begins when the victimized begin to discover themselves not as culpable for their suffering—some kind of divine chastisement—but precisely as victims of an unjust system of avarice and aggression. In the recognition that God does not legitimize the unjust ways and structures of society, the true mind and heart of God become known and proclaimed. The experience of God is deepened and clarified when the victimized realize that they should not try to overthrow the agents of violence through their own means of aggression, but rather through nonviolent alternatives of life which refuse to imitate and duplicate the schemes of the violent in this world. The living out of this conviction even unto martyrdom is one of the deepest and most authentic experiences of God. It is in these moments that we can truly see and experience the brilliance of God's glory in the midst of the human condition: "Now is the Son of Man glorified and God is glorified in him" (Jn. 13:31).

Notes

[1]Jon Sobrino, "500 Years: Structural Sin and Structural Grace," *SEDOS* 24 (15 May 1992).

[2]Leonardo Boff and Virgilio P. Elizondo, *1492-1992: The Voice of the Victims* (London: SCM Press, 1990).

[3]James G. Williams, *The Bible, Violence and the Sacred* (San Francisco: Harper, 1991) 78, 168.

[4]For a fuller discussion of the Galilean identity of Jesus as the identity of a victim, consult Virgilio P. Elizondo, *Galilean Journey: The Mexican-American Promise* (New York: Orbis, 1983) and "*Mestizaje* as a Locus of Theological Reflection" 159-175 above.

[5]M. Salinas, "The Voices That Spoke for the Victims," in *1492-1992: The Voice of the Victims*.

[6]Ignacio Ellacuría, "Utopia y profestismo desde América Latina," *Revista Latinoamericana de teología* 17 (1989): 141-184.

PART FIVE

Beyond Borders

INTRODUCTORY ESSAYS

Virgil Elizondo

Practical Theologian, Prophet, and Organic Intellectual

John A. Coleman

As I reread Virgil Elizondo's writings, I asked myself: "How do I name the kind of theology which Virgil does? Just what type of theology is it?" This man of *mestizaje* and the borderlands, this spokesman for the Mexican Americans who are not "quite" Mexican and not "quite" American, this "international" theologian who has, nevertheless, inserted himself in the very local and particular church at the Cathedral of San Fernando in San Antonio, this learned scholar who has avoided the usual haunts of academia, what can theology, more generally, learn from his *oeuvre*?[1]

I know full well that to name is to delimit and pin down, and there is a danger in any easy labeling of Virgil. Pastor, communicator, religious educator, liturgist, television "personality," entrepreneur even, with graduate degrees in religious education from the East Asian Pastoral Institute in Manila and in systematic theology from the Institut Catholique in Paris, Virgil will not, to be sure, ever be content to be pinned down. He revels in what the anthropologist Clifford Geertz has called "blurred genres."[2] Even at the international Catholic journal *Concilium*, where Virgil served as editor for twenty years, he was a protean character. He began as coeditor, with Tubingen's Norbert Greinacher, of the annual issue on practical theology. Later, with Leonardo Boff, Virgil coedited the issues on third-world theology. But he also frequently contributed articles to the issues on spirituality.[3] He has written widely on Mariology and ecumenism.[4] He has reflected broadly on culture and inter-cultural dialogue.[5] At *Concilium* he anticipated, by some years, the emergence of a regular feminist theology issue!

But to name—at least provisionally—is also to identify, to illuminate, and to give some preliminary guideposts. So, I want to name Virgil's theology with three phrases. Virgil's theology is: (1) a practical theology, (2) a prophetic theology (but a unique brand of prophetic theology which also blurs genres), and (3) a theology of an organic intellectual.

A Practical Theology

Elizondo writes of the need for theology to be " returned to its legitimate place as a pastoral service in the midst of the believing community."[6] He has also written on the stages of practical theology and, for six years, edited the *Concilium* issue on practical theology.[7] Clearly, he engages in practical theology. Just what is this brand of theology?

Practical theology may be, in ways, the most unfairly beleaguered and "minimized" of the theological disciplines. At times, it is reduced to an amorphous "pastoral theology." In the United States, often, it is trivialized to a kind of "skill-building" discipline, focused on preaching, worship, pastoral care, and religious education. Yet practical theology deserves to be ranged, with systematic and historical theology, as one of the three main arches in the edifice of theology. In a profound sense, it reminds *all* of theology that theology must be a reflection on the praxis of the church. All of theology should be practical. If the *lex orandi* (the rule of prayer) is the legitimate *lex credendi* (the rule for orthodox believing), more generally all of theology must be rooted in a critical reflection on the actual practices of the church.

In his classic statement about the triadic branches of theology, Friedrich Schleiermacher organized the discipline into philosophical, historical, and practical theology. Schleiermacher saw the latter as, primarily, theological reflection on the task of the ordained ministers or the leadership of the church—a kind of systematic analysis of the ministerial role as preacher, catechist, liturgical leader, and specialist in congregational care. Schleiermacher, however, held a deductive and subordinate view of practical theology. One simply "applied" the theory, derived uniquely from philosophical and historical theology, to shape the lived praxis of ministry.[8]

More recently, practical theologians such as Germany's Norbert Mette (a colleague of Elizondo at *Concilium*) and North American Don S. Browning have challenged some of the received notions about practical theology, deriving from this paradigm of Schleiermacher.[9] They have broadened the scope of the field beyond the minister's role, to a "critical reflection on the church's ministry to the world."[10] They have explicitly added and included social-action ministry to the earlier fields of practical theology: liturgics, homiletics, pastoral and congregational care. This makes clear that practical theology does not just focus on the inner life of the church.[11]

The new practical theologians have insisted that rather than a deductive move from theory to praxis, as in Schleiermacher, the preferred move is from a beginning in praxis to a theorizing about it (since all praxis is implicitly theory-laden) and a subsequent return to praxis. Praxis does not get all its theory from the outside. It congeals its own variant of practical reason.[12] Browning sees practical theology as "critical reflection on the church's dialogue with Christian sources and other communities of experience and interpretation, with the aim of guiding its action toward social and individual transformation."[13] Practical theology asks how the practices of the church form the very questions we bring to the historical sources of Christian faith. Even the return to and retrieval of historical sources is not just "objective." Our situation, our interests, and current problematics inform our very recourse to historical texts and roots. Practical theology is concerned with testing the practical validity claims of the Christian faith. It envisions transformations of persons and structures. Conversion is one of its key categories.

As Browning has argued it, practical theology involves:

(1) A doing of theology in close connection with description of situations. Something akin to a sociological analysis of the situation for the church—what Browning calls a "thick description"—is a necessary component of practical theology. Browning calls this moment "descriptive theology." It embodies more than a positivist map of "facts," since practices embody congealed wisdom, a practical reason. Practical theology is done in close dialogue with the social sciences. It may even generate its own sociology![14]

(2) An honest and explicit situating of the researcher's social location. Practical theology is hermeneutical through and through. It knows that we are interested knowers and that our initial situation shapes the kinds of questions we ask. Our horizons of meaning shape the very questions we ask as we meet quite different horizons of meaning embedded in historical texts and traditions. Practical theology cannot remain sociologically naive about the impact of social location on the cultural constructions of reality.[15]

(3) A privileged focus on the concrete praxis of the church. From this derives the sociological component in order to describe, accurately, that practice. But the assumption is that the theologian does more than merely describe. He or she also looks to the deeper wisdom ingredient in practices, as well as at their deformations and their needed transformations. What begins in practice moves finally, once again, to practical interventions that sustain, retrieve, or challenge current practices in the church.

Browning assumes that a practical theology will ask the following four questions:

(1) How do we understand this concrete situation (in all its particularity) in which we must act?

(2) What should be the praxis in this concrete situation?

(3) How do we critically defend the norms of our praxis in this concrete situation?

(4) What means, strategies, and rhetorics should we use in this concrete situation?[16]

In the concrete, the practical theologian gains an entry into and a lens on the field by an immersion in one or other of the main disciplines of church practice: liturgics, religious education, congregational care, pastoral care, preaching. For example, in his book on practical theology Browning focuses strongly on congregational care (in an exercise of a branch of sociology now called "congregational studies") and religious education. He draws on his expertise as a pastoral psychologist.[17]

Elizondo as Practical Theologian

Elizondo, too, insists on privileging concrete situations. "The theological questions will emerge out of the common needs, struggles, questions, and tensions of the community. The fundamental books to be consulted will be the life-tensions of the community. The language to be used will be that of the people as conditioned by their own historical and cultural identity . . . Analysis will assist the local group to understand and appreciate its own situation in the light of the tradition of the church, especially the foundational traditions of the New Testament."[18] Elizondo begins several of his major works with a careful "thick description" of the Mexican-American situation.[19]

For Virgil, as the Vatican Council document *Lumen Gentium* enunciated it, the local church is truly the concrete embodiment of the universal church.[20] I can remember vividly his spirited response at a *Concilium* meeting when Hans Küng had suggested an issue on "Universal and Particular Theologies" (for "universal" read European!). In Virgil's understanding, all theology—to be authentic—must be local, must attend to local needs and practices. "Every concrete Christian community has the privilege and obligation to reflect on the meaning of the faith."[21] Universalism lies in the communion of many churches, in their dialogue and communal sharing of spiritual goods among and across local churches and not in a hegemony of the Roman or Western European models of theology (which, alas, are very parochial without knowing it and too little rooted in praxis). Universalism must also obey the law of the incarnation and attend to—a favorite word of Elizondo's—the concrete mediations. The very humble acceptance of the localness of every church leads Virgil, as Browning suggests, to explore an honest and explicit situating of his own social location as a Mexican American. But the rest of us too must accept biblical humility which "means that we accept ourselves as we are—historically and culturally conditioned."[22]

Virgil's preoccupation with popular religion and popular devotional life enables him to find the wisdom, the practical reason, and fittingness distilled and lurking in these practices. Perhaps nowhere has he done this more brilliantly than in *Guadalupe: Mother of the New Creation.*[23] Many of Virgil's writings take off from his rich immersion in the field of religious education.[24] *San Fernando Cathedral: Soul of the City* is rightly seen as a major contribution to congregational studies.[25] Clearly, Virgil sees theology as practical. It looks not only to present practices but to transformation. As he once put it, "what all theology should do [is] animate, strengthen, correct, and nourish the life of the faithful."[26]

One also expects to find somewhere, in almost every talk or essay of Elizondo's, an appeal to the word *experience*. In his treatment of religious education, he insists on the role of experience as primary.[27] In his essay on "Hispanic Theology and Popular Piety," included in this volume, he contends that we must " theologize seriously out of the living faith experience of our people."[28] Our access to experience is often mediated through the social sciences. The social science of choice that Virgil employs as an integral part of his practical theology is anthropology. This has played a central role at the Mexican American Cultural Center, which Virgil founded. In *Galilean Journey*, for example, he appeals to " the laws of anthropology": inclusion, exclusion, social distance.[29] Mainly, he is interested in what anthropologists refer to as "acculturation," that is, the meeting ground of different cultures and the transactions and transmissions (both borrowings and conflicts) from one culture to another that create something new. He is attracted to the symbolism of Galilee precisely because it was "a crossroads of cultures and peoples with an openness to each other."[30]

Anthropology also informs Virgil's brilliant essays on pilgrimage. He evokes what Victor Turner has referred to as the breakthrough of *communitas* over structure where "ordinary social divisions fade out and pilgrimage sites break away from the recognized centers of organized religion and from control of their authorities."[31] He also elicits the powerful image of *liminality*, the thresholds and the "between and betwixt" stadia in which the search for new stages of life can achieve breakthrough. A good way to see Virgil as a practical theologian is to read, back-to-back, his two essays on pilgrimage in the *Concilium* volume he edited on the topic. The first essay, Virgil's introduction to that volume, is phenomenological and anthropological in character: "Pilgrimage: An Enduring Ritual of Humanity." In it he appeals to a "deep anthropological need of the human soul to be connected with mother earth."[32] This first essay is paired to an essay on concrete pastoral application: "Pastoral Opportunities of Pilgrimages," which addresses Browning's fourth question: "What means, strategies, and rhetorics should we use in this concrete situation?"[33]

In a more modest fashion, social psychology also informs Virgil's practical theology. He sees the original genius of the Christian message in its ability to interweave "with the local religious traditions so as to give the people a deeper sense of local identity (a sense of rootedness) while at the same time breaking down the psycho-sociological barriers that kept nationalities separate and apart from each other so as to allow for a truly universal fellowship (a sense of universality). In other words, *it affirmed rootedness while destroying ghettoishness*."[34] Virgil also appeals to social psychology to limn the consciousness of the oppressed.[35] Elizondo can feel so confident that the future is *mestizo* because our deepest and formative past, when Greek and Jew combined in Galilee at the dawn of evangelization, was *mestizo*!

The Prophetic Theologian

In his methodological paradigm for doing practical theology, Don Browning insists that a dialogue between practical theology and theological ethics is a necessary component.[36] This is so because practices are never morally neutral. They embody values and further or impede justice. Cultural practices can be a means of resistance to oppression. They can also, at times, be a source of oppression or veil structural injustices. An overly *culturista* analysis can be used to avoid facing structural contradictions. So, the natural movement of a reflection on praxis must move to the formally ethical, in order to answer Browning's third question: "How do we critically defend the norms of our praxis in this concrete situation?"

Elizondo's practical theology does not explicitly formalize the ethical. Instead, it appeals to the prophetic tradition of the scriptures to ground its ethical vision. But Elizondo's prophetic theology is a prophetic theology with a difference: (1) It joins any denunciation of injustice to a vivid imagination of alternate possibilities. (2) It combines the mystical and the prophetic. (3) Because it roots the prophetic so closely in culture, it surprises by synthesizing the prophetic with the festive. I want to say something briefly about each of these three traits of Elizondo's prophetic theology.

Denunciation and Imaginative Hope

In the classic tradition of the Hebrew Scriptures, the prophet denounces the injustice, names the oppressor, convicts of sin. Virgil has written of the sin of racism in American society as the Mexican American suffers it.[37] He has also written eloquently on the bloodshed and nightmare destructions during the European conquest of the Americas.[38] He decries the illusions of any truly authentic "evangelization" in the context of conquest. As he notes in the essay in this volume on "Hispanic Theology and Popular Piety": "we have always been evangelized by missioners from groups that have conquered, dominated, and controlled our lives."[39] He names as the "ultimate violence" the violation of culture just as, conversely, the stubborn retention of one's own cultural identity is a potent resistance to oppression.[40] Elizondo knows the power of cultural resistance from the many-layered history of the Mexican Americans in San Antonio. He speaks forcefully, however, of the concrete suffering and marginalization of Mexican Americans and of the poor. He describes Mexican Americans as a "people who have been forced to become foreigners in their own land, who have been driven from their properties, and who have been pushed around by the powerful in the way the mighty wind blows the dust around."[41]

I have felt the bite and judgment of these denunciations of injustice when I have heard or read them from Virgil. Yet Virgil is a prophet with a difference. He is a prophet who smiles a lot! This smile is more than only (although, perhaps, partially that too) the residue of Mexican-American polite deference in face of the conqueror. The smile is the smile of a prophet who imagines the new, the unexpected, the hopeful. I cannot begin to count the times Virgil evokes the phrase "the new" in his writings. He speaks of a new race, a new creation, new categories, a new cosmo-vision, new models of humanity, "the good news of a new humanity."[42]

Virgil is also always using phrases such as "creative dreams," "utopian dreams," "reimagining." He insists that "out of crisis, suffering, and misery, the prophets of old dared to proclaim a new heaven and a new earth."[43] In *San Fernando Cathedral: Soul of the City*, he asks us to engage in "imagining the city of God."[44] Virgil stands in the inclusive prophetic tradition of Second Isaiah. Note that his typical move, even in prophetic denunciation, is always "to transcend categories of defeat or victory" with a vision of inclusive solidarity.[45] Prophecy is not a zero-sum game of winners and losers. In Virgil's voice, prophecy is also a welcome embrace to those who must convert from their sinful ways. It is primarily a call for a new imagination and a new solidarity. Here the theologian merges with the humanist and the artist.

Indeed, the Virgil who can speak of an evangelization in *rostro y corazón* looks to "the triumph of the imagination over the known architectural and theological sciences."[46] In this respect, Virgil's profound *Concilium* essay "I Forgive But I Do Not Forget" is quite illuminating. He underscores how those sinned-against can run the risk of fixating on the past, resorting to a kind of violence as repayment for injuries unjustly suffered. They must forgive but not forget or ignore. Prophecy is a kind of generous hosting which allows a new way of being. "Forgiveness is not understanding, nor forgetting, nor ignoring. It is an act of generosity which deliberately overlooks what has been done in order to remove the obstacle to our friendship and love."[47]

Virgil consciously models his prophetic theology on liberation theology. He speaks of the impact on his life and thought of the figure and works of Gustavo Gutiérrez.[48] He has been active in the Ecumenical Association of Third World Theologians (EATWOT). But he tries to take the basic insights of liberation theology, forged primarily in Latin America, and apply them to the different social structures and cultural milieu of the United States.

Virgil once invited me to team-teach with Gustavo Gutiérrez in a summer session at the Mexican American Cultural Center. Our topic was "Liberation Theology in the Two Americas." I have often felt that the invitation was not only a lovely grace (as every meeting in my life with Gutiérrez has been) but a gentle nudge from Virgil to get on with the vast challenge to justice raised by liberation theology for my work as a sociologist of North America. Imagination, freedom, and cultural creativity are at the core of Elizondo's prophetic theology.

The Mystical and Prophetic Combined

As I have argued elsewhere, the distinctively Catholic prophetic imagination usually couples the prophetic with the mystical.[49] To be sure, there is a possible and ever lurking tension between the two. The mystical can tame the Catholic prophetic imagination and divert it into other channels concerned more with union to God than justice on earth. As David Tracy (another colleague of Elizondo's at *Concilium*) has put it: "Neither the Christian prophet nor the mystic can live easily with one another." Yet, Tracy continues, "as the liberation, political, and feminist theologians now insist, only a mystico-prophetic construal of Christian freedom can suffice. Without the prophetic core, the struggle for justice and freedom in the historical-political world can too soon be lost in mere privacy. Without the mystical insistence on love, the spiritual power of the righteous struggle for justice is always in danger of lapsing into mere self-righteousness and spiritual exhaustion."[50]

The best of the liberation theologians turned, at a crucial point, to a deepening of the mystical, the spiritual. Gustavo Gutiérrez wrote his small classic *We Drink from Our Own Wells* and his profound meditation on the Book of Job and Jon Sobrino turned to the mysticism of the Ignatian spiritual exercises in his work on spirituality of liberation.[51]

It was precisely at *Concilium* that Gutiérrez first announced the indispensable (and profoundly Catholic) both-and (prophecy and spirituality) and the insepa- rable conjunction of the mystical and the political.[52] Virgil followed his friend and colleague Gustavo in this too, as is evident in his prayerful reflections on "conver- sations with God" in *San Fernando Cathedral: Soul of the City*.[53] But even earlier, Virgil's preoccupation with "the other" and "the different" (both, in a sense, mir- roring the impact on him of French thought, influenced by Emmanuel Levinas) hides a transcendent thrust. He insists that God, "the third 'other' [in all dialogue between the different] offers to us the possibility of the new."[54] In any event, for anyone who thinks that liberation theology is merely horizontal social analysis and strategic thinking, Virgil cuts to the quick: "Only a true image of God can give us a true image of who we truly are as human beings."[55]

A Synthesis of the Prophetic and the Festive

Because of the centrality of the cultural in Elizondo's theology, he is not a stark ascetic or a puritan. He loves a *fiesta* and he knows that the poor, even in their poverty, also know how to party, to celebrate joy and sorrow. I can remember drinking beer with Virgil in the Market Square in Leuven, Belgium, and eating heartily with him in restaurants in Rome (where, as in the Jesuit rule, the "soul" also had its food!). I also fondly remember singing lustily with him to mariachis in San Antonio. Even during Holy Week, on Saturday noon, he hosted us "scholar- visitors" to San Fernando Cathedral with conversation, wine, and laughter. So, Virgil's prophetic theology is always an evangelization in *flor y canto*.[56]

One citation from many will capture this point about how Virgil is a prophet with a difference: "The prophetic without the festive turns into cynicism and bit- terness or simply fades away. On the other hand, the festive without the prophetic can easily turn into empty rituals or even degenerate into drunken brawls. It is the prophetic-festive that keeps the spirit alive and nourishes the life of the group as a group."[57] Even in his prophetic theology, Elizondo crosses borders, transgresses categories, and blurs genres. But a hospitable, mystic, and festive prophecy, a prophecy which smiles and laughs a lot, is not less prophetic, but it does prophesy in a unique and different key. Somehow, it helps me hear the prophetic denuncia- tions and calls for conversion with less resistance!

The Theology of the Organic Intellectual

Finally, Virgil is self-consciously an "organic intellectual." He does his theol- ogy from that stance. The term is from the Italian revisionist Marxist Antonio Gramsci, who, like Virgil, was primarily interested in culture. Gramsci was a Marxist who saw a positive role for religion. He complained that the ordinary intellectuals were deluded. They thought that they were above class structures and struggles and only served "objectivity" when, in fact, they were most often in the employ of the hegemonic classes who paid their bills. But Gramsci recalled cer- tain priests from his native Sardinia who had truly "accompanied" their people, helped them to find voice, aided them in popular forms of religion which were also a resistance to oppression from the industrial north of Italy. These became his model for his "ideal-type" of the organic intellectual.

The "organic intellectual" stays close to the people, shares their life and joys, and helps them to give voice to their pains, hopes, and imagination. Intellectuals cease to be elites. They are not cut off from the struggles for justice and liberation. They are organically rooted in the very struggles of their people. They become the articulators of the reality which their people experience. The true "organic intellectual" is a collective, not a lone individual.[58] The true test of the truth of the organic intellectual's analysis lies in the acceptance by the people, their spontaneous "aha" and "yes" to what the intellectual has voiced.

Gramsci's notion came to have wide relevance in Latin American liberation theology, especially as a background assumption in the works of Gustavo Gutiérrez. But Virgil shows the same penchant when he says of theology: "The new theologians . . . should be concerned that they are truly exercising their ministry of theologizing with and for their own local church. It is there that the validity of their work has to be verified."[59] And again, "It is the acceptance of the people, not of the academy, that is the first and most important verification of our work's validity."[60] One of the deceptive signs of Virgil, the organic intellectual, is that he wears his immense learning so lightly. Of course, he knows and implicitly refers to the works of such thinkers as Victor Turner, Emmanuel Levinas, Clifford Geertz, and Antonio Gramsci. But he is unlikely to cite it explicitly, to wear the learning openly. The theory behind his practical theology is deeply present but disguised and appropriated into words more ordinary people can themselves appropriate and understand. Nowhere is this disguising of immense theoretical learning more apparent than in the eloquent and seemingly simple and available language Virgil uses in *San Fernando Cathedral: Soul of the City*. Don't be deceived. An immense learning and theoretic apparatus (about liturgy, about public theology, about civil society) lurks behind this ordinary sounding prose!

And the challenge of this theology to the rest of us? What can we learn? We can learn that doing theology only in the academy is a mistake. Even professional theologians will need a concrete insertion into a local church and interaction with a real ministerial locale. We can learn to combine prophecy with worship and fiesta and to remind ourselves that *all* theology is called to be practical, to transform, to be a form of mystical prayer. We can learn to be humble about any "universal" pretensions and, accepting our limited social situation and location, engage more broadly in dialogue with other places and locales. Like any classic, Virgil has taught us that it is precisely by being *deeply* in touch with the particular that we also touch edges of reality which resonate more universally. I know that that pixieish Mexican American has taught this Irish American a different—I would argue a better—way to do theology.

Notes

[1]For *mestizaje* see Virgil Elizondo, *Galilean Journey: The Mexican-American Promise* (Maryknoll, NY: Orbis, 1983); for San Fernando Cathedral, Virgilio P. Elizondo and Timothy M.

Matovina, *San Fernando Cathedral: Soul of the City* (Maryknoll, NY: Orbis, 1998).

[2]For the concept of blurred genres, Clifford Geertz, *Local Knowledge: Further Essays in Interpretive Anthropology* (New York: Basic Books, 1983).

[3]Virgil Elizondo, "I Forgive But I Do Not Forget" 208-216 above. See also Elizondo's "Evil and the Experience of God" 225-232 above.

[4]For Mariology, besides Elizondo's *Guadalupe: Mother of the New Creation* (Maryknoll, NY: Orbis, 1997), see his "Mary and the Poor: A Model of Evangelizing Ecumenism," in Hans Küng and Jürgen Moltman, eds., *Mary in the Churches* (New York: Seabury, 1983) 59-65. Among Elizondo's treatments of ecumenism, see "Ecumenism: An Hispanic Perspective," *Ecumenist* 22 (July-August 1984): 70-74.

[5]See especially Elizondo's entry "Church and Culture" in *The New Catholic Encyclopedia*, vol. 17 (New York: McGraw-Hill, 1979) 167-168.

[6]Virgil Elizondo, "Conditions and Criteria for Authentic Inter-Cultural Theological Dialogue," in Virgil Elizondo, Claude Geffré, and Gustavo Gutiérrez, eds., *Different Theologies, Common Responsibility: Babel or Pentecost?* (Edinburgh: T & T Clarke, 1984) 21.

[7]Virgil Elizondo, "Stages of Practical Theology," in Paul Brand, Edward Schillebeeckx, and Anton Weiler, eds., *Twenty Years of Concilium: Retrospect and Prospect* (New York: Seabury, 1983) 20-26.

[8]Freidrich Schleiermacher, *Brief Outline on the Study of Theology* (Richmond, VA: John Knox Press, 1966).

[9]Norbert Mette, *Theorie der Praxis* (Dusseldorf: Patmos Verlag, 1980); Don S. Browning, *A Fundamental Practical Theology* (Minneapolis: Fortress Press, 1991).

[10]Browning, *A Fundamental Practical Theology* 35.

[11]Ibid. 57.

[12]For practical reasons cf. ibid. 34-54.

[13]Ibid. 37.

[14]Browning does generate his own sociological surveys in Don S. Browning et. al., *From Culture Wars to Common Ground: Religion and the American Family Debate* (Louisville: Westminster/John Knox Press, 1997).

[15]The classic statement on social location and the construction of knowledge is Karl Mannheim, *Ideology and Utopia* (New York: Harcourt, Brace and World, 1936).

[16]Browning, *A Fundamental Practical Theology* 55.

[17]For "congregational studies" see James Wind and James Lewis, eds., *American Congregations*, 2 vols. (Chicago: University of Chicago Press, 1994); Nancy Ammerman, *Congregation and Community* (New Brunswick: Rutgers University Press, 1997).

[18]Elizondo, "Conditions and Criteria" 20.

[19]Elizondo, *Galilean Journey*; Elizondo and Antonio Stevens-Arroyo, "The Spanish Speaking in the United States," in Antonio Stevens-Arroyo, ed., *Prophets Denied Honor* (Maryknoll, NY: Orbis, 1980) 7-13.

[20]*Lumen Gentium* #26.

[21]Elizondo, *Galilean Journey* 3.

[22]Elizondo, "Conditions and Criteria" 22.

[23]Elizondo, *Guadalupe: Mother of the New Creation* 100-114.

[24]See "Transmission of the Faith in the U.S.A.," in Virgil Elizondo and Norbert Greinacher, eds., *The Transmission of the Faith to the Next Generation* (Edinburgh: T & T Clark, 1984) 100-105.

[25]See the introduction by James P. Wind in Elizondo and Matovina, *San Fernando Cathedral* xi-xv.

[26]Elizondo, "Editorial," in Leonardo Boff and Virgilio P. Elizondo, eds., *Theologies of the Third World* (Edinburgh: T & T Clark, 1988) xv.

[27]Elizondo, "Transmission of the Faith in the U.S.A." 102.

[28]Elizondo, "Hispanic Theology and Popular Piety: From Interreligious Encounter to a New Ecumenism" 280 below.

[29]Elizondo, *Galilean Journey* 17; see also *"Mestizaje* as a Locus of Theological Reflection" 166 above.

[30]Elizondo, *Galilean Journey* 50.

[31]Elizondo, "Pilgrimage: An Enduring Ritual of Humanity," in Virgil Elizondo and Sean Freyne, eds., *Pilgrimage* (Maryknoll, NY: Orbis, 1996) ix.

[32]Ibid. vii.

[33]Elizondo, "Pastoral Opportunities of Pilgrimages" 133-139 above.

[34]Elizondo, "Popular Religion as Support of Identity" 127 above.

[35]Elizondo, *Galilean Journey* 23.

[36]Browning, *A Fundamental Practical Theology* 139-170.

[37]Elizondo, "A Report on Racism: A Mexican in the United States," in Gregory Baum and John Coleman, eds., *The Church and Racism* (New York: Seabury, 1982) 61-65.

[38]Elizondo, *Guadalupe: Mother of the New Creation* 25-33.

[39]Elizondo, "Hispanic Theology and Popular Piety" 281 below.

[40]Elizondo, *Galilean Journey* 10.

[41]Elizondo, "Popular Religion as Support of Identity" 130 above.

[42]Elizondo, "The New Humanity of the Americas" 272-277 below.

[43]Ibid. 273 below.

[44]Elizondo and Matovina, *San Fernando Cathedral* 99-113.

[45]Elizondo, "The New Humanity of the Americas" 272 below.

[46]Elizondo and Matovina, *San Fernando Cathedral* 9.

[47]Elizondo, "I Forgive But I Do Not Forget" 215 above.

[48]Elizondo, *Galilean Journey* 3.

[49]John A. Coleman, S. J., "Catholic Wellspring for the Prophetic Imagination," in Denise and John Carmody, eds., *The Future of Prophetic Christianity* (Maryknoll, NY: Orbis, 1993) 67-75.

[50]David Tracy, "The Prophetic-Mystical Option," in his *Dialogue with the Other: The Inter-Religious Dialogue* (Louvain, Belgium: Peeters Press, 1990) 117-118.

[51]Gustavo Gutiérrez, *We Drink from Our Own Wells* (Maryknoll, NY: Orbis, 1984); Gutiérrez, *On Job* (Maryknoll, NY: Orbis, 1987); Jon Sobrino, *Spirituality of Liberation: Toward Political Holiness* (Maryknoll, NY: Orbis, 1988).

[52]Claude Geffré and Gustavo Gutiérrez, *The Mystical and Political Dimension of the Christian Faith* (New York: Herder and Herder, 1974).

[53]Elizondo and Matovina, *San Fernando Cathedral* 51-65.

[54]Elizondo, *Galilean Journey* 63.

[55]Elizondo, *Guadalupe: Mother of the New Creation* 125.

[56]Ibid. 76.

[57]Elizondo, *Galilean Journey* 120.

[58]Antonio Gramsci, *The Modern Prince and Other Writings* (New York: International Publishers, 1987).

[59]Elizondo, "Conditions and Criteria" 20.

[60]Elizondo, "Hispanic Theology and Popular Piety" 281 below.

Crossing Theological Borders

Virgilio Elizondo's Place among
Theologians of Culture

Alejandro García-Rivera

An *homenaje* counts as a moment in which the life work of a great theologian is measured and celebrated. This brief reflection on the works of my dear friend and mentor, Virgilio Elizondo, attempts to do both these tasks. My formal doctoral education consisted of liberal nineteenth- and twentieth-century Protestant theology as well as Roman Catholic theology that led up to and included the theology of the Second Vatican Council. As a Hispanic who wanted to study in a serious way the reflections and analysis emerging out of the growing field of Hispanic theology, I found myself in an unenviable position.

At that time, some theologians considered Fr. Elizondo's work too contemporary or too specialized to be counted as "classical" theology. It was considered either "pastoral" theology (in the pejorative sense) or "descriptive" theology that did not engage the great theologians of the twentieth century. Part of the dangerous task I faced as a graduate student was convincing the theological faculty of my school that Hispanic theology and, more specifically, Elizondo's theology was indeed "serious" theology. Toward that end, I wrote various papers comparing Elizondo's thought with Tillich, Troeltsch, and even Schleiermacher. As my own maturity in theology has increased, I've come to recognize that Fr. Elizondo's thought deserves more than finding an equal standing with nineteenth- and twentieth-century theologians. Fr. Elizondo's work has wrestled with an issue that will, I believe, also find him a place among twenty-first-century theologians.

As I will argue in this reflection, Elizondo's work deserves equal standing among the great nineteenth- and twentieth-century theologians who attempted to articulate the relationship between culture and the gospel. His theology compares favorably, even extraordinarily, with the works of Troeltsch, Tillich, and Schleiermacher.[1] Yet, there is a cutting edge in Elizondo's thought that makes it more a work of the twenty-first century than a work of the twentieth century.[2] He has dealt with an issue European theologians have neglected since the beginning of modernity: what is the relationship between cosmic order and Christian redemption? This question was raised in the context of the evangelizing efforts of the first missionaries in the New World.[3] The missionaries came preaching a gospel of redemptive transformation while the indigenous practiced a religion of harmony within the cosmic order. These two seemingly incongruous views of salvation led to a new and vibrant ecclesial tradition born in the Americas. Though this tradition found little favor in the official Tridentine church that became the norm during the Counter-Reformation, it continued as the people's religion, or the popular religion of the Latin American faithful. It was not until the fresh winds of Vatican II and Medellín began to blow that the church's theologians began to seriously investigate this ignored tradition.

The first look, however, at the tradition that is popular religion was less than sympathetic. Liberation theology, the first important Latin American theology emerging after Vatican II and Medellín, responded to the reality of popular religion with either outright condemnation or sympathetic suspicion.[4] Only Fr. Elizondo, living out the Latin American ecclesial tradition in the context of the United States, took popular religion as a serious *topos* for theological reflection. His work on the semiotics of the popular tradition of Our Lady of Guadalupe transformed liberation theology's poor from being the *object* of liberation to being the *subject* of redemption.[5] In doing so, Fr. Elizondo was led to a truly innovative theological anthropology, namely, his anthropological notion of *mestizaje*, the biological and cultural mixing of peoples in the violent and unequal encounter of cultures.[6] *Mestizaje* reveals the Latin American church's answer to the relation between cosmic order and Christian redemption. Nature and culture intermix in the Christian gospel of redemption. Redemption is more than the "purification" of culture. It is a new creation. Redemption is more than a human undertaking. It is the human creature participating in a great cosmic adventure that the Jewish biblical scholar Jeremy Cohen called the "cosmic frontier."[7]

In this conception, the great Jesuit theologian Pierre Teilhard de Chardin guided Elizondo. I contend that Elizondo transformed Teilhard's evolutionary cosmology into a Latin American anthropology that answered the question of the relation between cosmic order and redemption. It is here, then, that I would like to place the significance of Fr. Elizondo's life work. It is both part of the larger dialogue with the great tradition of the theologians of "culture" as well as a work whose foundational insight, the relation between cosmic order and redemption, has yet to be explored as we approach the twenty-first century. Toward this end, I intend to demonstrate the affinity of Elizondo's work not only with the theology of culture but with the theology of evolutionary cosmology as proposed by Teilhard. As such, I hope to reveal that Elizondo's greatest theological contribution is laying the foundation for an even greater contribution to the theological thought of the twenty-first century.

The Theology of Culture

The great project of liberal theology, especially liberal Protestant theology, is arguably an attempt to relate popular culture to the gospel message in a sympathetic way.[8] Such an endeavor was launched in the wake of three important events which some claim formed the age now commonly referred to as modernity: (1) the religious wars of the Reformation, (2) the encounter of European (or, rather, classical) cultures with the cultures of the Americas, and (3) the early achievements of the natural sciences.[9] Ironically, the origin of liberal nineteenth-century

Protestant reflection on the theology of culture was also occasioned by an encounter with the cultures of the Americas as well as the issue of cosmic order and redemption raised by the natural sciences.

These events triggered the question whether "religion" belonged to the cosmic and metaphysical order studied by philosophers and theologians, or the cultural milieu that defined a people. In one sense, such a view of "religion" recognized a tension between "official" religion (religion as expounded by philosophers and theologians) and "popular" religion (religion as expressed by a people's way of life). As expressed in liberal theology, however, it also illuminated a dualist cosmology, a separation of cosmic (and metaphysical) realities and cultural realities. It is this double tension inherent in European Protestant theologies of culture that both demonstrates an affinity with as well as difference from Elizondo's engagement of popular religion. As such, Elizondo's thought is found to cross another "theological border." It doesn't merely cross the "border" between nature and culture but also the ecumenical "border," the "border" between Protestant liberal theology and Roman Catholic thought.

Theologians of Culture

Among liberal nineteenth-century Protestant theologians of culture, one can include Troeltsch, Schleiermacher, Harnack, and, in a sense, Paul Tillich. Tillich viewed the task of a liberal Protestant theology of culture as "stating the truth of the Christian message and interpreting this truth for every new generation."[10] Such an understanding of the theological task places before the theologian the challenge of accounting for the unity of the Christian message across the centuries while recognizing the capacity of the Christian message to address men and women with fresh vitality in different ages and in different places. These two aspects of the Christian message, its unity across the ages and its capacity to speak anew in the midst of change, require a concept that integrates universality and particularity. Indeed, these two aspects also define the essence of the culture concept. As Robert Schreiter notes, the concept of culture necessarily deals with the issue of unity and social change.[11] Troeltsch, for example, compared his own civilization to others and asked: Where do we and our God fit in all this variety?[12] Tillich asked: Where do we find God in a civilization that has lost its unity and become diverse within itself?[13] Elizondo, however, asked the question of culture in a more profound way: Where do we find God among a people caught in a culture-shattering experience and who now are conscious of a many-faceted sense of identity? Elizondo, I contend, asked of the culture concept a more profound question than any of these great liberal theologians of culture. Indeed, Elizondo's question needed not simply a "cultural" answer, but a "cosmic" one.

Elizondo's Theology of Culture

The sense of the "cosmic" is foundational in the Latin American ecclesial experience and can be seen as a principal element in the work of the "early" Elizondo.

In his first book, *The Human Quest*, he writes:

> As a former student of chemistry, biology, and mathematics, I share the fascination for the physical sciences, a fascination that I have discovered in people today. I truly believe that, while not "providing God," the sciences manifest more and more both the evident and the hidden glories of our evolving world.[14]

Elizondo's love of and fascination with the natural sciences, I believe, is also the love of and fascination with the cosmic order that is part of his ecclesial heritage. Indeed, *The Human Quest* is organized along cosmic lines. He begins with a chapter titled "Genesis," leads up to a chapter titled "Preparation for a New Creation," and then begins to sound his fundamental themes with his chapter on "New Creation: Christogenesis." The theological heritage of *The Human Quest* is easily discerned. Of thirty-two citations, nineteen are credited to the works of Teilhard de Chardin.[15]

Teilhard's influence on Elizondo's theology has been little noticed.[16] Yet, it is here that Elizondo as a theologian of culture distinguishes himself from previous theologies of culture such as Troeltsch's and Tillich's. While Troeltsch and Tillich saw culture as separate from nature, Elizondo, like Teilhard, sees not a dichotomy but a mysterious unity. As such, Elizondo follows the intuition of the great religions that existed in the Americas before Christianity came. The Maya, for example, based their sophisticated astronomy on the basis of the number twenty. Twenty, however, also stood in Maya religion as a symbol of the anthropos, the human creature. Just as the human creature has twenty fingers and toes, the cosmos is ordered according to this number. The human and the cosmic unite in this mystical anthropological cosmology based on the number twenty. This intuition, I have argued elsewhere,[17] becomes part of the Latin American ecclesial tradition born out of the early missionary efforts in the Americas. As a theologian of this ecclesial tradition, Elizondo must account for this sense that the natural and the cultural participate in a redeeming unity.

Elizondo, however, is not Mayan. His concern is to explain, like Troeltsch and Tillich, the "truth of the Christian message" in the context of a new generation. The consequences of such accounting in the context of Latin America's ecclesial tradition, however, results in a theology of culture that goes far beyond the scope of Troeltsch or Tillich. It is Teilhard who gives Elizondo the key "New Creation" theme that will be heard in all his writings. As we shall see, Elizondo weaves nature and culture in exquisite patterns as he develops his theology of culture. He goes beyond the concerns of liberal theology about the relationship between the gospel and culture and provides a foundation for a theology of the twenty-first century—the New Creation.

Mestizaje

Elizondo's theology of culture finds its basic shape in his doctoral dissertation.[18] He asks a question that continental theologies of culture failed to ask. What is the function of culture in the violent and unequal encounter of cultures? In other words, what does a theology of culture look like in the face of cultural evil? In his dissertation, Elizondo describes the near cultural genocide of the indigenous Mexican people and the subsequent U.S. conquest of northern Mexico. The conquest of a people is not only an historical "event" but also a cosmic experience. Out of the biological and cultural rape of a people, a new people are born who are biologically and culturally mixed. This "cosmic" experience results in the creation of the *mestizo*, a biological offspring of two different races, as well as the description of a new consciousness that finds itself at home in both of the two cultures and yet realizes it cannot rest peacefully in either.

It is the uniqueness of the question that sets apart a theology of culture and, in Elizondo's case, takes into account the Latin American experience of *mestizaje*. The *mestizo* makes a liberal theology of culture problematic. A multivalent existential situation describes the reality of the *mestizo*. Which culture provides the forms for the *mestizo*, Iberian, Native American, or African? The answer is all of these and none of the above. One could argue that the *mestizo* is a new culture and that is the situation provided for a theology of culture. The problem with this argument is that it does not take into account the multivalency of the *mestizo*'s cultural identity. It is not the case that the *mestizo* is a culture or that the *mestizo* has no culture. The reality of the *mestizo* is that he or she identifies with different cultures and yet fits in none of them. The multivalent identity of the *mestizo* makes problematic the culture concept's role of providing unity of essence in existential change. The root of the problem for liberal theology is its systematic exclusion of the cosmic. Liberal theology concentrated on culture as something radically separated from nature. It is here that Elizondo's appropriation of Teilhard's thought sets him apart as a theologian of culture.

In his first book, Elizondo asks the question of meaning:

From our earliest years, we begin to ask questions. As we grow, we seek to know the meaning of the realities that we encounter around us; increasingly, our questions become more penetrating. We begin to discover our uniqueness. We become aware that we are conscious, and begin to ask the meaning of this consciousness. Who am I? What is life? Why am I here?[19]

This traditional question, however, is transformed by Elizondo's orientation. He orients his work to complexity, the complexity of the human being in his or her cosmic and cultural environment. In Elizondo's words:

As humanity evolves, [we] discover more and more that vast complexity called [the human]. We continue to discover the meaning and working of creation, to learn how to improve and manipulate nature, to master the universe, yet the basic questions are still asked by every person at every stage of history. The more we discover about our universe, the more we seek to know just who is man? Who is woman? Who am I? From a simple analysis of experience, from the discoveries of our education, and from the demands of daily living, we begin to discover that there is more to life than mere existence. Science unfolds to us the gradual and beautiful evolution of the cosmic order toward a greater complexity and perfection.[20]

Indeed, Elizondo found this cosmic redemptive unfolding already at work in his native San Antonio:

I often ask myself the question: Is the frontier between the United States and Mexico the border between two nations or is it the frontier zone of a new human race? . . . It is not just the border between two countries, but the border between two humanities: between two worlds, two periods of time, two historical processes, two languages, two drastically different ways of life, two core cultural ideologies. The 3500 kilometers between the two countries is the political border between two nations, but it is much more. It is the meeting point and often the site of violent clash between two radically different civilizations . . . In the Southwest of the United States, the North of planet earth is meeting the South, and the result transcends old barriers by fusing North and South into a new synthesis. In this portion of the earth, differences are not destroyed, hidden, or ignored; they are absorbed to become the active ingredients of a new human group. The borders no longer mark the end limits of a country, a civilization, or even a hemisphere, but the starting points of a new space populated by a new human group. To be an intimate part of the birth of this *nueva raza* is indeed a fascinating experience.[21]

Here the influence of Teilhard becomes self-evident. The *mestizo* for Elizondo becomes a "new phylum of humanity." Nature and culture interweave in this theology of culture, asking something new of the culture concept. Unity now needs to be explained in the midst of essential (i. e., natural) change. Elizondo ingeniously provides this explanation by speaking of the *mestizo* as a "New Creation."

Elizondo finds the model for the "New Creation" in his christology. In his *Galilean Journey*, he makes the case that the Galilee of Jesus' time was very similar to the Southwestern frontier of the United States, concluding that Jesus is also a cultural *mestizo*. As such, Elizondo's christology is definitely "from below," but with a difference. The cosmological dimension of Jesus' cultural context is emphasized. In other words, Elizondo's christology becomes the flesh-and-blood Jesus of Nazareth.

The mind-blowing originality of Christianity is the basic belief of our faith that not only did the Son of God become man, but he became Jesus of Nazareth. Thus like every other man and woman, he was culturally situated and conditioned by his time and space. The God of Jesus cannot be known unless Jesus is known . . . yet we cannot really know Jesus of Nazareth unless we know him in the context of the historical and cultural situation of his human group. Jesus was not just a Jew, he was a Galilean Jew and throughout his life he and his disciples were identified as Galileans. In order to know Jesus, efforts must be made to know the Galileans of his day. It is only in their identity that the identity of the Word of God, made flesh, is to be found.[22]

Galilee was "the land of mixed peoples." Assyrian, Babylonian, Persian, Macedonian, Egyptian, and Syrian "rule, infiltration, and migration" established the character of the region as an international and cosmopolitan region.[23] Its name derives from the Hebrew *ha-Galil* or *Gelil ha Goyim*, which means "land of the heathen." This sets up Galilee as a region of "natural, ongoing biological and cultural *mestizaje*." As such, "the natural *mestizaje* of Galilee was a sign of impurity and rejection" for the "pure minded Jews of Jerusalem." Moreover, "Galilean Jews were doubly despised as being of mixed-blood and, generally speaking, ignorant—in both cases, they were considered impure." This image of the Galileans perceived by the Jerusalem Jews is "comparable to the image of the Mexican Americans to the Mexicans from Mexico, they were not pure Jews." On the other hand, "the image of the Galileans to the Greco Romans is comparable to the image of the Mexican American to the Anglo population of the United States." Thus, both the Galileans and Mexican Americans reflect the dynamic of Elizondo's *mestizaje*: "They were part of both [root cultures], and despised by both."

This Galilean mixing of cultures introduces a binary condition into the notion of the culture concept. Jesus as Galilean connects to the cultures that historically formed Galilean identity while at the same time having an authentic identity that is truly his own and separates him from his parent cultures. Jesus as Galilean is both an authentic (i. e., unique and particular) yet connected subject at the same time. As such, the binary condition of the Galilean complicates the discernment of identity in a special way. The mixing of cultures and races complicates the search for identity but in the violent and unequal encounter of cultures. Moreover, Galileans leave few written records.[24]

In identifying Jesus as a Galilean, Elizondo does not solve the problem of the cultural identity of Jesus, but shows that the intractability of the problem is in itself a guide to that identity. The intractability of Jesus' cultural identity represents an authenticity that is not amenable to description or definition. As such, Jesus' cultural identity resists assimilation or dismissal by the powerful. His cultural identity is not so much a content but an authenticity which is "otherness," an "otherness" that not only resists being involved in the enslaving social processes of creating human categorical boundaries but also breaks through to a new way of being human. Yet this is not all that is involved in the cultural identity of Jesus.

Jesus' ultimate identity resided in his uniqueness which was his unprecedented intimacy with God or "Abba."

> The fundamental proclamation of Jesus that God is our Father sounds so simple that it is easily deceiving . . . Jesus will not only refer to God as "my father," which went beyond all Jewish custom, but, going ever further, he uses the Aramaic language and refers to him in a most intimate way: ABBA! . . . [As such] he inaugurates a new relationship with God as Father, since the following of Jesus makes others capable of also being sons and daughters of God . . . On revealing God as the Abba of everyone, Jesus offers a new and radical understanding of human beings—by reason of being human, every person has the inherent ability of entering into a relationship of intimacy with

a common other. This opens up new possibilities for the structural basis of any and every society.[25]

Thus, part of the cultural identity of Jesus is his intimacy with the Father which allows a radical connectedness to the "other." By identifying the presence and activity of God the Father in the very intractability of identity, Elizondo is able to affirm differences even while purporting a cosmic process which will someday unite the human family. God becomes the "third other" through which the seemingly paradoxical relationship of difference and fellowship between two dissimilar groups or individuals can occur without sacrificing authenticity.

Thus, Jesus' mission was to reject the marginalization of exclusion by putting on the "existential nothingness" of the *mestizo* in order to bring about the unity of the human family. The unity of the human family guides Elizondo's reflection throughout his works. It is, in a way, the identification of the unity of the Christian message with the unity of the human family. The integrity of that message depends on the integrity of the human family. It is not so much a concern that belief in the true nature of God can be lost in the changes given by history, but that the human family, like nature, is seen as works of God throughout history. Yet God whose Son became *mestizo* and our Savior does not simply work existentially in this world. God is at work essentially through a New Creation. The *mestizo* is a product of that New Creation and Elizondo visualizes the day when a global *mestizaje* will occur.

Thus, by looking carefully at the cultural roots of the gospel message, namely, Jesus of Nazareth, Elizondo transforms the problem of liberal theology. It is not the "hiddenness" of the identity of the gospel in cultural forms that is the subject of a theology of culture. Rather, it is the very intractability of that identity that is the key to the relation between gospel message and cultural form. As such, Elizondo shows not only his affinity with Teilhard's thought but also his unique approach to the New Creation. Elizondo's transformation of the cultural concept as a way of explaining unity in existential change to a concept that explains unity through essential change is not a strict developmental or evolutionary concept. It distinguishes from an optimistic idea of development in that the New Creation was born of the conflict of conquest. It distinguishes itself from an evolutionary framework in the sense of an historical change through essential discontinuities as opposed to change through existential transformation. Thus, Elizondo's theology of culture sees, like Teilhard, the work of God through building a New Creation. For Teilhard, however, this New Creation takes place through a christology from above; for Elizondo this takes place through a christology from below.

Summary

Elizondo transformed the culture-concept of liberal theologians of culture by taking into account the biological and cultural dimensions of our humanity. As such, Elizondo was inspired by Teilhard de Chardin's great cosmic theology, thus crossing a great theological "border," the border between a theology of culture and a theology of creation. This accounting of the cosmological into the cultural separates Elizondo from liberal theologies of culture. Such accounting, on the other hand, unites him to Latin American theology. For in exploring the role of the cosmological in the redemptive dimensions of culture, Elizondo pursued a quint-essential Latin American theological *topos*: the relation between cosmic order and redemption. Elizondo's answer is rooted in his analysis of the redemptive nature of *mestizaje*. It shall prove, I believe, a continuing inspiration for theologians well into the twenty-first century.

Postscript

I first met Virgilio in San Antonio at the 1990 Hispanic Summer Institute sponsored by the Fund for Theological Education. The Hispanic Summer Institute, a blessed vision of the great Methodist theologian Justo González, sought to bring young Hispanic theologians in conversation with established thinkers. It proved for me a life-changing event. My first contact with Virgilio was electric. Indeed, Virgilio and I hit it off immediately. One reason for this spontaneous camaraderie (outside of Virgilio's magnetic personality) became clear during our first conversation. We both shared a common background in the natural sciences. In fact, the reason for our first conversation was advice I was seeking on an article comparing the Valladolid debate on the rationality of the American Indian and the debate over the nature of artificial intelligence. Virgilio was delighted with the subject and we had a wonderful conversation over the role of the natural sciences in theological reflection. This first conversation endeared Virgilio to me not only for his gracious openness to hearing the fledgling thought of one yet untried in professional theological reflection but also for the joy and delight of Virgilio's sharp intellect and his scientific-like curiosity in areas of thought yet to be explored.

It is this willingness to examine the unexplored, in my estimation, that marks Virgilio Elizondo as one of the great theologians of this century and the next. Virgilio, the discoverer-theologian-scientist, has opened entire worlds for fruitful theological exploration. It is one of these many worlds he discovered that I have described in this short essay. In doing so, I hope I have demonstrated the great range of Fr. Elizondo's thought and located it among the great twentieth-century theologians of culture. The next century, I believe, will see other theologians sailing down the territory that his great inquiring mind has already charted.

Notes

[1] The interested reader might want to explore my essay comparing the thought of Schleiermacher and Hispanic theology. See "The Whole and the Love of Difference: Latino Metaphysics as Cosmology," in *From the Heart of our People: Latino/a Explorations in Systematic Theology*, ed. Orlando O. Espín and Miguel H. Díaz (Maryknoll, NY: Orbis, 1999) 54-83.

[2] "The New Face of America: How Immigrants Are Shaping the World's First Multicultural Society," special ed. *Time* 142 (Fall 1993).

[3] The interested reader might want to consult Alex García-Rivera, "Creator of the Visible and

the Invisible: Liberation Theology, Postmodernism, and the Spiritual," *Journal of Hispanic/ Latino Theology* 3 (May 1996): 35-56; also, Alejandro García-Rivera, *The Community of the Beautiful: A Theological Aesthetics*, with a foreword by Don Gelpi (Collegeville, MN.: The Liturgical Press, 1999).

⁴See, e. g., Segundo Galilea, *Religiosidad popular y pastoral* (Mexico: Ediciones Cristiandad, 1979); Juan Luis Segundo, *Liberación de la teología* (Buenos Aires: Ediciones Carlos Lohle, 1975).

⁵Virgilio Elizondo, "Our Lady of Guadalupe as a Cultural Symbol" 118-125 above. See also Michael R. Candelaria on the distinction between the poor as subjects or as objects of liberation. Candelaria, *Popular Religion and Liberation: The Dilemma of Liberation Theology* (Albany: State University of New York Press, 1990).

⁶Elizondo first defined his understanding of *mestizaje* in his dissertation *Mestizaje: The Dialectic of Cultural Birth and the Gospel* (San Antonio: Mexican Cultural Center Press, 1978), which he later turned into a book, *Galilean Journey: The Mexican-American Promise* (Maryknoll, NY: Orbis, 1983). Fr. Elizondo continued to expand his thought in *The Future Is Mestizo: Life Where Cultures Meet* (Bloomington, IN: Meyer Stone, 1988). The notion of *mestizaje*, however, is not peculiar to Latin Americans. The biologist Jacques Ruffié considers *le Métissage Humain* of Cromagnon and Neanderthal peoples in chapter 7 of his second volume on the biological significance of race in Jacques Ruffié, *De la biologie à la culture*, new and rev. ed. Champ Scientifique (Paris: Flammarion, 1983).

⁷Jeremy Cohen, *"Be Fertile and Increase, Fill the Earth and Master It": The Ancient and Medieval Applications*, ed and introd. Baron F. von Hügel (New York: Meridian, Living, 1957).

⁸The interested reader may wish to consult Ernst Troeltsch, *Christian Thought: Its Theory and Applications*, ed. and intro. Baron F. von Hügel (New York: Meridian, Living, 1957).

⁹This is the thesis of Jacob Preus in *Explaining Religion: Criticism and Theory from Bodin to Freud* (New Haven and London: Yale University Press, 1987).

¹⁰Paul Tillich, *Systematic Theology*, vol. 1 (Chicago: University of Chicago Press, 1951) 4.

¹¹See, e. g., chapter 4 in Robert J. Schreiter, *Constructing Local Theologies* (Maryknoll, NY: Orbis, 1985). Also note that the culture concept as such is also a variation of the classical aesthetic principle known as "unity-in-variety." See, e. g., Wladyslaw Tatarkiewicz, "The Great Theory of Beauty & Its Decline," *Journal of Aesthetics and Art Criticism* 31 (1972): 165-179.

¹²Troeltsch saw the unity of the gospel message expressed as faith in the regeneration of the human alienated from God. This regeneration is effected by knowledge of God in Jesus Christ. However, this unity is mediated through the ages as a group of cultural values (*Kulturwerte*) welded into a system (a cultural synthesis) by a unifying principle, the "religious principle." See, e. g., Troeltsch, *Christian Thought*.

¹³In Tillich's days, the days of cynicism and despair brought about at the end of World War I, the question was not so much what to believe but why believe at all. Tillich approached the question by looking afresh at how the Christian message relates to the existential situation. In essence, the question came down to showing that meaning exists even in the existential situation of post-World War I Europe. Tillich explored this situation in his classic book *The Religious Situation*, trans. H. Richard Niebuhr (N.Y.: Henry Holt, 1932).

¹⁴Virgilio Elizondo, *The Human Quest: A Search for Meaning through Life and Death* (Huntington, IN: Our Sunday Visitor, 1978) 13 (first published as *A Search for Meaning in Life and Death*, 1971).

¹⁵These nineteen citations come from three major works of Teilhard: "L'énergie spirituelle de la souffrance," in *Oevres* 7 (Paris: Editions du Seuil, 1963); *The Divine Milieu* (New York: Harper and Row, 1960); and *The Phenomenon of Man* (New York: Harper and Row, 1965).

¹⁶A personal conversation with Fr. Elizondo confirmed Teilhard's influence on his thought.

¹⁷See chapter 2, "A Different Beauty," in García-Rivera, *The Community of the Beautiful: A Theological Aesthetics*.

¹⁸Elizondo, *Mestizaje*.

¹⁹Elizondo, *Human Quest* 17.

²⁰Ibid. 18.

²¹Elizondo, *The Future Is Mestizo* x, xi.

256   ALEJANDRO GARCÍA-RIVERA

[22]Elizondo, *Galilean Journey* 47.

[23]The following paragraph quotes pages 427-434 in Elizondo, *Mestizaje*. Elizondo bases this conclusion in the vast literature on the subject started by the then groundbreaking work of Ernst Lohmeyer, *Galiläa und Jerusalem* (Göttingen: Vandenhoeck and Ruprect, 1936). Since Elizondo's writing, however, the material on Galilee has undergone new evaluation (see, e. g., the references in Roberto Goizueta's essay in this volume 157 above).

[24]I am referring here to the issue of education and access to prestigious positions in institutions that would foster the kind of documentation usually needed to leave an historic trail. Gutiérrez calls this dimension of the "other" in the violent and unequal encounter of cultures the "underside of history." Gustavo Gutiérrez, *Teología desde el reverso do la historia* (Lima: CEP, 1977).

[25]Elizondo, *Mestizaje* 451, 465.

The Confrontation between the Theology of the North and the Theology of the South

Rosino Gibellini

I met Virgilio Elizondo in August 1975 at a Latin American theological meeting on the topic of "Liberation and Captivity" that took place in Mexico City. We became friends at once. Our friendship has been strengthened on various occasions and in many different cities around the world at congresses of the Ecumenical Association of Third World Theologians (EATWOT), to which I was invited as a guest observer, and also at the yearly general assemblies of the international journal of theology *Concilium*, where, for years, Virgilio Elizondo directed the section on "Practical Theology" (with Norbert Greinacher) and, subsequently, the section on "Theology of Liberation" (with Leonardo Boff). As a Mexican American theologian, Elizondo has always served as a bridge between the theology of the North and the theology of the South. And now, in his honor, I would like to reconstruct the sometimes tense relation between these two cultural and theological forces to which Virgil Elizondo has brought a decisive contribution, both in terms of his thoughts and actions. Thus, in this essay his work will be situated in an ecumenical and international context.

The *Geschichte der katholischen Theologie* by the German historian Martin Grabmann—one of the classical texts of theological historiography in this century, published in its first edition in 1933 (and often reedited until the last photocopied edition of 1983)—completely ignores the theology of Latin America, but it does mention the theology of North America, even though only in a few lines and in the last paragraph. Only the Spanish edition of this same work, published in Madrid in 1940, included the original German edition with "Brief comments on theology in Latin America."[1] The emergence of the Latin American theology of liberation in the years 1968-1972 represented, therefore, an event of considerable theological, ecclesial, and cultural relevance[2] which would become even more expanded with the establishment of EATWOT at the Conference of Dar es Salaam (Tanzania) in August 1976.[3] Let us reconstruct the main stages of the confrontation that had been looming as early as the seventies between the theology of the area of Europe/North Atlantic (theology of the North) and the emerging theology in Latin America, Africa, and Asia (theology of the South).

Doing Theology in a Revolutionary Situation

The first confrontation, which can be better defined as a clash, took place from May 1 to May 5, 1973, in Geneva, where the World Council of Churches organized a symposium on the new theological realities that were emerging in the Americas and, more specifically, on Black theology and on the Latin American theology of liberation.[4] At the 1973 Geneva symposium, Black theology was represented by James Cone and by Eduardo Bodipo-Malumba from Africa. The Latin American theology of liberation was represented by two Brazilians, Hugo Assmann and Paulo Freire.

The symposium was conducted for the first time as a discussion forum and it led to two results, over and beyond the fact that European theologians took note, first hand, of the changes that were occurring in the area of theology. To be precise: (a) The discussion was harsh and the first conclusion that asserted itself was the inability to communicate with different theological and somehow opposed realities. James Cone admitted: "As long as we live in a world of oppressors and oppressed, communication will be impossible. I do not believe that the oppressed and the oppressors can communicate with one another because of the different realities which condition their symbols and their language."[5] (b) This observed lack of communication should not be interpreted as an exclusively negative fact since it also had its positive side: it enabled one to discover the other as different from oneself, without simple and hasty assimilation. Hugo Assmann noted: "The basic contradiction in our days is that we are conditioned by the diversity existing in the Third World, the world of the oppressed. However, this experience of 'incommunication,' which I have lived so many times, is also a creative moment. It is the recognition of the other as a person."[6] It is significant to note that the Acts of the 1973 Geneva symposium were edited under the title of "Incommunication."

This first meeting, therefore, was not a happy one, and it is on the basis of this proclaimed "incommunication" that Jürgen Moltmann's "Open Letter" of 1975[7] can be explained. It was addressed to the Argentine evangelical theologian José Míguez Bonino, the author of *Doing Theology in a Revolutionary Situation* (1975).[8]

In his letter to Míguez Bonino, Moltmann introduced himself in these words: "After Hugo Assmann told the 1973 Geneva Conference that with European theologians, because they are Europeans, there was only room for incommunication instead of dialogue, my being available to take criticism into account had grown thin. Instead, you say that you want to critique Metz's theology and mine in order to further the dialogue rather than to interrupt it. This is an invitation."[9] Further on in the letter, there are objections to the Latin American theology of liberation, especially as it is found in texts by José Míguez Bonino, Rubem Alves, Juan Luis Segundo, and Gustavo Gutiérrez: (a) First of all, Moltmann rejects the criticism of abstraction directed at the theology of hope and political theology: "In terms of what concerns the theological criticism of European theology, there is a contradictory impression: it is harshly criticized and then one discovers, with surprise, that in the end, the critic says in his own words what had already been said."[10] (b)

Liberation theology is accused of an uncritical use of Marxism which, in the final analysis, is a sociology elaborated in Europe.

If Moltmann did not really grasp the newness of liberation theology in his letter, Bonino (and other Latin American theologians) thought that Latin America was in a revolutionary or prerevolutionary situation. Beyond the diversity of contexts and political assessments, the German theologian stated that he was open to the confrontation:

> The most important difference between the Latin American theology of liberation and the political theology of Europe is found in the assessment of the different historical situations. I believe that there is a large consensus on what is necessary on the subject of world politics. But the different countries, societies, and cultures are not yet living synchronically in the same time . . . The goal is a human world society in which people no longer live against one another but rather, with one another. Latin American orthopraxis could have a different appearance from European, Western orthopraxis. In our differences, what matters is a common perspective.[11]

Moltmann's "Open Letter" was present in the discussions of the first 1975 Detroit (USA) Conference, "Theology in the Americas," in which the Latin American theology of liberation entered into dialogue, for the first time, with the new North American realities, and, specifically, Black theology and feminist theology.[12] I myself was present as a guest observer at the Detroit Conference and, on that occasion, I became the coordinator of a response from the Latin American theologians to Moltmann's "Open Letter." The concerted text of this "Response to Moltmann" exists only in manuscript form in the archives of Brescia's Queriniana Publishing House, which had published *Theology of Hope* by Moltmann and *A Theology of Liberation* by Gutiérrez and which was making plans to translate *Doing Theology in a Revolutionary Situation* by Bonino. The texts of this unanimous "Response" reached me in the years 1976 and 1977, but when the text was already all but definitive, the project was dropped with the previous agreement of the authors. What had happened? In the meantime, the process of preparing for the Puebla Conference (1977-1979) had started and liberation theologians were beginning to have difficulties within the Latin American church. In addition, a campaign of defamation against liberation theology as a "subversive theology" and as a "theology of Marxist infiltration" had been opened in Germany. It would have been counterproductive to start a controversy between Latin American theology and European political theology and to make it public. In a particularly delicate ecclesial juncture, it was more productive to find all the points of convergence and possible alliances, which would later prove to be valuable in the years of the ecclesiastical controversy (1984-1986).[13] Here, however, I can present a few ideas from the unpublished "Response to Moltmann" (and to European political theology) in this first phase of the confrontation which can be situated between the Geneva symposium (1973) and the start of the process of preparing for the Puebla Conference (1977-1979).

In his "Response to Moltmann," Hugo Assmann[14] quickly cleared the way from useless misunderstandings by relativizing the "incriminating" text of the Geneva symposium on account of the "scant representation of isolated texts." Even if "incommunication" had been mentioned on that occasion, it was a question of going to the real problem, which was the future of Christianity in the perspective of the future of the oppressed world.

To Moltmann's objection that Latin American theology of liberation did not have the newness that Black theology, African theology, and Japanese theology represented, Juan Luis Segundo[15] responded that the problem of liberation was not to be "distinctive" or "characteristic" in accordance with academic models: a theology born of praxis and aimed at illumining the praxis with faith "has to assume much more concrete and situational elements than those which academic theology is accustomed to making its own and to studying." The problem consists in adjusting *problematic* and *theology* in Europe as well as in Latin America. The real problem is not to attach an exaggerated importance to being "Latin Americans," but rather, to be realistic and to do theology within a determined historical context. These observations were confirmed by the fact that there is also a theology of liberation in Africa and in Asia. In the report presented to the Third EATWOT Congress in Wennappuwa (Colombo, Sri Lanka) in 1979, Singhalese theologian Aloysius Pieris of Sri Lanka would be the one who identified liberation theology as a *third-worldness* dimension of the theology of the Third World even in the differentiation of the problematics of the different continental contexts.[16]

José Míguez Bonino,[17] the addressee of Moltmann's "Open Letter," focused his attention on the relation between liberation theology and Marxism. Liberation theology does not limit itself to a "speculative confrontation" as political theology does but it does establish a "more operative confrontation" with Marxism as a historical fact, as part of a broader historical becoming, of a historical process "to which we have to strive to give a more human future." Bonino blamed European political theology for its abstract formulations: "There is a kind of Apolinarianism [in political theology] through which faith assumes a historical function although, paradoxically, in a quasi a-historical way, without becoming incarnated in the particular form of an ideology." In other words, political theology would limit itself to assuming a critical function toward society, but not in a concrete project of liberation as is the case of liberation theology.

In his response, Gustavo Gutiérrez anticipated the essay "The Emergent Gospel: Theology from the Underside of History," published in a small volume in Lima in 1977 and inserted in the final section of *The Power of the Poor in History*, published in 1979 after the Puebla Conference. In this essay,[18] Gutiérrez develops a clear analysis in which he indicates points of difference and points of rupture between what he calls progressive European theology and the theology of liberation. While liberation theology is incomprehensible without being inserted in the struggle for liberation, European political theology finds its reference in the modern world or, according to Bonhoeffer's formulation, in the world come of age (*die mündige Welt*) without realizing that individualism is the most important characteristic of modern ideology and bourgeois society. Therefore, the theology of liberation comes from *another horizon*, in fact, from a *historical contradiction* between the bourgeois subject as author of modernity and "the people left out of history," that is to say, exploited classes, oppressed cultures, races discriminated against, and women. These are the ones who, in Latin America, are becoming the subject of another historical process which is a process of liberation of the people: "It is a calling into question of the social, economic, and political order which oppresses and marginalizes them and also of the ideology which claims to justify this domination. The challenges of faith coming from the world of the exploited can only be understood in this context. Such a provocation seeks to go to the roots of the poverty and the injustice which are being experienced in Latin America and in other parts of the world and this is the reason why the way is social revolution, rather than a reformism of half measures. Liberation, not a theory of development. Socialism, not a modernization of the ruling system."[19]

Gutiérrez's criticism of European theology became sharper in his article "The Limits of Modern Theology: A Text by Bonhoeffer," published in *Concilium* (1979/ 5) and taken up again at the conclusion of *The Power of the Poor in History* (1979). For Gutiérrez, the "coming of age," that is to say, modernity, with which modern theology contends, has been built upon a world of poverty and exploitation: "But if Bonhoeffer was attentive to the fascist enemy who was stabbing liberal society in the back, he was less sensitive to the world of injustice on which such a society was leaning."[20]

In summary, the planned "Response to Moltmann" was becoming more, in general, a "Response to Modern Theology." It was calling into question the historical bases on which the modern world was built and, as a consequence, it showed the lack of reliability of the very project of modern theology.[21]

Doing Theology in a Divided World

If one should want to determine the starting date of the confrontation between theology of the North and theology of the South under the banner of dialogue, one could indicate the ecumenical congress promoted by EATWOT in Geneva from January 5-13, 1983—ten years after the above mentioned Geneva symposium—on the theme "Doing Theology in a Divided World."[22]

EATWOT had initiated a process of reflection that, in five congresses from Dar es Salaam (Tanzania) in 1976 to New Delhi (India) in 1981, had led participants to review and examine the new theological realities emerging in the Third World. In Geneva, for the first time, the process led to a confrontation of representatives of third-world theology and representatives of European theology. As indicated by Sergio Torres, the secretary of the Association, one can assume that 1983 marked the start of a confrontation under the banner of fruitful dialogue.

At that meeting, Dorothee Sölle introduced into theology the dialectics of enlightenment which, if it sounded critical of European culture as a culture of domination, also sounded critical of European theology that did not succeed in overcoming sexism, capitalism, and militarism. Instead, it had cultivated a "theology of apartheid."

I mean the concept of apartheid both in terms of political disunion and spiritual disunion. Our theology of the First World is polluted by our living in apartheid. We are not allowing our brothers and sisters from the Third World to enter in our thoughts and feelings, in our hearts and in our prayers, in our way of reading the Bible and in our way of doing theology . . . Living in rich countries of the First World means being part of apartheid by our lifestyle and our ideology.[23]

From the start, in his written works, political theologian Johann Baptist Metz had been in solidarity with the requests of liberation theology. In his intervention, Metz summarized the positions of European political theology in a few theses: (a) He proclaimed the end of the Eurocentric era of Christianity and the passage from a culturally monocentric church to a culturally polycentric church. "Empirically, the Eurocentric period of the church is coming to an end. The Catholic church of the present day does not have a church of the Third World, it is a church of the Third World with a European/Western origin." (b) He illustrated a new concept of reform on a world scale: "The second reform will not come from Wittenberg, Geneva, or from Rome but it will come from the poor churches of the Third World." (c) Metz invited the building up of a new culture capable of a new praxis: "Within Christianity, this polycentrism has to be based on a culture of resistance/liberation. Otherwise, we will never succeed in collaborating for a culture of peace . . . inspired by faith and discipleship as a productive and unifying force in our divided world."[24]

French theologian Georges Casalis confessed: "We have begun to be struck by the irruption of the Third World. We have started to listen to the cries of the poor and of those who have no voice. The first elements of a new theology are emerging from the context of a socio-political conversion."[25]

The 1983 Geneva meeting made the following points especially evident: the contribution of feminist theology as a theology of liberation elaborated in the First World and under the challenge of the theology of the Third World, as well as the emergence of new theological currents in the First World. The final Geneva Declaration reviewed them in the following way: "Feminist theology, theology of resistance, European theology of liberation, theology of conversion, theology of crisis, political theology, and radical evangelical theology are a few of the initiatives which express the fresh air of repentance and of renewal in the First World"[26] and valorized, above all, the awareness that the emergence of the theology of the Third World represents an epochal turning point in the history of Christianity and its theology.

Modern Theology and the Theology of Liberation

The relation between modern theology and liberation theology as a common dimension of the theology of the Third World is now included in the European theological agenda, and here I would like to recall the most significant interventions.

An illuminating example was the debate, which took place in Europe, on the future of the Enlightenment. Immediately after the Second World War, Adorno and Horkheimer published the *Dialectics of Enlightenment* (1947), in which the two philosophers from Frankfurt showed how the historical process of enlightenment had turned into its opposite, into universal alienation in the sense that historical reason had become the *ratio* of domination (*Herrschaft*) over human beings and nature.[27] Forty years after the publication of that work (1987), which stated the debate on enlightenment and the history of its effects (*Wirkungsgeschichte*) in new terms, a group of eminent scholars decided to go over the *Dialectics of Enlightenment*.[28] For Jürgen Habermas, it could lead to a *Gegenaufklärung*, to a counter-Enlightenment, which is what characterizes the historical pessimism of today's conservative or neo-conservative cultural expressions, or else, by recovering the most authentic thinking of the two philosophers of the *Dialectics of Enlightenment*, it could lead to an *Aufklärung über Aufklärung*, to an enlightenment on enlightenment capable not only of criticism but also of self-criticism: "By its own nature, enlightenment has to be clear about itself and on the misfortune (*Unheil*) that it has caused."[29] For Habermas, it was a question of identifying the "rational nucleus" of enlightenment over and beyond historical ambiguities. This rational nucleus is a legacy to keep and to develop in order to face new problems "which, in any case, can be resolved only in the light of the sun, only with the cooperation and only with the last drops of a solidarity almost drained of blood."[30]

The main representatives of European political theology, the theologians Metz and Moltmann, have also brought their own contributions to the context of this critical revision. For Moltmann, the culture of enlightenment "is not threatened from the outside, for example, by the 'conservative syndrome,' by 'religious counter-revolutions,' by prophecies of 'the end of the modern era,' by the 'post-modern' era or by the 'New Age,' but it is certainly threatened by the contradictions of enlightenment itself."[31] The "three great contradictions" are as follows: *first*, the structural contrast between the progress of the First World and the misery and poverty of the Third World; "Either the culture of enlightenment succeeds in leading the people of the Third World to political freedom, social justice, and cultural autonomy or else it destroys two-thirds of humankind. This is why that culture has, as it were, to go beyond itself, namely beyond its European form";[32] *second*, the system of *nuclear terror* by which the *Neuzeit*, the modern period, is threatening to be overturned into the *Endzeit*, the end period; *third*, the *ecological crisis* which the techno-scientific civilization of enlightenment has come up against, a crisis that is in danger of leading to the collapse of nature. Moltmann writes: "The *culture of enlightenment* will be able to keep its ideals and to fulfill its promises in agreement with ecumenical and political Christianity in the perspective of the theology of liberation and the theology of peace."[33]

For Metz, if the culture of enlightenment wants to have a future, it has to open itself up to the contribution that can be offered by the "memory of God" (*Gottesgedächtnis*) of the biblical and Christian tradition, "which even today enables one to speak of humanity and solidarity, oppression and liberation, and to protest against an injustice which cries out to heaven and which can, therefore, render practical a maturity (*Mündigkeit*) capable of politics."[34]

But the debate is also present in other areas. In *Liberation and Progressive Theologies* (1987), Christian Duquoc set up a confrontation between the requests of liberation theology and progressive theologies. The French theologian distinguishes three types of theology: (1) One is the *classical theologies* that use ontological instruments and do not directly confront the problems of society. Polemically speaking, these theologies are antimodern or, in their abstraction, they ignore modernity and the problem of praxis. (2) *Progressive theologies* (political theology in particular) confront modernity and, from modernity, they take up the demands of critical rationality and freedom. (3) *Liberation theologies* embrace those who are left out of history and assume the preferential option for the poor; they also become critical of modernity. "The major problem of the *theologies of liberation* is not emancipation but rather, exploitation. These are not theologies of freedom but, rather, theologies of liberation."[35]

Paradoxically, it so happens that in this triangle of theologies, classical theology and liberation theology are both critical of modernity. The first one fights it directly because of its secularism and the second one is suspicious of it and bypasses it because there is "a complicity"[36] between progressive theology and the logic of the West. Duquoc thinks that

> In spite of some rather strong reservations toward the theology of liberation, Roman authorities prefer these theologies to the progressive theologies that came from the Enlightenment. Rome considers the former less subversive for the Catholic church: the struggle for the poor can be assumed without any further drama for the structure of the Catholic church, whereas the theology of freedom secretly undermines it.[37]

But it is not possible to go back to traditional neoclassical theology, in that it is dated and driven by strategies of immunization from the problems of freedom that came with modern times. Given the importance of the appeal for freedom, which is the driving force of political theology, and the appeal for the option for the poor that mobilizes liberation theology, the last conclusion of Duquoc's diagnosis is the following: "Perhaps, in the pluralistic space of today's world, these [theologies] cannot do anything else than coexist and mutually question one another."[38]

At the 1992 El Escorial (Madrid) meeting where Johann Baptist Metz developed the theme "European Theology and the Latin American Theology of Liberation," he went much further. In his presentation, Metz started "from the premise that the theology of liberation is something more and something different from a mere social theory from the left or from a subsequent pastoral strategy. It is theology."[39] This insight reflects a biting precision aimed at appraisals not exempt from neo-scholastic suppositions and laissez-faire arrogance.

For the political theologian, there is a convergence between European political theology and the Latin American theology of liberation. And this convergence can be identified on several fronts: (a) Both theologies are characterized by their sensitivity to the history of human suffering and, as a result, to the problem of theodicy. (b) Both theologies can be characterized as post-idealist theologies in the sense that they include the question of the relation between reason and faith within the question of the relation between theory and praxis and, from there, they develop either the mystical or the political dimension of faith. (c) From this is derived the commitment of these theologies "to support the transition from a European church for others to a European church of others . . . It is a question of building up a post-idealist hermeneutic culture, a culture which acknowledges others in their being others, in their otherness."[40]

The problem of the relation between modern theology and liberation theology was taken up again with a particular reference to Gutiérrez's criticism of Bonhoeffer in the report "Bonhoeffer, Modernity, and Liberation Theology" that was presented by North American theologian Clifford Green at the 1992 New York Congress organized by the Bonhoeffer Society. Its proceedings were published in 1994, on the occasion of the fiftieth anniversary of the *Letters from Prison* written by Bonhoeffer from April to August 1944.[41] And it was precisely on the basis of one of these letters, written on June 8, 1944, that Gutiérrez conducted a more general criticism of modern theology. In a careful analysis of Bonhoeffer's texts and their interpretation by Gutiérrez, Green agreed that Bonhoeffer's analysis of *Mündigkeit* and modernity (which relies directly on Dilthey, as Ernst Feil and Christian Gremmels have demonstrated)[42] was "a very partial and incomplete analysis."[43] It lacked an appropriate social analysis capable of assessing the costs of the process that led Western people to the emancipation of modernity: "Here Gutiérrez's clear words are pertinent."[44] But at the same time, Green wondered if the criticism brought by Gutiérrez against modern theology which attempted to respond to the challenges of modernity did, in fact, discredit too strongly an undertaking that still had value, and he thought that Gutiérrez had gone beyond the positions expressed in the final essays of 1977 through 1979, in his *The Power of the Poor in History* (1979).

Among the subsequent texts, a particular text was adopted. It is taken from *La Verdad los hará libres* (1986), a book that immediately followed the 1984-1986 ecclesial controversy about liberation theology. The book in question is worth mentioning. After having pointed out the differences between modern theology, which is addressed to nonbelievers, and the theology of liberation, which is addressed to nonpeople, Gutiérrez continued:

> Those addressed in modern theology are different, and it is only right to take this fact into account. Modern theology is called upon to answer the questions raised by the modern consciousness and perceptively expressed by the Enlightenment. For if theology is done in the service of evangelization, then it must find the language needed for the Christian message to be effectively present in the modern world, the world in which the church, too, is living. Modern theology is therefore a necessary theology that has to meet the challenges of unbelievers and counteract the secularizing influence these challenges exert in the Christian world.[45]

Clifford Green's analysis concludes, therefore, not only with a relativization of the theory of modernity in Bonhoeffer's writings but also with the recognition of the path accomplished by the theology of liberation in its assessment of modern theology: "It seems, therefore, that Gutiérrez went from the concept, according to which the theology of liberation supersedes modern theology, to the concept, according to which each of these theologies has legitimate roles with regard to particular social and historical contexts."[46]

Green's analysis was confirmed at the congress organized by the University of Münster (Germany) in 1987 (and not taken under consideration by the North American theologian) on the theme "Europe and Latin America in Dialogue" with the participation of Latin American and European theologians.[47] On that occasion, Gutiérrez confirmed a primary contention of the theology of liberation about theology: experience precedes theory. Yet this is also valid for the great projects of modern theology, and he referred to Bonhoeffer's example:

> I believe that theology is an attempt to respond to the questions of experience. For example, a significant part of modern theology is based on the question which was formulated by Bonhoeffer: How can we speak about God in this adult world? The adult world was his own experience . . . I think that the question about the possibility of speaking about God in an adult world, to be developed in a "technical" Christian and ecclesial sense, is a pastoral question and, as a result, a concrete question.[48]

Gutiérrez justified Bonhoeffer's question as a question that flowed from an experience and, in this sense, as a pastoral question. But he also immediately pointed out the different question to which the theology of liberation strives to respond: "In Latin America things are different. Our question would rather be: How can we speak about God in the presence of the suffering of the innocent? How can we find a language about God that would derive from the suffering of innocent human beings?"[49]

At that same congress, Leonardo Boff explained the difference and even the contrast between the European traditions of freedom and Latin American thinking about liberation. The European traditions of freedom have their own intrinsic value, although they contradict themselves in that historically speaking they are made to be valid only for Europe and the Western world. Hence, it is necessary for "the option for integral liberation" to be assumed by Europe and by Latin America and for both processes to be brought to flow into a single, historical, and political process capable of including freedom and liberation as its expressions. In this context, Boff recognized the contribution of Metz's political theology and of Moltmann's theology of hope and solidarity: "They have helped the churches to make their own contribution to this gigantic—I would even say, messianic—process of integral liberation."[50]

Moltmann was also following this line of confrontation and collaboration. In *Political Theology and Liberation Theology* (1991), the author of the 1975 "Open Letter," which started a debate and polemics, developed a concise comparison between the two theological perspectives: (a) First of all, Moltmann distinguishes European progressive theology from political theology. If progressive theology has liberal roots and considers religion as a "private matter," political theology presupposes "the public testimony of faith and political discipleship of Christ."[51] (b) In addition, if the theology of liberation has a single theme, the main theme of political theology is complex and it goes from the theology of peace, to ecological theology, to the theology of human rights, to European feminist theology as political theology.[52] (c) Every theology has its own context and this is true for liberation theology and for political theology but "each theology is truly a theo-logy and, therefore, it is universal."[53] (d) And, in the name of this affinity, he concludes by asking for a pact of dialogue and collaboration: "Political theology is the internal criticism of the modern world. Liberation theology is the external criticism of the modern world. At this point, is it not time for the critical theology of the First World and the theology of liberation of the Third World to enter into some type of agreement?"[54]

The harsh confrontation between European/North Atlantic theology and liberation theology as the common expression of the theology of the Third World is now developing into a fruitful dialogue, at least in the most vibrant sectors of Catholic and ecumenical theology. The decisive contribution did, however, come from Latin America and from liberation theology, which have questioned the kind of universal, tacit normativeness of European theology. From the South came radical demands that prompted the theology of the North to rethink its theological model, the relation between experience and theory, between orthodoxy and orthopraxis, and also its relation with modernity, far beyond Bonhoeffer's already exacting demands.

Doing Theology beyond Borders

Paul Tillich, the German American theologian, summarized his life experience which had led him from Europe to the United States in a short book, *On the Boundary* (1966). In this book he wrote: "The boundary is the best place for acquiring knowledge."[55] That experience gave rise to the method of correlation between Christian revelation and human culture. It had its expression and application in the great *Systematic Theology* (1951-1963). And, in an article titled "On the Boundary Line" (1960), written after a trip to Japan on which he had encountered Asian wisdom, Tillich foresaw the possibility of overcoming what he called "Western provincialism"[56] by way of opening significant opportunities for dialogue between cultures and religions, a dialogue that represents one of the most difficult themes of the contemporary cultural and theological debate.

If Tillich's theology is a theology *on the boundary*, American Hispanic theology, with Virgil Elizondo as its initiator and its best-known representative, is a theology *beyond borders*. It becomes the interpreter of a new human reality that is expanding.

I recall when the Foundation of the international journal of theology *Concilium*, represented by Edward Schillebeeckx, decided at Gustavo Gutiérrez's suggestion to nominate Virgilio Elizondo as a member of the board of directors, presenting him as a *theologian of the borderlands*. For twenty years, from 1979 to 1999, the theologian from San Antonio, Texas, has carried out this role with theological and pastoral creativity. Thus, American Hispanic theology made its entrance into the context of international theology as it developed its role of connecting the theology of the North with the theology of the South.

I also remember having received as a gift, in the seventies, the typewritten text of Virgilio Elizondo's doctoral thesis, which was presented and defended at the Institut Catholique of Paris. For a European, the title *Mestizaje* was somewhat mysterious. Later on, this text would flow into the book *Galilean Journey* (1983). In addition to describing the journey of Jesus from Galilee, culturally *mestizo*, to Jerusalem, the city of the resurrection, under the category of *mestizaje*, this book pointed out the promise of which Mexican Americans were the bearers. The concept of *mestizaje* became a hermeneutic key to rereading the Gospels but also to reinterpreting the dynamics of culture, as Jacques Audinet expressed in the preface to the work: "Elizondo points to a new frontier . . . His treatment of Mexican American *mestizaje* leads naturally to thoughts about global *mestizaje*."[57] By its hermeneutic newness, this book marked the beginning of a path of reflection and of a theological movement already well structured and present on the theological map of the end/start of the millennium.[58]

The most widely read work of Virgilio Elizondo in Europe is *The Future Is Mestizo* (1988). With autobiographical flair, it took up Virgilio's major work and it served to bring this new, complex cultural and theological category to the attention of European theology. Léopold Sédar Senghor has pointed out the convergence of Virgilio Elizondo's theological discourse with the vision of Teilhard de Chardin, who anticipated the "*civilisation de l'Universel*"[59] at the threshold of the third millennium.

With the paper "Toward an American Hispanic Theology of Liberation in the U.S.A." (1981), presented in the context of an international conference of the Ecumenical Association of Third World Theologians (EATWOT, New Delhi, 1981), Elizondo very early and authoritatively inserted this problematic into the broader context of the theology of the Third World at the time when contextual theologies were being defined. At this session, Elizondo stated: "We are . . . witnessing the beginnings of properly Hispanic theological productivity."[60]

As an active member of the board of directors of *Concilium*, published in seven languages, and in keeping with the vocation of American Hispanic theology, Elizondo has contributed to the building of a cultural bridge between the theology of the North and the theology of the South. Among the articles written for *Concilium*, the text "The New Humanity of the Americas" (1990) especially deserves to be mentioned. There we have the best expression of the *mestizo* and, at the same time, the universal spirit of Virgilio Elizondo, his dream and his vision of a new humanity of the Americas as the paradigm for a new humanity of the world.[61] Once Virgilio expressed himself in these words: "The more specific you are, the more particular, the more universal you are."

This is a dialectic of the particular and the universal, lived in his own flesh, celebrated in life, combined with anthropological and theological reflection and made concrete in a praxis of resistance, solidarity, and liberation. At a time when we are theorizing on the clash of civilizations, this is the gift that Virgilio Elizondo

and American Hispanic theology are offering to the universal church and to our society on its way toward multiculturalism and universal *mestizaje*.
Ad multos annos, Virgilio!

(Trans. Colette Joly Dees)

Notes

[1]Cf. M. Grabmann, *Die Geschichte der katholischen Theologie seit dem Ausgang der Väterzeit* (Freiburg im Breisgau, 1933; Darmstadt, 1983); Spanish edition, *Historia de la teología católica* (Madrid, 1940).

[2]Cf. C. Geffré and G. Gutiérrez, eds., *Prassi di liberazione e fede cristiana. La testimonianza dei teologi latino-americani*, in *Concilium* 1974/6; R. Gibellini, ed., *La nuova frontiera della teologia in America Latina* (Brescia, 1975).

[3]Cf. S. Torres and V. Fabella, eds., *The Emergent Gospel: Theology from the Underside of History*, Papers from the Ecumenical Dialogue of Third World Theologians, Dar es Salaam, August 5-12, 1976 (Maryknoll, NY, 1978).

[4]Cf. World Council of Churches, ed., *Incommunication: A Symposium on Black Theology and Latin American Theology of Liberation* (Geneva, 1973); trans. Italian *Teologie dal Terzo Mondo* (Brescia, 1974).

[5]J. Cone, in *Teologie dal Terzo Mondo*, cit. 120.

[6]H. Assmann, in *Teologie dal Terzo Mondo*, cit. 121.

[7]Cf. J. Moltmann, "Lettera aperta a José Míguez Bonino," in R. Gibellini, ed., *Ancora sulla "teologia politica" il dibattito continua* (Brescia, 1975) 202-217.

[8]Cf. J. M. Bonino, *Fare teologia in una situazione rivoluzionaria* (1975) (Brescia, 1976).

[9]J. Moltmann, "Lettera aperta" 203.

[10]J. Moltmann, "Lettera aperta" 205.

[11]J. Moltmann, "Lettera aperta" 211, 215.

[12]Cf. S. Torres and J. Eagleson, eds., *Theology in the Americas* (Acts of the Detroit Conference, August 1975) (Maryknoll, NY, 1976).

[13]On the controversy concerning the theology of liberation, cf. R. Gibellini, *Il dibattito sulla teologia della liberazione* (Brescia, 1986); J.B. Metz, ed., *Die Theologie der Befreiung: Hoffnung oder Gefahr für die Kirche?* (Düsseldorf, 1986); A. F. McGovern, *Liberation Theology and Its Critics: Toward an Assessment* (Maryknoll, NY, 1989).

[14]Cf. H. Assmann, *El futuro del mundo oprimido y el futuro del cristianismo* (typewritten text, 1976).

[15]Cf. J. L. Segundo, *Teología latino-americana: ¿por qué, cuánto, cómo?* (typewritten text, 1976).

[16]A. Pieris, "Toward an Asian Theology of Liberation: Some Religio-Cultural Guidelines," in V. Fabella, ed., *Asia's Struggle for Full Humanity: Toward a Relevant Theology*, Papers from the Asian Theological Conference, January 7-20, 1979, Wennappuwa, Sri Lanka (Maryknoll, NY, 1980) 74-95.

[17]Cf. J. M. Bonino, *Los usos del marxismo en teología. Peligros y promesa de una relación controversial* (typewritten text 1976).

[18]Cf. G. Gutiérrez, "Teologia dal rovescio della storia" (1977), in *La forza storica dei poveri* (1979) (Brescia, 1981) 211-273.

[19]G. Gutiérrez, *La forza storica dei poveri*, cit. 242.

[20]G. Gutiérrez, "I limiti della teologia moderna. Un testo di Bonhoeffer" (1979), in *La forza storica dei poveri* 281.

[21]The planned "Response to Moltmann" was also supposed to include the text of the report by historian Enrique Dussel, "Sobre la Historia de la Teología en América Latina," held at the Latin American meeting of theology in Mexico City in August 1975: cf. the proceedings, E. R. Maldonado, ed., *Liberación y cautiverio. Debates en torno al método de la teología en América*

Latina (Mexico D.F., 1976) 19-68. Cf. also in this same volume J. Sobrino's interesting contribution to our theme, "El conocimiento teológico en la teología Europea y Latinoamericana" 177-207.

²²Cf. V. Fabella and S. Torres, eds., *Doing Theology in a Divided World*, Papers from the Sixth International Conference at the Ecumenical Association of Third World Theologians, January 5-13, Geneva, Switzerland (Maryknoll, NY, 1985).

²³D. Sölle, "Dialetics of Enlightenment: Reflections of a European Theologian," in *Doing Theology in a Divided World*, cit. 82.

²⁴J. B. Metz, "Standing at the End of the Eurocentric Era of Christianity: A Catholic View," in *Doing Theology in a Divided World*, cit. 89, 90. On the same theme one can also consult F. X. Kaufmann and J. B. Metz, *Capacità di futuro. Movimenti di ricerca del cristianesimo* (1987) (Brescia, 1988).

²⁵G. Casalis, "Methology for a West European Theology of Liberation," in *Doing Theology in a Divided World*, cit. 118.

²⁶Cf. "Final Statement," in *Doing Theology in a Divided World*, cit. no. 56.

²⁷M. Horkheimer and Th. W. Adorno, *Dialektik der Aufklärung* (1947); Italian trans. *Dialettica dell' illuminismo* (Turin, 1966). Cf. W. Oelmüller, *Die unbefriedigte Aufklärung. Beiträge zu einer Theorie der Moderne von Lessing, Kant, Hegel* (Frankfurt am Main, 1969); M. Lamb, *Solidarity with Victims: Toward a Theology of Social Transformation* (New York, 1982).

²⁸J. Rüsen, E. Lámmert, and P. Glotz, eds., *Die Zukunft der Aufklärung* (Frankfurt am Main, 1988) (the volume contains the proceedings of the congress held at Frankfurt am Main in December 1987).

²⁹J. Habermas, "Die neue Intimität zwischen Politik und Kultur," in *Die Zukunft der Aufklärung*, cit. 64.

³⁰J. Habermas, in *Die Zukunft der Aufklärung*, cit. 66.

³¹J. Moltmann, "Die Zukunft der Aufklärung und des Christentum," in *Die Zukunft der Aufklärung*, cit. 77.

³²Ibid. 78.

³³Ibid. 79-80.

³⁴J. B. Metz, "Wider die zweite Unmündigkeit: Zum Verhältnis von Aufklärung und des Christentum," in *Die Zukunft der Aufklärung*, cit. 85.

³⁵Ch. Duquoc, *Liberazione e progressismo. Un dialogo teologico tra l'America Latina e l'Europa* (1987) (Assisi, 1989) 23.

³⁶Ibid.

³⁷Ibid. 40.

³⁸Ibid. 40.

³⁹J. B. Metz, "Teología europea y Teología de la liberación," in J. Comblin, J. Gonzáles Faus, and J. Sobrino, eds., *Cambio social y pensamiento cristiano en América Latina* (Madrid, 1993) 263. The volume includes the proceedings of the Second El Escorial Conference, July 1992. Cf. also J. B. Metz, "Die Dritte Welt und Europa. Theologisch-politische Dimensionen eines unerledigten Themas," in *Stimmen der Zeit* 118 (1993): 3-9; J. B. Metz and H. E. Bahr, *Augen für die Anderen. Lateinamerika—eine theologische Erfahrung* (Munich, 1991).

⁴⁰J. B. Metz, in *Cambio social y pensamiento cristiano en América Latina*, cit. 265.

⁴¹C. Green, "Bonhoeffer, Modernity, and Liberation Theology," in W. W. Floyd and C. Marsch, eds., *Theology and the Practice of Responsibility: Essays on Dietrich Bonhoeffer* (Valley Forge, PA, 1994) 117-131.

⁴²For the context of the discussion, cf. R. Gibellini, *La teologia del XX secolo* (Brescia, 1992) 109-127.

⁴³C. Green, in *Theology and the Practice of Responsibility*, cit. 127.

⁴⁴Ibid. 125.

⁴⁵G. Gutiérrez, *The Truth Shall Make You Free: Confrontations* (Maryknoll, NY, 1990) 113-114.

⁴⁶C. Green, in *Theology and the Practice of Responsibility*, cit. 120.

⁴⁷Cf. J. B. Metz and P. Rottländer, eds., *Lateinamerika und Europa. Dialog der Theologen* (Munich-Mainz 1989) (proceedings of the Congress, Sept. 28-Oct. 2, 1987, on the theme "*Europa*

und Lateinamerika im Dialog"). Cf. also J. B. Metz, *Zum Begriff der neuen Politischen Theologie, 1967-1997* (Mainz, 1967).

[48]G. Gutiérrez, "Theorie und Erfahrung im Konzept der Theologie der Befreiung," in *Lateinamerika und Europa*, cit. 48-49.

[49]Ibid. 49.

[50]L. Boff, "Europäische Freiheitstraditionen und lateinamerikanisches Denken," in *Lateinamerika und Europa*, cit. 45.

[51]J. Moltmann, "Political Theology and Liberation Theology," in *Union Seminary Quarterly Review* 45 (1991) 208.

[52]Cf. J. Moltmann, *Politische Theologie—Politische Ethik* (Munich and Mainz, 1984); idem, *Dio nella creazione. Dottrina ecologica della creazione* (1985) (Queriniana, Brescia, 1986); idem, *La giustizia crea futuro. Una politica ispirata alla pace e un' etica fondata sulla creazione in un mondo minacciato* (1989), (Queriniana, Brescia, 1990); *Jahrbuch der Europäischen Gesellschaft für die theologische Forschung von Frauen* (Kampen-Mainz, 1993ff.).

[53]J. Moltmann, "Political Theology and Liberation Theology" 215.

[54]Ibid. 217. Cf. also "Dire Dio dopo Auschwitz, durante Ayacucho. Dialogo tra Jürgen Moltmann e Gustavo Gutiérrez," in *Mosaico di pace 4* (1993/2): 13-26; J. Moltmann, *Theology and the Future of the Modern World,* American Academy of Religion/Society of Biblical Literature, Chicago, 1994 (Pittsburgh, PA, 1995). Cf. also J. Moltmann, *Gott im Projekt der Modernen Welt. Beiträge zur öffentlichen Relevanz der Theologie* (Gütersloh, 1997).

[55]P. Tillich, *On the Boundary: An Autobiographical Sketch* (New York, 1966) 13.

[56]P. Tillich, *The Essential Tillich*, ed. B. Forrester Church (New York, 1987) 210.

[57]J. Audinet, "Preface" to V. Elizondo, *Galilean Journey: The Mexican-American Promise* (Maryknoll, NY, 1983) ix-xi.

[58]Cf. E. Fernández, *U.S. Hispanic Theology (1968-1993): Context and Praxis* (Pontificia Universitas Gregoriana, Facultas Missionologiae, Rome, 1995).

[59]Léopold Sédar Senghor, *"Préface"* to V. Elizondo, *L'Avenir est au Métissage* (Paris, 1987) 7-10.

[60]V. Fabella and S. Torres, eds., *Irruption of the Third World: Challenge to Theology*, Papers from the Fifth International Conference of the Ecumenical Association of Third World Theologians, August 17-29, 1981, New Delhi, India (Maryknoll, NY, 1983) 54.

[61]V. Elizondo, "The New Humanity of the Americas" 272-277 below.

ESSAYS BY VIRGILIO ELIZONDO

13. The New Humanity of the Americas

(1990)

Virgilio Elizondo

1992 calls not for a celebration but for a new creation! It calls not for breast-beating but for deliverance. It calls not for historical continuity but for rupture—a cutting of the umbilical cord from mother Europe and Western civilization. The time has come for the spiritual declaration of independence of the Americas.

The only way to go beyond simplistic condemnation or arrogant triumphalism is to transcend categories of defeat or victory and see the beginning of the Americas for what it truly was: the long and painful birth of the new human person—a new human individual, community, civilization, religion, and race. Anthropologically speaking, five hundred years is a very brief period in the birth of a race, and that is precisely what we are witnessing in the Americas.

Nothing as painful, as far-reaching, and as fascinating has happened in the history of humanity since the birth of the European some 35,000 years ago, when the Cro-magnons migrated, conquered, massacred the native Neanderthals, and mated with them to produce the basis of today's European peoples. The only similar event in world history is the arrival of the Iberians in the Americas which marked the beginning of the new American race—the *mestizo*! A new genetic and cultural group was born. It would take centuries to develop. But a new race had been born.[1]

The greatest undiscovered wealth of the Americas is the rich genetic pool—cultural, religious, and biological—which constitutes the Americas. We must rediscover not only our great European past, but equally the rich heritage of our native ancestors: Quetzalcoatl, Nezahualcoyotl, and many others. We truly have the opportunity to create a new humanity like the world has never known. It will not be easy, but it can and must be done if America[2] is to survive. The long, scandalous, and painful process of the past five hundred years has been well brought out by various authors. Now, we must dream and work creatively for a new beginning. Out of the crucified peoples of the Americas of yesterday and today, a new humanity will resurrect. We have no doubt of this. The God of life will triumph over the forces of death.

It has taken Europe many centuries and generations of progress and upheavals; of wars and agreements of peace; of crisis, confusion, and new synthesis; of universalization and regionalization. Their rich Greco-Roman-Gothic past has constantly been rediscovered, reinterpreted, and synthesized with the new ideas of the day to announce unexpected and more exciting possibilities for the human spirit.[3] Finally, in 1992, Europe is coming together to work as a united Europe. Not necessarily a uniform Europe, but definitely a united Europe for the good of all its peoples. The new age of continents has arrived. A new Europe will be born—but will a new humanity be born in Europe? There seem to be no signs of this at the present moment.

We in the Americas are very young! We cannot wait 2000 years to come together as a united America for the good of all Americans—from the tip of Argentina to the upper tip of Newfoundland. The growing inner failure of the United States/American dream of a good life for all coupled with the massive increase of impoverished, undernourished, and medically uncared-for peoples throughout the Americas demands nothing less than a radical and creative new beginning.

Creative dreams can and will transform reality from battlefields to farmlands, from opulence at the cost of starvation of others to a new human family of concerned neighbors, from corruption of the mighty to a spirit of authority for the sake of service, from individualism to a sense that it is only within a healthy community that healthy individuals will arise and flourish, and from a sense of nationalism to a sense of continental identity and solidarity. However, these creative dreams will not emerge from those whose present-day wealth and security are safeguarded by the cultural and socio-economic structures of today's world. They will struggle and fight to maintain the *status quo*. The creative dreams can only come from where they have always come: the prophetic cries and the utopian imagination of the victims.[4]

Out of crisis, suffering, and misery, the prophets of old dared to proclaim a new heaven and a new earth. Today, it is the crucified peoples of the Americas that will come forth with the utopian dream of the new and truly universal (inclusive of all) humanity of the Americas. The great paradox, as Jon Sobrino brings out, is that those whose body and blood the dominant society has taken in order to enrich itself[5] will now become the instruments of the new life of the Americas. It is they who will become God's agents to usher in the new humanity. It is the Juan Diegos[6] of today who will bring hope to the hopeless and salvation to those who are perishing in their materialistic securities without even knowing it.

Our challenge for 1992 is to begin building the New America—the new humanity which will be something really new in the midst of a world ripped apart by wars, materialism, power-games, consumerism, racism, and the like. The challenge: how to get started? Why not convoke the first Ecumenical Council of the Americas?

Our ancient foundational stories about the origins of life in these lands tell us how in the very beginning the gods took council at Teotihuacan in order to give birth to men and women. So why not convoke a new Council at Teotihuacan to search for the new humanity of the Americas? This would be an inspired way to make a true beginning in 1992.

Such a Council should involve representatives of all the leading religions and churches of the Americas. It should also involve men and women who truly represent the exploited, excluded, and suffering peoples of the Americas. The fundamental credentials for participating in such a Council would be the personal acceptance that much of our Western American civilization is failing humanity, that more patchwork will not help, that the signs of decay and the end are more and more in sight, and that a radical new beginning is the only way to guarantee life in the new millennium. The models cannot be provided by those in the dominant groups, for they are too attached to their securities to think clearly.

Those coming together would assemble—perhaps in a tent city—at Teotihuacan, the ancient city of the gods, to fast, pray, and abstain together so as to be open to the great Spirit of God rather than defenders of petty interests. As Moses went into the desert for a new beginning, as Jesus went into the desert truly to discern the will of God and had to struggle against the temptations of the average good person of this world, so too would the members of this religious assembly of the Americas go into the desert to discover God's way.

We could repent together for our sins of the past, give thanks for the blessings of the past, and begin to forge a new future together. Out of the best of the roots of our past traditions—the ancient nations of this land, the Iberian world, the Anglo-Saxon world, the African world—a truly new American synthesis could begin to be worked out. Our native ancestors saw the earth as the sacred living entity which constantly gave birth to new life. Our European ancestors saw the God of heaven as the author of life and, in the name of the Lord of heaven, proceeded to possess and destroy Mother Earth. Today the sacredness and unity of heaven and earth can be celebrated in the new life of the Americas. Without question, today's America has not only impoverished the original native peoples of this world by robbing them of their lands, their cultures, their religion, and their humanity, it has impoverished itself by ridiculing their beliefs and ignoring and destroying their values! Isn't it amazing how through the failure of our Western American civilization in relation to questions of the environment, we are today discovering the great truth and wisdom of the sacredness of Mother Earth as lived and proclaimed by our ancient ancestors of this land?

This Council would not be called to discuss church questions or dogmas such as the nature of God, revelation, priesthood, sacraments, episcopacy, but to search our most sacred and ancient traditions in order to discover the image of the human which we should be living and promoting. The truth of God leads us to the truth about man and woman. It is not a question of relativizing the sacred doctrines of any one group but rather seeking what we have in common in favor of the human family.

Nor will this Council come together simplistically to condemn Western civilization as such. Throughout its centuries of struggle Western civilization has made great contributions in favor of the human family: the quest for learning, the development of the arts, science, technology, the quest for freedom and justice. The human and humanizing aspects of life that Western civilization has been accumulating across the centuries are great treasures. But the materialistic and individualistic extremes to which Western civilization has gone are threatening to destroy it from within at the same time that it is destroying the weak and poor of this world—almost consuming and feeding upon their bodies and blood in order to satisfy its apparently insatiable appetite.

Furthermore, it will not be a matter of simply listening to the problems of the poor and suffering of the Americas and trying to solve them according to the Western models of becoming human. Much more than that, it will be asking them to share with the rest of the Americas the very humanizing values which, despite their marginalization, they have managed to keep alive and pass on from generation to generation. Salvation and new creation always come out of God's poor.

What a world-shaking event it will be! Here the Quechuas, the Aymaras, Tetzalos, the Mayas, the Navajos, Quiches, the Yaquis, the Tarahumnaras, the Protestants, the Catholics, the Orthodox, the Muslims, the Jews—all the religions which live in this land—will come together in the most ancient sacred site of the Americas, geographically in the very center of the Americas, to take counsel and listen to the divine spirit at work in us. Coming together not to argue about God, but precisely because we believe in the God who is the creator of men and women, to seek ways of truly bringing new human life into these Americas that God has entrusted unto us. What an incredible wealth of religious knowledge in favor of men and women coming to the fullness of life! What a tribute to the creator that we in the Americas could become fully alive! This would be more than a celebration; it would be a marvelous manifestation of the glory of God.

The Ecumenical Council of the Americas will be a far greater event than the arrival of Columbus in 1492. It will truly be a first in world history—various religions coming together for the sake of men and women, respecting each other's sacred doctrines and traditions, but praying, dreaming, and working together for the sake of humanity. What a power it will be if all the religions and all the churches, each respecting their own doctrines and dogmas, can agree on the fundamental principles of what it means to be truly human, of what it will take to build up the new family of the Americas, of what are the vices that must be struggled against and the virtues that must be promoted to truly build up the human family.

"In my Father's house there are many mansions." Can you imagine the great gift the Americas will be to the world if the great religions, rather than ignoring or fighting one another, find ways of working together for the common good? The Pope and the leaders of the great religions of the world prayed together at Assisi; why can we not go even beyond this in the Americas? No one needs to surrender, but each one can work for the good of all. All will be enriched, and the God who is beyond all human expression will be glorified.

A new family of the Americas! If Europe can be a united family by 1992, why cannot the Americas be one? No more national borders separating us one from the other. People will easily, and at will, travel throughout the Americas. What a cause for celebration—no more "illegals" in the land. America will finally be the common home of all its peoples. Efforts and monies for military defense will be re-routed for affordable housing, education, medicine, agriculture, mass transit, sports, and the arts. Land and home ownership will not be reserved to the few who can afford it, but will be available to all the peoples, and there will be plenty of public lands for all to enjoy equally. The goods of the earth will be enjoyed but no longer worshiped. The individual will be important in the context of the primacy of the community, for it is healthy communities that give rise to healthy individuals and not vice versa. There will be rich racial and ethnic diversity, but not discrimination. Men and women in community will be the central focal point of priorities and concerns.

There will be privacy but not isolation, individuality but not individualism, ethnic identity but not ethnocentrism. There will be many religions, but not religious domination, hatred, insult, or division. There will be material resources for all, but not misery. It will be a humanity of freedom with responsibility; of humanizing work with leisure time for enjoyment of action and contemplation; of love and sacrifice. Yes, the new humanity of the Americas needs to be conceived and born!

From this Council should come personal commitments and a plan of action, how to bring the "good news of a new humanity" to the people. We will need the commitment and help of those who today shape the modern mind and heart: the athletes, the songwriters and singers, the script-writers, the playwrights, those who produce radio and TV commercials. The preachers, religious educators, and teachers all must work together for a new mind-set and new values which will determine our priorities of everyday life.

According to the Mayan scientist/priests who devoted themselves to the mathematical calculations of the ages, the Fifth Sun (age) in which we are now living will come to a catastrophic end in the year 2011. Judging by the increase in pollution, weapons, and new diseases, and by the general loss of confidence in our present economic, social, and religious values, it certainly seems that our present world could easily self-destruct soon.[7] Maybe these predictions are correct. But they will not be the end—they will simply be the end of human imagery and civilizations as we have created them for the benefit of some and the degradation and death of others.

As in the ancient beginning of the Americas, when the gods took counsel at Teotihuacan so that the original humanity of today's Americas might be born, so too today, from this sacred holy ground of the Americas, men and women of God can come together to take counsel so that the new humanity of the Sixth Sun may be born and spread throughout the Americas. The end of our civilization will come. There is no doubt of that. But there is no fear among the crucified peoples of this land, for they know that in them and through them, new life is already being offered to all the peoples of this land—rich and poor, native, *mestizo*, or immigrant. An age will come to an end, but life will not come to an end. It will be our resurrection—the rebirth of the Americas.

Notes

[1]Jacques Ruffie, *De la biologie à la culture* (Paris: Flammarion, 1976).

[2]Note: whenever I refer to America in this article, I am not limiting it to the United States but use it in reference to the entire American continent—North, Central, South, and Caribbean—and hence include all the inhabitants of these lands in the term "Americans."

[3]Michel Banniard, *Génèse culturelle de l'Europe* (Paris: Editions de Seuil, 1989).

[4]Ignacio Ellacuria, "Utopia y profetismo desde América Latina," *Revista Latinoamericana de teología* 17 (1989).

[5]Jon Sobrino, *The Principle of Mercy: Taking the Crucified People from the Cross* (Maryknoll, NY: Orbis Books, 1994).

[6]Juan Diego was the low-class Indian to whom Our Lady of Guadalupe appeared in 1531, asking him to be her messenger. He was the first and foremost evangelizer of the native peoples of Mexico. See "Our Lady of Guadalupe as a Cultural Symbol" 118-125 above.

[7]Frank Waters, *Mexico Mystique: The Coming of Sixth World Consciousness* (Chicago: Sage, 1975).

14. Hispanic Theology and Popular Piety

From Interreligious Encounter to a New Ecumenism

(1993)

Virgilio Elizondo

[Editor's Note: This presentation was a keynote address to the 1993 annual meeting of the Catholic Theological Society of America.]

Introduction

Welcome to San Antonio, welcome to the Southwest, welcome to the frontier and crossroads of the two great religious-cultural traditions of the Americas, welcome to one of the most unique borderlands of the planet! You have providentially come to one of the most interesting regions of the world for the subject which this conference addresses: ecumenism, interreligious relations, and cultural diversity. For those of us who are Mexican American, interreligious relations have not been an intellectual option nor an ecclesial choice, but a necessity which arose from the deepest level of the life process: the new being which was born out of our corporal relations. From the very beginning, the Catholic Iberians (who themselves were the products of the eight hundred years of Islamic, Jewish, and Christian coexistence in Spain) conquered and mated with the Amerindians of the Nahautl culture and religion. In so doing, these Nahuatl and European peoples gave birth to a new race, a new culture, and a new religion: the *mestizo* Latin American Catholic. Later on, U.S. Anglo Protestants along with French, Irish, and German Catholics came into our lives and started a new intermingling. As Mexican Americans of the Southwest, we have been twice conquered and three times evangelized, yet never fully welcomed into the fullness of ecclesial life. Perhaps this has providentially prepared us to be the *avant garde* of the future church! The people who evangelized us were concerned about our souls, but seemed to despise our bodies. Generally speaking, the evangelizers have not taken the time to really know us, to ask us our name, or to enter into our collective soul: our religious expressions.

Why do I theologize? I suppose out of my love/disgust relationship with my Catholic Church. I grew up in a Mexican American neighborhood here in San Antonio in which the Catholic parish was the center of life. The parish was the only institution in the city where we felt fully at home, fully free to express ourselves in our own language, our singing, our festivities, our worship. Popular devotions were an integral part of life in our home, neighborhood, and parish. Our Catholic religion gave me life and a deep sense of belonging and I love it.

As I went through theological studies, however, I started to distance myself from the living faith of my own Mexican American people. The religious practices of my people started to appear, from the perspective of Western theologies, as simplistic, backward, superstitious, and even pagan. I had somewhat accepted these theological teachings as correct and was trying to implement their pastoral consequences among my people.

During my early years as a priest, I discovered that great numbers of our Mexican American people had a very negative experience of church and had to rely entirely on the popular faith expressions of our tradition, for they could not rely on the services of the institutional church. In many U.S. Catholic parishes my people were made to sit in the rear of the church or barred from entering at all. It was not uncommon to be told: "Go to the Mexican church. This is not your church." Pastors and others often made us feel like dirty and unwanted foreigners. Why the people kept going to a church in which they were insulted and rejected is a great mystery. It has to be a tribute to the very deep faith of our people and our acceptance of the human sinfulness of our church. I had received so much from my Catholic tradition and I believed in it, yet the Catholic Church of the United States, which was the official custodian and interpreter of this tradition, seemed determined to destroy our Mexican Catholic tradition or get rid of us. As Mexican Catholics it was clear we were not wanted. As Archbishop Flores stated during the First National Encuentro de Pastoral in Washington, D.C.: "The Church was like the mother who chose not to hear the cries of her young daughter who was being raped so that she would not have to do anything about it!"

In the early 1970s, we were having a vocation conference at the Mexican American Cultural Center. There were several bishops, priests, religious, and many Mexican American laity. All kinds of suggestions were made as to how we could recruit more Mexican Americans into the priesthood and religious life. One couple came up to the podium and told us why they hoped and prayed that none of their sons or daughters would ever become religious or priests. They stated: "We don't want to lose them from the family." Everyone was stunned! They were against the very purpose for which we had all gathered. I immediately reacted (as I am sure many others did) by thinking that we too had to be generous and let go of our children so that they could become priests or religious. But before I could respond, they had already started to explain themselves:

If one of our sons or daughters became a religious or priest, and the Church sent them to Africa, China, or some other distant place, and we never saw them again in our lives, that would not be losing them from the family. In fact, we would be gaining the people they worked with into our family and we would be honored and proud.

What we mean by losing them from the family is that when one of our daughters or sons goes to the convent or seminary, they come home to visit us ashamed of who we are, especially of how we pray and how we express and practice our faith. This is losing them from the family!

There was a profound silence in the room. No one dared to respond; no one at that moment had an answer. These simple and unassuming *barrio* parents had pronounced a prophetic word which was immediately evident. They had identified the root of the problem: U.S. Catholicism was ashamed of our Mexican Catholicism and thus to become good priests or religious in the United States, we had to assume that shame of our own people. To go through any formation program successfully, we had to become foreigners to our own people—we had to abandon the very sources of our faith and the deepest bonding of *nuestro pueblo*. No wonder that over half of the ordained Mexican American priests at that time did not want to work with Mexican American people. This couple's simple word from the heart immediately revealed to me why I had felt a certain anger and disgust within me at the theological formation that had turned me against my people and especially against the very expressions of the faith through which I had come to know and love God, Jesus, Mary, and the saints in a very personal way. I had never verbalized this, even to myself. But this was the naked truth: theology had caused me to abandon rather than understand the living faith tradition of my people. This was a betrayal both of theology itself and of my people's faith. Paradoxical as it sounds, theological formation had made me and others like me dishonor our parents and ancestors; it had made us break the fourth commandment. Our theological formation was preparing us to destroy the faith basis of our Mexican American existence.

It was at this moment that I, as a diocesan priest who had never been too interested in academic or university theology, decided that either we ourselves must begin to theologize seriously out of the living faith experience of our people, or theology would continue to alienate Mexican American priests and religious from our own people and thus damage our people's faith. We had to theologize ourselves or be destroyed by the theology of others, not because other theologies are bad, but because Western theologies arose out of a totally different historical journey and world view. We had to theologize not against others, but alongside those who had other perspectives and faith experiences within the church. We needed their help, but we did not need them to do it for us. This was one of the main reasons we started the Mexican American Cultural Center (MACC): to begin a serious, critical, and creative process of theological reflection from within the living faith tradition of our people. Gustavo Gutiérrez made us aware of the all important theological category of "the poor" and from there we ourselves discovered a specific dimension of our poverty: our biological margination and rejection—a body and blood, skin and soul type of existential poverty.

We have come a long way but are the first ones to realize that we have a much longer way to go. In the beginning MACC was alone; today we have several centers around the country and many of our women and men are theologizing professionally and creatively out of our people's faith experience. We just completed our annual colloquium of the Academy of Catholic Hispanic Theologians of the United States (ACHTUS) and it was outstanding. Out of our common struggle as U.S. Hispanics/Latinos, we are emerging with some exciting insights into the mystery of God, Christ, Mary, tradition, church, liturgy, and prayer that I am sure will be enriching not just for our own people, but for the church at large. We are finally beginning to break through and theologize out of the living faith tradition of our *mestizo* Latin American peoples in the United States.

As exciting as Hispanic theologies are, today I will limit myself to theologizing out of my own Mexican American experience. This is not because I am not interested in the other expressions of Hispanic theology or do not consider them important, but because I think it would be arrogant for me to speak for the Puerto Ricans, Cubans, and others. Hispanic theologies have some commonalities, but at this moment each group is attempting to theologize out of their own particular experience. This, I might add, is one of the distinctive features of our new Hispanic theologies: each of us theologizes out of and in communion with the faith journey of our people. And it is the acceptance of our people, not of the academy, that is the first and most important verification of our work's validity. Are we making sense to our own Christian people? If our work makes sense to our people, then we will have something of value to share with you, our co-workers in the ministry of theologizing. Thus I will speak out of my own experience and that of my people in the Southwest of the United States, or as some Mexican geography books say, that part of Mexico which is presently occupied by the United States.

The Three Evangelizations:
Conquest, Evangelization, Domination

To appreciate who we are as a believing people, it is important to note that we have always been evangelized by missioners from groups that have conquered, dominated, and controlled our lives. Until the most recent times, we have not been allowed to be ourselves. Our ecclesial life has been dictated by outsiders, while our faith life has developed quite independently of the clergy or religious through the priesthood of the simple *barrio* people of the land. In our experience, there has always been a type of coexistence between official ecclesial life and the faith expressions of the people. Sometimes the two meet, but usually each goes its own way. Today, we are trying to bring them closer together in various ways. It is not an either/or situation, as the Latin American Bishops' document of Puebla states, but a mutuality which enriches both the people's popular expressions of piety and the official expressions of Catholicism.

We came into being—we were born—out of the totalitarian interreligious encounter between Catholic Spain and the peoples of the indigenous religions of Mexico, an encounter that began in 1519 with the arrival of Hernan Cortéz. The conquest was holistic in that the Iberians conquered the lands and the peoples and immediately started to bear children through the native women. The missioners attempted to evangelize in the context of conquest. It was difficult and even contradictory to speak about the God of love when the people of this God had just conquered, massacred, enslaved, and raped. At the official level, there was only imposition and not real dialogue—although a few efforts were made in the very beginning to bring about dialogue. However, profound and creative dialogue did occur, but not in the suspected places. As a people we came into being through the bodily encounters in the bedrooms, through the creation of new foods and new thought in the kitchens, and through the sacralization of our new life in our home *altarcitos* (home altars) and shrines. The Christian Iberian fathers started the bio-logical-religious process, but it was the native mothers who cultivated it creatively and brought it to maturity in the kitchens and *altarcitos*. These kitchens and *altarcitos* were the places where natural dialogue took place between the ways of our ancestors and the new ideas about God introduced by the missioners. This is the biological-cultural-religious beginning of the Christian tradition of Mexico and Mexican Americans in the United States. Just as the East and the West have their traditions, we are the beginning of a new tradition in the communion of believers.

It would not be too long before the Mexican *mestizo* Catholic would begin to be challenged by the arriving WASP colonizers from the northern United States. The people of the United States were filled with expansionist dreams and projects. They were convinced that it was their Manifest Destiny to expand the United States throughout the entire continent of the Americas. Northern Mexico would be the first step. This would begin the violent clash between two totally different and even opposing cultures, religious expressions, and ways of life—even be-tween two very different forms of Roman Catholicism. Hostilities broke out in the 1830s and fifty percent of Mexico would soon become the Southwest of the United States. You are in the very city and actually on the very grounds where some of the most bloody battles took place. Thus many of our Mexican families found themselves to be in the United States without ever having migrated a single mile. Unlike most of the people of the United States, we Mexican Americans are not immigrants who live in some type of continuity with the Christianity—Prot-estant or Catholic—of European ancestors.

As a Mexican American people, we are the product of two violent conquests: the Iberian conquest of Mexico beginning in 1519 and the U.S. conquest of north-ern Mexico (Texas to California) beginning in the 1830s. We were born from the violent and unequal encounter in each of these two colonizing enterprises. Our men were killed or enslaved, our lands were taken away from us, our women were raped, and our *mestizo* and mulatto children were condemned to a life of margin-ation and inferiority.

As *mestizos*, our flesh and blood identity has consistently marginated us from both parent groups. We have been too Spanish for the Indians and too Indian for the Spaniards, too Mexican for the United States, and too "Gringo" for our Mexi-can brothers and sisters. Our non-being has been our being! It is the multiple rejection and margination which have constituted the deepest pain and shared commonalty of our people. Yet, like the Hebrew peoples in captivity, we continue to multiply and increase. Others try to destroy us, but we continue to affirm and propagate life!

Beginning in 1519, Iberian Catholics of Europe evangelized our indigenous peoples of Mexico. Then the Anglo Protestants and the French, Irish, and German Catholics of the United States evangelized the Mexican American Catholics after the U.S. conquest of northern Mexico in the mid-nineteenth century. Finally, in contemporary times we are being evangelized by the Fundamentalists. All three evangelizations have proceeded from a conquest paradigm as the missioners came with the colonizers and presupposed that their religious expression is the only way to salvation and their cultural life the only way of life possible for the "saved." Thus evangelization and "civilization" (church and school) are presented as interwoven aspects of salvation. In this model, the sacred customs and traditions of our ancestors are looked upon as pagan, evil, and even diabolical. Only the missioner and his/her people know the way to God and they alone have a monopoly on the truth, the beautiful, the dignified, and the right way of living. Thus, in the name of God, people are exhorted to accept the missioner's cultural-religious way of life for no other lifestyle is worthy of God's people. In this sense, the missioners of all three evangelizing efforts have functioned in the same way. Their good will has been accompanied by an arrogant approach which holds that they are the sole possessors of truth and condemns everything else as false. This religious arrogance has been the typical demon of all the evangelizers who work out of the conquest paradigm of evangelization.

The Three Churches: A Religious Caste System

The New Mestizo *Church: Rooted in the Culture*

Whereas the missioners of all three groups have proceeded from essentially the same paradigm, the type of church which has come about has been quite different in each case. Many Iberian missioners abhorred the Amerindian religious "idols" and rituals but admired their culture and language. They loved the natives, their language, and many of their customs. At the same time, they were disgusted with their own European Catholic culture which they saw as debased and corrupt. They saw many values in the native cultures which were much more evangelical than the values of "Christian" Europe. Hence they sought to protect the culture and even to guard it from Spanish contamination. Their dream and their plan was to bring about a truly new church, different from anything Europe had known before. These dreams were great, even utopic, but the devastating reality of the conquest made the realization of these dreams most difficult. There were many serious obstacles and dialogue with the natives was next to impossible, until the unexpected apparition of Our Lady of Guadalupe. Had it not been for her, the Mexican church would not have been born or be here today. We are only now beginning to appreciate the full impact and implication of that miracle at the very beginning of the Americas. She opened the doors for a new trialogue between the Amerindians, herself, and the leaders of the official church. This trialogue eventually brought about the profound synthesis of symbols which is the basis of the *mestizo* church of Mexico. Through her, absolute religious barriers were bypassed, a new common sacred space appeared, and new religious expressions started to emerge.

Although some effective catechetical programs were carried out, it was the emphasis on image, ritual, and symbol which prevailed and became the basis of Mexican Catholicism. One of the very positive aspects of the new church was that it provided common space and common symbols for all: conqueror and conquered alike. Here, they were all equal before God and in God's presence. Yet, there was also a negative aspect in that a very strongly enforced racial-religious caste system was developed which sacralized and institutionalized the racist and classist basis of Latin American society. Natives, Africans, mulattos, and *mestizos* were not allowed into religious life or sacred orders. They were not considered worthy of the religious habit or of priestly ministry. They would be ministered to, but would not be allowed to minister officially in the church; admonished, but not listened to; spoken to, but not allowed to speak.

The *mestizo* Christian religion became deeply ingrained in the entire cultural fiber of Mexico and even though the religious evolution took place in the homes, neighborhoods, and ranches, the official church of this religion continued to be ruled and dominated by white European outsiders. Hence classism and racism continued to be reinforced and sacralized by the church—this continues in many ways to this very day! To be dark-skinned is to be distanced from the inner circles of power and authority.

The U.S.-American Church: Church against the Mexican Culture

As the United States started its western expansion movement in the 1800s it was inevitable that it would come into contact and conflict with the borderlands of the old Spanish Empire in the "New World." The WASP model of a "good, true, virtuous, and beautiful" human being fueled the doctrine of Manifest Destiny and not only justified but mandated the conquest of those who were "less human." The United States appeared as the new Israel meant to bring civic-religious salvation to the entire world. It was our sacred duty and responsibility to take our way of life to the rest of the Americas and throughout the globe.

The civic missionary mentality became an integral element of the national soul. Literature about the early contacts leaves us no doubt whatsoever about the way the Anglo Americans viewed the Mexican inhabitants of the borderlands: as an abomination! The Mexicans were the very contradiction of everything WASP: brown, *mestizo*, and Catholic! Since the Anglos had a profound disdain for both everything Spanish and everything Indian, the *mestizo* was looked upon as the mongrel who inherited the worst of two already degenerate peoples. The encounter between WASP-U. S. and *mestizo*-Mexico was truly the encounter between absolute otherness: each was the absolute opposite of what the other considered a "good, virtuous, true, and beautiful" human being. Thus the clash would not just be a political one, but a deeply anthropological one.

Whereas the Spanish missioners who conquered in the 1500s admired and loved the natives they encountered, the U.S. missioners despised the Mexican *mestizos* whom they met. This made a major difference in the type of church that would be produced through the evangelizing efforts of the missioners—whether Catholic or Protestant. The new Catholic missioners saw Mexican Catholicism as superstitious and pagan and the Mexican people as degenerate, devious, and backward. They had little or nothing good to say about the new Catholics they encountered in the borderlands and considered ministering to these people a burden and even a form of punishment. The Protestant missioners shared this negative view of the Mexican people. However, they identified Roman Catholicism as the main cause of their poverty and misery.

This second evangelization took place not within the culture but against the culture and since there was no mediating symbol (as Guadalupe was in the first evangelization) the dialogue was strictly between the people and the church. Actually, there was very little dialogue since the missioners taught and the people were supposed to accept and change from their backward ways to the ways of the missioner. To become a true Christian, the missioners demanded that the people break with their traditions and language so that they might develop into good human, civic, and religious persons. Assimilation into the United States culture and civilization was an integral component of the evangelizing efforts of the new missioners—whether French, Irish, or German; whether Catholic or Protestant.

Actually, the traditional expressions of the people's faith could have been a good medium for a life-giving trialogue between the people and the leadership of the church, but since the church never acknowledged or recognized as legitimate the piety of the people, it kept this trialogue from taking place. The churches demanded that we break radically from the religious ways of our ancestors. Some of our people have tried and have found it very painful, others have managed to survive while still others have just given up altogether. It has been a painful journey of "either/or" but there has been no synthesis.

The positive effect of this second wave of evangelizers was that they helped the Mexicans living in the borderlands to enter into the cultural and linguistic space of the United States. Their emphasis on education contrasted sharply with the desires of the new U.S. *conquistadores* who wished to keep the Mexican people ignorant and exploit them as cheap labor. In fact, an unofficial "pass without learning" policy was effected in Texas so that the Mexican Americans could go to school (as required by law) but not learn enough to organize, defend themselves, or go for higher education. Thus the educational emphasis of the churches—Protestant and Catholic—was a great contribution toward the development of the Mexican American people. It is interesting to note that many of our outstanding leaders went through a religious school: Henry Cisneros, Willie Velasquez, and many others. However, the educational effort of the churches was limited to only a few of the people—less than one percent. Most of the people remained outside the educational opportunities provided either by the churches or by society.

The emphasis on education and knowledge of the faith meant that Mexican Catholics of the Southwest were confronted with a more verbal, rational, institutional, and regulation-oriented Catholicism. In this approach to Catholicism, the emphasis was more on church than on religion. Mexican Catholicism was deeply rooted in the culture itself while U. S. Catholicism and Protestantism were rooted in the local institutions with their precise confessions of faith and strict moral codes. Thus the former emphasized life and death, sorrow and fiesta, family and people, while the latter focused on institutional belonging, clear-cut regulations, and strict accountability to those in authority. Concerns like parish registration, weekly attendance, regular contributions, and reception of the sacraments were basic for belonging to a church in the United States. Mexican Catholicism was comfortable and secure in the realm of sacred mystery, while U.S. Catholics and

Protestants needed to know dogmas and doctrines to feel secure. Nonetheless, through these differences, Mexican Americans were enabled to learn about and enter into the institutional frame-reference of the U.S. way of life.

On the negative side, the U.S. churches also continued the effects of the conquest model in that they continued the religious caste system initiated by the first missioners. Separate churches were built so that the Mexicans would not contaminate the purer Christians of the United States. Protestants ordained Mexican Americans but kept them in an inferior status, while Catholics did not even allow Mexicans into the seminaries or religious life. When Mexican Americans were invited into religious life, it was only to become brothers or sisters working in the kitchens and laundries of the White Anglo-American religious. As in the first evangelization, the Mexican *mestizo* was still not considered to be fully developed, capable, or worthy of full ministry and communion. In many ways, this distanced belonging is still the ordinary experience of church today—whether Protestant or Catholic.

Bible Churches: The Abomination of Catholic and Mexican Religious Symbols

The third wave of evangelists to approach our people have been the Fundamentalists. In many ways, their fervor in seeking to destroy "pagan idols" resembles that of the first Franciscan missioners. Fundamentalists abhor the "pagan idols" of the people, which for them are the Latin American expressions of our Catholic-Christian faith. They are convinced, like the early Franciscans, that they have to uproot all the pagan idolatrous images and practices. Thus from the very beginning of their interaction with the Mexican Americans, they set out to discredit everything Catholic: the pope, the Mass, priests and religious, Mary, the saints, etc. For them, the Pope is not the Vicar of Christ but the anti-Christ. They even go to the extreme of presenting Catholicism as the whore of Babylon and the monster of the apocalypse.

Their sole source of authority is the Bible as they interpret it. The Bible alone is the source of power and truth and only by confessing the name of Jesus as Lord can one be saved. All previous expressions of Christian faith are considered to have come from the perversity of the Catholic Church and its hierarchy and thus are not Christian faith at all. Tradition is not only ignored, but totally discredited. The religious ways of the ancestors are looked upon as an abomination to God. This leads to the absolute rejection and hatred of all the sacred imagery and tradition which is the very basis of Mexican American historical and cultural identity. Fundamentalism proceeds to systematically destroy the ultimate roots of our Mexican culture and replace them with the ethic of spiritual and material prosperity in which cultural differences are simply ignored.

The dialogue is now between the Bible and myself. Each person is called upon to read the Bible and proclaim what he/she hears from a particular text. Charismatic individuals quickly become the leaders of local churches. This in fact has been one of the positive contributions of Fundamentalism to the development of the Mexican American. For the first time in our history, our own are coming forth to minister to our own and, in the Fundamentalist churches, we finally have our own space which is not under the control of outsiders. Fundamentalism has given us our own churches, our own ministers, access to and love of the Bible, and especially of Jesus, and our own style of worship which is more in keeping with the original *mitotes* (Native American religious celebrations) than anything the European-based churches have ever imagined or permitted. The cost of welcoming Fundamentalism is very high, however: we have to give up our most revered traditions. But the result is overwhelming: we can finally be ourselves and be liberated from the tutelage and control of foreigners.

This has been a great experience of liberation. We love our Catholic traditions yet we equally love our newfound liberty. The new type of *Tejano* religious music, charismatic preaching intermingling the Bible with our *barrio* talk, and the freedom to speak out in our own way is very appealing to a people who have been traditionally silenced and dominated. Ministers from our own ranks who answer primarily to our own people and not to some foreign institution or hierarchy give us a new church experience of ownership, communion, and participation. We are free and responsible; thus we have to learn how to work together and not rely on some higher authority to work out our differences for us. All this is a great liberation from the tradition of subjugation. Yet the cost is high and painful. And behind this new ecclesial freedom, there is the realization that even this is still being used to keep us segregated: some of the rich Anglo Fundamentalist churches finance the ones in the Mexican areas of town so that the converted Mexican Americans will not invade their Anglo churches. They take us away from the Catholic communion of our own people, but do not want us fully in the Fundamentalist communion.

The final very painful and negative result of Fundamentalism is that it divides our families in deeply painful ways. It provokes even a hatred of those family members that remain Catholic. Fundamentalism guts and defleshes Mexicans and Mexican Americans of our deepest being and commonalty. It offers us a disincarnated Jesus who destroys us while attempting to save us. This religious divisiveness is the most negative and destructive aspect of Fundamentalism.

Beginnings of a Common Theological Reflection

About fifteen years ago, the Fund for Theological Education brought together U.S. Hispanic theological doctoral candidates at the Mexican American Cultural Center (MACC) in San Antonio to meet one another and some of the few Hispanic doctors in theology. As far as I know, it was the first ecumenical academic theological symposium. At the first social on the evening of arrival, everyone— Pentecostal, Lutheran, Methodist, Baptist, Presbyterian, Catholic, Disciples, Adventist—expressed how much at home they felt at MACC. Our denominations had fought each other in the field, but here on our common ground it was more like a family reunion. There was not so much an awareness of difference as of profound similarity and commonalty. We all knew that many of our churches had functioned as rivals and even enemies. Yet here in one of the only institutions in the country that was truly our own—*nuestra casa*—what we experienced was not division but loving and caring *familia*! We conversed, we laughed, lamented, ate, prayed, sang, and worshiped together. Here we could speak our own language and meet with our own experts without having to explain why we were the way we were. It was an incredible life-giving experience. Many interdenominational friendships and cooperative efforts started here. It was the birth of a new ecumenism. Today, this experience is being continued through the annual Hispanic Summer Program sponsored by the Hispanic Theological Initiative.

From our first encounter, we came to the realization that before being of any one denomination, as Spanish-speaking *mestizo* Hispanics we are one flesh and blood. This was our common heritage. We have a similar skin, the same blood mixture, and a common language. Before or after any religious divisions, we are *un pueblo, la raza!* As such we all had one other thing in common: rejection! Our mother churches had all made efforts to convert us and bring us into their fold, but in effect had only allowed us in so far. We were always marginal to the centers of our churches. The academy had not helped either. Scholars either ignored our wisdom or considered it simplistic, if not pagan. Even our ways of thinking and reasoning were considered illogical, confusing, and irrational. We were told that we were too emotional—that we needed to grow up! In many ways, all our churches and theologians kept telling us we were nothing and had nothing of value to offer the wider church. Salvation would come when we would give up our heritage and become like them in every way. They had told us to come and join them, but had never allowed us all the way in, nor accepted and valued us as we are. Out of this common experience of rejection, we began to discover the Jesus paradigm of evangelization. The Son of God divested himself of all power and prestige to enter our human situation in absolute lowliness. He did not come to conquer or impose but to liberate and invite into communion. In the gospel stories, those who had nothing to say according to society and religion were the first witnesses of the Good News: the Samaritan woman, Mary Magdalene, the cured leper. In Jesus, the outcasts become the privileged spokespersons of the new creation. The very Gospel that had been used to subjugate, dominate, and control us would now become the power of our liberation.

Because the faithful had been neglected and marginated from the centers of official authority, the people, moved by the Spirit, had developed their own forms of worship and religious expression. We discovered that this was the common experience in all our churches—Catholic, Protestant, or Fundamentalist. This was our living *sensus fidelium*. Nowhere else had God been more intimately incarnated than in the God-language and expressions of the simple people of faith. Our tradition of faith was emerging from the images of our *Papás* who could easily joke with God, the friendly visits of our *abuelitas* with the *Virgencita de Guadalupe*, the songs of praise in the pentecostal church, and other such expressions. The official discourse about God was like a foreign language to us, but the God-language of our people arose out of our daily struggles for dignity, belonging, and survival.

In the ridiculed, insulted, and crucified Jesus, we knew that God had not abandoned us for the nice and fancy churches of our society, but that God in the person of the suffering Jesus carrying his cross was right there with us in our struggles. God was not with the high priests, the Herods or the Pontius Pilates of today's society, but among the suffering poor who were daily being scourged, crowned with thorns, and crucified by the church and society of the dominant. The silent suffering of Jesus had been our way of life. All of us Hispanics had experienced this suffering even within our own churches. But now, it was time to begin the resurrected existence. As God raised Jesus from the dead, God would bring new life through our crucified peoples.

Often marginated and ridiculed by those in control, we started to discover our own hermeneutical keys through which we could read the life-giving message of the Scriptures. We were at the bottom of the social scale of our U.S. culture, but had not the Son of God emptied himself of all social rank to enter our human world as the lowliest of all (Phil. 2:7)? Because he became our own condition of lowliness, today we have privileged access and unsuspected insights into the Son of God. Since the "stone rejected by the builders has become the cornerstone" (Acts 4:11), our own social and religious rejection by the builders of our society and churches is the basis for God choosing us at this moment of history and in this space of the globe. God chooses us to begin something truly new which can by-pass the tragic mistakes and divisions of the past. Thus our painful rejection and margination is the very basis of our present-day election for a creative mission. We are not called to just enter and conform to the old church models whose missioners gave birth to the Hispanic churches, but to create new expressions of church wherein others will not suffer the segregation and rejection which we ourselves suffered—churches that will be ever more Christian. In and through us the kingdom must begin in a new way: we must work to break down all the barriers of human divisions and hatreds.

Out of our biological, social, and religious "poverty"—what others have seen as our inferiority—we are called to be the artisans of a new creation. Even though Mexican Catholics, Protestants, or Fundamentalists have had different popular expressions of our faith, they have all functioned in the same way. They have used the language of self-affirmation, resistance, and celebration. Through our religious expressions, whether of Our Lady of Guadalupe or pentecostal prayer meetings, we have experienced God's unconditional love for us. Even though the social and ecclesial world we live in might have considered us inferior and unwanted, God loved us and wanted us.

As the trialogue between the Amerindians, Our Lady of Guadalupe, and the Iberian church allowed a new church to be born in the 1500s, so today through the new trialogue between our diverse Hispanic religious expressions, our common U. S. experience of margination, and the person of Jesus, a new ecumenical spirit is emerging. What Our Lady of Guadalupe was to the birth of Mexican Catholicism, the person of Jesus is today for the birth of the new ecumenical Hispanic church of the United States. Our denominational and doctrinal differences are not done away with or relativized, but we begin to perceive them in a new way: as diverse parts of the one body of Christ. We are discovering that differences do not have to be obstacles for unity; rather, they can be diverse elements of a more vibrant and dynamic unity. We are discovering that our Hispanic Christian family can be inclusive of all its children: Baptist, Lutheran, Catholic, etc. and that our diversity can be a source of enrichment to all of us. We should not eliminate differences, but celebrate them and enjoy them.

What I am speaking about is just barely beginning, but it is beginning! At the grassroots there is still a lot of competition, mistrust, and even disgust. But as each one of us deepens our faith journey from that which we have in common—our experience of rejection and our belief in Jesus who saves—we begin to re-image and expand our understanding and appreciation of church. We might easily say that we are all becoming less sectarian (without ceasing to be who we are) and more catholic. Yes, even the Roman Catholics are becoming more catholic in the process. While Western ecumenism seems to be carried out at the level of seeking a common understanding of doctrines and dogmas so that we might all arrive at a common articulation of faith, Hispanic ecumenism is developing precisely in the way we accept and affirm our doctrinal differences without trying to reconcile them. It is in our re-imaging the value of difference itself that we find a new and positive value in our denominational differences. We are discovering that we can all help one another become better Christians through our mutual contacts.

From our experience of interdenominational fellowship, we are discovering the basic need for interrelatedness. All of us can and need to help each other understand Jesus better. But in today's world, we must go even further. We are discovering how intimately interrelated all life is within our planet. The ecological movement is certainly making us aware of this. It seems to me that the Aztec cosmology was much closer to the truth of the universe than our individualistic philosophies which have been so removed from the earth. The Aztecs were correct in believing in sacrifice for the sake of cosmic survival. Their crucial mistake was in thinking that by sacrificing human beings—the bodies of others—they could save the universe for everyone. What we need to discover today is that we need human sacrifice for survival, but not the sacrifice of others. We need to sacrifice our arrogance and self-righteousness that allows us to think that we alone possess the truth. As the new *Catechism of the Catholic Church* states, God made the nations diverse so as to keep any one nation from becoming too proud and arrogant. We need one another in our diversity to become complete.

Just as we need a new interrelatedness within the communion of Christian churches, so we need a new interrelatedness within the communion of world religions. It is no longer a matter of converting the people of one religion to another, but of helping each other to truly live out the principles of the religion we confess! Conversion to one's own religion is much more challenging and difficult than going out to convert other peoples to our way! Each religion has to repent of its past intolerance and arrogance and recommit itself to the most humanizing elements of its own tradition. I know this is possible because it has already begun.

San Fernando Cathedral is a very traditional Roman Catholic Mexican American church. Yet each year, on the feast of Thanksgiving, Muslims, Hindus, Buddhists, Jews, Native Americans, Christian Protestants, Catholics, and Fundamentalists gather there to pray together—each in their own way. It has been an electrifying experience of God's presence. This is not mere tolerance, but a profound spiritual communion. The wife of a rabbi stated that it was like being in

Noah's ark preparing for the new creation. An elderly Catholic lady, holding her rosary in her hand, told me after the Thanksgiving service: "Father, the picture of the Last Supper has always been my favorite. Today, I had the feeling I was taking part in the Last Supper at the end of time!" Because we are praying together, a new paradigm of human and religious interrelatedness will bring about a new humanity—from enemies seeking to destroy one another, to friends working together. We know it is being born within us. It is just beginning. It is ambiguous, it is dangerous, it is fascinating, and it is exciting. Thus from our original interreligious encounters of the 1500s, through our various evangelizations and religious divisiveness, we have begun to forge a new ecumenism and now a new interreligious family of all God's children.

Welcome to San Antonio where the future humanity of the planet has already begun.

TABLE OF ORIGINAL PUBLICATION

1. "Educación religiosa para el México-Norteamericano." *Catequesis Latinoamericana* 4 (January-March 1972): 83-86.

2. "A Bicultural Approach to Religious Education." *Religious Education* 76 (May-June 1981): 258-270.

3. "Cultural Pluralism and the Catechism." In *Introducing the Catechism of the Catholic Church*, ed. Berard L. Marthaler, 142-162. New York: Paulist Press, 1994. © 1994 by the Missionary of St. Paul the Apostle in the state of New York. Used by permission of Paulist Press.

4. "Benevolent Tolerance or Humble Reverence? A Vision for Multicultural Religious Education." In *Multicultural Religious Education*, ed. Barbara Wilkerson, 395-406. Birmingham, AL: Religious Education Press, 1997. Reprinted from *Multicultural Religious Education*, edited by Barbara Wilkerson, and published by Religious Education Press.

5. "Our Lady of Guadalupe as a Cultural Symbol: 'The Power of the Powerless.' " In *Liturgy and Cultural Religious Traditions*, ed. Herman Schmidt and David Power, 25-33. New York: Seabury, 1977.

6. "Popular Religion as Support of Identity: A Pastoral-Psychological Case-Study Based on the Mexican American Experience in the USA." In *Popular Religion*, ed. Norbert Greinacher and Norbert Mette, 36-43. Edinburgh: T & T Clark, 1986. Reprinted with permission.

7. "Pastoral Opportunities of Pilgrimages." In *Pilgrimage*, ed. Virgil Elizondo and Sean Freyne, 107-114. London: SCM Press, 1996. Reprinted with permission.

8. "Le mestissage comme lieu theologique." *Spiritus* 24 (December 1983): 349-375. Translated and republished as "*Mestizaje* as a Locus of Theological Reflection." In *The Future of Liberation Theology*, ed. Marc H. Ellis and Otto Maduro, 358-374. Maryknoll, NY: Orbis, 1989. Also in *Frontiers of Hispanic Theology in the United States*, ed. Allan Figueroa Deck, 104-123. Maryknoll, NY: Orbis, 1992. And in *Mestizo Christianity: Theology from the Latino Perpsective*. Ed. Arturo J. Bañuelas, 7-26. Maryknoll, NY: Orbis 1995.

9. "Transformation of Borders: Border Separation or New Identity." In *Theology: Expanding the Borders*, ed. María Pilar Aquino and Roberto S. Goizueta, 22-39. Mystic, CT: Twenty-Third Publications, 1998. Reprinted with permission.

10. "I Forgive But I Do Not Forget." In *Forgiveness*, ed. Casiano Floristan and Christian Duquoc, 69-79. Edinburgh: T & T Clark, 1986. Reprinted with permission.

11. "Unmasking the Idols." *SEDOS* 24 (15 May 1992): 131-140. Reprinted with permission.

12. "Evil and the Experience of God." *The Way: Contemporary Christian Spirituality* (January 1993): 34-43. Reproduced from *The Way Supplement* by kind permission of the Editors, Heythrop College, Kensington Square, London W8 5HQ.

13. "The New Humanity of the Americas." In *1492-1992: The Voice of the Victims*, ed. Leonardo Boff and Virgil Elizondo, 142-147. London: SCM Press, 1990. Reprinted with permission.

14. "Hispanic Theology and Popular Piety: From Interreligious Encounter to a New Ecumenism." *CTSA Proceedings* 48 (1993): 1-14. Reprinted with permission.

BIBLIOGRAPHY

Virgilio Elizondo's Writings

Books

1971   *A Search for Meaning in Life and Death*. Manila, Philippines: East Asian Pastoral Institute. Also published as *The Human Quest: A Search for Meaning Through Life and Death*. Huntington, IN: Our Sunday Visitor, 1978. The Spanish version was also published twice: *Hombre quien eres tu? El enigma del hombre en el tiempo y en el más allá*. Mexico: Instituto de Pastoral Catequetica, 1971. *Quien eres tu? El enigma del ser humano*. San Antonio: Mexican American Cultural Center Press, 1983.

1974   *Religious Practices of the Mexican American and Catechesis*. San Antonio: Mexican American Cultural Center Press.

1975   *Christianity and Culture: An Introduction to Pastoral Theology and Ministry for the Bicultural Community*. Huntington, IN: Our Sunday Visitor.

1978   *Mestizaje: The Dialectic of Cultural Birth and the Gospel*. San Antonio: Mexican American Cultural Center Press, 3 volumes.

1980   *La Morenita: Evangelizer of the Americas*. San Antonio: Mexican American Cultural Center Press. A somewhat abbreviated Spanish version is *La Morenita: Evangelizadora de las Américas*. Ligouri, MO: Ligouri, 1981. Bilingual version now available from Mexican American Cultural Center Press, San Antonio.

       Virgil Elizondo and Angela Erevia. *Our Hispanic Pilgrimage*. San Antonio: Mexican American Cultural Center Press.

1981   Virgilio Elizondo, Dolorita Martínez, Carlos Rosas, and Daniel Villanueva. *Creemos en Jesucristo*. Ligouri, MO: Ligouri.

1983   *Galilean Journey: The Mexican-American Promise*. Maryknoll, NY: Orbis; 2nd edition, 2000.

       Virgen y Madre: Reflexiones bíblicas sobre María de Nazareth. San Antonio: Mexican American Cultural Center Press.

1987   *L'Avenir est au Mestissage*. Trans. J. Pierron. Paris: Nouvelles Editions Mame. English version *The Future Is Mestizo: Life Where Cultures Meet*. Bloomington, IN: Meyer Stone, 1988; reprint, New York: Crossroad, 1992; reprint, San Antonio: Mexican American Cultural Center Press, 1998. Spanish version: *El Futuro es Mestizo: Vivir donde se juntan las culturas*. Trans. Rosa María Icaza. San Antonio: Mexican American Cultural Center Press, 1998.

1992   *The Way of the Cross of the Americas*. Maryknoll, NY: Orbis (also published in Spanish, Italian, and German).

1997   *Guadalupe: Mother of the New Creation.* Maryknoll, NY: Orbis (also published in Italian and German).

1998   Virgilio Elizondo et al. *A Retreat with Our Lady of Guadalupe and Juan Diego: Heeding the Call.* Cincinnati: St. Anthony Messenger.

        Virgilio Elizondo and Timothy Matovina. *Mestizo Worship: A Pastoral Approach to Liturgical Ministry.* Collegeville, MN: Litugical Press.

        Virgilio Elizondo and Timothy Matovina. *San Fernando Cathedral: Soul of the City.* Maryknoll, NY: Orbis.

Edited Volumes of *Concilium*

1980   Virgil Elizondo and Norbert Greinacher. *Women in a Men's Church.* New York: Seabury.

1981   Virgil Elizondo and Norbert Greinacher. *Tensions between the Churches of the First World and the Third World.* New York: Seabury.

1982   Virgil Elizondo and Norbert Greinacher. *Churches in Socialist Societies of Eastern Europe.* New York: Seabury.

1983   Virgil Elizondo and Norbert Greinacher. *Church and Peace.* Edinburgh: T & T Clark.

1984   Leonardo Boff and Virgil Elizondo. *The People of God amidst the Poor.* Edinburgh: T & T Clark.

        Virgil Elizondo and Norbert Greinacher. *The Transmission of the Faith to the Next Generation.* Edinburgh: T & T Clark.

        Virgil Elizondo, Claude Geffré, and Gustavo Gutiérrez. *Different Theologies, Common Responsibility: Babel or Pentecost?* Edinburgh: T & T Clark.

1986   Leonardo Boff and Virgil Elizondo. *Option for the Poor: Challenge to the Rich Countries.* Edinburgh: T & T Clark.

1988   Leonardo Boff and Virgil Elizondo. *Convergences and Differences.* Edinburgh: T & T Clark.

1990   Leonardo Boff and Virgil Elizondo. *1492-1992: The Voice of the Victims.* London: SCM Press.

1993   Leonardo Boff and Virgil Elizondo. *Any Room for Christ in Asia?* London: SCM Press.

1995   Leonardo Boff and Virgil Elizondo. *Ecology: The Cry of the Poor.* Maryknoll, NY: Orbis.

1996   Virgil Elizondo and Sean Freyne. *Pilgrimage.* London: SCM Press.

        José Oscar Beozzo and Virgil Elizondo. *The Return of the Plague.* Maryknoll, NY: Orbis.

1999   Virgil Elizondo and Jon Sobrino. *2000: Between Reality and Hope.* Maryknoll, NY: Orbis.

Collaborative Video Projects

1996   "Soul of the City/Alma del pueblo." Produced by JMCommunications, Houston in collaboration with San Fernando Cathedral, San Antonio.

"Nuestra Señora de Guadalupe: Madre de las Americas." San Antonio: Mexican American Cultural Center.

1997   "Catecismo de la Iglesia Católica." Washington, D.C.: United States Catholic Conference.

1998   "A Walk through Scriptures." Allen, TX: Resources for Christian Living.

1999   "La gran posada." Hollywood, CA: Family Theater Productions in collaboration with Hispanic Telecommunications Network, San Antonio.

"Abré tu biblia." San Antonio: Catholic Television of San Antonio.

Articles and Book Chapters

1969   Virgil Elizondo and Alan Oddie. "San Antonio International Study Week of Mass Media and Catechetics: A Report." *Living Light* 6 (Winter 1969): 67-74. Reprinted under the title "Documento final de la semana internacional de estudios sobre medios de comunicación social y catequesis." *Catequesis Latinoamericana* 2 (January-March 1970): 78-87.

"The Mystery of Human Fulfillment." *Good Tidings* 7 (September-October).

1970   "Crisis of Our Times." *Good Tidings* 9 (July-August): 83-90.

"Il misterio della vita e della morte." *Catechesi: Revista di Pastorale Catechistica* 39 (December): 9-19.

"Segni dell'autorivelazione di Dio." *Catechesi: Revista di Pastorale Catechistica* 39 (May): 5-9.

"Segni della autorivelazione di Dio all'interno dell'esperienza di ogni uomo." *Catechesi: Rivista di Pastorale Catechistica* 39 (February): 16-17.

"Toward a Definition of Pastoral Theology." *Good Tidings* 9 (January-February): 3-7.

1972   "Educación religiosa para el México-Norteamericano." *Catequesis Latinoamericana* 4 (January-March): 83-86.

1974   "Biblical Pedagogy of Evangelization." *American Ecclesiastical Review* 168 (October): 526-543.

1975   "A Catechetical Response for Minorities." *Colección Mestiza Americana.* San Antonio: Mexican American Cultural Center Press. 92-109.

"A Challenge to Theology: The Situation of Hispanic Americans." *Catholic Theological Society of America Proceedings* 30: 163-176.

"Expanding Horizons in Ministry." *Colección Mestiza Americana.* San Antonio: Mexican American Cultural Center Press. 83-91.

"Pastoral Planning for the Spanish Speaking in the United States." *Colección*

Mestiza Americana. San Antonio: Mexican American Cultural Center Press. 57-69. See also *Prophets Denied Honor: An Anthology on the Hispano Church of the United States*. Ed. Antonio M. Stevens-Arroyo. 183-187. Maryknoll, NY: Orbis, 1980.

Virgil Elizondo and John Linskens. "Pentecost and Pluralism." *Momentum* 6 (October): 12-15.

"The Biblical Pedagogy of Evangelization: Its Signification in Our Times." *Colección Mestiza Americana*. San Antonio: Mexican American Cultural Center Press. 1-19.

"Theological Interpretation of the Mexican American Experience." *Perkins School of Theology Journal* 29 (Fall): 12-21.

1976   "Politics, Catechetics, and Liturgy." *Religion Teacher's Journal* 10 (November-December): 30-32.

"San Antonio Experiment." *New Catholic World* 219 (May-June): 117-120.

1977   "Our Lady of Guadalupe as a Cultural Symbol: 'The Power of the Powerless.'" *Liturgy and Cultural Religious Traditions*. Ed. Herman Schmidt and David Power. New York: Seabury. 25-33.

1979   "A Second Bethlehem: Christ Comes to the Americas." *Today's Catholic Teacher* 13 (November-December): 28+.

"A Theology of Evangelization." *Priest's Councils/USA: Ministry—Evangelization—Community*. Chicago: National Federation of Priests' Councils. 7-20.

"Culture, Church and." *New Catholic Encyclopedia*. 19 vols. New York: McGraw-Hill. Vol 17. 167-168.

"Response to Theological Education and Liberation Theology Symposium." *Theological Education* 16 (Autumn): 34-37.

"The Catechumen in the Hispanic Community of the United States." *Becoming a Catholic Christian: A Symposium on Christian Initiation Organized and Directed by Christiane Brusselmans*. Ed. William J. Reedy. New York: Sadlier. 51-57.

"The Pope's Opening Address: Introduction and Commentary." *Puebla and Beyond*. Ed. John Eagleson and Philip Scharper. Maryknoll, NY: Orbis. 47-55.

1980   "The Christian Identity and Mission of the Catholic Hispanic in the United States." *Hispanic Catholics in the United States*. New York: Spanish-American Printing. 61-71. See also Virgil Elizondo and Angela Erevia. *Our Hispanic Pilgrimage*. San Antonio: Mexican American Cultural Center Press, 1980. 1-16. This presentation also appears under the title "The Treasure of Hispanic Faith." *Origins* 10 (11 September 1980): 203-208; and in abbreviated form as "Identidad Cristiana y misión de los Católicos Hispanoamericanos en los Estados Unidos." *Catequesis Latinoamericana* 2 (1981): 99-105.

"The Mexican American as Seen from Within." *Prophets Denied Honor: An Anthology on the Hispano Church of the United States*. Ed. Antonio M. Stevens-Arroyo. Maryknoll, NY: Orbis. 5-7.

Virgil Elizondo and Antonio M. Stevens Arroyo. "The Spanish-speaking in the United States." *Prophets Denied Honor: An Anthology on the Hispano Church of the United States*. Ed. Antonio M. Stevens-Arroyo. Maryknoll, NY: Orbis. 7-13.

1981   "A Bicultural Approach to Religious Education." *Religious Education* 76 (May-June): 258-270.

"Ministry in Education from a Pastoral-Theological Perspective." *Ministry and Education in Conversation*. Ed. Mary C. Boys. Winona, MN: Saint Mary's Press. 45-73.

"The Gospel Mandate—Implications for the Future." *Proceedings of the National Catholic Educators Association Curriculum Conference*. 18-28.

"The Hispanic Church in the USA: A Local Ecclesiology." *Catholic Theological Society of America Proceedings* 36: 155-170. See also "A Local Ecclesiology: The Hispanic Church in the USA." *Japanese Missionary Bulletin* 9 (September 1983): 487-497.

1982   "A Child in a Manger: The Beginning of a New Order of Existence." *Proclaiming the Acceptable Year*. Ed. Justo L. González. Valley Forge: Judson Press. 64-70.

"A Report on Racism: A Mexican American in the United States." *The Church and Racism*. Ed. Gregory Baum and John Coleman. New York: Seabury. 61-65.

1983   "By Their Fruits You Will Know Them: The Biblical Roots of Peace and Justice." *Education for Peace and Justice*. Ed. Padraic O'Hare. San Francisco: Harper & Row. 39-65.

"Christian Challenge and the Disadvantaged." *Linacre Quarterly* 50 (August): 242-245.

"El idioma de la resistencia, la superviviencia y la liberación." *Vida y reflexión: Aportes de la teologia de la liberación al pensamiento teologico actual*. Lima, Peru: Centros de Estudios y Publicaciones. 235-248.

"Le mestissage comme lieu theologique." *Spiritus* 24 (December): 349-375. Translated and republished as *"Mestizaje* as a Locus of Theological Reflection." *The Future of Liberation Theology*. Ed. Marc H. Ellis and Otto Maduro. Maryknoll, NY: Orbis, 1989. 358-374. Also in *Frontiers of Hispanic Theology in the United States*. Ed. Allan Figueroa Deck. Maryknoll, NY: Orbis, 1992. 104-123. And in *Mestizo Christianity: Theology from the Latino Perspective*. Ed. Arturo J. Bañuelas. Maryknoll, NY: Orbis, 1995. 7-26. Printed in Spanish as "Mestizaje como Locus para la Reflexión Teológica." In *Secularidad y cultura contemporánea: Desafíos para la teología*. Ed. Ezequiel Castillo, Carlos Mendoza, and Francisco Merlos. México, D. F.: Universidad Pontificia de México, 1998. 134-154.

"Mary and the Poor: A Model of Evangelising Ecumenism." *Mary in the Churches*. Ed. Hans Küng and Jürgen Moltmann. New York: Seabury. 59-65.

"Stages of Practical Theology." *Twenty Years of Concilium—Retrospect and Prospect*. Ed. Paul Brand, Edward Schillebeeckx, and Anton Weiler. New York: Seabury. 20-26.

"Theological and Biblical Foundations for Communidades de Base." *Developing Basic Christian Communities. Proceedings of the Annual Meeting of the National Federation of Priests' Councils*.

"Toward an American-Hispanic Theology of Liberation in the U. S. A." *Irruption of the Third World: Challenge to Theology*. Ed. Virginia Fabella and Sergio Torres. Maryknoll, NY: Orbis. 50-55.

1984   "Conditions and Criteria for Authentic Inter-Cultural Theological Dialogue." *Different Theologies, Common Responsibility: Babel or Pentecost?* Ed. Virgil Elizondo, Claudé Geffre, and Gustavo Gutiérrez. Edinburgh: T & T Clark. 18-24.

"Ecumenism: An Hispanic Perspective." *Ecumenist* 22 (July-August): 70-74.

"Transmission of the Faith in the U.S.A." *The Transmission of the Faith to the Next Generation.* Ed. Virgil Elizondo and Norbert Greinacher. Edinburgh: T & T Clark. 100-105.

1986   "I Forgive But I Do Not Forget." *Forgiveness.* Ed. Casiano Floristan and Christian Duquoc. Edinburgh: T & T Clark. 69-79.

"Mary in the Struggles of the Poor." *New Catholic World* 229 (November-December): 244-247.

"Mexamerica: Une galilée des nations." *Catéchèse* 102 (January): 99-107.

"Popular Religion as Support of Identity; A Pastoral-Psychological Case-Study Based on the Mexican American Experience in the USA." *Popular Religion.* Ed. Norbert Greinacher and Norbert Mette. Edinburgh: T & T Clark. 36-43. See also "Popular Religion as Support of Identity Based on the Mexican American Experience in the U. S. A." *Voices from the Third World* 14 (December 1991): 132-146. Original essay reprinted in *Perspectivas: Hispanic Ministry.* Ed. Allan Figueroa Deck, Yolanda Tarango, and Timothy Matovina. Kansas City, MO: Sheed and Ward, 1995. 105-113.

"Response to the Article by C. Peter Wagner." *International Bulletin of Missionary Research* 10 (April): 65-66.

1987   "Hispanic Evangelization—A Lost Cause?" *Paulist Evangelization Association.*

"The Mexican American Religious Education Experience." *Ethnicity in the Education of the Church* (June): 75-89.

"The Ministry of the Church and Contemporary Migration." *Social Thought* 13 (Spring/Summer): 120-132.

1988   "America's Changing Face." *The Tablet* 242 (23 July): 832-834.

"Elements for a Mexican American Mestizo Christology." *Voices from the Third World* 11 (December): 97-117.

1989   "A Paradigm for Cultural Study." *Journal of Catholic Education* 3 (Melbourne).

"Mary and Evangelization in the Americas." *Mary, Woman of Nazareth.* Ed. Doris Donnelly. New York: Paulist. 146-160.

1990   "The New Humanity of the Americas." *1492-1992: The Voice of the Victims.* Ed. Leonardo Boff and Virgil Elizondo. London: SCM Press. 142-147. See also "A New Humanity." *North Dakota Quarterly* 59 (Fall 1991): 17-20.

1991   "The African Way." *Tablet* 245 (23 February): 253-254.

1992   "El pueblo de Dios en marcha/The Pilgrim People of God." *Visión profetica: Reflexiones pastorales sobre el plan pastoral para el ministerio hispano/Prophetic Vision: Pastoral Reflections on the National Pastoral Plan for Hispanic Ministry.* Ed. Soledad Galerón, Rosa María Icaza, and Rosendo Urrabazo. Kansas City, MO: Sheed and Ward. 44-52 (Spanish), 218-226 (English).

"Mestissage: La naissance d'une nouvelle culture et d'une nouvelle chrétienté." *Lumière et Vie* 208 (July): 77-90.

"Retrieving the Dream: One Priest's Story." *Priests and Community: Their Stories, Their Future. Proceedings of the Annual Meeting of the National Federation of Priests' Councils.* 17-25.

"Toward a New Educational Center: Creating Something New, Catholic Schools as New Life Microcells." *Educación Hoy* 2 (July-September): 37-62.

"Unmasking the Idols." *SEDOS* 24 (15 May): 131-140.

1993   "Evil and the Experience of God." *The Way: Contemporary Christian Spirituality* (January): 34-43.

"Hispanic Theology and Popular Piety: From Interreligious Encounter to a New Ecumenism." *Catholic Theological Society of America Proceedings* 48: 1-14.

1994   "Cultural Pluralism and the Catechism." *Introducing the Catechism of the Catholic Church*. Ed. Berard L. Marthaler. New York: Paulist Press. 142-162.

"Popular Religion as the Core of Cultural Identity Based on the Mexican American Experience in the United States." *An Enduring Flame: Studies on Latino Popular Religiosity*. Ed. Anthony M. Stevens-Arroyo and Ana María Díaz-Stevens. New York: Bildner Center for Western Hemisphere Studies. 113-132.

1995   "Carissimi fratelli e sorelle della Chiesa d'Italia." *Adista* 69/70 (14 October): 92-95.

1996   "Cultura moderna y cristianismo: Inmigrantes pobres, evangelizadores del mundo." *Evangelio e iglesia*. Acta de 16o congreso de teología de España. Madrid: Centro de Evangelio y Liberación. 33-50.

"De un encuentro interreligioso a un nuevo ecumenismo." *Cristianismo y liberación*. Ed. Juan José Tamayo. Spain: Editorial Trotta. 65-82.

"La Madre indiana delle Americhe: La nascita di una nuova umanità. *Cammino e visione: Universalità e regionalità della teologia del XX secolo. Scritti in onore di Rosino Gibellini*. Ed. Dietmar Mieth, Edward Schillebeeckx, and Hadewych Snijdewind. Brescia, Italia: Queriniana. 119-131.

"Pasion du Christ: Chez les peuples d'Amérique Latine." *SEDOS* 28 (15 May): 151-155.

"Pasion du Christ en Amérique Latine." *Spiritus* 142 (March): 50-59.

"Pastoral Opportunities of Pilgrimages." *Pilgrimage*. Ed. Virgil Elizondo and Sean Freyne. London: SCM Press. 107-114.

1997   "Benevolent Tolerance or Humble Reverence? A Vision for Multicultural Religious Education." *Multicultural Religious Education*. Ed. Barbara Wilkerson. Birmingham, AL: Religious Education Press. 395-406.

Virgilio Elizondo and Timothy Matovina. "From the Guest Editors." *Journal of Hispanic/Latino Theology* 5 (August): 3-5

"Guadalupe: An Endless Source of Reflection." *Journal of Hispanic/Latino Theology* 5 (August): 61-65.

"Incarnation and Culture." *Momentum* 28 (October-November): 67-69.

"The Mexican American Cultural Center Story." *Listening: Journal of Religion and Culture* 32 (Fall): 152-160.

1998   "Transformation of Borders: Border Separation or New Identity." *Theology: Expanding the Borders*. Ed. María Pilar Aquino and Roberto S. Goizueta. Mystic, CT: Twenty-Third Publications. 22-39.

"Pluralismo y verdad: Espacios de tolerancia, fraternidad, y comunión en la sociedad y en la iglesia." *Secularidad y cultura contemporánea: Desafíos para la teología*. Ed. Ezequiel Castillo, Carlos Mendoza, and Francisco Merlos. México, D. F.: Universidad Pontificia de México. 79-94.

1999   "The Sacred in the Latino Experience/Lo sagrado en la experiencia latina." *Americanos: Latino Life in the United States/La Vida Latina en los Estados Unidos*. Ed. Edward James Olmos, Lea Ybarra, and Manuel Monterrey. Boston, New York, London: Little, Brown, and Company. 20-23.

"Theology's Contribution to Society: The Ministry of the Theologian." *From the Heart of Our People: Latino/a Explorations in Catholic Systematic Theology*. Ed. Orlando O. Espín and Miguel H. Díaz. Maryknoll, NY: Orbis. 49-53.

Published Interviews

1980   Pablo Lopez de Lara. *Ejercicios espirituales en, desde, y para America Latina*. Torreon, Mexico. 5-14.

1981   "Hispanic Catholics: They Don't Fit into the Melting Pot." *U. S. Catholic* 46 (October): 24-29.

"Virgilio Elizondo: La teología integrada a la vida de la Iglesia." *Páginas* 6 (December): 14-16.

1984   Mark R. Day. "San Antonio Theologian Links U. S., Latin Poor." *National Catholic Reporter* 20 (27 January): 1, 22.

Introductions to Works of Other Writers

1981   "Foreword." Isidro Lucas. *The Browning of America: The Hispanic Revolution in the American Church*. Chicago: Fides/Claretian. ix-xiii.

1983   "Preface." *The Mexican American Experience in the Church: Reflections on Identity and Mission*. Ed. Moises Sandoval. New York: Sadlier. 13-19.

1989   "Foreword." Allan Figueroa Deck. *The Second Wave: Hispanic Ministry and the Evangelization of Cultures*. Mahwah, NJ: Paulist Press. xi-xvi.

1990   "Foreword." Justo L. González. *Mañana: Christian Theology from a Hispanic Perspective*. Nashville: Abingdon. 9-20.

1994   "Foreword." Jeanette Rodriguez. *Our Lady of Guadalupe: Faith and Empowerment among Mexican American Women*. Austin: University of Texas Press. ix-xv.

"Foreword." *Hispanics in the Church: Up from the Cellar*. Ed. Philip E. Lampe. San Francisco: Catholic Scholars. vii-viii.

1995   "Foreword." Alex García-Rivera. *St. Martín de Porres: The "Little Stories" and the Semiotics of Culture*. Maryknoll, NY: Orbis. xi-xii.

1998   "Foreword." *El Cuerpo de Cristo: The Hispanic Presence in the U.S. Catholic Church*. Ed. Peter Casarella and Raúl Gómez. New York: Crossroad. 9-20.

List of Contributors

Jacques Audinet is professor emeritus at l'Institut Catholique de Paris. He first met Virgil at Medellín in 1968 and later directed Virgil's acclaimed doctoral thesis. Over the past three decades he has worked with Virgil on numerous projects, especially through his long-standing collaboration with the Mexican American Cultural Center. Audinet's distinguished publishing career includes his recent works *Ecrits de théologie pratique* (1995) and *Le temps du métissage* (1999).

John A. Coleman, S.J., is the Charles Casassa Professor of Social Values at Loyola Marymount University in Los Angeles. His numerous publications include *An American Strategic Theology* (1983) and *One Hundred Years of Catholic Social Teaching* (1991). He served with Virgil on the editorial board of *Concilium* and has taught at the Mexican American Cultural Center.

Orlando O. Espín is professor of theology and director of the Center for the Study of Latino/a Catholicism at the University of San Diego. He is author of *The Faith of the People* (1997), coeditor of *From the Heart of Our People: Latino/a Explorations in Catholic Systematic Theology* (1999), past president of the Academy of Catholic Hispanic Theologians of the United States (ACHTUS), and the founding editor of the *Journal of Hispanic/Latino Theology*. Elizondo and Espín were among the eight original members of ACHTUS.

Alejandro García-Rivera teaches systematic theology at the Jesuit School of Theology, Berkeley and is a past president of the Academy of Catholic Hispanic Theologians of the United States. He first met Virgil in 1990 at a theological institute and subsequently Virgil has been a constant friend, mentor, and colleague. García-Rivera's publications include *St. Martín de Porres: The "Little Stories" and the Semiotics of Culture* (1995) and *The Community of the Beautiful: A Theological Aesthetics* (1999).

Rosino Gibellini holds doctorates in theology (Gregorian) and philosophy (Università Cattolica, Milan) and is currently the literary director of Editrice Queriniana, a publishing house in Brescia, Italy which specializes in theological studies. He worked most closely with Virgilio on the editorial board of *Concilium* and continues to serve as director for the Italian edition of that journal. His publications include *La teologia del XX secolo* (1992).

Roberto S. Goizueta is professor of theology at Boston College. He has served as associate editor of the *Journal of Hispanic/Latino Theology* and as president of the Academy of Catholic Hispanic Theologians of the United States. In 1996, he received the Academy's Virgilio P. Elizondo Award. His book *Caminemos con Jesús: Toward a Hispanic/Latino Theology of Accompaniment*

(1995) received a 1996 Catholic Press Association Book Award and is largely based on his experiences as a participant with Virgil in the San Fernando Cathedral Project.

Justo L. González is director of the Hispanic Theological Initiative and the Hispanic Summer Program on Theological and Ministerial Education. He has been a leader in theological education for three decades and has published extensively on church history, biblical hermeneutics, and Latino issues. His friendship and collaboration with Virgil also date back several decades.

Thomas H. Groome is professor of theology and religious education at Boston College's Institute of Religious Education and Pastoral Ministry. He is an internationally recognized expert on religious education whose extensive publications include the recent *Educating for Life: A Spiritual Vision for Every Teacher and Parent*. Professor Groome first met Virgilio Elizondo through their mutual friend, Gustavo Gutiérrez, and they have remained close friends and collaborators ever since.

Gustavo Gutiérrez is a native of Lima, Peru, from which he continues to articulate a theology that integrates his extensive studies with his experience living and working among the poor. His acclaimed international influence on Christian thought is reflected in numerous works such as the recent volumes *Gustavo Gutiérrez: Essential Writings* (1996) and *The Density of the Present: Selected Writings* (1999). Over the past three decades he has collaborated with Virgil on the editorial board of *Concilium*, at the Mexican American Cultural Center, and on various other projects.

Gloria Inés Loya, P.B.V.M., is a faculty member and coordinator of the Instituto Hispano at the Jesuit School of Theology, Berkeley. She is a native Californian and a noted analyst and practitioner of Hispanic ministry. Her first encounter with Virgil was in 1978 at the Mexican American Cultural Center; like numerous other MACC participants she testifies that the MACC experience changed her ministry and her life.

Anita de Luna, M.C.D.P., is from San Antonio, Texas and has extensive experience in pastoral work and leadership at the local, regional, and national levels. She is a frequent speaker at various forums on faith, culture, and catechesis and has published on these topics in various journals. Her publications include her contribution to Virgilio Elizondo's *A Retreat with Our Lady of Guadalupe and Juan Diego* (1998). She did her graduate studies in theology and spirituality at the Graduate Theological Union, Berkeley, and currently is a faculty member at the Mexican American Cultural Center and a collaborator with the Oblate School of Theology.

Timothy Matovina is assistant professor of theological studies at Loyola Marymount University in Los Angeles. He first met Virgil in 1982 as his student at the Mexican American Cultural Center. Since then they have worked together on various projects and have coauthored *San Fernando Cathedral:*

Soul of the City (1998), *Mestizo Worship: A Pastoral Approach to Liturgical Ministry* (1998), and a special issue on Our Lady of Guadalupe for the *Journal of Hispanic/Latino Theology* (August 1997).

Carlos Mendoza-Álvarez, O.P., is professor of theology at the Pontifical University of Mexico in Mexico City. He is an expert in the theology of revelation and has collaborated with Virgil on several international symposia dealing with Latin American theology.

Jeanette Rodriguez chairs the theology and religious studies department at Seattle University and is a past president of the Academy of Catholic Hispanic Theologians of the United States. She is the author of *Our Lady of Guadalupe: Faith and Empowerment Among Mexican American Women* (1994), *Stories We Live* (1996), and numerous articles on U.S. Hispanic theology, spirituality, and cultural memory. Her collaboration with Virgil has been particularly evident through their mutual interest in Our Lady of Guadalupe.

R. Stephen Warner is professor of sociology at the University of Illinois at Chicago, where he directs the Youth and Religion Project. A past president of the Association for the Sociology of Religion, he is author of *New Wine in Old Wineskins* (1988) and coeditor of *Gatherings in Diaspora* (1998). Virgil Elizondo's influence on his thinking is evident in his article "Religion, Boundaries, and Bridges" (*Sociology of Religion*, Fall 1997).

Index

undefined identity, 160-63, 167; universal, ix-x, 268; "unpacked," 110; violent birth of, 118, 282
"Mestizaje as a Locus of Theological Reflection" (Elizondo), 147
Mestizaje: The Dialectic of Cultural Birth and the Gospel (Elizondo), 1, 249-50, 268
metanoia, 20-21, 92
Metz, Johann Baptist, 262-66
Mexican-American Cultural Center (MACC): Gutiérrez and, vii-viii, 280; influence of, 19; *Madre del Sol* performed at, 110; and production of local materials, 84; theology at, 280-81; training of ministers at, 18-22; workshops at, 1-2, 241, 287-88
Mexican-Americans: and Elizondo, 30-32; families of, 66-68; identification with church, 15-16, 49-57, 60-61, 279-80, 283-86; knowledge of Spanish, 49-53; as *mestizo*, 160-63; as new humanity, 58-61, 173-75, 179; "oppressed, never crushed," 5-6, 160-63; patriotism of, 65-66; Protestant evangelization of, 282-88; religious symbols of, 128-31, 283-85; in San Antonio, 48-49, 51-53, 278-79; in servitude, 229, 285; as sinned-against, 200-3; struggle for belonging, 163-67; view of life, 66-67
Mexico: Spanish conquest of, 111-13, 119-22, 131, 145-46, 161-62, 281-82; U.S. takeover of territory, 48-49, 128, 131, 161-62, 229-30, 282
migration, 128, 148, 176-86, 192, 252
Míguez Bonino, José, 258-59
"Misa de las Americas" (Mass in the Americas) (broadcast), 1, 32-33, 72
missionaries, 119-21, 130, 226, 246-47, 281-82
Moctezuma II, 111-12
modernity: bourgeois subject as author of, 261; crisis of, 189, 196; criticism of, 192-93, 264-66; formation of, 247-48
Moltmann, Jürgen, 258-61, 263, 266-67
money as idol, 204, 219-20
Morenita, La: Evangelizer of the Americas (Elizondo), 32, 109
mystical, the, 241-42
Nahuatl culture and language, 110-16, 120, 278
nationalism as U.S. religion, 127-28
"nation" concept, 75-76
Native American religion, 111-16, 119-23, 127-30, 203-4, 246-47, 249, 274-76, 281-

82, 287
new creation: in Americas, 272-76; of church bodies, 94-99, 123; of cultural identity, 163-64, 173-75, 184-85, 249-52; of the human being, 87-88, 93-94, 123-24, 148-49, 167, 179-86, 240-41, 268, 291
"New Humanity of the Americas" (Elizondo), 268
Nican mopohua, the, 112-13
offending the offender, 209-12
On the Boundary (Tillich), 267
"Open Letter" (Moltmann), 258-60
pastoral action: based in community, 17-18, 149; and pilgrimages, 133-39, 239; and popular symbols, 118-24
pastoral formation, centers of, 59-60, 84
"Pastoral Opportunities of Pilgrimages" (Elizondo), 239
Paul VI, x, 16
pilgrimage, 133-39, 239
"Pilgrimage: An Enduring Ritual of Humanity" (Elizondo), 239
poor, the: cry of, 217-18; and Guadalupe, 109, 123-24; in history, 260-61; preferential option for, 20, 172-74, 198; as scapegoat, 165; solidarity with, 42
popular religion: in CCC, 81-82; cultural interpretation in, 105-7; Galilean Judaism as, 152-55; Guadalupe in, 113-14, 146-47; and identity, 126-31; and institutional church, 278-80, 283-91; as liberating, 122-23; pilgrimages as, 133-39; in theology, 101-7, 124, 146-48, 238-39; translation into dogma, 103-4
Plaza de las Tres Culturas, 178-79
pleasure as idol, 204, 220-21
Political Theology and Liberation Theology (Moltmann), 266-67
power: human vs. God's, 205-7; as idol, 223-24
Power of the Poor in History, The (Gutiérrez), 260-61, 265
prayer: inculturated, 82-83; insight from, 94-95; and pilgrimage, 134-35, 137-38
prophetic, the, 21, 27, 40, 63, 69-70, 111-12, 121, 175, 224, 239-42
Puebla Conference, 259-60
Quetzalcoatl (returning god), 111-12, 272
racism, 55, 84, 88-90, 128, 206-7, 221-23, 284
Ramírez, Ricardo, 19
religions, the: and diversity, 76; feasts of, 85; gathering of, 4-5, 274-76
religious education: against cultural idols, 63, 219; barriers in, 36-45; and the fam-